TIN SEA

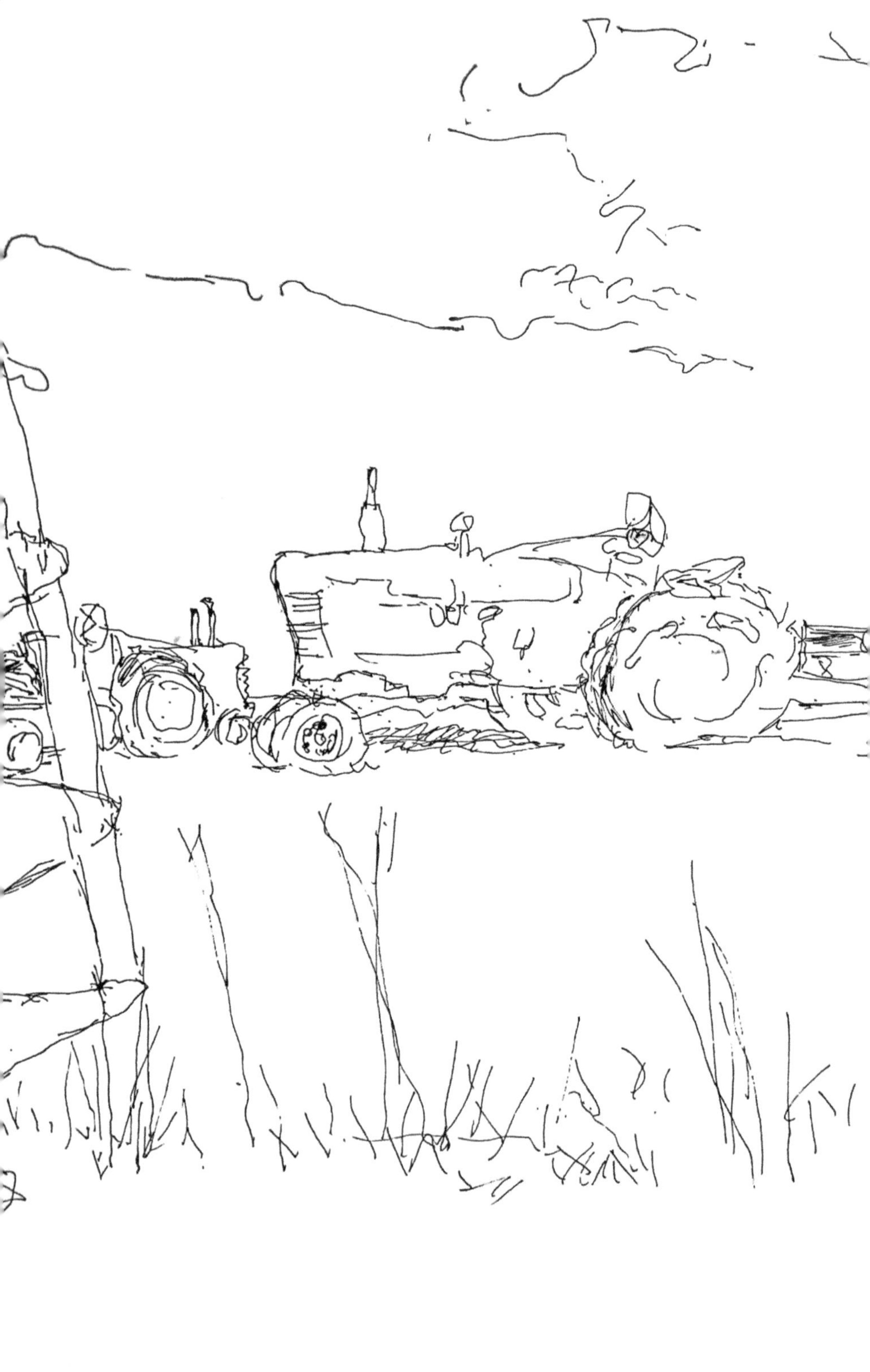

TIN SEA

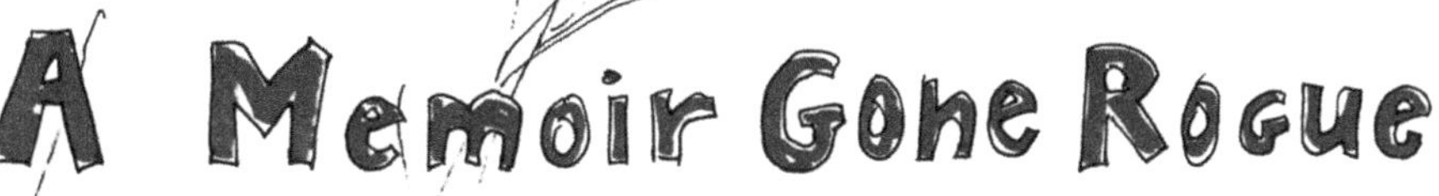

By Garrett M. Brown

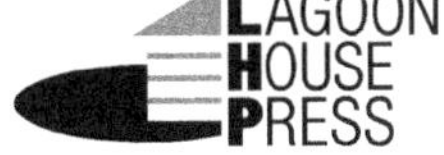

This is a work of memory and fiction. Some names and places are actual; others are invented. My recollection of events may differ from those who witnessed or were part of these same events. Any resemblance to actual persons, in some instances was intended, but mostly, is purely coincidental.

Garrett M. Brown, garrettmbrown8@gmail.com

Artwork by Garrett M. Brown
Author photo by David Zaugh

ISBN 978-0-9972609-8-4
Library of Congress TXu2-425-624

Printed in the United States
Lagoon House Press
Long Beach, CA
lagoonhousepress.com

For Kathleen Jane and Johnny D.

*In memory of Lexie Helms and her boys,
Sam and Mike.*

"I don't like work—no man does. But I like what is in the work—the chance to find yourself. Your own reality—for yourself, not for others—what no other man can ever know. They can only see the mere show and never can tell what it really means."

– Joseph Conrad, *Heart of Darkness*

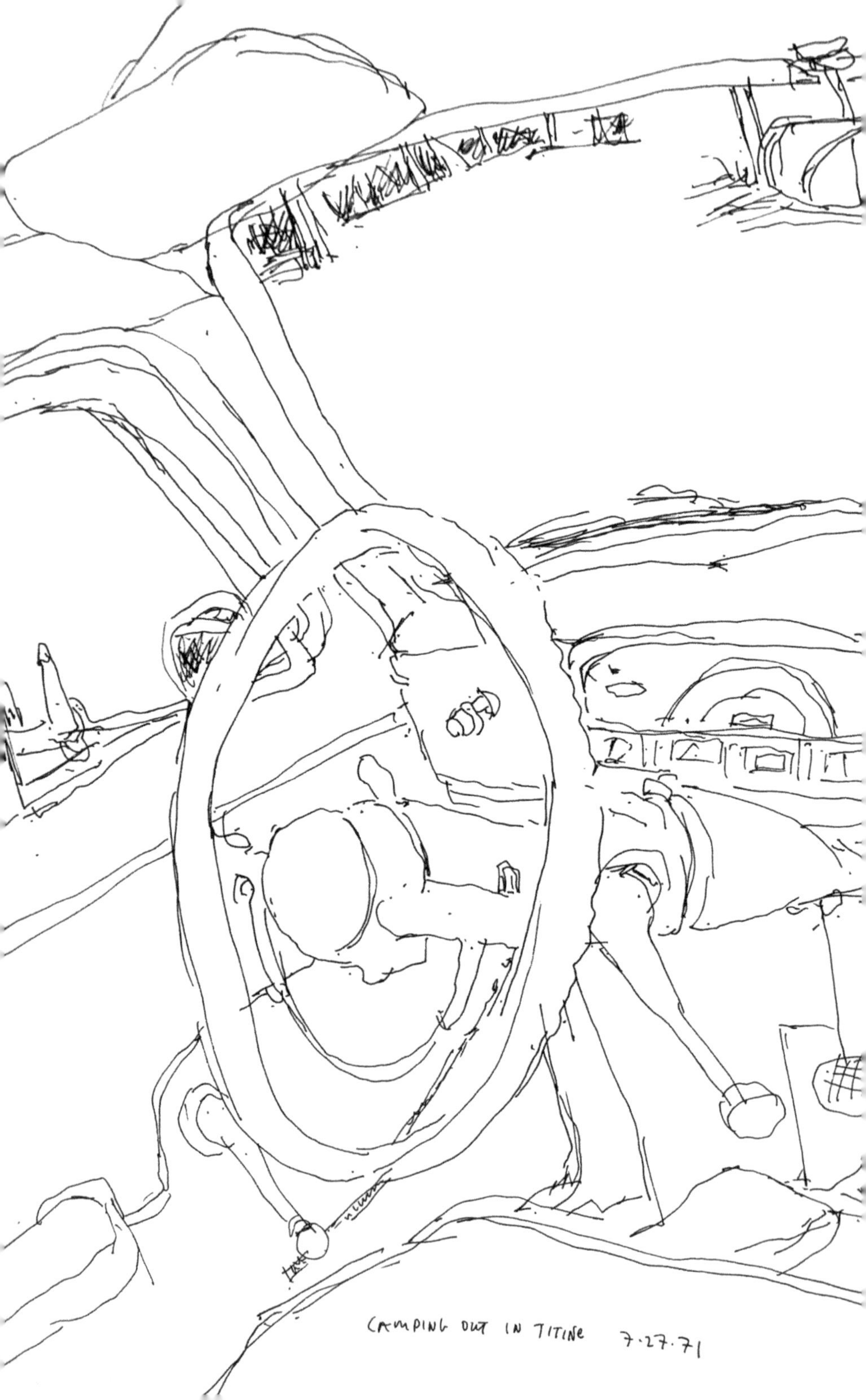

CAMPING OUT IN TITINE 7·27·71

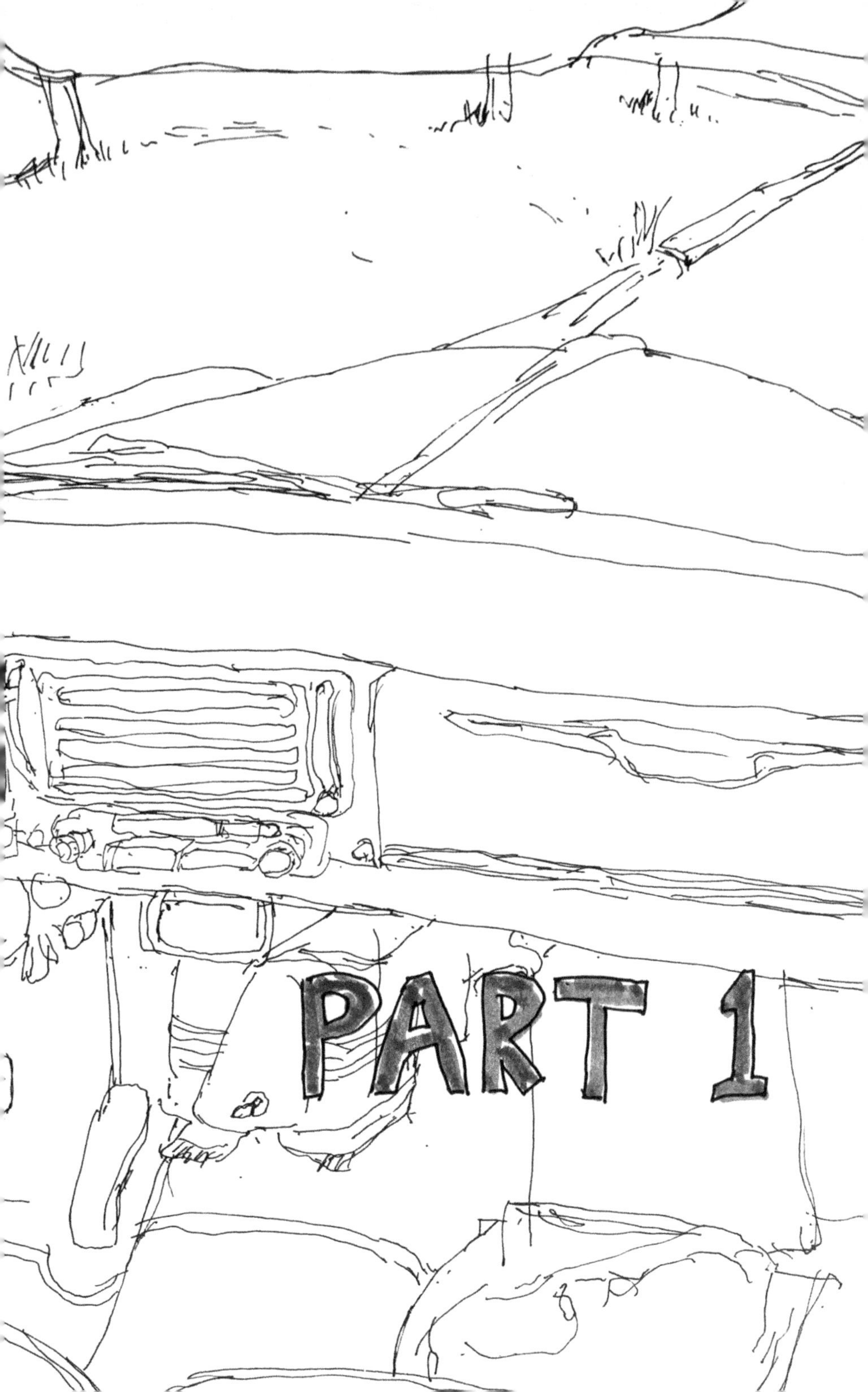
PART 1

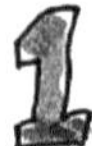

It was a summer of light. It was a summer of longing and wonder and fear. It was a summer of newfound freedom—of anger, too, and frustration and helplessness. It was a summer of wanting so much and then being unable to reach that perfection or expectation. It was a summer of fitfulness and blue moods and depression—of boredom, too. And it was a summer of great and wonderful solitude as much as it was a summer of loneliness.

Everything began to unravel that spring, 1971. To come undone and fall into place, at the same time: Kathy was finally responding to me, even getting a little clingy. My best buddy John Durland had phoned with summer plans. In two weeks, all of us, the classes of 1971, were going to graduate. There was a bright sadness in the air. There was an urgency as well as a laziness, as in: no more. Enough. And, of course, there was this curiosity about the "real world"—what was that? If college hadn't been real, what had it been? Where had I been the last four years?

But the main intrigue for me was this slowly evolving inner dictum, *I'm going to be an artist, a painter and, somehow, express things.* Perhaps even bring a new way of seeing into the world. Of course, this was all basically unspoken, internal, and confused. I was a young upstart from suburban Connecticut who was supposed to become a doctor but defaulted. Broke the ranks. I'd never felt totally comfortable among these mostly well-to-do prep boys and now it was okay. That alienated persona had joined the late '60s, early '70s milieu of hippie, strange, offbeat, and for some reason, I was fitting in again. As an outsider. The existential *artiste.* Which already was becoming so well defined that it might show up in a VW ad if we weren't careful:

Buy a VW bug. It'll make your dad's house look bigger, and—your existential artist friends will want to sit around, get high, and ponder it.

Or something like that. But the thing is, I didn't have a lot of existential artist friends. None that I knew of. I'd become a kind of loner. I was a straight arrow, too. Oh, I did let my hair go somewhat, enough to discover that this once-athlete's crew cut was harboring these "wonderful, lush curls" (Kathy's words). That's another thing. I was a jock, played frosh football, basketball and then the rest of my college career I actually starred on my college hoops team, was co-captain senior year.

And now I was an artist?

But I was. I had this gift, had it since I was a kid. I used to copy the characters from Archie Comics. I loved those big-busted Veronicas and Bettys. Superman, too. Muscles and flying through the air. When I was twelve or so, I stole into my dad's closet and his Playboy bunnies became my models. A book in our Darlington town library said, "If you can draw the human form, you can draw anything." So, I did that: I drew all manner of human forms, particularly female ones, and drawing anything else was easy. Those three dimensions made into two. Perspectives, illusions, subtleties—master those, and the other wrinkles become doable.

In junior high, Mr. LaVigne taught us how to do woodcuts, silkscreen, even how to create our own handmade books. We did mosaics as well. He was a great fan of Ben Shahn but I had no notions of becoming an artist. It wasn't something you even thought about in the bedrooms of New York City, where doctors and lawyers and businessmen raised their families.

In high school, Mike Johnson did these wonderful pen and ink figures in our yearbook and I did the inked blocky headings. The one hold-over from all that I'd learned from a very intent and keen Mr. LaVigne was the silk-screening: down in the basement on my once-upon-a-time ten-foot by six-foot plywood tabletop that had housed my HO train set, I'd created a silk screen platform where I did all the posters for our Darlington High school plays, Theatre 308. That was it.

Three years later, my junior year at Amherst, the art impulse had revived. Out of necessity. But it rose up in me with such desire and ability, too. I needed some easy classes to offset my pre-med requisites, Organic Chemistry and Thermodynamics. I took a writing class with Mr. Clark where we were writing short, autobiographical essays. I loved it: I'd get a thematic notion on Monday and by Wednesday I'd begin writing it in my head, type it up on Thursday, and hand it in at Friday's class. Studio 101 was an actual painting class, in oils. When I was twelve, I had a set of oil paints, did a very heavy-handed oil painting of a single sailboat at sea; now we were painting from a live model, a buxom girl named Maggie, from Smith, and I was enamored—with her and with painting. Funny, there were two other jocks in the class, Ted and Doug: Ted was truly gifted and would become a gifted painter and eventually an art teacher; Doug, not so much—his talents remained on the football field and eventually a career in medicine. But in that painting class, all the labels dropped off: we were not jocks or math whizzes or chemistry nerds but varying degrees of would-be painters. Those classes, the writing, the painting, became these resurrected joys.

The middle of my junior year, early winter, 1969 about eleven a.m., the Dean of Students had me sit down in his spare white-walled office. The "Marine Dean" we called him. Red hair, crew cut, a hefty man who had served in the Marines, a straight shooter who could be funny, too. "So, Garry, we got good news and bad news."

"Oh?"

"Yes." He kept eyeing me, quietly, almost sullenly.

"Um. Okay."

"This pre-med thing."

"Yes?"

"Okay, look." He was eyeing an open file on his desk. "You're flunking Organic Chemistry and you're getting a C in Thermodynamics."

"Oh no. Really?" I bowed my head. Oh God.

"But this is the strange thing which I don't quite understand."

"Yes?" I raised my head even as I already felt dizzy, forsaken.

"You're getting an A in this Painting 101 with Mr. Porter and an A in Mr. Clark's writing class . . . What's going on?"

A bit numb, it was a cue. I mumbled and muttered but, essentially, I told the Dean that I needed to sort things out, that I would get back to him. He nodded and said, "Yes, I hope you will—get back to me. And soon."

I shook his hand and thanked him. He gave me that very straight, sincere, and thorough eyeing. I did not linger.

From the Marine Dean's office in Johnson Chapel, I marched across the main Common, past the Robert Frost library, down the hill to what was once a grand piece of nineteenth-century architecture, the Fayerweather Physics building, now converted into this burgeoning Arts confab, where labs had been turned into lecture halls and art studios. And, where Mr. Fairfield Porter, the first-time newly appointed Artist in Residence also had his modest studio, just as you come up to the second floor and veer to the left, away from the bigger studio space where thirteen of us were learning how to paint in oils.

His studio door was ajar. I knocked lightly, once. "Yes? Come in."

As I entered, along the weathered wooden wall to the right of this very thin corridor were several taped-up postcards, one of a Giacometti pen and ink and another of a very fine pencil rendering by de Kooning of his wife, Elaine (I was surprised that late morning—I knew de Kooning only as an abstract painter).

Once through this brief hall, around its corner, to the right, stood Mr. Porter, brush in hand eyeing a big canvas, at least six by eight feet, a tight fit in this smallish nook of a studio.

"Oh, hello, Garry."

"Hi, sir." We both paused. He continued to watch the canvas. I continued to watch him, and then the soft painterly pastel images in oil on the canvas:

> *A dog was standing on the first step of two, waiting to enter the screen door along the ribbed siding of a grey house. Beyond the dog were lawn and trees and then the grand view of a bay with several boats, sailboats and row boats and beyond them, on the horizon, distant hills that were actually islands, with a sultry blue sky above.*

"I don't like that boat . . ."

"Sir?"

He pointed and I focused on the foremost boat, pinkish shading, port to bow, left to right.

"I don't think it quite works."

"I like that shade of pink," I said. "But I wonder if it shouldn't be more like a . . . lavender?"

"Maybe so. Did you want something?" Mr. Porter was not one for small talk, which was refreshing in these often much-too-academic halls of verbal dexterity and bravado. He was a contrast to the then-stars of Amherst, Leo Marx, Benjamin DeMott, and George Kateb.

"I just met with the Dean of Students, and well, I'm not doing so well in my pre-med classes but in painting and writing, my grades are very good, and I guess I need to know—"

"You are an artist."

"What?"

"I think you should look at Corot's paintings. That nude study you did, it reminds me, take a look."

"Okay."

"Also, those watercolors of yours, the way you don't go right to the edge, the way you leave bits of white space?"

"Yes?"

"Take a look at Maurice Prendergast."

"Yes, sir. Okay. Thank you."

"Anything else?"

I watched him as he so gently but evenly eyed me. There was no flourish about him. He wore a blue linen long-sleeve shirt, the sleeves rolled up, as well as his usual light brown corduroy slacks. Next to him on a high stool was his palette, an expanse of eighteen-by-twenty-four-inch clear glass, the pigments dotting across the top, the oil and turpentine in small bottles nearby, the mixings below the colored line-up; the one medium-sized brush still in hand was now at his side as he watched me and then checked again with the painting.

"No, sir. Thank you."

He nodded. I nodded, turned, and departed. (It was after the winter break, when I returned to Mr. Porter's studio that he showed me the finished painting. I was stunned: the pink boat had been changed to lavender!)

I immediately returned to Johnson Chapel, the Marine Dean was still in his office and I told him, "Sir, I'd like to become a Fine Arts major."

"You're sure?"

"Yes, sir."

"Okay then. I will make the necessary changes. Fine Arts it is."

"Thank you, sir."

I remember the mid-day sun barely breaking through the wintry New England clouds. And fast-walking down the hill to the Social Dorms. A fast-walk that became an exultant jog, saying to myself, Omigod, I'm going to become an artist! *An artist! OMIGOD! What in the world am I doing?*

And yet, I was ecstatic—I was a free man!

Now, two years later, with a cockeyed sense of confidence—this mix of innocence, naivete, and an emboldened curiosity—I was going to graduate with my Amherst class of 1971 and become an artist. Madness.

And yet, my folks—well, this was the phone call when things first unloosened. "Hey, Mom . . . Dad, you there?"

"Yeah, we're here," said Dad.

"Oh, Garry, how ARE you?"

"Fine, Mom. So, listen. I don't think I want to become a doctor."

"Oh?" says Mom. Dad is silent.

"No. Had a meeting with the Dean. You know this man I've told you about—Mr. Porter, well, he thinks, you see—I'm going to become a Fine Arts major."

"Oh, Garry, really?" Mom actually sounded pleased.

"And teach," said Dad.

"No. No, Dad—paint."

"What—houses?"

"Maybe, if I have to support the painting, but—I think I really want to become an artist, a painter."

"Oh, Garry, you're so gifted. You really are. This is very exciting, isn't it, Brownie?"

"Yeah. Real exciting. I need a refill. Caroline? I'm up in the kitchen, you want another?"

"No, honey, you go ahead. I'm fine."

"G'night, Dad. See ya. Love ya."

"Yeah. Same here. See ya." Click.

"Oh, Garry darling, this is very exciting. Are you pleased?"

"Yeah, Mom. Yeah."

We spoke a little longer. But. Actually, I think my dad was relieved. My older brother Sandy was finishing up med school, in the last year of a residency at Henry Ford Hospital in Detroit. Dad had idolized his father, who'd been a doctor in Boston, the first one to own an X-ray machine. No question, Dad lauded the medical profession. But perhaps one doctor in the family was enough. But. An artist. A painter. I had no idea what I was doing.

And then, that spring of 1971, a few weeks before graduation, I saw this quirky, wild movie over at Jim Goodwin's frat house. It was called *Harvey* and starred Jimmy Stewart.

That's when things somehow fell into place.

2

It was a weekday night at the Sigma Ki frat house. James Goodwin, known as the Goodwink, also the Good-Dude, was up from Connecticut visiting. He'd graduated the year before, he and Linda had married last summer, hadn't quite settled yet. Jim had invited me to come over. I'd never joined a fraternity, wasn't real keen on groups of young men drinking beer. Neither was James, really, but he had made some good friends there and had always urged me to come hang out. I stood there eyeing the TV and the empty sofa.

"You coming down? I'll buy you a brewski."

"Sure. What is this?" I pointed to the TV.

"This? *Harvey.* Jimmy Stewart. The big white rabbit, that no one can see but him? You've never seen this movie?"

"No. I like Jimmy Stewart, though."

"You'll love him in this. Listen, stay. Watch it. I'll come up in a bit, okay? I love this flick, it's so out there. You want tap or a bottle?"

"Tap—?"

"Your beer."

"Oh." I looked at James, tall, thin, his gold wire-rims. "What am I thinking? James, I don't drink. Remember?"

"I was wondering, you ol' jock."

"How about a ginger ale?"

"Or Coke?"

"Fine."

He left. I stayed, mesmerized. I'm not sure now if James ever did join me. I was lost, immersed, charmed, intrigued, aroused, enlivened, and finally, somehow—transformed.

A middle-aged man, Elwood P. Dowd, played by Jimmy Stewart, has a friend, a close friend: a drinking buddy named Harvey. A compadre. A soul brother. Alter ego? No. A rabbit. A six-foot-tall rabbit. But—this rabbit, named Harvey, is invisible. Only this man, Elwood P. Dowd, can see him. And for this he is considered—mad, loopy, crazy.

Yet, this man Elwood is so charming. So present, so interested, so alive and curious and tender, understanding.

He'd gone to Yale, was en route to be a big success, a Somebody in that town. Took care of his mother, lived with her, in fact. Never married. When she died, the house became his, the monies, all, and he continued to work. And then, not. He invited his sister, Vita, and her daughter, thirty-year-old Myrtle Mae, to come live with him. His sister saw the change in him, after their mother's death. It was also about the time Harvey joined him.

"Oh, Mother, you talk about 'Harvey' as if he really did exist," says Myrtle Mae.

"Myrtle Mae, there are some things you must learn in life—and I hope you never do."

Myrtle Mae, tall, gangly, a blonde Olive Oyl, so wants to meet a man. A true love. And yet she can't, living there with her crazy Uncle—Elwood.

I made myself comfortable on the sofa, the dusk outside the frat house blending into this curious black and white movie that I continued to watch. Alone. Gradually, I'd get hints of a party slowly beginning to gather, as sounds would drift upstairs: the clatter of glasses, beer bottles, laughter, songs.

It tickled me, this movie. It moved me.

"For you see," says Jimmy Stewart in his slow, chivalrous drawl, "no one ever brings anything small into a bar . . . and then I introduce them to Harvey and he's bigger and more impressive than anything they've ever told me . . ."

Harvey.

Elwood's sister, Vita, is finally persuaded to try and put Elwood into an asylum, Chumley's Rest—where Dr. Chumley's wife comes to pick up her husband and she encounters the warm and chivalrous Elwood, who begins to explain who and what Harvey is: "Oh yes, Mrs. Chumley. A pooka. And my best friend, too. Many's the time Harvey has said to me, 'I'd do anything for you.'"

Harvey.

"Allow me to give you my card. Harvey and I would love you to join us for dinner. How's seven o'clock? Fine. Oh, if you need to reach me, use that number. This one is no longer in use."

Harvey.

"That's right," says Elwood, "Harvey can look at a clock and stop it. And then you can go anywhere you like, with anyone you like, for as long as you like, and when you return, not one second will have passed . . . Harvey's not only taken care of time and space but any objections, too."

Harvey.

It was not a movie. It was a manner. A code. A way of living. And, as the movie reached its tender conclusion, it struck me:

> *This is what an artist is. An artist has a vision; like Elwood, who sees and talks with the invisible Harvey, so does an artist behold and carry and see this vision of his work, which he dialogues with, invisibly, since no one else can see it. Often times, the artist is considered weird, unfathomable, even crazy—just as Elwood was being treated. But, in fact, like an artist with a vision, here comes a way of seeing the world, in all its detail, magic, and wonder. And like* Harvey, *Art, too, be it poem, book, film, music, or painting—time stops and as Elwood says in the movie, "You can go anywhere you like, with anyone you like, for as long as you like"—within that work of art.*

I never got my ginger ale. I'm not sure I even said good-bye to Jim. I just eased my way off the sofa and out the door. I was both present and not. I was still with Elwood P. Dowd and I was on my way back to my dorm.

Instead of returning by way of side streets and parking lots, I decided to walk along through the Amherst town Commons. Down the center green strip, with the bus depot to my right. No more bus trips to and from Skidmore where Kathy was doing what tonight? And, on a bit of a diagonal to my left, Grace Episcopal Church, where

I'd taught Sunday School to sixth graders for the last three years. That had finished up a few weeks ago. No more Sunday School.

Winding down, final exams, papers. Closing shop, all of us. A couple more weeks and we'd be college grads. Kathy invited me to come to her commencement. A man named Edward Villella, a dancer, would be giving the commencement address. Curious, a man who danced, ballet. My class of '71 had finally gotten someone, a poet named Robert Bly. I'd found one of his books a few weeks ago, about snow and Minnesota. I started reading it; I liked the poems: something very sad in them, never flip. Honest, too. Straightforward.

I was enjoying this slow late-night ramble back to my dorm. It was so quiet. The air was cool and damp, all of May and spring become sweet and a little sad, too—this was all about to end. There was the green embankment and on top, the big old Octagon building, looking like a darkened ship. I stood across from the Administration building, lit up as if some musical were about to be performed among its multitude of steps and Greek-like columns.

I remembered the rally once held there, one of the Vietnam War protests. I'd had one of my sketchbooks out and poised as I hurriedly inked in faces, the crowd, the swish and swill of light, dark, so many students, mostly guys but girls from Holyoke, Smith, UMass also, a few. I was not a protester, not really. I didn't believe in this war, misguided, bullying—it was not the America I believed in. My draft number had been low—51—was that what had motivated me? I wanted to savor life, relish it—paint it and create it, really, as art can sometimes do. Not kill it. True, I had my moments of rage on the playing fields, which felt murderous. But, day in, day out, to go off killing? No. So I conscientiously objected. Prepared papers. Procured statements from my teachers, my friend Joe who was a Marine, a minister, also Mr. Porter. They bore witness to my conscience, my anti-war feelings, and beliefs. Then my mother, my dad, too, reminded me of how bad my acne had been over the years. My acne? I revisited Dr. Clary who re-examined me, updated my medical papers and recommended that I not be considered for the military. The Springfield, Massachusetts medical board agreed: "open wounds," the papers noted, "not fit for service in Southeast Asia." What? That's it?

Had I somehow cheated? What about serving as a CO in the military? Everyone said, Drop it. Let it go. Be thankful. And my CO papers, the letters I'd collected? They became pieces of my puzzle, an autobiographical collage, a marker, that called up in me a gathering honesty: who am I? What do I really want to do with my life?

"You want to spend the summer together?"

It was Durland's voice on the phone. I was back in my dorm room, alone. It was a full throttle May evening, late night, not cold, not hot, and Durland was probing, "Gar, you there?"

"Yeah, yeah. Kinda."

"You want me to go over it again?"

"Please."

"So. This will be our last summer together as best buddies, as bachelors."

"Why?"

"Brooke and me. Come on! You're going to be our Best Man."

"Right."

"You know this. We talked about this."

"A while ago."

"Gar, did I wake you up or something?"

"No, no, it's just, I saw this—"

"You and me, buddy, and Tennessee."

"What about Tennessee?"

"Gar, that's what I'm telling you. I got four other guys lined up. You'll make five. That's my crew. We drive to Nashville the first week of June. They tell us a few things, we get our books and then door to door, buddy. We make some good money and have one last big summer together, right?"

"What about Brooke?"

"What about her?"

"Then you're *not* going to marry her?"

"Gar, I'm marrying her. She's marrying me. But that's *next* summer."

"Next summer . . . okay. And this summer is . . ."

"Tennessee. Selling books. Best buddies."

"Right. This summer."

"I mentioned this to you, oh gee, about a month ago. You didn't have any plans then. Have things changed?"

"No. That's just it. I think I've been looking forward to having no plans. No classes. No, you know, schedules. Just—life. Living. Seeing."

"Well, we will. Once we get to Nashville. Get our assignment. And Big Jim, my point guy, promised me he'd put us together in the same territory."

"'Territory'?"

"Town. You know, somewhere in Tennessee."

"Right. God. Where is Tennessee?"

"In the South. Down there somewhere. We'll find it."

"Right. Okay."

"So—you're in?"

"Like Flynn."

"Great, Gar. This'll be so good. Going door to door. You're a natural. That big smile of yours."

"Durl, don't sell me, okay? You're my best friend and I want us to be together. That's why I'm doing this."

"Thanks, Gar."

"Have you ever seen this movie *Harvey*?"

"The big white bunny?"

"Yeah."

"No."

We talked some more. I tried to tell John about *Harvey.* He didn't get it. Well. I didn't get it either. Not yet. But, this movie. It had excited me, or catapulted me, or—what? What had it done to me? What was going on?

The Big Picture. The Bigger Picture. College, sure. Tennessee, okay. But John, my best buddy. Our lives. Our families. The journey ahead. A move toward something grand and yet quite simple.

"Here's my card."

"Have you met my friend Harvey?"

"When? When can you come for dinner?"

Time. We do have time. But. Time is money, I'd been constantly told. Time is of the essence. Do you know what time it is? It's later than you think.

"'And the evening wore on.' Isn't that beautiful? I'd like to say that again, 'and the evening wore on . . .'"

Something had clicked. Perhaps—snapped. I was getting off. This is my stop. Stop. Yes. No more. Thanks for all those classes. All those books. All that reading and hustling, "Hurry, you'll be late, class starts in—", thanks for all the schedules and formats and, "Three exams today, one on Friday, that final paper is due next week." Oh God. Oh Time. Thanks. And good-bye to all that.

Please? Can I go now? Can I start my life?

Could I, at least, have it, be with it, savor it? Find it first, okay, but—love, marriage, kids, career—whoa, whoa. Slow down. Let's graduate first. End. Begin. Begin what?

"Here's my card: Dowd, Elwood P."

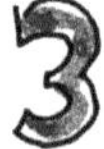

Kathy's graduation from Skidmore was a week before Amherst's. Her commencement speaker, Edward Villella, the dancer, was short, muscular, like a svelte athletic gym teacher. He spoke with great enthusiasm, had a sense of humor and—a sense of timing: he only spoke for ten minutes. Everybody loved him.

At my graduation, Amherst class of 1971, two moments stood out: the climactic dictum of the poet Robert Bly's commencement address, and, after lunch, still packing up, my dad's urgency to get on the road and return home.

Mom loved Robert Bly. My dad, couldn't figure him out. Myself, I wasn't sure at first. A poet. A writer. A bit of a showman. Shaman? Perhaps I'd say that now. But then? The climax of his talk, that stuck. Years later, I'd realize he was one of those rare few who was profoundly trying to speak truth to power, because Amherst, then and now, the Little Ivy, like the bigger Ivy, catered to and groomed elite young men then, along with women now, who came from and would return to—some degree of power, influence, tippy top of the hierarchy: those worlds of politics, law, medicine, finance, education, but the arts? A few.

In his colorful shawl, beads, and lion's mane of white hair, here was an ally. An artist in the world. A voice in a kind of cultural wilderness.

And I still wasn't sure. This man recited poems, waved his arms, fluttering his right hand as if tracking the path of a butterfly; elongating words, phrases—pausing—looking deep into this sea of dressed-up bonhomie. We watched him closely, poised as he was before the steep hillside to our left (the once mountainous and profound labor of broken breath and pride, those dreaded wind sprints) and to the right and beyond, the mottled forest of the Connecticut Valley with its oceanic breadth and history.

He also made everyone laugh. A bit of the King's jester. His crack about Nixon, "Talk about lying—perhaps Nixon and Pinocchio are related. Look at those noses . . ." Then he stopped everything, mused aloud, and spoke to each one of us, spoke to me:

> *"Look, you've had a grand time here. I hope. It is a special place, Amherst. A special, even elite education. Costly, too, I'm sure . . . So, I say to you—stop! Ask your folks for another five hundred bucks, say, and stop everything. Before you go on, into your grad schools, your law schools, your med schools—just go somewhere, sit under a tree, or like Thoreau, beside a lake, and just look around. Pause. Long enough to consider, ponder, reflect on all you've done and lived so far. Take a look into your very own heart, see what it is you truly believe, you profoundly want . . . Thank you, and good luck."*

Thunderous applause. The class of 1971 stood, clapped, cheered. I was touched. A chord struck. An impression made. Who was this man/poet, really? And what had he just, quite bravely and intimately, told me?

The incident with my dad happened after lunch, in my dorm room. Kathy was not present as she had taken a load of things to my car. I had just finished packing the last suitcase. I was hauling it up from my single bedroom—one of the four that neighbored five steps below, off the main room, and shared the fluorescent-lit bathroom—to join two other suitcases, a box of books, a box of appliances, i.e., my clock-radio, two lamps, plus my sketchbooks, more books, a few T-shirts which I used to cushion the breakable stuff. I had some other clothes in hand including a red cashmere sweater—I remember that sweater—when Dad entered. No one else, just Dad.

"Hey, Dad."

"Hey." He stood there. "So, you ready? Let's go."

"Right," I said.

Dad continued to stand there, his chesty sports jacket, thin slacks, his striped tie now absent, collar open. I could sense his impatience. I was feeling loose, playful, even giddy. I'd just graduated. I was a free man, glad to be "on my own." I said as much to my father: "Dad—you know what? I really don't want to rush. This is it for me. My last hours here. It's been a great day. I'd like to savor it, you know? And," (this had an edge to it, to match my dad's impatience) "I really don't want to rush things, okay?"

"Why you—" Dad grabbed the red sweater, "fucking ungrateful little bastard!" and he flung it in my face. The sweater grazed my left cheek, flapped thwat! into my chin and chest. The lovely flow of the day, now bright afternoon, bird song, distant hum of radio, stereos, a few lone dorm rooms emptying still—it was all gathered up and held.

And stopped. As if all the air, sound, light had been scooped out of the room, now etched into my dad's grimacing, perspiring face. I watched him, waited.

"Jesus fucking Christ!" Dad muttered, as he now charged down the stairs, into the bathroom.

"Dad?!"

"Goddammit!" I heard from below. I placed the sweater on the box I was packing, then hurried down the stairs, knocked on the door. "Dad?"

"What?"

I slowly opened the door. He was at the sink, washing his hands. His hands still wet, he rubbed and patted his face. I stood there. He then reached for the dispenser, grabbed some paper towels. "What?" he repeated, almost matter-of-fact, though his face was flushed.

"You okay?"

"Sure, sure. Jesus."

"Listen, Dad—"

"No, no. I'm sorry, okay? I just want to get going."

"I know and—"

"Look. You're a good kid. I'm tired. It's getting late. I know it's a special day. I know that."

"Thanks to you, Dad, these four years—"

"Right."

"Look, Kathy and I—there's still a little more to do, but—you don't have to wait. We'll just come along when we're all packed, okay?"

"Right." He threw the paper towels in the small bin. I followed him up the stairs.

He didn't look back. Didn't say good-bye. Or wave. His shoulders hunched, he marched down the main stairwell. I held the dorm room door, watched him go. Watched him head from shadows into the brightly lit pavement fringed in Quad grass. It was a steady walk with a light, almost gliding step for a big-chested six-footer. I saw him hesitate, turn his head both ways and then raise his right arm and wave. He saw Mom, and started after her.

That late May afternoon, I was twenty-two, would be twenty-three in November. Dad would be sixty in August, in his prime as an executive with General Foods. In five years, he'd be forced to retire. Though he seemed older, thinning hair, some grey, creased and tightly combed in place, the style among so many businessmen then, and still, today.

And he *was* tired. During those years, he and Mom traveled a lot as ambassadors for General Foods—conventions, cities, a lot of parties, entertaining clients. Business pressures, family pressures. I was the last of four that he had finally put through college. These graduations were old hat. And yet, he never seemed to enjoy them, never seemed quite comfortable. Out of his element. He wanted to get home, be home. Fix a drink, swim in his pool, watch Walter Cronkite. Or, go to work, where people knew him, where he was known, a Somebody.

Of course, he was an alcoholic, which wasn't understood or dealt with then. Everyone drank in Dad's crowd, social drinkers, all. A way of life, in the suburbs, in business. But, on this day, it felt like something else. Dad had gone to the University of Vermont, but just for two years. It's where he met my mother. He'd gone to a prep school, Governor Dummer's Academy, hated it. Made sure none of us were sent off to prep schools.

In fact, he was one of those rich preppies who I never liked while I was at Amherst: spoiled, entitled. Often either too slick or too clearly opportunistic, ambitious, or the worst, trust fund layabouts. Yet, Dad was not like that. He'd overcome his prep-dom. Yet he never seemed like a college man either. He was a Working Man, down to earth, not Upper Crust. None of that affect. When he was relaxed (was it only when he was drinking? In his later years, it seemed so), he could be so charming, lovable, magnanimous, a real man of the People. But. College. He'd never finished college. He'd been called away—his father, a physician, died of heart disease toward the end of his sophomore year. It was the Depression, there was no money. College? No, he had to work, and work he did. College years? Grad school? Travel? No.

Work. Then marriage. Family. And—work. Years and years of it. Musing? Pausing beside a lake, under a tree, to consider things?

No. Work. And—going on.

4

It starts slowly and builds, music on the car radio, a movie of my life finally unfolding—my life, the credits rolling, the car passing houses, yards, summer afternoon light—home from college!

And kids, faces smiling, heads thrown back, laughing. I'm going home, and the car is singing—full of song and hopes and dreams—this moving picture of Life In America. And I am going to be this artist, a chronicler of My Life and Times. It's a wild song, a wonderful ride!

John called. I agreed. I took my John Marin book, my sketchbook, my Bible, a journal to write in, my watercolors, my pens, my black ink, some clothes, and filled up my car, Titine, a '68 grey Peugeot, the shape of a bowler hat. With Kathy beside me, we met John and the other guys that next morning. Three days after graduating cum laude from college. I was going to be an artist, a painter.

Yet, here I was on my way to go South, a twenty-two-hour trip, from Darlington, Connecticut to Nashville, Tennessee, to learn how to sell dictionaries door to door. I was going but I was hesitant. Selling. Dictionaries. I was tired of trying so hard. I was tired of keeping up and learning and doing and trying so hard.

I watched Kathy slip into the seat beside me as she sighed and we looked at each other. My mom stood in the driveway watching, pink robe, her arms folded until she began to blow kisses. Kathy waved to her, smiled. It was a coolish morning for June with that warm humid hint of things, weather, to come. The car wouldn't start. It was getting late, we were supposed to meet John and the guys, the rest of his crew, at eight a.m. at the Howard Johnson's near the 95 freeway.

Titine. My grey Peugeot. French. Temperamental. My last two years at Amherst, winters, when I delivered *The New York Times* on campus, she was the only car that functioned those frozen mornings.

How so? Because of Titine's secret weapon.

I got out and I used it: from under the driver's seat, I took the grey metal bent hook, crowbar-like, placed it in the slot below Titine's hood, and with a firm hold, firmer grip, and a solid twisting motion—crank! Crank! This ratchet action would produce combustion and—blast off! When every other car wheezed in the winter, my Titine was the only one who whirred. Which she was doing now.

My mother marveled, "Oh, Garry, you can just crank her like that?"

"How 'bout those Frenchmen, Ma? The French kiss, French fries, AND the crank-it-yourself auto! C'est merveilleux, n'est-ce pas?"

As I stuffed the mini-crowbar under my seat, Mom came over. I stood, she hugged me, then with both hands, gently pushed me into my seat—"Now, go! Hurry! I'll tell your father good-bye for you. I'm sure he's sorry he's missing you. Go! I love you. Write please, or phone, too."

"Okay, Mom. Love you, too. Don't worry."

"I can't stand this anymore." She wiped tears, then hugged herself in her pink robe, said, "I'm going inside—good-bye!" And she did.

As we backed out of the driveway, she turned, blew another kiss, then disappeared. We were off. First stop, ten minutes away—Howard Johnson's.

"Your mom's cute," Kathy said. "She sure does love you."

"Yeah. And—I sure do love you."

"Yeah?"

"Yeah." And then really asking, I said, "How ya doin'?"

"Fine."

"You wanna sell dictionaries door to door?"

"Naw."

"Me neither."

"Then why you goin', Gar?"

"Durl. My best bud. You know. Our last summer together before he and Brookie, y'know, and, it's an adventure. I'll meet people. I'll draw. I'll paint. I'll miss you. Will you write this time, please?"

"Sure. I did last summer."

"Once."

"No! More than that."
"Kath."
"Well . . . it got busy."
"Yeah."
"I'm sorry."
I nodded, kept driving.

Did I mention the cookout the night before, Dad's crack about Van Gogh? Or later, Mom and Kathy, in the house, washing dishes, readying for bed—Dad and I, after watching cars depart, turned toward the big two-story house, a ghost ship on the dark waters of suburban lawn. How Dad kicked my car. The left front wheel.

"Going to Tennessee, are you?"

"Yup."

His broad barrel chest bending. Was he looking for a dropped cigarette? Then, an abrupt rise from the earth, right leg lunging, a perfect follow-through, and, in a moment of madness, this heavy powerful BLAM! in the quieting warm summer night, a startling song. The record suddenly scratched, a punch as if to my soul.

Why, Dad, why?

"Fuckin' car. Think she'll make it?"

"Hope so. You okay, Dad?"

"*Me*? Take a good look."

We bent close, eyes locked, faces sharing the same sweet air, only Dad's was sweeter, pungent, the reek of alcohol stinging my nostrils. "Huh? I never been better . . ."

A woman's voice calling. Background music. "Brownie? Oh Lord, come on to bed, you two. Garry's got to get up early and, oh, look at you!"

Dad didn't look back, just roared, "Shaddap!" Mom's voice fading, her shape a receding shadow.

"Christ! Go to fuckin' bed. Who cares, huh, kiddo?"

"Yeah, Dad. Come on."

"Hey." His eyes blurry, watching me. A long pause. A moment now to look, really see this sweet tormented man try to work out the lyrics of his latest late-night ballad.

"*Hey.* I'm talkin' to you. You hear me?"

"I do, Dad, but—"

"Hey . . ."

The slump of his broad shoulders, shake of his short sleeves, long gorilla arms, big chest, and those sad watery eyes, grinning now, chuckling: "Tell me. Come on."

"What, Dad . . ."

"You think you'll ever amount to somethin'?"

Now I pause, watch him, try to make a joke. "I'm thinking, I'm thinking . . ."

Oh, Dad.

The stillness now. Party voices silenced. Cars droned up the lane, gone. The traffic of the universe as if slowed but for the ticking of the crickets and the moths' tap-tappings over by the driveway lamp-post.

That lamp-post and my dad's triumphant act of forgiveness when I was eleven and shot BBs into it. He was supposed to roar and scream but that evening—had Mom coached him? He delicately fingered the lamp-lid, a professor outlining the Mysteries of Science, saying finally, "Ah, but you missed the bulb. A hole on either side. Fine shooting, son, but never again, okay?"

The lamp tonight shone bright, replacing the moon, gone off, scraped across the sky and, like the rest of the party, wise thing, gone to bed. But not my dad. Or me.

Oh, and into this sphere of consciousness and self-inquisition, maybe I've never returned since, not really. Oh, I have longed to. I go on, don't I? But, Dad, I miss you—I've wanted to go on and I've wanted you to go on.

I'm here now, by your side: I want to be your son. Will you be my father tonight, please? Talk to me, something wise and comforting. I've finished college—I'm out there now. Out *here,* this world. What do you think? Are you happy for me? What was your first summer like after college—were you scared? Did you know what to do? But you worked right away, didn't you? The Depression. You never finished school. Marriage then, soon kids, pressures. You never took a ride, girlfriend on your arm, off to the Wild Blue. Is that why you kicked Titine's wheel? Dad?

He hung there, a floundering maudlin scarecrow, waving, grinning—

"Dad? What were you going to say to me—"

"Say what?"

"Just now. You said, 'Hey' and . . . You know I'm going South tomorrow, to sell books door to door, right?"

"Yeah?" As if this were news. He was over in the grass, just past my old basketball hoop, its long pole reaching up into the dark night. He faced the bushes, a wealth of bulky darkness. He was peeing. "Ahhhh," he said. "Come on over here, Garry. Nothin' like a midnight pee outdoors. Ahhh . . ."

"Sure." I joined him.

"Ahhh . . . 'The water's cold' . . . 'Yeah, deep, too.'"

"What?"

"An old joke. Whew!" He zipped up. Its force pulled him off balance. He bumped me. We both fell. He landed on me, the grass, wet, cool. "Christ! Whaddya doin'?"

"*Me*? What are *you* doing?"

"Hey . . ."

There it was: that long pause, silent night. The bathroom light clicked on above the garage. Its click noise called attention to the steady drone of the air conditioner. A humid night. Dad's breath. Oh, sweet cool night but this sadness still clammy all over me. Dad's chin now on my crushed shoulder.

"You really want to be an artist?"

"I want to try."

A rip in the air, a torch lit, as my mother shouted, "Brownie, come to bed!"

Dad's face lifted and turned, the eyelids heavy, shutting, opening, as if it was the appropriate response.

"It's okay, Mom. We're coming," I called up to her. The swoosh sound of bathroom window closing. Stamp of wood sealing our resumed privacy.

"Dad . . ."

"Hey."

Another long pause. I wanted an answer, *Dad, come on, where are you?*

". . . He says you can do it. He says you got what it takes. He says—"

"Who, Dad. who? John? He says I can sell books?"

"NO! You know—*him*—your teacher—that *man.*"

Oh. Dear Fairfield. My mentor, my teacher, yes. My example. My permission. My guide. My friend and, also, the good father. But I love you, Dad. Do you love me? Dad?

He burped. "*Him.* You know."

"Yes."

"He says you can so . . ."

"Don't worry, Dad." I was trying to get up and pulling him with me.

"Who's worrying? Do I look like a worried man?"

"Come on, Dad." I was impatient. I wanted to move.

Oh, Dad, I wanted so much from you that night. I kept pushing us, rushing us but—you *were* saying things, weren't you? You were trying to tell me something and I was tired. It was late. "Come on, Dad, *please*—upsy-daisy, okay?"

"HEY . . ."

We were up. I bent over, dusted off. I'd give him this one, this last lengthy pause, this short circuit. Oh, Dad, you fallen angel man, you God forsaken wilderness, speak it, say it—*please*—

"Listen . . . Oh Christ. Never mind. It's late, huh?"

"Yeah."

Dad was walking now. The moths tapped the lamp box glass, the crickets whirred, and the stars were noticeable, a few brilliant and warm. We made our way toward the open mouth of garage. The bathroom light above still on, the whir of air conditioner was steady, somehow reassuring in this sudden oasis of suburb.

"You go on, Dad."

"Huh?"

I had roused him from his trying to walk a straight line to bed. "I just want to take a few moments. I'll turn off the lights and lock up. Go to bed, Dad." He didn't look at me, just nodded. He entered the dark mouth of the garage, swallowed. Then sputterings, "Christ! What the—?" He tried to find the steps and the light switch. Click!

A cloak of white grabbed me, the garage lit, my dad hanging there, a gorilla about to be sucked into the cavity of house and cage and civilized sleep. After his rumblings of breaking and entering, a sudden silence.

My face turned to the stars now, the beckoning night sky. "HEY." I turned back—that long pause. Then, were they words or a clearing of the throat? The screen door slammed, an abrupt slap of punctuation. And silence.

"What?" I quietly asked.

Dad had gone, disappeared. *Hey . . .* this man of rumblings and grumblings, so much shadow, so violent, so abrupt, so boring, so big and blustery and so confusing. Confused? Dad. I know now. What you said. I couldn't make it out that night. But.

Yeah, it's late. It's always late, isn't it?

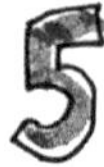

Picturing Kathy that morning. Asleep in what had been Gammy's bedroom, the curtains blowing softly.

Her gentle touch, or was it my mother's, waking me? I'd slept in my attic bedroom, the bottom of my bunk beds. Mom's pink kitchen and countertop.

"Oh, let me fix you breakfast—*please*? It'd make me so happy." Fried eggs, toast, bacon, juice. First morning light through the kitchen window slowly overcame the artificial kitchen light.

"Got everything, you kids? Here, I'm going to pack some sandwiches. From last night's steak."

"Mom, no, we'll be fine."

"Yes. You eat them. Kathy, you make sure."

"Yes, Mrs. Brown." She nodded, gave me a smile.

"Thanks, Mom."

Bathroom, brush teeth, all packed. My sleeping bag, my suitcase filled with shorts, T-shirts, sweater, sweatshirt, running gear, jeans, my Marin art book, Bible, journal, sketchbook, pen, watercolors. Was I reading a novel then? That would be later. And Kathy's light, more delicate gear. Ready. Out the downstairs door, through the garage, into the driveway. First smells, grass, heat, early June. Brightening sky.

"You drive carefully . . ."

Opening the trunk, loading our stuff, clunk noise shut. Drum roll, please.

"Oh, Garry . . ." Tears. Oh, Mom, dear Mom.

Big long hug . . . Mom's hugs, always too long. I break first, always—embarrassment, shame—what? Dear Mom, I do love you. Now. Then. But. So loaded. So much pain. I thought I had to say things, do things, fix things, somehow make your life better. I never felt I could just be on this earth. Is that why I became an artist?

Always thought it was Dad's approval, but I wanted yours, too—or was it to somehow translate this pain, which I felt, too, looking into your face, your face then become mine? Or, as a way to move beyond, to hide from these tears? How lonely you've been, Mom. I know now. Because I am, too. Have been. I cried that summer, sure. Alone, homesick, but now, these years, when I cry, it becomes clear, very clear, that sometimes I am you crying. They are for a moment not my tears but yours, your heaves, your pain. How can this be? Still a mystery, as was your love, then, now.

That morning, your sweet, generous send-off, but in that hug, you almost tried to grab me back, not let it happen: you thought I could fill places that Dad so neglected. That summer and beyond, I thought so, too. I wanted so to be a man, a hero, respected, a savior of sorts. Fix everybody. Somehow my art was a rebellion against all that. I'd left pre-med, gave up my missionary zeal. I'd begun to touch another honesty, a different voice deep within began to speak up. One who still cared but now understood there were limits. I was no doctor. I was no god. Though there were moments, Mom, in our confidences, our walks and talks, our emotionally incestuous intimacies, when I believed I was so endowed, so gifted.

As long as I stayed your son, your little man. And yet, this trip South, that summer, it was time, and you did let me go.

Titine sputtered. I shifted gears. Titine was going. We were going. We passed houses, lawns, porches, reshaped by the light of the just-risen sun. Mist, wetness on everything. My window partly cracked, gave off cool air. I reached for Kathy's hand, then I squeezed her leg. We both wore jeans, sneakers—I wore a short-sleeved shirt, she had a blouse—loose, full, bosomy. Wonderfully bosomy. Bosoms. Or, as Mrs. Smith used to say in eighth grade, "boo-zums," lengthy accent on the "boo," as in "Evangeline's *boo*-zum," from that poem, "The Song of Hiawatha."

Kathy's *boo*zums, her freshness, her sweet sexy shyness. The fright from her big open-mouth kisses. A farm girl from Iowa, though not really, a family full of doctors. And Kathy's twin sister, Chrissie,

Chris—thank God, fraternal, just as sweet as Kathy but very different. Was it Kathy's obvious shyness that made her alluring, mysterious? Her lithe strong legs, from synchronized swimming. Wrestling matches, our legs tangled, she really was stronger.

Told John after I'd spotted her in her red dress at a freshman mixer, "She's like a cross between my mother and my sister Carol"—this gentle, feminine stuff: the way she buttered bread, smoothing the knife across it, gently wiping it on the crust edge. That delicate touch. Sensuality.

For three years I idolized her, never knew her sexually. Until the fall of our junior year when I'd lost my virginity with Anne from Mount Holyoke, who'd been in my English writing class. The following weekend, Kathy surprised me, a group of girls had carpooled in from Skidmore. I told Kathy about my experience with Anne, more in the spirit of friendship and, hey, isn't that something? This did it, we turned a corner—she wanted to share this mystery of the flesh. She took my hand, pulled me into my dorm bedroom. We shut the door and began a new adventure. Which became loving and obsessive and fleeting and deepening, and, finally, inexplicable. Always cat and mouse. Always giving me so much and then pulling back, confiding in me her fears but reassuring herself and hurting me by saying, "I love it but I'm saving myself. I'll only have an orgasm with the man I marry."

Dear Kathleen, I wanted so to please you. I tried so hard, didn't I? I was a good lover, wasn't I? But, oh, if you could know me now. Yes, there were times when I'd wanted to call you—in Iowa, Minnesota, Connecticut—all these years. Call you, charm you, seduce you—just to take you to bed and show you—fuck you, yes, until you'd come and cry and ache and love me, want me, more and more—Oh, Gar—Oh Gar—that wonderful deep dark moan—from the toes, from the world beyond, deep within, from those secret places—and you'd tell me. You'd ache and gnash and paw and scratch and grab and lick and love it, and oh, you'd tell me, yes, all your secrets—that I was the one, the only one, I wanted you to love me so much.

But you didn't, did you? Neither of us did. We were cautious. We were friends.

That spring of our senior year, you did come closer to me. You were anxious about leaving school. I was not. I was ready. You saw this yearning in me, this strength, and you wanted some of it. I became powerful for a time, less needy. I began to pull away from you—a first. I wanted to be an artist. And you, you wanted—well, you weren't sure.

Funny how we never talked about marrying or family. I was so afraid you'd reject me. Think I wanted you to ask me. I'd tell you I love you, out loud. You never did. You never said I love you to me. You'd squeeze my hand or hug me or smile or look away or, in letters sometimes, a "Love, Kathy" but never from your sweet mouth. How I longed to hear you say it, out loud, with pride, with longing, with passion and even some degree of possession. But, no. Even that morning, as Titine revved and we finally departed, you said, "Your mom's cute . . . she sure does love you . . ." As if telling me, Gar, you're lucky, your mom loves you and that should be enough. I'm just a good friend. And I said, "Yeah," and then, faster than a speeding bullet, "I sure do love you." You said, "Yeah?"

"Yeah," I said and without pausing (to get hurt), I asked, "How ya doin'?"

A habit: not to expect a reciprocal endearment. No. Move on. And I was moving on. Maybe some element, a new one, a scent, yes, of manhood, was asserting itself. I was on a journey, a rite of passage, a young man entering the world, an artist (oh, what is that, Lord?).

You would come with me as far as Tennessee, then fly from there to Iowa to spend another summer as a counselor at your beloved Y camp. And, in the fall? Perhaps together, we'd backpack through Europe. Perhaps not. Things were loosening, the years ahead were no longer structured, known—real life was seeping in.

Titine was steady now. We idled at the stoplight, on the Post Road, Darlington's Main Street. Ahead of us a big brown and grey railroad underpass. Then moving again, under the tracks, along Main Street, past the Sugar Bowl, the movie theatre, Bob's Sports, the public library, a side road off to the right—past memories, former lives, all quiet this Saturday morn, all increasing in brightness, warmth, that reverent glow as one leaves a beloved place. Further along, another light, then a short right (alongside and opposite the Connecticut Thruway) and there, among cement islands and grass, beside the orange and aqua and white mirage of HoJo's, the guys were sprawled, waiting.

"Christ, Brown." Durl spit out a piece of chewed grass. "I was just about to call your house. You oversleep?"

"Sorry. Car wouldn't start."

"Really? Is it okay—will she make it?"

I pointed to John's partly shiny and partly rusted green Plymouth Valiant. "Green Monster meet the Grey Monster. Okay, the Grey Bowler, actually." No one laughed. Kathy smiled.

"Okay. Well. Let's do introductions fast and get going, alright?"

"Sure."

"Kathy and Brown One, this is . . ." John pointed to four young fellow college grads, one was a junior—Brad. The others were Chuck, Kram, and Monroe. Everyone nodded, mumbled greetings as they pulled themselves up, dusted off, and got into our respective cars. Southward Ho!

We abruptly stopped. John's back passenger door crunched open. One of the crew pushed his way out, ran off. "Kram has to pee!" John called. Which started me thinking. I looked at Kathy. She shook her head. "You?" I shook my head. The car hummed. We waited. I began to feel my body. Maybe I did have to go. Naw. But. I wasn't sure. I'd better go. Insurance. Then Kram ran out of HoJo's, popped into the car. Nope. I'd wait.

But like so many things that summer, I wasn't sure that I could.

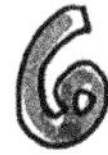

I drove most of the trip: from Darlington, Connecticut, to Nashville, Tennessee, twenty-two hours straight, or thereabouts. Early Saturday morning in the Nutmeg State to early to mid-morning in the state of the Volunteers. A long, hard trip. Nonstop. Okay: a few, to pee or grab snacks. No sight-seeing, no real meals, and a few outbursts of minor existential angst. Or, was that simply car sickness?

There is a wonderful initial high, a euphoria once en route, a veritable liberation as a journey to a strange land commences. This colors the way one sees things, friends, oneself.

Vision. On the road now, passing other cars, following John and his antic caravan, as they hooted, hollered, made signs, signals, faces, until the revelries and even politesses settled finally into the reality of a long car ride. Informed by moods: is that an ugly landscape or is that landscape simply reflecting my mood, my state of mind? (a crude paraphrase of Simone Weil).

Again, vision. I was trying to become an artist. It was more than practice—drawing, painting, day in, day out, the discipline, the technique. All this had to be informed by my attitude, my belief systems, and finally, and simply, my life. How do you see her face? I watch her. Absent of desire or need or willfulness, I simply look, see, remember. Mental notes: the passage of light across her face, through the windshield, its deflection and the sun's increasing glare, mid-day, the highway, a truck's shadow, a bird's flickering, cars whirring in nearby syncopation; the guys up ahead, heads bobbing to music, making their faces—Kathy's laughter; the flex of her mouth, teeth shining, her sound, her smell, the texture of her clothes as she crosses her legs, looks back over her shoulder out the rear window and waves. The guys now behind us, also waving, shouting, hooting; the motion, like the sea, unceasing, of heat and asphalt and wave after wave of highway, into the late afternoon, that June Saturday on the road.

I did take one nap while Kathy drove. It was early evening. We'd gone from the main highway on to route 81. Car sounds, the car itself: leather seats, bucket seats in front, the heat from the day stayed in the leather, warmed us as the sun set. Somewhere in West Virginia the night grew cool. The sensuality of her lap, its heat, coziness, where I tucked my head between her thighs and tummy. Her gentle smells, the occasional light touch of her hand on my hair, my forehead, as she drove and I napped.

Titine had a hole in her bottom left floorboard, between the driver's seat and where the pedals were—brake, gas, clutch. The metal underneath rusted, rotting. Air, rain, or snow—weather entered there. I used to joke: if need be, I could just put my foot through that hole and push off. A bad joke because it was a bad hole. It worried me. Titine. My car, could she make this trip? But I'd been told, like the VW, the body always goes before the engine. Swell. While the engine's cruising around, where are you?

Deep down, it pleased me that Titine might act up. Titine would allow me, and John, too, to be scared, and thus, spontaneous, alive, challenged, maybe even thrilled and victorious. Titine might help break the rigid format of the trip: twenty-two hours straight, no stops, a marathoner's (John's) dream: a challenge, a mountain to climb, sheer-faced and steep. No thanks. But John? He loved it.

The trouble didn't really begin until well after nightfall. No longer four lanes, the highway had narrowed to two, very dark, and Kathy and I were tired. By late afternoon, we'd eaten our steak sandwiches. It wasn't until this stop that we finally had something to drink. Thirst. Fatigue. Crankiness. What else could go wrong? Murphy's Law? What can go wrong, will go wrong. I pulled up close to John, honked and then signaled with various hand gestures, mostly Kathy's, that we needed to stop. After a few vulgar interpretive gestures from a couple of the guys in the back seat—I was no longer laughing—John got the message that we needed gas. At the next exit sign, "Gas Ahead," we pulled off.

I turned off the engine, told the kid attendant to fill her up, and went to pee. Kathy also went—John, Kram, Chuck—Tom, Dick, Harry—we all went to pee. I sighed, inhaled the deep dark night air. Crickets sounded. A sky full of stars. Cool air, no breeze, just damp coolness. A fall night in June. Strange. Ah, only the beginning.

Kathy and I stocked up on snacks—peanut butter-filled Saltines, cheese-filled crackers, chips, pretzels, and a few sodas. All of which John kind of snubbed as I continued inserting quarters and pumping the machine's pinball-like lever.

"You plan to eat all that, Brown?" I pulled the lever again. Kathy retrieved the crackers. "Uh, well, not all alone but yeah. Why? Want some?"

"*Brown.* You kidding? That stuff's poison."

"I know. But, do you see any Good Shepherd Granola around?"

"Yuck."

"You're the runner, not me."

"Brown, you're an athlete."

"Was—*was* an athlete."

"Oh? Don't you care about your body?"

"Johnny. Come on. This is just a snack, not a regular diet."

"Sure. Come on. Let's ride."

Kathy and I watched John walk off, her arms filled with our midnight snacks. Kram joined us at the machine.

"Don't mind him," offered Kram. Short, dark curly hair, a mole to the left of his mouth, eyeglasses.

I remembered Edward Kram from a trip to Trinity College during our junior years. He was in a Moliere play, very hopped up, and quickly tried to become my friend. John had told him of my leaving pre-med to become a fine arts major, a painter. He was Mr. Twenty Questions: how's it going? What made you change? Do you paint every day? How will you make a living once you graduate? Any favorite painters? A part of me loved the questions, forcing me to think them through a little. I appreciated his intensity, his ready warmth, his being that interested in me. Which is where I began to balk: WHY is he so interested? Is this guy queer—what's really going on here?

But that was then. (To this day, I'm still wary of these Twenty Questions People, endemic to the suburbs where silence is unheard of . . . And how old are you now? You've grown, haven't you? What do you want to be when you grow up? Where are you going to school? What will you major in? What will you do with your life? A form of false intimacy but with Kram, perhaps nervousness.)

No. Kram loved John, with a non-athlete's idolatry—of a star, a running star, dear Johnny D, captain of one of the top small college track teams in the country. A rigorous, disciplined, ambitious athlete. Kram assisted the track teams, indoor and out, while studying English and Poli Sci and doing a college play when he could.

"He misses Brooke," said Kram, rattling the machine.

"Who?" asked Kathy.

"You know, his fiancée. Brookie. The Smithie. Smitten he is. Next year they're tying the knot."

"That's right," I sighed.

"She's really very sweet." A pause. Kram hammered at the machine with his fist. "Damn Butterfinger—grrrr!"

"Butterfinger?" I said. "And you're driving with the stiff?"

"Yeah, I just tell him to fuck off."

"He means well," I offered. Kathy nodded.

"Yeah," said Kram. "He's a stiff but hey, he's our stiff, right?" Turning to Kathy, Kram said, "Excuse me, but I don't think we've really—*really*—met. I've heard so much about you—you're Kathy!"

"Oh yes!"

"I'm Ed, Edward Kram." He offered his hand, which had the Butterfinger in it. "Ha! You want a Butterfinger?"

"Oh, no thanks."

From across the lot came John's shout, *"Hey! It's time, let's move it out. How 'bout it?"*

Kram waved and called back, "Coming, Sahib!" We dispersed. I was angry. I was muttering. Kathy tried to calm me: "Come on, Gar, you know John. He's probably nervous, and it's his show anyway, right?" Sure. But. I did not like this rush job. His being God and Judge, Mr. Righteous, and by the way, where was my best buddy amidst all this Wagons Ho stuff?

I paid the attendant, ate some more of my peanut butter saltine, and started the car, still muttering. John, his lights ablaze, a turn signal blinking, beneath a dark night, hovered. Waiting. I took my time. So did Titine: the engine was not turning over. Instead—a click, click—with each turn of the ignition key.

"Oh-oh," said Kathy.

"Naw. Don't worry." I got out, grabbed my grey wrench as I called to John, "She won't start!"

"What?" he shouted back.

I shouted louder, *"She won't start!"*

"Oh." His silhouetted figure slumped.

The attendant said, "What?"

"No problem," I told him as he walked over, "I can start it."

The attendant, short, T-shirt and jeans, bubble gum, and teenaged insouciance, said, "Let me hear it again."

I looked at him.

"Turn the key, let me hear her try to turn over."

"Sure . . ." I got back in, turned the key.

Click . . . click . . .

"Open the hood," said the kid.

I did. He fingered around.

"Now try it."

Click . . . click . . .

"Wall . . ." his Southern accent, soft spoken and sincerely concerned, "you got a problem." John came running over, the night growing cooler, I could feel the breezes from his anxious approach. "What's wrong?"

"Wall . . ." I began in a mock Southern drawl, "we got a problem."

"See," the kid began, "there's this lil grey box what's doin' the clicking. The batt'ry feeds it, which then gets the engine revved and hopping."

"Christ." John hung his head.

"Let me test the battery." The kid walked off. He tested the battery, and the plugs—the battery did need charging. The click-click continued until somehow this gum-chewing young mechanic got Titine going. How he did it, still not sure. Maybe he patched it with some of his bubble gum. A half-hour later we were making left turns, headed for the highway and the Dark Night of The Road. With this warning, "Do not turn off the engine until you get to a real mechanic. This here car needs work."

You drive with a certain degree of tension—attention, too—when you know you cannot let your car engine turn off. There's a metaphor here, about my own life, about the life of this trip. Tied to the building pressure I was feeling from John, this pressing toward Nashville, with such myopia, intensity, and so little pleasure. Except for a few midnight snacks, which we ate too quickly, adding indigestion to the mounting list of grievances.

And so. We drove through the night. We made one more stop, an all-night gas station in northeastern Tennessee: a young man in a grey jumpsuit with little pink badges sewn across his chest and shoulders came running out. I explained about not turning off the ignition due to engine trouble. No problem, he said, did I want him to look at it? No. Just fill her up. He did, very carefully, and we drove on.

It was near dawn when we played the Little Engine That Could routine. A gargantuan hill. A very suburban feel, houses on either side of this major north-south route, but picket fences, nice lawns, not a wealthy neighborhood but clean, kept up, and this HILL. Steep. Deceptively so.

John was ahead of us. We followed until about three-quarters of the way up, I had no more gear to shift, no more gas or punch in the pedal. Titine whined, maybe it was a whinny. Whatever: she slowed, coughed, and we were visibly losing altitude. John kept on, and I'm not sure when he became aware of our absence. But. Thank God, there was no traffic. I backed Titine down into a near driveway. We sat there, engine idling, perplexed, fatigued. Was this really how I wanted to spend my summer?

Within five minutes, John and the guys appeared. We waved, he shouted, I tried to explain. The rest of his crew was asleep, though not for long: this was the fun part.

Once John spotted us, he went and turned around, called to us that he would follow, push us if necessary. Fortunately, the sun just rising, there were very few cars on the road.

We pulled out and as we began the ascent, Titine began to fail again and fall back into John's front fender. Then his Green Monster began to slow. Not enough speed. He couldn't accelerate or even hold steady. John waved us over. He had a plan: Kathy should squeeze into his car. He'd take everyone up to the top of the mountain. I should turn around, return down the Sisyphean slope, and wait for him. Alone in his car, John would head back down, meet me where it was fairly level, get up some speed and push me and Titine up the slope.

Which is just what we did, with a bit of a nod to Sisyphus himself!

There was a fair amount of banging and clattering, my back fender on his front. But—John's intensity and my sense of the ridiculous—a bumpy parallel: John pushed, Titine coughed, wanted none of it, even as I lunged repeatedly at the accelerator, and finally, we reached the top, where there was cheering, clapping, screaming. We'd crossed an imaginary Finish Line, broken the tape, and together we'd won! I was very excited, John smiled, we slapped hands as our cars idled. We all piled back in and continued on.

Yes: we'd won and, shifting gears, I could see the sun was up and bright. I smiled at Kathy, she laughed—this sense of accomplishment and relief and—but what, what had we won?

7

Nashville, Tennessee. I remember a yellowed city skyline, late afternoon, sun trying to set, colors dissipated, washed out. Hot. Muggy. We came off the highway and slowed into the patterns, the hems and haws of local traffic. Titine was still running. Shaky, but running. We stopped at a gas station for directions, Titine idling.

The Hermitage Hotel, downtown Nashville, 6th St. North. We parked in the hotel lot, Titine finally coming to a stop, a prolonged rest. It was Sunday: we'd go find a mechanic later that week. The Hermitage: old, a huge lobby, marble fountains, leather chairs, ornate rugs and everywhere, on rugs, on walls—images of the South, homes, countryside, farms, families, histories.

John checked us all in. Our rooms were on the fifth floor. John and the crew in one room. Kathy and I in another, down the hall.

That evening, after we'd settled in, I went for a long, solitary jog. The summer dusk slowly getting murky, especially as I moved from downtown Nashville into the outskirts where I saw Black families lounging on their porches, talking, playing music, a group of men playing cards, a brother and sister jumping rope. One little boy tried to run beside me. I smiled, he frowned, and then finally smirked and stopped. I waved good-bye and jogged on. On my return to the hotel a small yappy dog followed me part of the way.

The next morning, Monday, almost ten, there were six of us making our way through the high-vaulted hotel lobby. White-railed balconies above, big loungers and white rocking chairs below. Groups of people checking in; other groups mingling, chatting.

John led with Kram close behind, Brad, too, then Chuck and Monroe. I brought up the rear, sketchbook in hand, wide-eyed and enthralled with the bustle of energies, the Southern pageantry of it all.

We were halfway into the lobby when through the turnstile doors, Kathy appeared. "Hey!" I called, went over.

"Hay is for horses."

"Whatcha doin'?"

"Looking for you." She had a small bag in hand.

"What's in the bag?"

"Oh, just something."

"Oh?"

"Oh yes."

John solemnly raised his hand. "Whoa," he said. The guys stopped and lined up near the doorway. "Gar." John smiled at Kathy and said, "Hi, Kath."

"Hey, John. Where are your books?"

"That's where we're headed, to get them. Gar, we're going to be late."

"Right," then to Kathy, "You wanna come?"

"Sure."

"Gar—"

"Kath's just going to take a peek, see what we're in for, okay?"

"Okay. But—let's go."

We went. Six guys and a girl. College grads, well, except for Brad. It was a clear blue-sky morning, the heat and humidity already kicking in. I watched Kathy as we marched along, her chirpy walk, her bouncing breasts. God, I was suddenly very desirous. Two blocks later, we were there.

The convention hall had these pseudo-Greek-columns ornate facade made of mostly concrete. Inside there was a big, long lobby with double doors, left and right, that led down lengthy aisles, either side, to a big, broad, brightly lit proscenium stage. Groups of mostly young men, a lot of them in white shirts and ties, were in variously sized groups, talking, nodding, as we entered, an excited energy in the air. Our group started through the double doors to the left when, up the aisle, aimed right for us, came this big, jolly man in a tan sports coat, dark slacks and bright red tie: Big Jim Osborn, John's significant connection and point man.

"Johnny boy, hey, you made it! God, almost gave up on y'all."

John straightened up. "No, no. We're here."

"'Course you are. And look at y'all, huh? Good lookin' crew."

"Thanks. You wanna meet everyone?"

"Sure, sure. Hey, y'all, I'm Jim Osborn. Mos' folks call me Big Jim, 'cause, well, I'm BIG for starters, and, I'm also one of the big honchos with Southwest. See, Johnny?"

He grabbed his yellow shiny tie clasp. "Gave me a gold-plated tie clasp. Fifteen years with Southwest. Not bad, right?"

"Yeah. Nice." John fingered the clasp. "Real nice."

"So, welcome, y'all . . ." And then, as if he'd become an inspired showman, Big Jim rattled off a Welcome Litany:

> *"Welcome to Orientation Week—welcome to Southwest Company's Summer Kickoff . . . Hey now . . . you Northerners, welcome to Nashville, yessir, welcome to Tin-Sea and the Good Ol' Boy South!" (Yes, that's when I first heard Tennessee pronounced as two words, Tin Sea. I liked it.) Then, patting John's shoulder, slower, more confidential, he added, "Any problems this week, you talk to John or me. We'll take good care o' you, y'hear?"*

We all waited for the Showman to continue. Then, watching us, a bit mystified by our actually listening, he said, "Me or Johnny, we got you covered, awright?"

We all nodded. Then, Big Jim, laughing, his big sports coat flapping, went one by one, shook hands, got names, gave each of us a warm welcome. Until he got to Kathy. "Oh-oh, sorry. No women allowed. Besides, you're much too attractive. You'd outsell all these boys. Nope. Can't have it."

"Oh. Okay. Bye, Gar." Kathy gave me a quick kiss, started to leave—

"Whoa! I'm just kidding. Kathy, is it? Come back!" Kathy turned. "Well, darlin', at least let me meet you first before you leave." Kathy smiled, returned. Big Jim apologized, we three briefly visited: I explained that Kathy hadn't planned to stay. She wasn't part of the crew, she was just my girlfriend.

"'Just'? Oh no. Not this lovely lady. She's not 'just' a girlfriend.

Uh-uh."

She laughed. I watched her, loved her, realized, oh God, that was true. Not "just" but given how lovely she was and with all that I was feeling that morning, it was very "*un*just." Big Jim insisted she could stay if she wished, but Kathy shook off the invitation, gave me a kiss, and departed. Big Jim joined me as we watched Kathy bounce up the aisle and disappear. He turned to us all.

"Ah, young love, huh, guys? Hey, believe me, there's a lotta romance in selling door to door, right, Johnny? Come on, guys, I saved seats for you. Front row, center, best in the house—come on *down*!"

Again, we marched, down the long aisle, deeper into this now packed auditorium.

Mid-morning. A Monday in early June. A beauty of a day outside and my girl, too, all of it gone, pushed aside for this book-selling jamboree about to unfold. I was curious, and, I dreaded it.

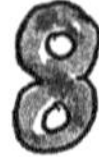

It was true: we did have the best seats. Front row center, with Big Jim on the aisle, then John, myself, then Ed, both of us in T-shirts and shorts; Brad, the junior, I realized was a carbon copy of John, pressed white dress shirt, sleeves rolled up, Bermuda shorts, jog shoes; Chuck and Monroe, both had pressed short-sleeve shirts and khaki pants, shiny shoes, a real pair. Big Jim never stayed put. He easily had ten other crews, from across the States, who he had to corral, charm, make ready. But he and John did seem to have a cozy relationship, which for some reason irked me.

My friendship with John dated from Middlesex Junior High in Darlington. Really though, it kicked in our sophomore year of high school, that basketball season, and never slowed: through high school, college, summers mowing lawns, painting houses, working out and training for sports, through car trips, the Montreal Expo of 1967, building Dr. Harper's house in Vermont, to driving cross-country in 1968, to selling dictionaries—now.

Yet, John and Big Jim carried on like old war buddies, which, of course, in a way, they had been. Big Jim's counsel probably had comforted "Johnny Boy" during the challenges and demands of the past three summers. Still, I was peeved. As much as he was a good ol' boy snake-oil salesman, you could tell he had a good heart, a big generous spirit. After shouting up the aisle and carrying on—at one point, doing this hefty jig of a dance, a combination of the Twist and the Monster Mash—Big Jim finally returned to us. "Okay, boys, you ready? Here we go!"

The lights dimmed. Music, a big band's clamorous overture, then a drum roll. A spotlight followed a tall man—in a white suit with that same red tie as Big Jim's—as he entered, came to center stage, where he stood just down front of a wooden podium, huge smile, waved, and the music stopped.

"Welcome, y'all—to the Southwest Company's twenty-third Annual Summer Kickoff! Will y'all please stand with me as we sing our country's National Anthem?"

We did. We stood, hands on hearts and sang, accompanied by a big band orchestration. The song finished, the tall smiling man clapped and waved. The whole auditorium erupted in cheers and shouts and whistles. Was this a ballgame, a church service, or the raising of the Confederate dead? It was strange, even perverse and—exhilarating.

Once things quieted, the tall man, all white teeth, called out, "Thank y'all and WELCOME!" Another round of cheers and applause and carrying on. The tall man waved us to be quiet. "May I have all the sterling studly stunning Southwest managers up here on stage, please? Come on, y'all!" Big Jim stood, smiled, clapped and then waved, as if calling the cavalry. Others like him, not as big perhaps, or as hearty, but all with tan suits or beige jackets, and those big red ties, first ten, then twenty, perhaps forty men were now on stage, greeted by catcalls, cheers, applause, and then this huge, thunderous stomping of feet. Oh boy. This continued all morning, as five different managers, including Big Jim, came and went from the podium, where they presented various aspects of selling, with each juncture punctuated by shouts, cheers, and foot-stomping.

We learned about respect, for the people whose doors we'd be knocking on, their points of view (a whole other topic, "How to Listen"), and especially, respect for ourselves, our wares. That is, "How to Dress and Present Oneself with Respect" (white shirt and tie was highly recommended, which John told me he'd stopped wearing the last two summers: "Smacks too much of Jehovah's Witness. No. A nice shirt, open collar, slacks, and either clean, decent jog shoes—you walk a LOT—or, a nice polished pair of shoes, Cordovans, say. This summer I might try those thick-soled shoes that servicemen and janitors wear. You can get them at the Army/Navy store.").

On the topic of "Respect for Our Wares," I learned that this huge throng of three thousand young American men, while two-thirds would be selling dictionaries, the other third, about a thousand or so, would be selling Bibles. This was news to me but not for Brad and Chuck. It was a big reason why they had come. Big Jim told us we each needed to decide on what we wanted to sell by the end of the day.

Of course, what we were selling, Big Jim clarified, with us and in his talk, was not these books. Not Bibles, not dictionaries, not cuckoo clocks, not Frigidaires to the Eskimos, though we could if we had to, because what we were really selling was ourselves. Big Jim's presentation, "The Hearty Soul of Selling," was a highlight that first morning. "Basically," he said, "and I don't mean to get metaphysical on you boys, but it's *you.* Who you are, how you live your lives, how you love, how you think. How you care about this world, how you love your fellow man. Quite honestly, fellas, the greatest salesmen are *the greatest lovers,* and that's why America is such an AMAZING country."

Cheers, shouts, and whistles, and—foot-stomping.

All of which got me to thinking about my dad. Big Jim, in fact, reminded me of my dad, on a good day. His charm, his boyishness, his big welcoming warmth, and, too, his ability to get quite serious and in your face, like a football coach, dispel your fears and rouse your spirit. My dad always said, No one can sell a salesman like a salesman. And it's not *what* you know but *who* you know. Which is when I realized how much I despised this whole display of pseudo-cozy Rah-Rah, Sis Boom Bah, macho-religio-jingo-God-Bless-America, Make Love/Make Money, Winners/Losers fraud. Because finally, it was about making money. About being a *winner,* not a *loser.* It was a performance, a series of not spontaneous goodwill gestures but furtively and carefully plotted steps toward breaking and entering not just a person's home but their heart, too. Creating a warm connection, and filling it with enormous need, fear, desire for status. It's you, your charm, your winning performance, finally. A nation of pearly-toothed salesmen.

Thanks. But, no thanks. Sadly, I could picture my dad bent over his third martini, watching Walter Cronkite and the CBS news; I saw my dad's loneliness, his emptiness. A shoeshine and a smile. My father, the businessman, the salesman, but when did the selling stop? In his rage? In his longing for his doctor dad, that huge roar of sadness? What about my dad's maudlin drunken recitation of how "the best is none too good," or, "Hey, I love you. You're a good kid, Garry, don't forget that, and good kids are hard to find." Was that a performance, too? Who, really, was he saying those words to? Or, was that *his* father talking to him in some old recycled drunken dream?

Selling books—dictionaries, Bibles—door to door. Oh, "Johnny Boy," I don't think so.

It was when we broke for lunch that I told John. So strange: the darkened auditorium, the spot-lit stage, with all the incentives lined up there: TVs, stereos, fancy suits, dress clothes, bicycles, motorcycles, barbells, treadmills, on and on, all sorts of items, big and small, and they can be YOURS, depending on how many books you sell! Not to mention the trips to Hawaii and Europe as well as Bonus Money Certificates, along with later that week, our being introduced to these rare individuals who had accomplished such feats, won these prizes. And again, foot-stomping, applause, as each one praised Southwest and shared their "wisdom of the road" as one very enthusiastic young man put it, gushing, laughing, further engaging us would-be salesmen/winners.

When we were dismissed for lunch and told to be back by two p.m., the lights came up, pow, as if windows had been opened, the drama and mystery and suspense suddenly lifted. Slowly, our crew made its way up the aisle. Others ran, the lobby doors, over and over, flapping open, with glimpses of sunlight. I stayed behind, sizing up the stage, now dulled, not quite so flashy, more like a busy, littered wood floor, not a showroom for Paradise.

Finally, the sun! Mid-day, this Southern city, Nashville. It was still a beautiful day out there. No. I cannot do this. There, out there, I need to be out there.

"Gar, what're you talking about?"

We were in the lobby, headed out the doors, then down a few streets and over, to the diner Kathy and I had found that morning. "I'm serious. I can't do this."

"*You* can't do this? Wait. Is this like when you told me you couldn't leave the baseball team to run track, and then—you burned up the place, running those incredible half-miles. Remember?"

"Durl."

"Gar, you *can* do this. In fact, you're a natural."

"Thanks, D, but look—"

"You *can.* You just don't *want* to."

"That's it: I don't want to sell books. I don't want to sell anything. In fact, I feel like that's all I've been doing my whole life. Junior high, high school, college, selling. Myself. Trying to impress. Always *trying.* Trying so hard, over and over, and, oh, Johnny, I'm tired. Enough already."

All of us were seated at the counter now. I thought maybe I should go find Kathy. We only had an hour for lunch. But. No matter. Maybe I'd take two hours. I wasn't going back in there. That dark labyrinth of bravado and hoo-hah. No way. John watched me, his brow furrowed. Then he fingered his jaw as he lowered his head, looked over the menu. Eddie was next to us, pretending to eye his menu but really eagerly watching our every move. This rebellion in the ranks thoroughly excited and delighted him. Monroe and Chuck sat looking at their menus. Brad kept watching John and then his menu, before we all put in our orders.

The waitress, who looked like a teenager but was probably older, freckles, big front teeth, a light grey uniform, took our lunch orders. When she got to me, I ordered a tuna melt and a 7-Up. After she took my menu, she said, "You awright?"

"Me? Fine. Why?"

She had this big goofy smile. "Just checkin'."

"Okay. Thanks."

"Sure."

"Why'd she say that?" I asked John.

"Probably thinks you're cute. See? You could sell her a dictionary. Right now. If you wanted."

"But I don't want to. I really don't."

"Okay. Let's eat and we'll talk about this."

"I don't think there's anything to talk about."

"Gar, come on."

Our drinks came first. Also, Eddie's chicken noodle soup. He said he liked things hot. It would cool him off. We all watched Eddie slurp his soup. Monroe asked Chuck a question which Chuck couldn't answer and called to John. John started to answer—the question was about the number of books a first-time seller should purchase for his first month of selling—and Brad, trying to be like John, spoke up. John chuckled, ducked his head, sipped his iced tea, and then nodded, laughing, "My protégé, ladies and germs, Brad German!" John reached around and patted Brad's shoulder. Everyone mock-applauded. Brad stood, took a bow.

The freckled waitress returned with a tray of our sandwiches, which she deftly placed before us. "And the tuna melt for you. With cole slaw. Sure you don't want fries?"

"Positive. Thanks."

"How ya doin' now?"

"Fine. Can I ask you something?"

"Sure." She stood there, goofy grin, waving her empty tray.

"What's your name?"

"Sarah Jean."

"Sarah Jean, why do you keep asking if I'm okay?"

"You remind me of this guy."

"Yeah?"

"He was real sweet. And cute. And he was selling books, too." John was listening now. "Last summer, end of the Welcome Week, like you're doin' right now—?"

"Okay . . ."

"He kind of went nuts."

John started laughing. Waved at Sarah Jean. A piece of his sandwich fell from his mouth. "That's right. I know who you're talking about."

"You know who I mean? Real sweet guy. Think he's in some mental—"

"Thanks, Sarah Jean, he doesn't need to hear this just now."

"Yeah, I do."

"I wasn't trying to interfere. My dad sells stuff. It's a good living."

"Okay," nodded John.

"Just, some people, it's not in their make-up."

"Right," said John, nodding way too much.

"You know who I'm talkin' about?"

"Tall guy, glasses, named Greg Something?"

"That's him. Great smile. Just like yours." She sweetly looked at me with that grin.

I finally spoke up, "Thanks, Sarah Jean. I like your smile, too. And your freckles."

She blushed. "Oh gosh, I can't help my big ol' blotchy freckles."

"They're nice."

"Thanks." She flushed. "So you guys got everything you need?"

"Yeah, Sarah Jean," said John. "Thanks."

"Just holler if you need somethin'." She walked off, waving her tray as if she were swatting flies.

Toward the end of our lunch, John, with Eddie leaning in close, told us about this Greg fellow. "He *was* a sweet guy. He was going to be a junior at a small religious college in the Midwest."

"Like a seminary?" I asked.

"No. A Baptist college in Missouri somewhere."

"Okay," I said.

"Greg had gone to an Ivy League school for two weeks, then transferred."

"Really?" This was Eddie.

"Academically he was a stand-out but emotionally, well, one night they found him running around naked, spouting off about Nietzsche and how the Military-Industrial Complex was his father, that he couldn't keep up. Crazy stuff. So, he was hospitalized. The school, his family, they all felt that Greg needed a smaller school, a simpler situation."

"Amen," I said.

"Look, Gar, the guy was already a loon, okay?"

"How do you know all this?"

John paused. Stared at me, then Eddie.

"Look, guys, this is strictly confidential . . . Big Jim told me. He felt horrible when he lost him last summer. Greg's dad had helped Big Jim, and Big Jim really wanted to help Greg become a young man in the world, learn things, make a living . . ." Now John zeroed in on me,

"Which is why you can't look down on this, Gar. It could be the most important experience of your life."

I nodded. "Right."

"Where's Greg now?" asked Eddie.

"Some mental facility near his home in Missouri."

Eddie continued, "What'd he do last summer—run around naked and quote Schopenhauer?"

"It was pretty disturbing." John stared at his soda.

"What? What'd he do?" Eddie leaned in even closer.

"I don't think he'd ever been with a girl. Supposedly, he went to this whorehouse with a bunch of the guys, and, after, how many floors is the hotel we're staying in?"

"Ten?" said Eddie.

"Eleven floors. He went to the top and threatened to jump."

"Jesus," said Eddie, and whistled.

"Yeah," said John.

As if on cue, the three of us went silent and stared down at our empty plates.

Sarah Jean joined us, stood there. "I know, empty plates make me sad, too." All three of us looked up. "How about some dessert? Gotta great rhubarb pie, pecan, even strawberry shortcake, whaddya say?"

"Well," said Eddie.

John shook his head, no.

"Rhubarb pie," I said.

"With nice creamy vanilla ice cream on top?"

"Please."

"Okay," said Ed. "Me, too. Why not? You only live once."

John returned to staring down at his plate. He fingered his soda, then, "Listen, Gar, I would really hate to lose you."

"Me, too."

Eddie excused himself. "Gotta pee."

I continued, "I really wanted to do this. I just didn't plan on this circus."

"I know, Gar."

"This selling thing. Winners. Losers. Omigod. I really see it now. It's such a mindset. It's how I was raised, what I've believed for so many years. What I've suffered, really, if I didn't win in sports or get the high grades."

"I know, Gar. Right."

"Durlie, please?"

"Sorry. Go on."

"Life. Art . . . the human condition isn't on a scale of one to ten. You're not an A plus or an F. You're John, my best buddy. What, Rembrandt's *Night Watch* is a B minus painting or Van Gogh's *Starry Night* was, in its day an F, but now an A minus? I can't do this anymore. He's a winner. Oh, him, big loser! Judgments. Twelve years, no, sixteen including college, I did this. But making art has done something to me. I see a small escape hatch. I've got this invisible rabbit with me now, and, all this measuring, defining, win, lose—big bucks or bust. No, that's a whole other way of life, which I'm not fond of. I can't, Durl. I really can't."

"Okay, Gar. Look. You made some good points."

"Did I sell you? Did I win big?"

"Gar, come on."

"But see?"

Eddie returned. "See what?"

"Eddie, we're talking, okay?" said John.

"Sorry." Eddie slipped back onto his counter seat. Then our pies arrived. Sarah Jean winked at me. Which made me laugh.

"What? What's so funny, Gar?" John was not handling this well.

"Nothing. She—" I pointed to Sarah Jean as she departed, but I had injured John, attacked his cause, his way of life the past three summers. While the others? Brad was outside looking at a map of Tennessee. Monroe and Chuck were both using toothpicks. Eddie devoured his pie a la mode.

John continued, "You got this 'invisible rabbit'? What does that mean?"

"Harvey."

"*That* invisible rabbit. Right." John shook his head.

"What invisible rabbit?" asked Eddie, ice cream drooling off the right side of his mouth.

"Eddie, please?"

"Sorry, John. Do you mean *Harvey*? I love that movie!"

"Isn't it a *great* movie?" I leaned back so I could see Eddie better.

"Omigod, it's so funny."

"Eddie, please, I need to talk to Gar," said John.

"Right." Eddie waved his spoon at me. "We'll talk later." Ed and I did talk later, not sure we ever got around to *Harvey.* As we walked back to the Convention Hall, John and I agreed: I'd take the afternoon off, be with Kathy. That day and each day after, the one thing John repeated was, "Gar, don't give up on this. Please. Just give it until the end of the week."

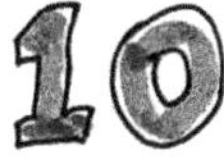

That first afternoon, Kathy, John and I stood in the Hermitage Hotel parking lot and watched as a red and white tow-truck pulled up alongside Titine, who sat there like a big grey beached whale. A lump. A load. Big Jim had recommended a garage called "Jolly's" out by the Twin Oaks Pass. I made a phone call and John offered to go with me and Kathy, in case we needed a ride back after delivering Titine. The garage, Jolly's Car Repairs, sent their own tow-truck into Nashville. I waved to the dark stubble-faced driver as he pulled up. We watched as the tow-truck guy, dressed in a grey uniform with a red sewn name of "Wally" above his left pocket, very quickly and efficiently unraveled chains, several of them, and then attached them to Titine, which he then levered and mechanically pulled up and secured.

It was hot in the sun. I said to John, "Johnny, really, you can get back to the Convention Hall. We should be okay."

"Gar, what if they can't fix it while you wait? No, I'll come, just in case."

"Really? After all I put you through at lunch?"

"Hey, I'm your best friend, remember?"

Kathy watched us and gave her sweet appreciative smile.

"Thanks, Durlie."

I nervously rode shotgun with Wally as Titine clamored and bumped behind us. But Wally drove as if we were just out for a Sunday cruise. John and Kathy followed in the Green Monster. It was a twenty-minute ride to just outside the city limits. Jolly's Car Repairs was a big high-ceilinged garage, white exterior, with an adjacent lot lined with cars, trucks, a few old refrigerators, too. Inside, two cars were being worked on. Wally backed Titine into the third slot.

A big husky man opened Titine's hood, had me start the car, or try to, in vain. They brought a charger over, attached wires. A young boy, fourteen or so, took my place behind the wheel and cranked the engine. It turned right over this time. I nodded to John and Kathy, who were standing near one of the other cars. It was nice to hear again Titine's sputter and chugging. The husky man, dour, serious, kept fiddling under the hood, touching wires, inspecting. He had the kid turn the engine off. Then, "Okay, Timmy? Start it again." Timmy did. The man fingered some more. "Okay, turn it off. Timmy?" He stood up, shut the hood, twisted his hand toward Timmy and called out, "Off!" Timmy gave a serious nod as he turned off the engine.

The husky man came over to me. Husky but not that tall. Solid, tanned, serious, he spoke with a Southern accent mixed with something Eastern European? I wasn't sure. His sentences were clipped. He didn't like to waste time.

"Alternator. Plus, a mess, that engine. Oil change, it needs, and some other fluids, things. So. Looking at about two hundred dollars' worth of work. Okay?"

"Two hundred?"

"You wanna pay more? I can make it three hundred."

I laughed. He stayed serious. I found out later that this was Jolly.

"No, no. Two hundred. I need to make a phone call first. I have this Mobil credit card. Is that okay?"

"Sure. You wanna phone? Timmy! Show this man our phone."

"Over here, Mister!" A fourteen-year-old calling me "Mister"? Okay.

Kathy joined me by the phone, which was on the wall next to a grimy doorway that had no door but led into a small dark office. John was over by one of the other cars, a blue Chevy sedan, talking to a thickly built mechanic with a bristly-looking mustache.

I was calling my dad's office. Finally, his secretary, Janeanne, picked up. "Oh, Garry, how are you?"

"Thanks, Janeanne, I'm pretty good."

"Are you down South now?"

"Yup. Arrived last night, in Nashville."

"Oh wow, Nashville! Is it hot there?"

"Hot and humid."

"It's pretty sticky here, too. You probably want your dad, don'tcha?"

"Is he around?"

"He was in his office a minute ago. Wait just a sec."

I waited. I watched Kathy, who stood close to me, fingering the seam on my right T-shirt sleeve. Then, when we made eye contact, she smiled, and quickly spotted something on my neck, and began fingering around the T-shirt collar, which wasn't a collar but a sewn neck opening.

"Here he is, Garry, have a great summer."

"Thanks, Janeanne."

"Yeah," my dad's dark baritone.

"Dad?"

"You never phoned. Remember? Your mom's been worried."

"I'm sorry. We drove all night. Like twenty-two hours."

"To Nashville?"

"Yeah. Got here last night. We started this sales indoctrination first thing this morning."

"Phone her. She'd like to hear from you."

"Right."

"What's goin' on?"

"Well . . . that twenty-two-hour drive, Titine had problems."

"Tit-teen? Who's that?"

"You know, my car."

"That French contraption."

"About halfway here, a garage guy said don't turn it off or it won't start up. We made it to Nashville, but, just now, we had it towed to this garage . . . the mechanic says it'll cost two hundred dollars to fix it."

"So? You got the Mobil card I gave you, right?"

"Right."

"So use it."

"But, Dad, I feel lousy."

"You should feel lousy. I told you that car's a piece o' junk. But you're a sentimental fool. So. It'll cost you."

"I'll pay you back. Please don't worry . . . I just feel bad."

"We'll figure things out later. Just make sure the car runs good—and you're safe. Okay?"

"Thanks, Dad."

"I gotta run. Call your mom."

"Will do. Love ya."

"Me, too. Bye."

Strange: I was crying. Kathy noticed. "Gar, you okay? What'd he say?" Then John came over. He saw me wiping my face with my T-shirt. "You okay, buddy?" Everyone was so sweet, it made me cry even more.

"Gar sweetie, your dad loves you. He's just so gruff." John nodded as he put an arm on my shoulder.

"You guys," I was teary and laughing, "he didn't yell or get mad. He just said . . ." I choked up again, "use the Mobil card and be safe."

"Really?" said Durl.

"Yeah . . . be safe."

"What a nice surprise," said Kathy, looking at John, then me.

"He also said that my car was a piece of junk and that I was a sentimental fool."

"So, he did give it to you."

"But he's right, Gar, you *are* a sentimental fool," said Kathy.

"And that's why we love you," added John.

When we returned to the hotel, Kathy decided to take a bath and freshen up. I went with John to see what the guys were up to, what the afternoon session had been like. They were taking turns practicing selling books.

John at one point asked, "So, did anyone actually sell a dictionary today?" Monroe raised his hand, as if he were still in class. "Chuck did a real good job selling me a Bible. I really think I would've bought it. Right, guys?" Brad and Eddie nodded. Then Eddie continued, "Yeah, I mean it got a little sticky with the spiritual stuff. But. If you were a believer, you'd have bought it. It was pretty good."

If you were a believer, you would've bought it. Eddie's words. They stayed with me. That evening, after Kathy came to the guys' room, we ordered a pizza. Eventually, Kathy and I left so they could watch a baseball game on TV. Everyone was exhausted.

If you were a believer, you'd have bought it.

I lay next to Kathy that night, thinking about those words, the day, John, Big Jim, Titine, this whirlwind gathering and book-selling circus and Nashville. I watched her sleeping, facing me, curled up. Her gentle, almost silent, breathing. The light through our hotel room windows, not moonlight—though it had that coolness—but the glow of the city itself, its hum and thrum and the streetlights' reflections, entering the windows, both of them open, curtained, the curtains now and then wafting with gentle breezes.

If you were a believer . . . but, I wasn't anymore. John knew this. I had told him. Yes, I'll stay the rest of the week. Attend morning sessions, but the afternoons would be mine. He was okay with that, "Just wait, Gar, you'll see." But I was seeing, wasn't I?

Seeing is believing. But what was I seeing now? What was I believing? There was a revolution going on inside me. And, I was confused: John remained so certain and yet, I was certain in another way amidst a path I'd chosen that remained very . . . uncertain.

11

Tuesday afternoon I took Kathy to the airport. At lunch, while Kathy packed and readied, John drove me to Jolly's garage where we picked up Titine. Jolly noted the rusted and rotted floorboard, driver's side, and some other external decay. He suggested a nearby body shop. I told him, Thanks but not now, paid with my dad's Mobil card, and then followed John back into Nashville. Titine hummed right along.

John came to the room with me to say good-bye to Kathy. They hugged, "Well," said John. He stood there, looked down.

"You guys have a good summer, okay? And, John, keep an eye on this crazy guy, will you please?" Kathy nudged John.

"Oh sure." John rubbed his chin.

"How's Brooke, by the way? I never asked you."

"She's got one more year at Smith and then next summer we'll wed."

"That's great. She's so sweet."

"She's working in a doctor's office this summer, not far from her folks in East Aurora."

"Tell her I said hi, will you?"

"Definitely. I'd better go find the guys." He turned to go, then turned back. "You have a good summer, too. Working at that Y camp again, right?"

"Right."

"Have fun." Then to me, "I'll see you later, Brown One."

"Yes, you will, Durlie."

We both watched as John loped down the hall. "He's a special guy, huh, Gar?"

"Very. Special. Like you."

"Oh pshaw." Kathy slapped my shoulder. "Come on. Take me to the airport."

Kathy had a small suitcase, her knapsack, and a purse. We loaded up Titine. "Titine's okay?"

"She's good. A little sad you're leaving but otherwise fine."

It was a forty-five-minute drive to the Nashville airport. I could already feel myself missing her. I tried to joke and make light, in vain. I told her about picking up Titine at Jolly's garage. "So Jolly," I began, "who doesn't seem so jolly—"

"Yes?"

"He noted the hole in Titine's floorboard."

"I'm glad he 'noted' it."

"Said I should get it fixed."

"He's right."

"But, Kathleen, that's how I keep this contraption moving."

"Whaddya mean?"

"My foot, sometimes my hand, I push off through this hole, see?" I began to demonstrate until, "Oh, never mind, a dumb joke."

"Oh. Ha. Funny, Gar."

Then, of course, there was Kink.

"Will Greg Kinkel be at the Y camp this summer?"

"You mean 'Kink'? I dunno."

We drove on in silence. Kathy looked straight ahead. It was an almost deserted freeway, straight to the airport exit. Beyond the city, empty lots, some suburban backyards, and then lots of fields, meadows on either side.

This would be Kathy's third summer at the Two Rivers Y camp, a couple of hours northwest of her home in Davenport, Iowa. She loved working there: a good, fun group of adults, and the kids all adored her. She was maternal, playful and athletic, too. She'd done synchronized swimming at Skidmore. Great legs, lithe, strong. She could be quite feminine with a dancer's flourish. And, she could be quite determined and competitive, so the boys loved her. She had been shy growing up, a bit of a tomboy, and then, athletically, much more adventurous than her fraternal twin, Chrissie.

Okay: I thought she was gorgeous. Her short cropped blonde hair (like a French cut), white skin that tanned to a wonderful umber, and a voluptuous, big-breasted figure—a body that was sexy, playful, and, because of her still remnant shyness, that much more attractive. She was an "Iowa farm-girl" (her description) who never saw herself as all that pretty. So, women and young girls were not threatened and boys saw her as one of their own. And camp counselors like Greg Kinkel—Kink—like me, thought she was hot, the end-all, be-all. Needless to say, I wasn't fond of Kink.

"Have you guys been in touch?"

"Who?"

"You and Greg."

"Everyone calls him Kink, Gar."

"I know."

"Yeah. He wrote me a while back."

"He didn't mention his summer plans?"

"Oh, Gar."

So, he'd be there. This would be his third summer, too. I'd met Greg Kinkel last summer, when I passed through Iowa on my way to visit Johnny D, who was selling dictionaries in Nebraska. I stopped in, saw Kathy's folks, spent the night. The next morning, on my way north and west to Omaha, I pulled into this elaborate pastoral playground of campsites, cabins, playing fields and a long blue lake. Kathy and I had lunch together. I met her girlfriends, a few adoring kids, and then this counselor who was her supervisor even though he was younger than she by a year or two. Greg Kinkel. Kink.

It struck me: he was a short, blonde version of me. He smiled a lot, was muscular (okay, more than I was), athletic (a gymnast or perhaps bantam wrestler), seemed like a fun guy, had a good sense of humor. He was sensitive, too. Damn. A good guy. I could see, as he watched Kathy, as she shyly tipped her head—as I watched him and then Kathy—oh God—they were attracted to each other. Like a jolt, I was flushed with heartache.

That was the summer I got the one letter from Kathy to my five. It wrenched me. It hurt. This was when I read my Bible, prayed, tried so hard to let go—let Fate or God or Whoever work it out. I told myself that, if I loved her, I couldn't own or control her. I had to believe that letting her go was the best way for me to love her. But, dear God, please, I didn't want to lose her. When Kathy finally wrote me near the end of that summer, it was newsy, cheerful, curious about how my summer had gone.

As our junior years began, we started seeing each other again, the Skidmore-Amherst commutes restored. That autumn she finally told me about Kink, that he was a devout Christian; how she relished the Y counselors' end-of-the-day get-togethers—the meals, trips to town, Bible studies, card games, board games, which were group activities for the most part. Until, one night, Greg—Kink—confessed to Kathy that he had fallen in love with her. Which surprised and pleased her. She told him about me, our friendship, and our love. I wanted more details and I didn't want more details.

Kathy then said, "He's young, Gar, and sweet. I really am fond of him as a friend, but you know."

Well. I didn't know. I was pretty sure they still had a mutual infatuation/admiration. Again, I was not going to beg or demand. I wanted Kathy to be with me because she loved me and wanted to be with me. Of course, I didn't know how to say this. I knew she cared about me. She knew I adored her.

And. We both knew that college was over now, that timeframe, that structure. Already there were instances when we were like an old married couple. But. We both knew that, first, we needed to find our work in the world, our callings. Kathy still wasn't sure about medicine. Her family was rife with doctors. So, perhaps teaching—she was so good with kids. Part of the draw of marriage, family, was how wonderful Kathy would be as a mother.

We'd never really talked about marriage. Now, with my clear-cut desire to become an artist, I knew I couldn't comfortably, or practically, ask Kathy to marry me. I needed to make my way in the world, establish myself. Too, there was this part of me that felt I was still too young to marry, too naïve, not ready. That is, I wasn't certain I could fit into or abide by that cookie-cutter pattern of the married and domestic as my siblings had, Kathy's, too. And now Durland was ready to fully commit next summer. No. I contained this resistance, this urge, to move out, move beyond. A deep need to see things, travel, wander, not be contained. Not yet. Maybe never. What did being an artist look like? I'd seen Mr. Porter, raising a family, writing (he'd shared with me an article he wrote about art and science), and I saw him painting, saw his work, but having a show, selling paintings? I had no real idea. I hadn't thought any of this through. I was still leaving the practical world where I thought I'd become a doctor, which meant years and years of further education, for this mythical world of becoming an artist, a painter. For me, that was about drawing, painting, learning this craft, observing. The only other counsel I'd had was that I should always find other work to do, so that I could make ends meet, while I continued to grow as an artist and develop a "body of work," whatever that was. If I ever did marry—Kathy and I had already felt this depth and desire—for my part, it would be Kathy. And for her?

"You think he's still in love with you?"

"Who are you talking about, Gar?"

"You know, your buddy at Y camp—Kink."

"Greg is a really good guy, Gar, but I don't know, he's a really devoted Christian, and, he's very determined to become a doctor."

"His name is *Kink,* Kath."

"What?"

"You said 'Greg.'"

"Funny, Gar. Ha Ha."

"Okay, look—"

"Gar. Let's not. I don't want to leave you talking about this. Please?"

"Okay. Yeah." There was no more highway. Just a right turn, a left turn, and another right turn. It was not a huge airport. Inside there were lots of photos of country singers and a big display ad for the Grand Ole Opry. Oh yeah. Nashville.

We hugged and kissed. Not a long romantic kiss but a pretty tender one. We both got a little teary. Kathy had Kleenex, wiped her eyes, fingered mine. We laughed. She promised that she'd try to write me. But not to worry. We still had plans to travel to Europe together in the fall, right? I nodded. We'd talked about it. Her family was flying over to England for her sister Ellie's wedding in September, and maybe

I'd fly, too, and then Kathy and I would backpack through Europe.

"You still want to do that, Kath?"

"Of course, you big lug."

"Okay."

"So just remember things, okay? Have a great summer, Gar."

"You, too, Kath."

We hugged a last time. She turned and quickly walked to the gate, a walk I cherished, a bit pigeon-toed, almost child-like. The attendant took her ticket, gave her the smaller portion. She turned. She waved. I waved. She disappeared.

I cried as I drove back to Nashville. Not sobs but tears. I said these dumb little prayers, too. Please God—about taking care of Kathy. About her and Kink: let them enjoy each other. Why not? Be friends. Good friends. But not that good, okay, God? Please? Silly things. About her love for me—does she really, God? My love for her—let it be whatever it's supposed to be. And this summer. And I'm scared. And this dictionary thing.

And Tennessee, or "Tin Sea," as they all seem to say it down here. And for John and the guys, our crew, and that Kathy travel safely. And my mom and dad, my sister and brothers, their families. It started kind of silly and then went on and on. Not the first of this sort of prayer, and probably not the last. Oh, take good care of my car, too, please. Dear Titine. Thank you, God. Amen.

12

With Kathy departed, the next few days I joined John and the guys for the morning session at the Convention Hall, and then after, for lunch. As agreed, the afternoons were mine. Mostly I'd just traipse around Nashville. Took my sketchbook and a book to read. Long walks. Glimpses. Sittings. Pen and ink sketches. Or, then just sitting, watching, waiting. And some reading. The only books I'd packed were the Bible and this big coffee table book, *John Marin on John Marin.* I've never liked carrying a Bible in public. Besides, that was mostly just for a brief reading to start the day. But the Marin book, as big as it was, often came with me. I appreciated Mr. Marin's kind of mouthy, cranky wit and wisdom. He loved life, art, drawing and painting, the sea, food, and a little bit of "Society," but not much. Which, given my present rebellious spirit, made him a keen and much needed ally.

The big twist came on Thursday night, the final night we'd all be together as a group. Instead of doing something en masse, we split up. Eddie and Brad joined two guys from Philadelphia who would be in their "territory," over toward Knoxville; Chuck and Monroe went off with three very devout Christian boys who would lead them into "the Promised Land" near Memphis. One of them liked saying about Elvis's home, "There's a divine reason why it's called Graceland. I just can't figure it out."

Big Jim invited John and me for dinner at his home, a little beyond the Nashville city limits. A small suburb called Hartsville, or as Big Jim called it, "Harts-vull," filled with developments until it became a section of bigger homes with big backyards and swimming pools. Big Jim and his wife, Kelly, lived in one of these. A creamy beige two-story, with a number of decent-sized trees, a small jungle-gym and swing-set out back, and, a pool. Just as we rang the doorbell, John whispered, "Don't ask about their kids."

"Why?"

"Just don't, Gar. I'll tell you later."

Kelly came to the door. "Hello, John." John offered his hand. "Oh, come here. Say hello." She gave John a big hug. "We're old friends now, right?" John blushed. "Right."

"And this must be Garry, the only one in the group with his head on straight. Hi."

I, too, offered my hand but, "No, no, you get a hug, too, for not getting sucked into this madness." She hugged me, quite nice and full. I didn't quite understand but I sure did appreciate it. Suddenly, I missed my mom. I missed Kathy, too.

"Well, come on in. Big Jim's upstairs, on the phone, in his office, on the john. I dunno, doin' somethin', but he'll be right down."

It was a simple house. Foyer. Stairs off, going up, a big living room with an L into the dining area and a kitchen adjacent. The living room had a big picture window that faced the backyard which seemed unusual. The backyard was big with a good-sized very blue kidney-shaped pool to the left with a grey wire and rail fence around it. The jungle gym and swings off to the right.

"What do you guys want to drink? Beers, wine, sodas, you name it."

"Oh," I said.

"A big glass of water is fine for me," said John.

"What kind of beer you got?"

"Gar!" said John, the scolding mother.

"Ha! Gotcha, Durlie." We eyed each other.

"What?" said Kelly. "I love beer. We have Coors, Bud, Bud Lite—those are Big Jim's. I'm a Heineken girl myself."

"No, no. Just pulling ol' John the Teetotaler's leg. A ginger ale's fine for me."

"7-Up, okay?"

"Perfect. Thanks."

Kelly was an attractive woman, brown hair done up, a pink blouse and light blue skirt, a cute figure, kind of busty. A cheerleader's energy with a truck driver's mouth. "Come on in the kitchen, guys, we're not formal here, and talk to me."

We followed her into a wood-paneled kitchen with lots of cabinets and a Formica counter. Windows over the sink looked out on a side yard. Late afternoon light (it was already past six) cut through the windows. An amber drink sat on the counter. Kelly's. Looked like the Scotch and rocks my dad often liked right after work. "So, come in. Sit."

We sat. Kelly began asking questions—as she opened the fridge, got my 7-Up, got John's water—about John's last year at Trinity, where was I from, where had I gone to college, and the one she seemed to take most delight in, "So, what're you guys going to do with your lives?"

John talked about becoming a therapist.

"You're still interested in that, huh? You were talking about that last summer."

John nodded, stretched, cracked his knuckles.

"And Big Jim says you're an artist, Garry. Is that true?"

"That's my dream, yes."

"Do you have a sketchbook?"

"I do."

"Can I see it?"

"Well, I left it in John's car."

"Could you get it? I'd love to see your drawings."

"Okay." As I left the kitchen, I heard John say, "He's really gifted. You'll see."

Going through the living room and out the front door, I realized that all the floors in the house, except the kitchen, were covered in this thick spongy white carpet. Outside, the heat was letting up, there were even a few breezes. But John's Green Monster, sitting in a last slat of sunlight, was warm inside. Stuffy. I grabbed my 9 x 12 ringed sketchbook and started back inside. Then, I hesitated. I paged through the sketchbook as if I'd suddenly become self-conscious or ashamed. Were there drawings I didn't want anyone to see? A few of Kathy, perhaps. Bra and panties. Nothing too risqué. Most of them were views through windows, or landscapes, and a bunch of quick ink portraits, faces: Eddie, Brad, Monroe, Chuck, and a bunch of John, my bud, as he and the guys sat there in that Convention Hall transfixed. Live models by default. A few watercolors, too, and some quick smudgy pencil doodles.

"Is that Big Jim?" asked Kelly. We were still in their kitchen, the sketchbook wide open on the white Formica, as Kelly paged through, John and I looking on.

"That's Big Jim," I said.

"Wow. You really caught him when he's in that kind of stupefied state of listening, which he rarely does."

"I heard that!" Big Jim had just entered the kitchen.

"Hi, honey. Come see."

"Hey, guys, you made it! Welcome!"

Big Jim had his white shirt still on, tie undone, green slacks. He came over, patted our backs, shook hands. Then he pecked Kelly on the cheek as he bent close and looked with her. "Hey, that's me!"

"That's what I'm saying. Isn't that a good likeness?"

"Jesus, you're good, Garry. Huh, honey? No wonder you don't wanna sell books, huh, John?"

"Well," John said.

"I know. We haven't given up on him yet." Big Jim winked. I looked at John. He shrugged.

"What're you drinking?" Big Jim asked Kelly.

"Scotch rocks. You want one? Here, you look. Start at the beginning. I'll fix it."

I turned the pages back to the front and Big Jim, John, and I looked. Kelly got ice from the fridge, then reached for the bottle of Scotch sitting on the counter. She poured the Scotch, added some water from the sink faucet, stirred it with her first finger, which she licked as she gave it to Big Jim. She then fixed another "Scotch rocks" for herself. All of us then continued looking at my sketchbook. Eventually, Kelly prepared a salad. An alarm went off on the oven. A casserole dish was inside.

At the dining table, John and I sat on either side with Big Jim at one end, Kelly at the end nearest the kitchen. Conversation continued as we ate Kelly's pasta casserole and salad with tomatoes. Wine was offered. I followed John's lead and declined. Kelly and Big Jim had a couple more Scotch rocks, then red wine. There was a big bowl of chewy rolls, warm from the oven, too, with real butter. It was a lovely home-cooked meal, food-wise, but about halfway through I realized what was going on. A last-ditch effort.

"You guys wanna go for a swim after dinner? You bring your suits, John, like I told ya?"

"Jim, I don't want anyone swimming in that pool, okay?"

"Honey, come on."

"They're nice boys."

"Honey, they're young men, for Christ's sake!"

"Jim, watch your mouth."

"Okay, okay. So, look, my question is this . . . Garry, you come all the way from Connecticut to Nashville" (pronounced 'Nash-vull'), "what're you going to do? Just tag along with John?"

"I suppose. Right, John? This is our last summer together as bachelors."

"Gar, you'll make a great salesman, you know that," said John.

"I think I would, yeah. But I don't want to."

"Look, when I met you, I knew right away, this kid's got it. I even told Kelly all about you, after that first day. Didn't I, honey?"

"You said he was tall, friendly, had a goofy grin and would probably be a damn good salesman."

"Thass right!"

"And then you said . . ."

"No, Kell, that's it. That's what I said."

"Right. But you also said—"

"Kell, that's it."

"No, honey. That's not it."

"Kell!"

"Jimmy!"

A stand-off. A pause.

"It's okay, Big Jim," I piped up. "What else did you say?"

"Well . . ." Big Jim looked down at his half-finished plate.

"What did you say, honey?"

"Well," said Big Jim, still looking down. "I'm not proud of this, okay?"

"Wasn't it something about how he'd be great at selling books if he, being Garry, with the winning smile, wasn't 'some kind of faggot artist'?"

Another pause, with John's gasp in it.

"Big Jim, really?" John was incredulous.

"Look, John—Garry—guys—I was tired, I'd been drinking. It was later in the week, right, honey?"

"Big Jim, it's okay," I said.

"No, it's not. But it was later, after I found out from John that you didn't want to sell. I got angry. Took it personal. I didn't even know you yet."

"Wow. This really upsets me," said John.

"What?" Big Jim looked at John. "Come on, Johnny, don't take it the wrong way."

"Open mouth, change feet, huh, honey?" said Kelly.

"Look, you shut your trap, alright? You're not helping."

"Oh? Well, I can tell you right now: Garry's no faggot. I'm a woman. I know these things."

"Oh?"

"Yeah. And another thing . . . sorry, John, to break Big Jim's spell. He *is* a great guy but, hey, he can be a jerk, too!"

"Kell," it was an intense whisper, "Will you please *shut up*?"

"No. I won't."

"I'm sorry. I need to go to the bathroom." John stood up.

"No, Durl, come on." I waved him to sit down.

"Hey, Johnny, come on, man. It was just a drunken slip of the tongue. I'm sorry. Really."

"No, Big Jim. It's okay. It's my contact lens. It fell out. I need to go to the bathroom, put it back in. Really. Be right back."

John departed, fingering his right lower eyelid, an actual clear contact resting on his adjusting finger.

Silence.

Big Jim looked at his empty wine glass. Kelly looked at Big Jim. I sat between them. My plate was empty. I was full. I sipped my 7-Up.

I stared out from the dining room through the front yard windows. Lights were coming on in the house across the street. It was a balmy summer night, the street darkening. Beyond, above rooftops and darkening trees, the sky was still bright, a gentle muted blue mixed with bright pink, oranges.

For a moment I remembered my mom and dad. This angry banter among the married. But my folks were so much older. Kelly and Jim were in their thirties. It depressed me. It scared me. I kept trying to think of something to say. I wished I was with Kathy, taking a walk down that darkening street. Holding hands. Quietly sharing things or just walking along, peeking in windows.

13

I wanted Jimmy Stewart to walk in, introduce Harvey to Kelly and Big Jim, pull up two more chairs, for the two of them, so that Elwood and Harvey could sit next to me, join us. Somehow, Kelly, wide-mouthed, would love Elwood P. Dowd and believe in Harvey. Big Jim would laugh at first but soon he'd become fond of Harvey, too. Elwood would admire Kelly's dining room, their home, the great meal she'd prepared, and then he'd invite them both to his home for dinner.

"When?"

"What," says Big Jim.

"When can you come for dinner?"

"Oh gosh, I dunno. Honey? When can we come?"

"Soon," says Kelly.

"How about tomorrow night? Say, around seven? Did I give you my card? Here." Elwood pulls a card from his vest pocket.

"Thanks," says Big Jim.

"Now don't call me on that number." Dowd is pointing to the card in Big Jim's hand. "Use this one, okay?"

"Fine," nods Big Jim. "Will Harvey be there?"

"He's always invited. Aren't you, Harvey?"

Dowd, Big Jim, Kelly—all three look up into the empty seat between me and Elwood.

"I like you, Harvey," says Kelly, still eyeing the empty chair. "You remind me a lot of our little boy, Charlie."

"Honey, don't."

"No. It's okay. Charlie is five years old now—forever—isn't he, Jimmy?"

"Please, baby."

"He died last summer, Mr. Dowd. Drowned in that pool out

there. Before we could put up that fence, right, Big Busy Handy-Man Jim?"

Big Jim whispered, "Kelly, honey . . ."

"Hi, Charlie." Dowd was talking to the empty chair where John had been sitting. "My name is Dowd, Elwood P. and—huh?"

"See, Jimmy, he *is* here with us."

"Honey."

"Oh," continued Dowd. "This is my friend Harvey. Yes, that's right, he *is* big for a bunny rabbit." Elwood laughed and turned to Kelly. "What a sweet little boy!"

"Isn't he? He's my precious . . ." She began to cry.

"Jesus, Kelly . . . sweetheart." Big Jim got up from his chair.

Then Elwood leaned in close to Kelly. "He's a wonderful little boy. He wants to know if he and Harvey can go for a swim in the pool."

"What?" Kelly raised her head.

"Oh God, no," said Big Jim, standing there, waving his hands. "No, Kell, right? That's *not* a good idea."

"Charlie said that? He wants to go swimming? Is that what you said, honey?"

"Please, Mommy?"

And there he was, their little boy, Charlie, getting up from John's chair, reaching for Kelly, his blonde tuft of curls waving, shimmering. "Please, can we?"

"Why, baby, of course, but first, give Mommy a big hug, okay?"

"Okay." He did. Kelly embraced this cute red-cheeked cherub, his eyes twinkling. As he squirmed out of her hug, I could see his dimpled smile, his eagerness and delight.

"Come on, Harvey, let's go. My mommy says it's okay."

"Why, Harvey," said Elwood, looking up, as Harvey was now standing, "I didn't know you knew how to swim. What? That's true, yes."

"What'd he say, Mr. Dowd?" asked Big Jim.

Elwood looked at Big Jim, smiled. "Harvey said that as close as we are, there's a lot I still don't know."

"Come on, Harvey. Let's go!" Charlie came over and looking way up, admiringly, he took Harvey's unseeable paw and they walked off.

"Be careful, Charlie."

"Okay, Dad."

"Please take care of my little boy, Harvey!" Kelly called after.

There was a pause. Then Elwood spoke, "What a lovely gathering. You know, you two make quite a handsome couple."

"Thank you, Mr. Dowd," said Kelly, using her napkin to wipe her eyes.

"Hey, you wanna drink, Dowd?" Big Jim started to move toward the kitchen.

"No, no. Maybe another time. Thanks for this wonderful little visit. I'll see you tomorrow night at seven, okay? The address is on my card. G'night."

"But—" said Big Jim.

"Good night, Mr. Dowd, and thank you," said Kelly. She waved her glass and then drank a last sip of her red wine. Elwood slowly got up, put back the two chairs, either side of the buffet, nodded to us, gave me a wink. Then, just before leaving the dining room, he stopped. He went to Kelly, where he leaned over and very gently kissed her cheek. He then stood and waved good-bye, as he strode out.

Kelly didn't look up or try to catch Elwood's eye. She just fingered her wine glass with her left hand and slowly, with her right hand, felt her cheek, where the kiss had been. So strange, and lovely, too. In reality, we hadn't said a word, the three of us, but just before John returned and sat down, out of this silence, Big Jim said, "Kell honey, you okay?"

"It's the funniest thing, Jimmy . . . I was just thinking about Charlie and how much he loved being in that pool."

"Kelly . . . honey."

"No. It's okay, Jimmy. I'm okay. It feels good. God, he loved to swim."

"He was good at it, too, huh, Kell?"

"Oh, Jimmy, not really but, God, how he loved to splash around."

They looked at one another, openly, honestly. Then John returned, his right eye a little red. He nodded, smile d. "Hope I didn't miss anything monumental."

"If you call dessert monumental—and I do—then you didn't miss it, right, Kell?"

"Oh yes! Who wants theirs warmed up with vanilla ice cream on top?"

John and I cleared while Kelly fixed the dessert: warmed-up, fresh-baked homemade pecan pie with large dollops of creamy vanilla ice cream on top.

Then, Big Jim and John, with me listening, discussed Big Jim's various crews, how things were coming along; John's crew and "except for Garry," Big Jim looked at me and winked, how did Johnny think things were going? Tomorrow was the rousing go-forth finale, were his guys ready? And, how much Big Jim admired John, hoped he'd consider, if therapy didn't pan out, moving to Nashville with his new bride and taking on a more advanced position with Southwest.

"Are you making me a job offer, Big Jim?"

"Listen, Johnny, you're the real deal. You're great with your crews, I've watched you these last three summers. You're a solid salesman, you care, you're fiscally conscious—you're also from the North. We need some new, Northern blood, and, I've been authorized by my superiors to make you, yes, a decent offer, upwards of twenty-five thousand dollars to start, a car, and a small advance toward the purchase of a house. Whaddya say?"

"The American Dream all rolled into one, and some pecan pie, too, if you care to change your mind?" said Kelly as she delivered ice-cream-covered pie to me and Big Jim (John had declined). Then she waited at the kitchen door for John's decision. John, smiling, looked at Kelly, who kept standing there. "What?" asked John.

"Well, have you decided?" asked Kelly, a cool eye on him.

"Omigod. This is too much, too sudden. No, Big Jim, I need to think this over."

"No, silly," Kelly chuckled, "I mean about the pie, got another nice piece all warmed up?"

"Come on, Durlie, it's not booze, it's just . . ." and I took a good, close-up look, "a delicious looking piece of gooey pecan pie all lathered up with oh yum, creamy ice cream. Come on!"

"What the hell? Yes, Kelly, thanks. Bring it on!"

She did. We all ate pie, wonderful, oozy pecan pie. Of course, Kelly and Big Jim had gone back to drinking, their Scotch rocks. Then things got weird again.

"So, John's got the American Dream waiting for him," said Kelly, slurring her words just a bit, and winking at John. "But what does Garry have? Just his little old sketchbook?"

"Hey, that's *his* dream, right, Big Guy?" said Big Jim.

"It's all pretty much unknown just now."

"But perhaps, wise," offered Kelly.

"If you talk to my dad, I'm a fool."

"A wise fool," insisted Kelly.

"My question is, how you gonna make a living? What's one summer with your best buddy, selling books? Save up some money," said Big Jim.

"Yeah, Gar, sell books, save money and have a final summer together."

"Guys, it's like a physical reaction. I'm not afraid of work, good, hard, physical work. I just can't sell anymore. I'm done."

"Anymore?" asked Big Jim.

"But, Gar."

"Durl, it's all I've done—is charm and smile and persuade and sell—*myself.* Remember when I was class president in high school? Remember some of those high school and then, even some of my college professors? Even my own dad. I can't do it anymore. I've had it."

"Okay, Gar. Okay, buddy," John spoke gently.

I guess I was near tears, which surprised me.

"There's a woman you boys should talk to, over at Big Jim's Southwest office," said Kelly. "Trudy Gilligan. Isn't that her name, Jimmy?"

"What about Trudy?" snapped Big Jim.

"Trudy knows things."

"Kelly."

"Ask her."

"Kell, just shut your mouth, dammit!" Big Jim was almost shouting.

"Big Jimmy, these boys should know the lies a good ol' American Dream is built on."

"Stop it right now. Jesus!"

"I'm just saying." Kelly looked at us. "Ask Trudy. Trudy Gilligan. Ask her what these books are worth."

"Kell, John and Garry both know what these dictionaries cost."

"Dictionaries, Bibles, not their *cost.* Everyone knows that, Jimmy. What they're really *worth.* Ask her."

"Okay." Big Jim clapped his hands and made a big laugh. "That fine lady of the fine pecan pie has spoken! Who wants more pie, besides me? Huh?"

It was as if Big Jim took a big eraser and just wiped and laughed and cleaned the blackboard of whatever had been written there: his pressuring of me, eliminated; discussion of the summer and crews and John's job offer, gone. All subjects changed. Moving on. Big Jim had another piece of pie. Kelly had a refill of now an iced and milky liqueur. Big Jim put on a Frank Sinatra record as we moved into the living room. Eventually, he and Kelly began to dance and carry on. Then Kelly pulled John up from the pink sofa to dance, too. Even me, toward evening's end, not slow songs but a slower song, she beckoned and I followed.

She was a good dancer, drink still in hand. While Big Jim and John began to talk at the far end of the living room, Kelly casually whispered to me, "Follow your dream, Garry. Follow it hard. These books are dirty, dirty money . . . I know we've been damned here but what are you going to do? It's the Good Life, right?" She reared her head and laughed. Big Jim looked over and called to her, "What's so funny, Kell?"

"The Good Life, Jimmy. It's a laugh riot, right, honey?"

"Right, baby . . . That's what ol' Blue Eyes says."

Just then Frank Sinatra was intoning, "It's the good life . . ." Kelly leaned in close, her breath, warm, sweet, boozy. "Talk to Trudy. Tomorrow. Trudy Gilligan. She'll set you straight."

14

A piece of moon was already halfway up in the darkened night sky as John drove us back to the Hermitage.

"Jesus, Durl."

"What?"

"It's after midnight."

"I know. I thought this was going to be like last summer, a bunch of crew leaders, y'know. A big cookout, which Big Jim loves, people coming and going. But, God, we couldn't just leave."

"Did their son drown?"

"That's probably why. End of last summer, their little boy."

"Charlie, five years old?"

"Yeah. Really tragic. Kelly took it very hard. Big Jim, too."

"I can imagine."

"Wait. Who told you? They tried to keep it hush-hush."

How did I know? I wasn't psychic and I'm not trying to say artists have magical, intuitive gifts. I didn't even think I was really an artist yet. I had a gift, yes, for drawing, and some of my paintings were pretty good. A vivid imagination, I had that. A vibrant fantasy life, too.

If I tell John about Elwood and Harvey's visit, well, he already questioned my mindset, given my anti-bookselling vehemence. Recounting this wishful encounter might really shake him. So, I made a joke: "Harvey."

"Who?"

"Harvey told me."

"Oh right, the big white bunny. No, Gar, come on, who told you?"

"Not sure. Maybe it was you?"

"I know I said don't ask about their kids."

"*Kids?* Plural?"

"Big Jim was married when he was like seventeen. An older woman, who had a daughter. Then they had a girl together, before he divorced."

"Oh man, life's complicated."

"Yeah."

As John drove, I sat there, riding shotgun. Both of us tired, it reminded me of the first years of our friendship. It had begun at Middlesex Junior High but took off in high school, especially when we both began to drive. The summer after our junior year had sealed it. We would hit Pear Tree Beach or Weed Beach, late afternoon, swim, throw the Frisbee, and after, go get a California Burger at this beat-up diner on the border of Stamford/Darlington. Then, we'd just drive around town, looking for girls.

That was the summer I thought I didn't know how to talk. I was so self-conscious. I'd been in Advanced English, sat next to Newly West, who was so verbal and bright but couldn't look you in the eye. She always looked at my forehead when we spoke. But, in that class, Mr. Adams, "The Porcupine" (he had a bristly crew cut that seemed to run from the top of his head down into his back since he had no neck to speak of), would call me Teddy Bear. The big Teddy Bear, making fun of my being a jock. He often put me on the spot. I'd stiffen and go cold, clam up. Vocal paralysis. Self-fulfilling prophecy: jocks can't talk.

We also lost games with me as quarterback on the varsity football team. I felt responsible. And, I felt a great deal of shame. But John stood by me. He really believed in me. That summer he said, "We're going to talk to people, all sorts of people, and regain our confidence, okay, Gar?"

And we did. We didn't meet any neat girls but we sure gained a lot of confidence.

As we entered Nashville, I said to Durl, "Feels like a California Burger night. Remember, Durl?"

"Yeah, Gar." He squinted his eyes, smacked his lips. "Those California Burger nights. Oh man, what I wouldn't give for a California Burger."

We kept talking about those burgers as we approached the hotel, parked the car. California Burgers. What made them *California* Burgers? Maybe it was the lettuce, tomato, onions. Avocados on burgers hadn't hit the East Coast yet. Or had they? Whatever. By the time we walked through the hotel lobby, low lit and empty, we'd gotten ourselves into a state of heightened hunger alert.

"You hungry, Durl?"

"You wanna?"

"But where at this hour?" We reached our floor, shaking our heads. "Naw," I said. "It's late."

"We gotta big day tomorrow. The big send-off," whispered John.

"D-man, I wanna go talk to this Trudy Gilligan."

"When?"

"What if we go first thing tomorrow, like nine a.m.? Talk to her and then be at the Convention Hall by ten and all?"

"I suppose."

"Can we?"

"Sure. Why not? Good night, Brown One."

"'Night, Durlie."

That's not how it played out. It was a rushed and ragged last morning. Both John and I overslept, as did Eddie and Brad. They, too, had stayed out late. Chuck and Monroe, having gone to bed by ten, eager to sell Bibles, were the ones to wake us. We all managed to grab breakfast in the hotel coffeeshop, check out, leave our bags with the concierge, and run over to the Convention Hall where things continued to feel rushed. Which apparently, by now, was the whole idea.

There were final pep talks by various crew leaders; a finale speech by one of the new young execs who had been recently promoted and knew well the rigors of door-to-door sales. He gave some final exhortations, full of what was considered hip wisdom and humor. His penultimate crack, "Keep your pants on!" went over very big. There was more music, flag-waving, foot-stomping, and then cheers as guys finally hurried off to buy their books and begin their adventures.

It was a beautiful day. The morning air had been clear, even a little cool, like a late June day in New England. But by mid-morning, you knew that hospitably Southern humidity would take over. By midafternoon, it did. As John and I drove over to the Southwest offices, the heat was in full and sticky bloom. But the skies remained bright and clear, that end-of-week energy was in the air, and, too, there was this whisper of joy (in me) that all this book-selling folderol was finally finished.

John had been to Southwest headquarters before. He knew the way. Not a long ride, it was on the edge of Nashville, between the city and Big Jim's house in Hartsville. Brick building, lots of glass windows, a grassy courtyard, and a surprisingly tall five stories. Like a tall elementary school building. Inside, lots of fluorescent lighting as well as natural light. Lots of small offices and cubicles. Wall to wall carpeting everywhere, and, of course, the immediate cool and shiver of constant air conditioning. Even in our shirts and shorts, a great relief.

Driving over, John had said he was concerned about Big Jim, that he never missed the finale Friday send-offs. But this Friday, no one had seen him. John had spoken to one of the other crew chiefs who said Big Jim had been there earlier but then something urgent came up at home and he quickly disappeared. If Big Jim wasn't in his Southwest office, John wanted to call him or go by his house to say good-bye.

So, we first went to Big Jim's office on the fourth floor. John explained: the bigwigs were on the fifth floor, the lesser execs on the lower floors. When John first met Big Jim three years ago, Big Jim had a small cubicle on the second floor. Obviously, he was doing well, a young gung-ho exec on the rise. But Big Jim wasn't in his office.

"A company man," I said, as we headed for the elevator.

"Whaddya mean, Gar?"

"You know: Rah-Rah, a Company Man."

"Meaning?"

"A Company Man. No doubts, full speed ahead."

"And?"

"Like my dad, for example."

"That's what I thought."

"What?"

"This book-selling disgust is coming from—"

"Don't. Come on, Durl. Let's just find Trudy."

"Right. To be continued."

To be continued? It *is* continued. These companies. These corporations. These anonymous elaborate collaborations. These men, these women. These armies. Even these institutions of higher learning, colleges, grad schools, even high schools. Even small towns. But. Groups. I was sick of groups. Their laws, their unspoken agreements. Their dress codes. Their moral codes. My dad had certain very high standards by day and then he got drunk at night. It all seemed stupid and ridiculous. What then, really, was it all about? Kelly was adamant that Trudy Gilligan knew things, not the books' cost but their *worth.* What did that mean, exactly?

We found Trudy down on the first floor.

"Ten dollars and twenty-five cents. That's right. The Bibles are even cheaper because their plates date from the twenties."

"What?!?" John was incredulous.

"Kelly called me, said you might come by. You must be Garry then? Nice to meet you."

Trudy was interesting. Perhaps in her fifties, she was a big woman, fleshy, big busted, a strawberry blonde with a kind of reddish Irish face, a Reubens body, voluptuous, really, but this prim, clipped, even edgy way of speaking, with little or no Southern accent. "That's 'cause I'm from up North. Massachusetts. Boston Irish. Followed a young man down here. He departed, I stayed. End of story. Or, just the beginning, I guess." She looked up, rolled her eyes and reared back with this big bosomy shake of a laugh. She wore a flower-print blouse, freshly ironed, and watched us both from where she sat, as we stood there like two guys who had just pulled away a drop rug, found a hidden door in the floor, turned its latch and pulled it open, to find this ruddy-faced woman looking up at us with a handful of mysterious playing cards that held all manner of secrets.

"So, wait a minute," John said, fingering the air.

"How is Kelly? She okay? What a loss."

"Yeah." Both John and I bowed our heads, nodding.

"He was something, that little boy. A rare one."

"Listen, Mrs. Gilligan—"

"Miss. Miss Gilligan but please call me Trudy. Big Jim's never been the same either. Think that little boy was a chance for them both to start over."

"Trudy, I'm sorry," interrupted John.

"What're *you* sorry about? You got your whole life ahead of you. Y'know, I've firmly decided, youth *is* wasted on the wrong people."

I laughed at this. John tried to get her attention.

"John, right? You've been with Big Jim for at least two summers now, correct?"

"This is my fourth."

"And this is the first time we're meeting? How strange. Anyway, you were saying?"

"The books."

"Big money makers. Ten bucks for the dictionary plates, five or so for the Bibles. You boys buy 'em for, what, twenty a dictionary, ten a Bible. Then sell 'em for—think it's up to like twenty-five a dictionary, fifteen a Bible, right?"

"Right." John nodded.

"Royal rip-off, if you ask me. But who's asking? Are you asking? Don't."

"What?" said John.

"Don't ask me. In fact, this is strictly confidential. I didn't tell you, okay? But. Now you know. Somewhat disillusioning. But it pays the rent and, I'm sure you've had three wonderful summers, right?"

"Right," said John. "Wow. This is crazy."

"Hey, welcome to my world."

"So, these plates, they're not even current."

"Let's talk in whispers, shall we?" Trudy leaned toward us conspiratorially. John and I leaned down toward her. Whispering, Trudy continued, "The dictionary plates are from the fifties."

"But it says 'New and Revised.'"

"Yeah, as of 1951. Which is twenty years ago."

"I can't believe this!" John took a fist of air and flung it.

"The Bible plates, well, it's the King James, they're from 1923, old plates. Look at the books, those pages. Pretty old looking. But with Bibles, people don't mind. They like old, they like history and the classics, religious people seem to. I'm just surprised folks haven't figured out how old those dictionaries are. But, they're not buying dictionaries, are they?"

"Whaddya mean?" John was almost defensive.

"Those people, most of them poor, rural, kind of innocent, right? You're selling them hope, their sons and daughters doing better than them. A future, right? Getting ahead, doing better. The good life, right?"

"Well . . ." John fingered his chin.

"It's true." I looked at Trudy. "That's what I said to John. It's a con job. They're buying him, his charm and something they don't really need."

"Gar, look. I never sold a person a book they didn't want."

"You know what I mean."

"Right. But it's not just Southwest. America sells things 'cause we need things."

"That much?"

"Gar, come on, our whole economy, our whole national psychology."

"Precisely."

"Then when does it stop?"

"Does it ever?" asked Trudy. "If it did, I'd be out of a job, and oh-oh." Trudy looked past us, down the hall. "If I don't stop, I will be out of a job."

Then she called and waved, "Hi, Big Jim!"

15

Emerging from the elevator, marching past the rows of cubicles and offices, was Big Jim, navy blue sports coat flapping, a brisk khaki-legged walk, as he nodded and waved and called out people's names on his way to us, "Hey, Trudy." Big Jim smiled as he swooped in to join us. "Hey guys. Jesus, thought I'd lost y'all. Got back to the Hall, y'all were gone."

John rubbed his chin. "Everything okay at home?"

"Yeah, Johnny. Damnedest thing though. You'll appreciate this, Trudy. So, our pool's been fenced off since last summer. But Kelly thought she heard swimmers in the pool last night. After you guys left, I checked. Nobody. This morning she calls me at the Hall, 'Come home, Jimmy, please.' She's all worked up, she's sure someone's in the pool. I get home, march her out to the backyard, swivel her head, force her to look. Of course, I'm just expecting our dumb ol' kidney full of blue water, right?"

"Kidney?" asked Trudy.

"The pool shape."

"Of course."

"Would you believe it? This big ol' white rabbit is treading water. Size of a big cat or a smallish dog. Big, beautiful rabbit. Charlie loved rabbits. Anyway, Kelly starts screaming, goes wild. Then, after I almost fall in trying to grab the crazy critter, she starts laughing hysterically."

"A rabbit. In your pool?" asks Trudy.

"Big. Furry. White. We dry him off. He doesn't move or try to scurry away. Just a big white lump. Those pink ears, pinkish eyes, y'know. Well. Kelly's sure it's a sign. So . . ."

"A sign?" asked Trudy.

"You know, to do with Charlie."

"Of course," nods Trudy.

"So. We're keepin' him. Had to run to the pet shop before I could get back to the Hall. She wants to feed him, find a nice spot for him, maybe in Charlie's room. Crazy, huh?"

John just kept watching Big Jim, nodding. It all made perfect, if somewhat eerie, sense to me.

"Does he have a name?" asked Trudy.

"Bartholomew. 'Call him Bart,' said Kell. No. Wait. She saw this movie a long time ago about this rabbit. Called *Harvey.* She might call him that."

"Harvey," said John.

"Oh, that's a great movie," Trudy laughed. "Jimmy Stewart and his invisible buddy Harvey! Ha!"

"Harvey," John said again, almost deadpan, looking at me.

"What?" I asked Durl.

"Gar, your guy—*Harvey*!"

"Not *my* guy, but, yeah."

"What are the odds?" John kept eyeing me as if I'd somehow cooked this up.

"What?" said Big Jim.

"Gar has this artistic vision thing that—"

"It's a long story." I cut John off.

"Not that long, Gar. Not yet," said John.

"True."

John then turned serious. "Big Jim, you and I need to talk."

"Great."

"That's a nice story, Big Jim," said Trudy.

"Thanks, Trudy. It's the happiest Kell's been in a lotta months. You good?"

"Never been better."

"Good, good. Sounds like John needs my undivided attention so if you'll excuse us . . ."

"Of course. Have a good weekend."

"You, too, Trudy," Big Jim said this as he tried to put his arm around John's shoulder. Very deftly, John slipped it off as they walked toward the elevator. I followed but I wasn't sure I was supposed to.

I hung back. I had my sketchbook. One thought was to go back and do a pen and ink of Trudy, sitting there. Then, no, what about one of John and Big Jim talking? I watched them. First John spoke, at length. Big Jim waved his arms, began his reply. Then they both looked back at me. Big Jim smiled, waved.

I waved back as I got my pen and opened my sketchbook. I kept standing there between Trudy, as she returned to her paperwork at her desk, and John and Big Jim getting into it over by the elevators. Then, in loud whispers, they began again, going back and forth. Fingers were used, hands. Now Big Jim's waving, then John's joining with his own waving. Whispered words, intent, pointed, and fingers waving. Some of this seemed to repeat itself. I tried to draw them but they were moving too much. Then Big Jim put his hands on his hips, looked away from John, toward the elevator. John bent close, waiting, listening. Big Jim looked back at me, didn't really see me, nodded, smiled, and again, tried to put an arm around John, as if about to tell a joke and walk him back toward me. No. This time John slapped away Big Jim's arm. "No, Big Jim," said John. "Stop. That's it."

"But, Johnny." Big Jim turned. They both faced each other. No words, just eyes locked. John, tall, dark haired, thin, intent. Big Jim, barrel chested, stout, thinning blonde hair—a big man in a navy sports coat and khaki slacks, just as intent. Stalemate.

"Okay." Big Jim put his hands in his pockets, standing there.

"Okay." John still watched Big Jim.

"You sure?" Big Jim looked down, rubbed his nose.

"I'm sure."

"Fine," said Big Jim.

"Fine," answered Durl.

"Okay then. You boys have a safe summer." Big Jim turned very abruptly, hands still in pockets, and headed for the elevator.

"You, too," said John as he turned, walked toward me. As Big Jim got in the elevator, I called out, "Good-bye, Big Jim, thanks for everything!" I saw a part of his hand give a slight wave as the elevator doors closed. As John approached, he didn't look at me. His eyes darkened as he passed. "Come on, Gar, let's go."

I closed my sketchbook and joined him. We marched past Trudy's desk. John said nothing. I waved to her and shrugged. As we neared the first-floor stairwell, Trudy called out, "Good luck, boys!"

The Green Monster was unlocked. John just stood by his driver's side door. So, I stood by the passenger door. His white shirt sleeves rolled up to just below his elbows, he placed both on the Green Monster's scaly rooftop. Which was very hot. But John stayed leaning there, keys jangling in his hands as he fingered them, his gaze way up, into the blue sky.

"Durl?"

"No. I'm okay." He kept watching the sky. His fingers and those car keys had more of a conversation than we did. With a sudden rise and swoop of his right hand, thankfully free of the car keys, John hammered the Green Monster's rooftop—THWAT!

"DAMMIT!" John cried out, "I don't fucking believe this! FUCCCKKK!" After a breath, he stepped back and began to wring his right hand and say, "Ouch." As he massaged his bruised fingers, he continued, "You were right, Gar. You were fucking right!"

"I'm not glad I'm right," I inserted. "You okay, Durlie?"

"Yeah. I just—OWWW! It still HURTS!"

"Want me to kiss it, make it better?"

"Come on, Gar, this isn't funny."

"Sorry."

"My summer just exploded. Disintegrated. Pow! Jesus. It's a fucking rip-off . . . and . . . you figured it out. The first day!"

"No, Durl, I just wanted to be outdoors. To paint. You know."

"Still. It's a con job . . . they get us kids to do their dirty work. Sell these 'great books' to the poor and ignorant . . . it's a fucking Children's Crusade. And then, Jesus, I thought *I* made good money. Holy cow! They rake in the bucks! While we sweat all summer going door to door. No way! That's it. Over and outta here! Come on. Let's go."

John pulled at his door. It wouldn't open. With his backside against the car, he brought his bruised fingers close to his face, where he kept massaging them.

"Durl?" I went over to assist.

"Shit." He was licking his fingers. "Jesus, they're like on fire!" He looked at me, held up his reddened hand. "See? This is what you call adding injury to insult . . . oh man . . . OW!"

I offered to drive but John insisted he was fine. We drove back to the hotel, got our bags. Ed, Brad, Chuck, Monroe—their bags were gone. Never got to say good-bye. John said they were good guys, they'd be fine. They might even sell some books. But he was done, wanted to get out of Nashville right now. Which we did.

We loaded up our two cars. I took in the Hermitage and environs, the Convention Hall was a few blocks away. The diner. The city streets surrounding the hotel, this whole rag-tag hodge-podge of old and new, rich and poor, city conglomeration, "So long," or as Durl was feeling it, "Good riddance."

But where were we going? "I don't know," said Durl. "It's the weekend, right? There's supposed to be a nice area northwest of Nashville—we'll just head there, find a motel, or we could camp out, Gar, how about that? Let's just get out of Nashville."

"Fine."

So, we didn't have a plan. Okay. But . . . "I don't like the idea of camping out."

"Why not?" Durl was not happy.

"I'm not a big camper-outer."

"It could be fun."

"Yeah. Not my style."

"Thought you were a Mr. Big Outdoors guy."

"For painting not sleeping."

"We'll get a paper then, find a furnished room. Who knows? Let's just get going."

We got going. Something occurred in John's car soon after we left the Southwest offices. One of those ways, as young men, we could feel close but without that sense of cloying, mushy sentimentality, although that's exactly what it was. I remember how John tapped the steering wheel with his good hand, how he smiled—beamed—and how I joined him. How happy we both were, this surprise gift after so much rushing, tension, those flurries of doubts, questions, and then outrage. It was a song on the car radio, "Oh, don't it hurt deep inside . . . Oh, don't it pain to see someone cry . . . especially if that someone is her . . ."

John heard its beginning chords, then turned it up. ". . . Silence is golden, golden but my eyes still see . . ."

John had always been basically a private young man. I was the chatty extrovert while John often hung back, listened, observed. The past three summers had been a real challenge for him, a stretch. They'd forced him to come out, talk to people, warm up to them, persuade them, charm them, and, yes, sell them. In a way, while he found he actually enjoyed people, enjoyed selling, he also found himself, this piece that was not unlike me. John had been emerging these last few summers while I was actually trying to slow down, go inward.

". . . Talking is cheap people follow like sheep . . . even though there is nowhere to go . . ."

Under that still blue sky of afternoon, as we reveled in relief and liberation, this song became magical. I joined Durl's voice, the two of us intoning . . .

". . . Silence is golden, golden but my eyes still see . . ."

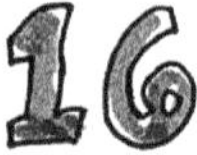

I followed John as we headed out of Nashville, the same highway that had led us to Hartsville and Big Jim's home. Only this time, as we passed the Hartsville exit, John pointed to it and gave it the finger. It surprised me as a bit extreme and totally unlike Durl. But he was still pissed off and might be for a while. I honked and waved back and started flipping numerous birds every which way, hamming it up as if it was all a big joke. John didn't respond except to look in his rear-view mirror, nod, and then leave his left hand dangling out his window with that raised finger still in place, like a trail of disgust. Like a record stuck on the words "Fuck you" over and over . . . fuck you, fuck you, fuck you . . .

About a half hour out of Nashville we stopped to get gas, grab sodas and snacks. Okay, I got a soda and peanut butter-filled cheddar crackers, John got a small orange juice. Plus, a local paper. When I came out, snacks in hand, John was sipping his juice, the local paper, *The County Bugler,* spread out atop the Green Monster's roof. He'd found the "Rooms for Rent" section and was slowly skimming over it with his finger.

"The guy inside said there's also a rec area with a lake and campsite about a half hour from here."

"Think I'd prefer a furnished room or a motel."

"Okay, Gar."

I opened my crackers and munched. John sipped. We both eyed the listings.

"How about that one?" I pointed.

John read it aloud, "'Nice home. Private furnished room. Gentlemen preferred. No pets. Fifty dollars per week'?"

"Here." I gave John my pen. "Circle it."

John did. We circled a few others. John said he remembered this other area northwest of Nashville from a few summers ago.

Not long after we got back in our cars, I followed John off the highway. Fortunately, most of the Friday night traffic was headed in the other direction which puzzled me until later, when John explained, "The Grand Ole Opry, Gar."

One furnished room was on a farm, fairly run down. John didn't want to bother, it was so shabby looking. But I was curious. The old woman was hunched and spoke in single Southern words I could barely understand. No.

The second stop was a small house next to a gas station where a group of young boys hung out, smoking, laughing, carrying on. The woman stayed in the kitchen. Her husband, half naked, hairy chested, beer in hand, chain-smoking, said he'd be glad to show us the room, but they didn't want "no homos." I assured him we were not. He took us upstairs. It was a child's bedroom with a tilted eaves ceiling that had both John and I stooping. As we departed, we thanked Mr. Beer-belly, who stood in the doorway, shouting at the boys over by the gas station. Just before he turned to go in, I grabbed Durlie, threw my arm over his shoulder and kissed him on the cheek.

"Gar!" John flinched.

Then Durlie, getting the joke, grabbed my butt as we skipped our way over to our cars. It was quite a moment: Mr. Beer-belly and the boys all stopped dead, watching. Then came a series of groans and hoots from the boys and a harsh door-slamming from the house. Boys will be boys. We drove on.

It was now early evening, clouds beginning to move in, a gentle darkening, dusk's slow moves to take over. Strange, how the sky had a darkening coldness but the air was still damp and hot, even steamy.

We pulled into a long narrow driveway, gravel tracks for the tires and a worn grassy middle. The woman was perhaps in her fifties, a worn white face, no make-up, a blue checked dress. She wiped her hands on a long grey apron as she welcomed us, nodded, invited us in.

She was very quiet, shy, and for the rest of our visit, in her living room, upstairs in the second-floor bedroom, and even as she stood there outlining the weekly rent, the few rules (no pets, no smoking, no loud music), she always seemed to retreat to a posture of standing on one leg, her right, holding her left hand, open-palmed, beside her left cheek. Her name was Mrs. May, polite and lovely. Her home and this furnished room did intrigue me. I was not put off.

"It's a very nice room," said John.

The light blue walls had a few framed reproductions of old paintings. One was Rembrandt's *The Jewish Bride,* where the husband is touching his young wife's middle. The white ceiling was high, which gave the room some space. There were twin beds, a dresser, a big old brown shaded lamp sat on the small mahogany night table between the two beds, which were nicely made up with plain grey coverlets.

I liked this room a lot.

"You have a lovely home, Mrs. May . . . this room is really nice."

"Why, thank you." She nodded, no smile but a worried look, her left hand firm on her left cheek.

"I'm sorry," said John, "what's the rent again?"

"It's a weekly. I have two other boarders. People come and go, so it's easier this way. Twenty a week."

"From each of us?" I asked.

"Oh no. For the room. However you split it, is up to you. But I do prefer cash. No exceptions. Also, now and then, I do offer a small breakfast, mostly just the weekends."

"Really?" I was getting hungry. I liked this room. Nice twin beds. Nice lady. Nice home. Why not?

"I don't know, Gar."

"But, Durl."

"Let's think about this for a minute."

"You boys talk it over. I'll be downstairs. Just call out if you have any questions, okay?"

I watched as Mrs. May wiped her left cheek with her left hand, then used that same hand to pull the door just about closed as she seemed to dance away, her grey apron a billowy slash, a grey gleam of exclamation point as she departed. I could see out the window it was now dark but for a twist of light on the horizon, beyond trees, where sparks of last sun mixed with fire, it seemed, for a brilliant sunset. I turned to John. "What's the problem? I really like it, don't you?"

"I do but I'm sort of curious about that rec area. With that lake."

"We could do that tomorrow, go swimming and all, but this could be our base of operations."

"Operations for what, Gar? What are we doing here?"

"I dunno. But, we're not selling books, right?"

"Right. No way."

"Look, we're calling 'time out'!" I made a "T" with my hands in front of John's face. "We're slowing down, and like we do, we'll figure out our next moves, okay?"

"Okay . . . but . . ."

"D-man, it's a really nice room. Great view out this window. She's very sweet. Not weird. Nice home. The price is right. A motel would be easily forty a night. This is like ten bucks each—*per week!* How can there be any hesitation?"

"Everything you're saying, yes, I agree but . . ." John's eyes twinkled. He had that slight dimple in his left cheek, that Cheshire cat grin.

"Oh no, Durl—*what*?"

He watched me. His eyes got big as he sidled over to the other side of the opened window, which we both now straddled, like on a seesaw. John motioned to the window.

"Smell that air, Gar?"

I took a whiff. "Yeah."

"Smell that good earth, that sweet pungent earthy night air?"

"Okay . . . yeah . . ."

He pointed now. "Look! See that sunset? It's on fire! It's beauty, nature, God's glory, Gar, unfolding right in front of us! But we're boxed in, stuck in this . . . granted, it's nice. But it's another room in a house. Small. Close. Suffocating. Stifling."

"Durl."

"Gar, look at that night sky."

"I see it."

"Pretty soon there'll be stars. A sky full of stars . . . this warm, sweet, earthy night air. Come on, Gar, you're the one who started this. Come on."

"Started what?"

"The Great Outdoors!"

"For painting!"

"Trust me, Gar. You're going to love it."

"Durl."

"One night. Try it for one night."

"*This* night?"

"Just tonight. If it's horrible, we come back here or find a motel room and I'll pay."

"You'll pay?"

"My treat. If you're not seduced by the stars and the summer night. Whaddya say?"

I watched my best bud. He was adamant, enthused, gesturing to the window, practically in the window and through it. He was performing. He was charming.

"You really want to do this, don't you?"

John tapped his good hand on the windowsill. "I do."

"Okay."

"Really?"

"Really." Oh God, what were we doing? We romped down her stairs, into Mrs. May's living room where she met us coming from her kitchen.

"Thank you, Mrs. May. We really like the room. We really like your home. In fact, we really like you," said John, a little out of breath.

"Oh, thank you." She quickly placed her left palm on her left cheek, her grey apron in her right hand.

"But, we're thinking of camping instead."

"That's too bad."

"I'm sorry?"

"I mean, good for you, too bad for me. You seem like nice boys. It would've been nice to have you here."

"Thank you." John nodded.

"It's nice weather for camping. Will you head to the mountains?"

"We heard there was a rec area with a lake about a half hour from here?"

"Up in Donelson. Old Hickory Lake. Real nice."

"You know it then?"

"Used to take my kids there, real nice, country setting. Very pretty."

"Great," John beamed.

"And if you don't like it—"

"It's an experiment," I cut her off. "I'm not a big sleep outdoors kinda guy."

"Okay." She looked at us both. "If the experiment doesn't work out, come back to me, okay?"

"That's just what we'll do. Thank you," said John as we both began to move toward the front door.

"Wait a moment, will you?"

"Sure." John and I looked at each other. Mrs. May disappeared into her kitchen. In only a few seconds, she reappeared with two plastic sandwich bags.

"Here. For later. A little snack."

"That's so nice."

"Wow," I chimed in. Both plastic bags contained similar portions.

"It's nothing. But it's fresh and warm from the oven. I was baking it for tomorrow's breakfast."

John and I both stumbled over each other with our litany of Thank Yous.

"Just an old recipe."

I kept wondering what it was, brown and yellow and cakey.

"My grandma's cinnamon and apple walnut coffee cake."

"Oh man, we may not wait for later. Thank you!"

"Sure," she nodded as she held her left hand to her left cheek and watched us leave, get into our cars. John and I both waved as we backed out. Mrs. May waved with her right hand, her left still on her cheek, unmovable.

17

I wasn't sure why but I felt a little sad, even tender, as we drove out of Mrs. May's driveway. Mothers, I guess, that kind of reaching out, thoughtfulness. Something John's mom would do, and had done, often. Her fruit bowls. Her cookies. My mom, too, though probably with a little more fanfare. A wave of homesickness hit me as we joined a two-lane road that took us through three little towns and into Donelson. Now it was nighttime, dark and damp. Streetlights were on, filled with flies, moths. We stopped at a small diner that looked like an old chrome railroad car named the Snack Shack. We both had burgers and fries and decided to celebrate our liberation with big gooey milkshakes, strawberry for John, chocolate for me, thick and delicious.

As we finished up, John asked our waitress if she knew the best way to get to the rec area and Lake Hickory.

"You mean Old Hickory Lake?"

"Right."

She held our cleared plates in her hands and just stood there, staring at the two of us. Later, I realized she was lining up her thoughts, trying to picture in her mind the best roads to take. This pause was curious and of course, I was enchanted: her name was Terri, a vivacious, curvy auburn-haired beauty, maybe in her forties, tanned with freckles, fire engine red lipstick, bright white teeth, and a killer smile. She seemed like one of those tomboyish girls who grows up to become a beauty. I wanted to know her. I wanted to paint her.

She turned and called to a man seated toward the end of the far counter, "Stan? Hickory Lake? Don't they want to go through town, past the duck pond, out to Andrew Jackson's, then make a left and go past Langford's farm?"

"Sure. Why?" Stan was maybe in his fifties, black hair, a darkness to him. Not dumb or mean, necessarily, but a kind of roughness.

"That's my husband, Stan. He knows everything," she turned back to him, "don'tcha, honey?"

"What."

"Know everything."

"Just about. Unless I'm having a bad day."

"But today was a good day, right?"

"Pretty good." He returned to fingering his newspaper.

"Yeah." Terri turned back to us. "I'm right. Want me to write it out for you?"

"No, it's okay," said John.

"Lemme write it down. Gimme a sec." We watched her turn and flounce away, her lovely shapely butt almost directing traffic as it moved side to side until she disappeared behind the counter and into the kitchen. I heard our dishes being dropped off.

"Wow," said John. "She's really interesting, isn't she?"

"Like she doesn't belong here," I said.

"She's got charisma, Gar."

"Elan vital," I offered.

"Elan vital?" asked John.

"You know—the Life Force."

"Right." John eyed me. "Where'd you get that one?"

"I dunno, some book."

When Terri reappeared, as she started for us, she waved a yellow paper toward the front of the diner. "Be right there, Georgie. Just a sec!" Then abruptly she placed the yellow page, red lined, in between John and me. "Hope you can read it. Holler if you can't. You boys want any dessert?"

"No," said John, "the shakes were it."

"Okay. Let me find your tickets." She shuffled through her yellow pad. "Here's yours, and, here's yours." She gave us both a big smile. Then, eyeing my sketchbook, she said, "What's in the big pad—your life story?"

I laughed. John watched her. "Kinda. But, no. Just some drawings."

"Oh! Can I see?"

"Sure."

"Wait. Mr. George's been waiting. Don't go away."

Are you kidding? A few minutes later, Terri returned. "Move over," she said to me. I did, making room for her on my side of the booth. I saw John's eyes widen. We both smelled her sweet perfume, which warmed the air between us. I moved the sketchbook over, in front of her. She touched the faded orange cover of it. "It's okay?" she asked.

"Please." I nodded, and opened it for her.

"Oh. Very nice." She fingered the first page, a pen and ink of an Amherst landscape, small hillside, row of spring trees in blossom.

I'm very sensitive to how people look at my drawings. The pace at which they page through my sketchbook, if they pause or linger, or if, as most often happens, they just turn pages automatically while talking about other things. That's the worst, the most humbling, none of the images really grab them. Or, the most indicative: they really don't care or know how to look, or it's just a clear signal of their own restlessness, discomfort. But then, I must ask myself, why do I care? This is my sketchbook, private, personal. My "notes," as it were. My impulses, notions, excitements. Essentially, for my eyes only. But, too, at this stage, they were a kind of entrée . . . perhaps I did need others to see and approve. Tell me I'm an artist.

Terri reminded me of Kathy. Kathy had always loved my pen and inks. She'd pause, ask questions, really look and marvel or laugh at the weird expression of a person's face, often hers.

Terri was doing this, which was a seduction in its own right. The way her first finger would point and query or pull across the page, then lift and move onto the next. She'd tap the page, or do a lovely feminine tra-la-la with her beautiful red enameled nails. Which she'd then pull to her mouth, smiling, watchful, all of her—face, fingers, buxom chest, swiveling hips—so animated.

Obviously, I was very pleased. John, too, smiled, watched her, watched me, and marveled. I was surprised that Stan, up at the counter near the front door, remained so oblivious, head in his paper.

"These are *so* good," Terri said, fingering the next drawing.

Then she stopped and seemed to really look at me. With a deep sigh, she said, "You are a real artist, you know? You have a really great gift. Really." She quickly turned back to the sketchbook, not waiting for my "Thank you" but now very intently looking, turning pages as if turning up evidence, or searching for a specific image. As she continued, she blushed. "I do watercolors now and then, but . . ."

"Really? That's great," I said.

"Yeah," added John. We were cheerleaders, eager to rally her from defeat.

"But these are real art. My watercolors, oh God. They say that watercolors are the toughest 'cause you can't erase. Oils you can do over, y'know? But pen and ink, too, very tough."

"Watercolors, really?"

"Oh, they're *bad*!"

"I have a hunch you're being modest," said John.

"No. They stink. Right, Stan?"

"What?" Stan's head in the newspaper still.

"My watercolors."

"What about 'em?"

"Come here, Stan, look at these."

"What?" Stan was turning his paper to the next page.

"Stan. Oh God." Terri pulled out of the booth, and, as if in one motion, moved to the counter, closed Stan's paper. "Hey!" he said. She pulled him over to our booth. "Stan, I want you to see this young man's drawings. He's a real artist. This is real art," and she tapped my open sketchbook.

"Good for him. I'm not finished with the paper. Christ." Stan barely looked at us. I noticed his dark black stubble and a pinkish scar on his left cheek. He watched Terri, spoke only to her and then, as he turned away from us, he suddenly raised his arms and cried out, "Augghh!" It was a big noisy yawn. "Oh God, I'm tired," he said as his arms collapsed. "How much longer you gotta work tonight?"

"I dunno. Please come see this boy's drawings."

"Place is almost empty. Christ. Fred!" he called out.

"Don't bother Fred. He'll let me go when he sees fit."

"Fred!"

"What, Stan?" A man appeared in the long window where the food orders were placed. He had thinning hair on the sides, shiny bald on top, a black mustache, and facial hair, dark, too, like Stan's.

"How much longer you need this girl? I wanna take her home and have some fun. It's Friday night for Christ's sake!"

"Oh Stan, please." Terri poked Stan, giggled, and looked back at John and me. She quickly called out: "Ignore him, Fred. He's just lonely and obnoxious."

"And horny, too, you little vixen." Stan grabbed Terri in a sudden quick headlock.

"Stan, stop that! Right now." Terry pulled away. "I told you, no joking. Not in public. Jesus."

"Oops," Stan mock apologized, his hand to his mouth.

"Go read your dumb ol' paper."

"Yes, ma'am."

Fred came around to the counter. He carried a plate of fries and a big plastic glass of clear bubbly soda. "Here, Teresa. For those boys over there." Fred nodded to the table by the door. A couple of teenage boys leaned toward each other, whispering, laughing.

"Once you're straight with your money and such, go on home. I'll close up," Fred said.

"Really, Fred? You sure?"

"Sure as shootin'. Go on."

Terri delivered the fries and soda. Fred leaned at the counter, then sat on a stool two spots down from Stan and his paper, toward the front. He just sat there staring out toward the front windows, the night dark but for the diner lights shining off the few parked cars.

Fred sighed, "Electrical storm."

"What?" said Stan, into his paper.

Terri returned. "The other boy wants a soda now, too."

Fred nodded. Terri went behind the counter—cup, ice, soda—and returned with it to the boys. Fred continued to stare out. When Terri returned, he pointed. "Electrical storm. See?"

Terri turned. "Where?"

"Up beyond the clock tower. See?"

"Sure enough. Stan, look. An electrical storm."

"What?"

"Out there." She went to Stan and spun him toward the front.

"Jesus, what?"

"See? An electrical storm."

"Oh yeah." Stan watched now, rubbing his neck.

"Fred, come here. Want you to see some real art."

I'd closed my sketchbook as Terri and Fred approached. John was ready to go. He'd been studying the yellow restaurant receipt of directions. Terri held Fred's elbow as she leaned in, tapped my sketchbook. "Can I show Fred your drawings?"

"Oh sure." I turned it toward them as they hovered there. Terri began to turn the pages as Fred hunched over and looked on.

"Wait." Fred stopped Terri's page turning and looked straight at me. "You did these?"

"Yes, sir."

"Oh!" said Terri, turning pages again. "This is one of my favorites. Isn't she lovely?"

"Beautiful. Who is it?" asked Fred.

"That's my girlfriend. Kathy."

"Does that look like her?" asked Fred.

"Pretty much. Yeah."

"Man, I never had a girlfriend that pretty."

"Oh Fred, you never had a girlfriend!" Terri nudged him and laughed.

"That's true!" Fred had an impish grin, then winked at John and me. "I just had wives." They continued paging through the drawings. John studied the directions, seemed a little distant, as if I was getting too much attention. I could see Stan now leaving the counter to go up front, where he stood looking out, up toward the flickering night sky.

Then I saw him. Could it really be? A lanky man walking past the diner windows, hands in pockets, a felt hat on his head, fairly well dressed, in a dark wool suit, maybe dark blue, but looking up, above eye level, talking to someone . . . who wasn't there. I stood up, it was so startling. "Excuse me," I said.

"Hey, Gar," called John.

But I was already up front by the windows, not far from Stan, this side of the teenage boys, who were throwing French fries at each other. I turned to Stan. "Excuse me but, who was that man?"

"What man?" Stan studied the light show high above.

"He just walked past."

"Dunno."

"He was talking to himself. Wore a nice dark suit?"

"That's Mr. Steward, right, Stannie?" Terri had joined us.

"Oh, him. Crazy bastard." The lit sky was flickering on both their faces. The man, Mr. Steward, was gone now, had turned the corner.

"Was he looking up and talking to himself?" asked Terri, now standing between me and Stan, her arm around his back and waist.

"Exactly," I said, looking for him again.

"Poor Mr. Steward. Sweetest man."

"Wealthiest, too," said Stan.

"Took care of his folks, his mom, actually. She died. Left him everything. Then he went off the deep end. Always wanted to be a grocer or a farmer. Mostly he takes walks around town, talking to himself. Not angry. Almost cheery. Some people think he's talking to his older brother who was quite tall, died in Vietnam . . . that's what they say . . ."

"Oh," I said. I watched the sky continue its lull and then flashings.

"Come on, Stan. I can leave now."

If this was Donelson, it was not just quaint but like the Snack Shack, it had its moments. It was quirky, and like this evening, amidst the streetlamps and flashing night sky and Elwood P. Dowd look-alikes, it had an eerie otherworldly quality. I liked it.

18

John drove at a steady, almost slow pace, for him. I followed, and watched, a sight-seeing tour, of sorts. The clock tower was nowhere near as tall as I'd imagined; the duck pond was well off the two-lane road we were on, with green park and trees in front, the pond in back with a small hill behind, a bluff of trees surrounding, and no ducks that I could see given the maze of streetlights' pockets of brightness edged into by lamp and tree shadows.

Andrew Jackson's Hermitage was behind a high wall, ivy covered, more like a small, darkened mountain than a mansion. We turned left there and then things got interesting. This was a road, not unlike the roads of suburban Connecticut, shrubs and trees nudging the tarmac from either side, glimpses of houses at first near the street, then set back, and then, these great broad expanses, which in the dull darkness I realized were pastures, fields, farms. They came to life when the sky flicked on and off like a basement light.

These were the rolling hills you hear about. We drove among them until we began a gradual descent that seemed to never end, with big black expanses on either side. When the sky brightened, I realized we were traveling down the grey artery that joined the two dark valves of this black heart: Old Hickory Lake. As the left section continued on, a black bounty of water, the grey road curled right. Signs and arrows indicated the recreation area, restrooms, and the tree-lined campgrounds.

We parked both cars in a small lot neighboring a small hillside, with an actual sidewalk about 100 feet from the grey and white boxy cinder block building that housed the restrooms and showers. We got out and, guided by the remnant light from the one shaded lamp pole next to the building, went in and peed. Walking back to our cars, John said, "Why don't we just sleep on this little hillside, right here?"

"Here?"

"There's trees for protection, and . . ." John lay down on the grass, his elbows under his head, and looked up, "a great view of that light-show sky. The grass is pretty soft. Whaddya say, Gar?"

"What're we going to sleep on?"

"Not on, in. Come see."

I joined John next to the Green Monster's trunk.

"See? One for you, and, one for me." John handed me a crusty old rust-colored sleeping bag with a flannel interior of cowboys and Indians. His was green, shinier, newer, with just a dull beige flannel lining.

"Okay?"

"Thanks . . . I think."

John and I locked our cars, spread the sleeping bags on the already dampening grass. We faced away from the restroom building. I kept my shorts and a T-shirt on, my clothes and shoes in a neat pile beside me. John did the same. We settled in. I kept my flap unzipped at first as the flannel got too warm too fast. John lay on top of his bag. There were night breezes, cool, moist. A few jarring caw sounds—crows, perhaps? Crickets continued nonstop, which annoyed me at first.

"Listen, Gar."

"What."

"Just listen."

Far away, not steady, was a dark deep "Ooh . . . Ooh . . . ," a long pause, and then, "Ooooh . . ." An owl. Not sure why it comforted me, but it did.

We lay there listening, watching the night sky, now and then saying things. I dozed off at one point only to be jarred awake by loud country music and the crunch of gravel. I bolted up as John pointed down right. "Just some campers, Gar."

Two big pick-up trucks, their radios blasting, crunched along the dirt road into the campsite. I could hear the twangy music fade as an announcer proudly called out, "And that's it, folks, good night from the Grand Ole Opry. Y'all come back and see us real soon, y'hear? Take us on out, Johnny!" The music got louder, twangier, lots of strumming, several voices, not just one, a big crescendo of happy sound, and then—not. Clicked off.

As did John and I, faded. Gone. Lights out. Asleep.

Which surprised me, upset me, too, as I told John the next morning. I'd wanted to lie there and watch the sky's continuing fireworks. And the stars that John talked about. Okay, I wasn't enamored of sleeping on the ground, on wet grass, and would there be snakes or wild dogs, coyotes, or other larger animals? But I forgot all that once we were collapsed on the grass in those sleeping bags. There was something kind of dangerous and thrilling, those stars and John and me, getting quiet and simple, and, so private. Like being with Kathy, without the stirrings of sex.

But there were stirrings of adventure and curiosity and not knowing. For the first time in many years: not knowing a thing about what was going to happen next. No classes. No books that had to be read. No papers except my journal and what I wanted to make note of. No family. No girlfriends. No familiar hometown, well-known streets, neighbors. No structure and none of the ivy-walled security of those college years. None of that. Except that same big sky, the damp earth, and me and my best buddy.

And a new morning coming: no alarm clocks, no appointments, no schedules, no demands. Kind of scary, but more than that, exhilarating.

That first night on the ground I have no idea what I dreamt. I do know I slept through the night and awoke refreshed. I didn't realize I'd slept so long. Waking up, I was a little slow, foggy. My flap was still unzipped and open. I was sweating, the inner sleeping bag heat and the heat from a well-risen sun. My eyes were burning. I put my hand over them at first.

"Come on, Gar, rise and shine."

I pulled myself up, put both arms behind me, propped on my elbows, took in the new bright morning: it was disappointing. It was sunny, already getting hot, a little humid. Last night's sound and light show was completely gone, transformed into cars, trucks, groves of trees and campground, and the traffic of bodies, a steady stream coming from and going to the restrooms.

"Come on. Let's go for a run. Want to?" Durl was already in his navy-blue shorts, jog shoes, ripped grey gym shirt, doing his stretches. His clothes were still piled neatly next to his rolled-up sleeping bag. My mouth was dry. I was thirsty, maybe even hungry.

"What about breakfast? What time is it?"

"A little after nine. You slept like a little baby."

"When'd you get up?"

"Ten minutes ago. I was pretty much lights out, too. Come on."

"A run? Now?"

"When better? Exorcise the week that was . . . all those fries from last night. Those celebratory shakes, right? A good sweat, a good swim after, in that lake. Wait till you see. A good shower, and then, man, devour a good, big breakfast. Whaddya say?"

"Oh boy." I wasn't thrilled but I knew John was right. The exercise would be good for body and soul. See the sights, the good earth, some deep breathing, all that. Sure. Why not. I went to Titine, grey and solemn. Got my jog shorts which doubled as swim trunks. Got in the passenger seat and changed clothes. Found my jog shoes. Rolled up the sleeping bag and put it and my clothes into Titine's rusted trunk. Then I hustled up to the restrooms, peed, joined John back on the hill with my own abbreviated set of stretches.

"You need more time, Gar?"

"No, no. I'm good." I re-tied my shoelaces.

We were off. The small hillside curb where our cars were parked came down and T'd into the dirt road that had bent to the right off the entry road. John and I jogged in place at that intersection.

"Which way," asked John, "left or right?"

"Right?" I could see around the dark row of trees, in the distance, a fringed horizon of blue waters. I wanted to see more.

"Left it is," said John, as he shot off, to the left.

Great. One of those runs. I chased John and caught up. Good long strides, side by side, this dirt road that seemed fairly abandoned, looked as if it had been dipped into a big cup of pekoe tea. This good earth had a distinctly orange tint to it. We kept a steady pace.

"Durl, I don't want this to be a competitive run."

"Right."

"But you went 'left.'"

"Did I?"

"Really, D-man, can't we just go for a leisurely run? Enjoy the scenery, and not try to set a world record?"

"Gar, you love to compete."

"Sure."

"You almost broke two minutes in the 880 in high school."

"True. But that's over, college, too."

"Gar, it's never over until, y'know, it's over."

"Durlie, come on, can't we just enjoy running?"

"I enjoy it. I'm enjoying this right now, aren't you?"

"Not really."

"Why not, Gar?" John pointed to the left green ledge, just off the orange dirt, as a pick-up truck approached. I followed, as we thinned into single file, John in the lead.

As the truck passed, I waved. The man driving, tanned, a straw hat, simply flicked his hand off the steering wheel in reply.

"Why do you always do that, Gar?"

"Do what?"

"Wave to everybody."

"I'm friendly, okay?"

"Okay." John veered again, this time to the right, as if he knew where he was going. He looked to our right, through the trees and shrubs, to a smaller portion of lake. I hadn't noticed it before. We kept on that side for a while.

"Why do you do that, Durl?"

"Do what?"

"Always take the lead . . . always have to be the one in charge?"

"I dunno. Because you let me?"

"I don't think so."

We ran quietly for a bit. Then, a little frustrated, I said, "Why do these runs always feel like they're a test of our manhood?"

John shrugged and said, "I dunno," then, he burst into a new gear and shot off ahead of me. Over his shoulder, he called out, "Because they are?"

This is where the American Way and Art—my allegiance to them, my love of them—get very confused in me. The athlete and the artist and ne'er the twain shall meet? Not really. But something about how achieving and striving don't quite fit with the act of creation. How do you achieve musing or observing? There isn't a world record for seeing, is there? Why, he just set a new world record for drawing a pen and ink!

John was a very fine runner. We'd both been dedicated athletes in high school. We'd played Little League, we were on the same Babe Ruth team. In high school, John left off baseball and just ran: cross country, along with outdoor track, the mile and two-mile, in which he set high school records that might still be standing. He was captain of those high school teams. He was a quiet almost defiantly internal, modest and stubbornly moral leader of those teams. I loved his intensity and dedication. I had those qualities, too, but I didn't feature them. It did seem, during college, as we moved on, that we began to exchange those colors: he became more social, I was becoming more introspective.

And now we were out for just an old-fashioned jog. But as John picked up the pace, it felt as if I were being punished. I wanted a leisurely run. He wanted a competition. All the anger about this past week's fallout, perhaps, plus throw in the attention my sketchbook was getting. We began to match strides along this still dirt road. Up a long hill, past a meadow, a slew of houses set back from the road, and then a familiar long grey tarmac that was lined with grass tufts, until the broad familiar strokes of pastures and fields. In the distance, we heard the drone of machinery. I could barely make out what looked like a big tractor that trailed hoop-like metal cylinders. A field of hay, I suppose, or long grass, was being mown.

This road, with farms on either side, was our approach from last night, now soaked in blazing sunlight: there, to the left below, that big glistening valve of lake.

"Shall we kick it in, Gar, to the lake?"

"Love to. Can't wait." I stayed with John, stride for stride, as we began our—okay, my—panting descent. I was surprised: when we landed lakeside, we were in a dead heat. I was out of breath, sure. But I was beaming, too. A Pyrrhic victory!

John stripped first, T-shirt, jog shoes, socks. I followed. With a roar and an Arrrgh! we both took off from the grass, across the thin strip of grainy sand, and threw ourselves, stretched long, hands and heads first, into the cool lake waters. We were noisy and splashy. It all felt so refreshing and wild, in contrast to the hot, contained and sweaty fury of our run. A great, invigorating release.

Eventually, we swam out toward the far side of the lake, a good distance off. The lake shimmered. There were wonderful cold pockets where my feet and knees chilled, my hot body was able to slow and be restored. John swam out even further. He suggested that we try swimming across the lake all the way to the other side. No. This was enough for me. While he swam, I floated. Finally, the slowness I longed for: I watched the sky, a sudden chase of birds, the dull drone of a small plane, and then nothing but blue with a few trinkets of clouds.

It was a great, glorious morning. I said a little prayer of thanks, that I was alive and able to be a part of all this. I'd lost sight of John swimming. As I turned over to start looking for him, my leg was grabbed and pulled down. Oh God! I wriggled and pulled and wrestled free as John resurfaced, laughing, "Boo!" He sputtered word and water. "Gotcha, huh, Gar?"

"You scared me!"

"Come on. I'll race ya in!"

"No thanks."

"I'm hungry!" John took off, a strong free-style stroke.

I wanted to just float there. Watch the sky. Watch the small shoreline of lake.

It was less peopled than I'd expected from all that restroom traffic. We'd put our shoes and shirts on the small picnic table nearest the lake's edge, which had a varied assortment of trees near it, along with a green trash container. Up the slope of grassy hillside, the trees got bigger and more numerous, along with about eight more picnic tables strategically placed. Further along to the left, there were dark metal rectangles with concrete footings, which I realized were outdoor grills.

At the crest of this lakeside hill, just beyond the trees and boulders and outdoor grills, were the restrooms. On the other side was the grassy glade where we'd slept and the small lot where our cars were parked.

John called to me, "Come on, Gar!" As he toweled off, waved, and indicated he was heading up to the restrooms to shower, I waved back. I continued to troll the waters, watching, taking in the beams of sunlight, the shaded stirrings of a few people, a family up to the left, three teenage girls just coming down the slope, carrying a small wood basket, towels, chattering, laughing.

19

It was a Saturday morning, mid-June, 1971, in a small town called Donelson, just outside Nashville, Tennessee, on a lake that seemed pretty big, called Old Hickory. Nixon was president; I had friends who were fighting in Vietnam; my dad would retire from General Foods in four years; my sister Carol had already had one nervous breakdown; brother Sandy and wife Judy and their two kids were now living in Kalamazoo, Michigan, my brother's internal medicine practice thriving; brother Chris's marriage, along with his college teaching, were falling apart: he was drinking, carousing, and his two little boys would be fatherless in about four years. Some of this I sensed back then, much of it I didn't know or understand.

Just then, I floated in this quiet lake's mellow waters, before the swimmers and motorboats and sailboats, too, would begin to cruise and enliven this lovely glistening sanctuary. All of it this morning was lit, picturesque, almost became hallowed. I wanted to draw it, paint it. I wanted to taste it, smell it, an urge, too, as if I wanted to not just eat it but devour it. This fascinating life, such a contrast to the years of so much academic regimen. These waters were for me a great unburdening, an enormous deep gasp of freedom.

"Gar! What're you doing? Come on!" Durl called from the hilltop, near the restrooms, as he towel-dried his hair and waved. I waved back. Slowly, I sloshed forth from what I'd briefly glimpsed and felt, these waters of liberation.

It didn't take me long to shower and put on some clean clothes, my last pair of clean underwear. We took just one car into town, John's Green Monster. We both agreed: after breakfast, we'd go find a laundromat. It'd been a week since we left Connecticut and the dirty clothes had piled up.

The sky had a deeper blue now, fewer clouds. The humidity didn't feel so cloying, helped by sweet breezes as we motored along, retracing the route that had brought us from town. Kind of fun to see the sights again, only in reverse: clear, fully lit, drained of all mystery and suspense. Fun, and a little disappointing, too, since as first impressions go, this modern small town didn't seem to have a lot of character. I loved passing by those big farms, either side, as we drove uphill, Old Hickory Lake behind us. The smell of cut grass, or was it hay? It was strong, reminded me instantly of mowing lawns back in Darlington. I wouldn't have to do that this summer. Who would? Dad, I guessed.

John loved the pop songs from the '50s, songs his older sister, Diane, had loved and even taught him the words to. But finding those songs from the '50s, '60s, or even contemporary rock on the radio dial in Donelson, Tennessee, just outside Nashville, was nearly impossible. There were mostly Southern preachers or else Southern good ol' boys, and a few good ol' gals, too, singing country songs. John kept fiddling though, trying to find the station we had listened to as we departed Nashville, in vain. Finally, he turned the radio off. We drove in silence, until John began to hum and sing his own version of "car radio." "Poison ivy—ay—ay—ay . . . Poison ivy—ay—ay—ay . . . Late at night while you're sleepin', poison ivy starts a-creepin' all around—ound—ound—ound . . ." Eventually, I joined him, as we crooned and laughed and made our way back to Donelson, in search of the best breakfast in town.

The day had that Saturday energy, people in the stores, families in town, a lot of sidewalk traffic. A nice bustling, cozy feel to it. We ended up back at the Snack Shack where breakfast did seem to be their specialty. Fred, still the master chef, was in the rear. We kept hoping Terri would appear. No luck. We never found out whether it was her day off or she just worked the later shift. An older woman, Hazel, very officious and no-nonsense, served us. Not as much fun, but we ate well, pancakes for me, a big waffle with strawberries for John. We both had burgers.

The one laundromat was quite busy. An Asian husband and wife ran it. Several Black families had most of the washers. But way in back we found a washer and dryer. We threw our clothes in together to make a pretty big load. A very thin woman, maybe in her fifties, with no front teeth, offered us her Tide detergent. We thanked her.

There were so many interesting people in there. Thought I might do a few pen and inks, kind of Walker Evans-style portraits, but as stark ink drawings, not photos. When I started for my car to get my sketchbook, John called to me, "Hey, Gar, how about some Frisbee?" I couldn't resist. There was a biggish parking lot outside, to the left. It wasn't paved, just a nice crunchy white gravel, a little dusty. John got his purple Frisbee out of the Green Monster's trunk.

It felt good to spin that well-worn disk, float it, style it, loft it high, boomerang style, of which John was a master. He was also very good at making dramatic catches of my looping off-center thrusts. John loved to go lunging, sliding in the crunchy, dust-billowed gravel as he'd pick the purple skeet from the air at the last minute, as if it were a bright clean napkin being offered at dinner.

We did our laundry, though the dryer never seemed to get hot enough or maybe the load was just too big. We left a few things, our jeans, our shirts, to dry out on the back seat of the Green Monster. We threw the Frisbee some more.

Then, leaving the Monster parked at the laundromat, we walked around town. There were lots of small shops. Also, a big department store, a one-story older building called Sloan's. A barbershop where a few older men stared back at us: they could've been John and me, as old men, looking at ourselves as young men. I wanted to find the library. In a small soda/ice cream shop, we got directions and realized we'd have to drive to it. So, after we folded our dried clothes and packed up, we drove back in the direction of Old Hickory Lake. Not far, but on the rise, just as we left behind the cluster of shops and fast-food eateries, there it was: it appeared to be a one-story shiny building, all by itself on a small hill with a glade of trees beside.

As we approached, there was a row of parking slots, a small circle for loading and unloading and then to the right of the building, a drive led downhill to a bigger parking area in back. We parked in front.

Above the glass doors, in big silvery metal letters, it read, "Donelson Public Library." On either side of those doors were even bigger glass windows. Through the glass I could see a big spacious lobby with skylights, and straight ahead, the long check-out counter. If you'd told me those women behind the counter were bank tellers, I wouldn't have been surprised. They were three older women—a younger woman was over among the stacks to the right, pushing a small metal book cart. I love libraries. While this one wasn't quaint or all that charming, I liked its spaciousness, its airy bounty of natural light.

"Okay, Gar. There's the library. Nice. Let's go."

"Whoa, Durl. A library. A reading mecca. Not even a quick look, a brief browsing?"

"No thanks."

"But, D-man, you love to read!"

"I do, but it's a beautiful day, Gar."

"Come on, just ten minutes?"

John looked at his watch. "It's two-fifteen. You got until two-thirty."

"Yes! Meet here in fifteen!" I started inside.

"Meet by the Green Monster."

"Deal."

John went left, into the periodicals section, with its small host of chairs, a sofa, several tables, set up in front of the tall glass windows. I went to the right, the Adult Fiction section. Further on, back to the left, was a smaller area where the children's books were shelved. Adult Fiction books were nearest the check-out counter, then Philosophy, Religion, Psychology, Social Sciences, and the big art books and monographs. Oversized art books were on the racks nearest the other section of tall windows, with its respective grouping of chairs, tables, but no sofa.

All during college and once out, I'd had a list of "Great Books" that I wanted to finally read. One that John had always touted was Thomas Wolfe's *Look Homeward, Angel.* They had it. Another was *The Great Gatsby.* They had it. Also, Ayn Rand, several of her books. Hemingway. The Brontë sisters. This was a very good library, with a surprisingly good selection. Among the art books, I found one on El

Greco that I wanted to borrow right then and there. I took it to the check-out.

A lovely older woman, with brown hair dappled grey—her name tag said "Lexie Helms"—said to me in a syrupy Southern accent, "You can't take that book, young man, unless you got yourself a library card."

"I have a library card," I said, in the same jousting spirit.

"You do? Lemme see."

I pulled out my wallet, shuffled a few pieces of plastic—my dad's Mobil card, driver's license, Social Security card—until I found it and handed it to her. Mrs. Helms stared at it through her grey reading glasses. "You must be joking."

"It's a library card, right?"

"'Darlington Public Library . . . Garry Brown . . . Darlington, Connecticut,'" she read aloud. "Oh my, this library card number is very long. Must have more people up there than here. Plus, that library's probably much older."

"Very old. It's New England. Y'know, the Mayflower and all."

She looked up from my bogus card, sized me up.

"New England, huh? I was in New York City once."

"Oh?"

"Hated it. Too fast. Nobody has time to look you in the eye and say 'Howdy.'"

"Well," I looked Lexie Helms in the eye and said, "Howdy."

"Ha!" She giggled. "You're a funny one. Alright. Whaddy'all want to borrow?"

"You're serious?"

She looked at the El Greco book, then up at me again. "I'm serious . . . just fill out this form," she pulled out a piece of paper from a drawer, "and give it back to me with a form of ID, driver's license, Social Security card or the like, and, one letter or bill with the address of where you're currently staying. Okay?" She gave me a big sweet smile.

John was already outside next to the Green Monster. I watched him come over to the glass doors, shade his eyes, and look in. "I guess maybe another time. Thanks." I started off.

"Wait. You really want this book?"

"Yeah, but I don't have the time to fill out that form and we're—I'll come back when I do have time."

"Here." She handed me the book. "Take it."

"What?"

"And take your Darlington card, too."

"But—"

"It's due in three weeks."

"But I don't have a card."

"I know. I do. Just make sure you bring it back on time or I'll get into a whole mess o' trouble, okay?"

"Okay . . ." I stared at her, somewhat mystified. "Thank you."

"No problem, Garry. I'm Lexie. Lexie Helms."

"Thank you, Mrs. Helms." I took the book. "Are you sure?"

"I am right now but if you don't go join your buddy, I might could change my mind, okay?"

"Okay. Really, thanks! And don't worry, I'll—"

"I'm not worried, Garry Brown. Go!" She waved me off. I smiled and waved back.

As if I'd just bought a new car, I felt so lucky, pleased, and this was a really good book, almost new, with great reproductions of El Greco's paintings. Very high quality. John was now just leaning, arms folded, on the Green Monster's rear fender.

"Gar, we need to talk."

"Okay."

"By my watch, it's almost quarter to three."

"Durlie."

"No, no. Listen, this isn't the first time, and, it's okay. Maybe we should just do things on our own for a while and then meet for dinner, y'know?"

"Durlie, we're on vacation. You can't be so rigid."

"I really don't like waiting."

"I'm sorry. I did lose track of the time a little."

"A 'little'?"

"Well, twelve minutes."

"Fifteen."

"Fine. Fifteen."

"I don't think this is going to work."

"What?"

"This summer. Together. We're just *so* different."

"Look, Johnny, you have your peccadillos, too."

"Do I ever keep you waiting?"

"Well, no."

"I tell you a time, I'm there, right?"

"True."

"What 'peccadillos'?"

"Well . . . I'm loose with time, you're rigid."

"It's not rigidity, Gar, it's respect!"

"Okay. Correct."

"Don't try to placate me . . . What're you thinking?"

"I dunno. Just, we have different styles, okay?"

"'Styles'?"

"I'm looser, you're more, um, controlling."

"Hey, who got all worked up that first day in Nashville?"

"True. I'm sorry. We've been having a great day. Let's get back to that, okay?"

"Well. Okay . . . what's the book?"

"El Greco."

"Can I see?"

I handed John the book. He carefully paged through it.

"You like this stuff, Gar?"

"Some of it, yeah. Look. Let me show you. This painting of Toledo at night, the dramatic sky. Hold on . . ." I paged through until I found it, this road leading upward to this skyline of towers and spires, a city high up with a swirling array of storm clouds in a night sky. "Look."

John looked at it for a moment, then, "Huh . . . Guess you had to be there."

"Really?" Now, I looked at it with him. The movement in this painting excited me. I wanted to paint like this. Its silence, its loneliness, it all seemed so immediate, so *there* to me.

"'El Greco,' huh?"

"Think he was Greek but ended up living and painting in Spain, which is where this Toledo is."

John paged through some more, fingering various reproductions, pausing, continuing until he raised a cocked eye to me and said, "Oh, that wasn't Toledo, Ohio?"

"Right."

"Gar, that was a joke."

"Oh. So, are we alright?"

"Fine. But I am getting a little hungry."

"Me, too."

"Let's get something to eat."

"And then what?" I asked.

"I dunno."

"We could go swimming back at our lake."

"'Our lake'?" John closed the book and handed it back to me.

"Yeah, or more Frisbee, or . . ."

"What about a movie?" said John, as we opened doors and got in the Green Monster."

"Really?" For some reason sitting in a dark movie house didn't really interest me.

"We'll think of something," said John as he started the car and backed out and we pulled away. And we did. We thought of a lot of things that summer. Some things we'd thought of before, and some were completely new and strange and unexpected.

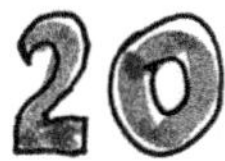

We ended up at a fairly new fast-food place called Burger King instead of the nearby McDonald's. We got burgers, sodas. It was here that I went back to ask for a refill and first learned that if you keep your same cup, the refill is free. John felt the fries here were much better than at McD's.

We sat outside on small concrete benches at concrete tables that would suddenly light up from the afternoon sun. It was here John overheard some kids talking about a roller coaster ride, some nearby fairgrounds. He was intrigued. I wasn't. But, feeling bad because I'd kept John waiting, I'd decided whatever John wanted to do, I'd go along.

We drove to the fairgrounds. About a half hour's ride (we got our second wind), it was beside a small lake with a huge parking lot that was completely filled. We stayed there from late afternoon into the early evening.

There was a carousel, a bunch of other rides. At the Arcade, it got a little competitive, which I tried to resist. A BB gun shoot; a pistol shoot; blowing hot air to knock down tennis balls; a basketball shoot, make three in a row and you get a stuffed bear, a very small pink one.

Cotton candy, foot-long hot dogs, ribs, sausage, a big roasted pig, steak sandwiches, chicken kebobs. A lot of food. Ice cream stands with vats of every flavor, including blueberry, cheesecake, and bubblegum. One woman had her own brand, Frannie's, some interesting combinations: gingerbread frappé and chocolate alligator twist. She, Frannie, was from Florida. "You've heard of chocolate turtles, right? This is just like it only better. Chocolate and caramel and molasses, too, with a bit of honeycomb. Wanna try a taste?" We did.

It was after ten when we returned to our Old Hickory Lake campsite. The Grand Ole Opry tunes were playing from several car and truck radios. One campsite was quite loud, a group of men and women, talking, laughing, a small campfire ablaze and cheery. John wanted to go for a late-night dip. I just wanted to lie down under those stars again. Reluctantly but true to my earlier pledge, I joined him. Once we parked the Green Monster next to my lonely looking Titine, I went and dutifully looked for my swim trunks. John stopped me, said, "Gar, you don't need a suit. Come on!"

"What?" I said and followed.

"Race ya!"

We jogged up toward the restrooms and down the other side. I let John lead, as we rattled through grass and stones and cover of trees until we landed together next to that same concrete picnic table.

"Skinny dip, Gar, come on." John stripped, T-shirt, shorts, jog shoes.

"Really?" I stood there, reluctant, a bit shy.

"Look, Gar, not a soul in sight. Just us, the lake, and the moon! Come on. Be great. After all this heat."

"Yeah . . ." I slowly peeled off my T-shirt. John, now naked, a dimly lit skeleton, took off and leaped arms first, missile-like, into the dark brew.

"Agh! Oh *man*! It's great, Gar, come on!"

There'd been such a lovely, almost dainty, white drizzle of moon reflected in the dark lake patina. It was gone now as John stroked and kicked and the waters churned.

I finished undressing and, not to be outdone, raced toward the now frothy waters, screaming, "Aaahhh!" I charged and leapt and plopped into the lake's anticipated chill wet. It was refreshing. Then it was warm. Like a big black tub, an embrace of warmth and comfort. Not hot, not clammy but refreshing.

"Huh, Gar?"

"Nice, Durl."

"You wanted the outdoors, remember?"

"I did. I do. Thank you."

"Don't mention it."

We swam and floated and John dove and touched bottom. "It's not that far down, Gar. Try it."

"No thanks." No way. The muck. Maybe creatures. Nuh-uh.

"Aw, Gar, scared-y cat."

"I am. I admit it."

"Look at those stars! We even got moonlight, see?"

I did. It did seem, too, that we were all alone. Along the far edges of the lake, there was the sporadic morse code of houses, lights. But mostly there was this gulf of silence. When we slowed or floated, we heard the faint strains of banjoes or guitars, and the Southern twang of country songs. But mostly, it was this luxurious black and starry night, the moon a small white coat hook. And I was with my best friend in all the world. We were far from our homes. And we were happy.

That night, our second under the stars, I was much more relaxed. Something I had at first resisted I now looked forward to: the marvel of all those stars. The solemnity of the night. The splendor and largesse but then the privacy, too, of it all. Our view was edged with leaves, tree branches, but the major content was this black ceiling board poked with white holes. A maze of bright white hieroglyphs.

John knew a few of the constellations. I knew none. We lay there, both on our backs, side by side, sleeping bags unzipped, half opened, our heads resting atop our scissored arms. It was glorious as well as a comfort. As if this right here—two best buds under the great night sky, collapsed, cooling from the hot day, soothed by a lake skinny dip, and a little weary—was quite simply the secret of life.

"That's Orion," said John. "See?"

"I think so."

"See how those stars line up? That's his bow."

"His bow, like in archery?"

"He was the archer, Gar. I'm surprised you don't know this stuff."

"Yeah. Well."

"And the Big Dipper is—"

"Over there, right? See, Durl, along this side, see? To our right."

"I don't think so. Wait." John got up and walked down to the where the cars were parked.

"Well?"

"It may be up and over toward the lake." John came back,

walked up toward the restrooms. "Oh yeah, there it is! Come here, Gar, come see!"

I rose and lumbered up the walkway and joined John.

"See?" John positioned me. "Just . . . there."

"Oh yeah. Nice."

We lay back down, continued our stargazing. I could feel the mix of cool night, sweet earthy smells, the few bird calls just starting up. John said he could hear that hoot owl again. Then, the music from the Grand Ole Opry. Voices laughing, muted, talking. This wonderful mix of night air, sounds, and stars . . . and drifting. Fatigue blending into dreams, images, and a kind of sweet joy. John was not sleepy. I was. I'd start to drift off—"Shooting star, Gar. Two o'clock." I'd wake and look. Too late. "You missed it."

"What'd it look like?"

"Y'know . . . Piece of whiteness dragged across the black sky, like Rickey Henderson sliding into third."

"How about Maury Wills?"

"Coulda been him. Think it was him."

"Nice . . ." I drifted off again.

"What're we gonna do, Gar?"

About Maury Wills sliding into third? Across the black night sky. That hoot owl is not happy. Hear him Boo-ing?

"I miss Brookie, Gar. Maybe I'll go back up North."

Maybe, maybe, someone hold the baby. Oh, this feels so good, cool night-air. Caw-Caw. Is that me or a crow at midnight?

"Might go visit my aunt first. In South Carolina."

Carolina. My dad sometimes called my mom "Carolina" . . . Carolina in the morning . . .

"Gar?"

Carolina in the evening. That lake. My feet. A cool drink of water. Carolina. Aunt Jemima, too . . . pancakes. Ooh yeah . . . Pancakes in the morning . . . Carolina.

21

The next morning, Sunday, stayed relatively cool. An overcast sky, though you could tell the sun was right there, behind the cloud cover, just waiting to pounce. It didn't. Not until late in the morning. John wanted to go for a run. I wanted to go down to the lake and do a few pen and inks. So that's what we did. John did his stretches while I went to the restrooms to wash up. When I returned, he was gone.

With the El Greco book, my Bible, my journal and my sketchbook, I sat at the concrete picnic table nearest the lake waters. It was quiet, peaceful. I slowly paged through the El Greco reproductions. With my Bible, I had this little morning ritual: holding the Bible by its black leather binding, I'd shake it, rapidly fingering its pages, like ruffling through a deck of cards, and then stop. I'd place my finger on a page and stop again, and look. I'd read whatever sentence my finger sat upon. This morning it said, "Rest in the Lord." Yes. Will do. A Sunday. Day of rest.

I wasn't a religious fanatic or even a devout Christian. I did have a spiritual hunger, or interest, which had begun when I was ten. I think perhaps it began when my dad's mother died in our home. Gammy. One Sunday, we came home from church, my brother Chris went up to call Gammy to join us for breakfast. He found her fully dressed, on her bed, asleep. He tried to wake her. Nope. She was dead. He freaked. I went kind of philosophical, even mystical. I'd been playing Doctor, had my pretend stethoscope. I walked around the house listening to things: plants, the stereo, my books, my mom's arm, her pulse. I watched another doctor, a real one, come to the house, and tell Mom and Dad how sorry he was but Alice (Gammy) was dead. I nodded. I didn't cry or carry on like my older brother. I just kept walking around the house, my stethoscope dangling from my neck, carrying my small black doctor's bag.

Gammy was gone, just like that. It was all very mysterious and somehow, enchanting. I liked that it was something so big, so enormous, so overwhelming that even all the adults couldn't understand it. It made things more equal, even.

Later, in high school, I had this desperate longing to believe in God. It seemed that everyone in my family had some kind of knowledge of God, which to me translated as belief.

My dad and my oldest brother Sandy, always, mantra-like, intoned their belief as "the brotherhood of Man and the fatherhood of God." My older brother Chris, so passionate and emotional, never spoke of God, but he seemed intent on believing, on faith. When I was still little and he was high school age, he did magic tricks at birthday parties. With his black top hat and cape, he became a real Magician: he could make objects disappear and reappear, and so he seemed to make God into a kind of magic trick. Now you see God, now you don't. His faith seemed to be tied to his magic shows and his ability to catch footballs. He became a star on the Darlington High football team, was All-State his senior year, a Little All-American in college at Allegheny, and was even drafted by the Chicago Bears as a small (six-foot, two-ten) tight end. But that's another story. His Darlington High teams went undefeated for three years. The one game they lost, he said was because ". . . We lost faith. We stopped believing."

My mom was the one outspoken True Believer. Carol, my sister and the oldest, seemed to follow Mom's lead. Carol never taught Sunday School like Mom, but she took it all many steps further; after marrying Dick, living in New York City for a time, and then returning to live in Darlington, she attended this charismatic Bible study. It was there she began to hear Christ's voice and receive instructions, guidance, and have visions. At first, we all were in awe of her profound connection, which blended suburban housewife with the mystical. She'd told Dick that she prophesied, it'd been a vision, that one day he would go into politics and become a great leader like JFK. Dick took this to heart. I think it scared him and thrilled him, until the day he came home from work to discover that all his suits had been donated to Goodwill. What finally turned it was the day she left all three of their kids (David, ten, Lor, eight, and Jess, five) unattended, at home alone, reassuring Dick, and all of us, "God in His great goodness, will take care of the kids, of everything." Admiring awe became real alarm and this grievous realization: Carol was not well. Something was very wrong. This is another story, too, and a sad and painful one, which continued for many years. But then, the summer of 1971, it was not fully evident yet, though already, Carol's spiritual distortions had tempered my longing for God.

I did teach Sunday School, too. In fact, I took over my mother's sixth-grade class, "The Life of Christ." Mom was going to join Dad on his out-of-town trips, ambassador-like conventions for General Foods. I was a sophomore at Darlington, loved kids, had baby-sat to make money, but how did Mom know I'd love teaching so much?

These sixth graders were a delight, curious, adventurous, funny, and we shared this same quest: is there a God? For real? And, how does one know God? How does one truly, deeply believe? There were books to help me structure the lesson plans for each Sunday. Too, there were other books, besides the Bible, the four Gospels, to track this man/God called Jesus—and these Big Questions—of Belief, Faith, Doubt, Death, Life, Mysteries. Every three weeks or so, I'd make up a quiz. I typed up and mimeographed questions like, "The four Gospels were written by whom?" (Matthew, Mark, Luke, John); "How old was Christ when he died?" (thirty-three); "Is it true that Christ was a door-to-door salesman?" (No, a carpenter and spiritual leader); on and on, with a few curves thrown in, like, "Is it true that blondes have more fun?" And for the boys, "Who will play in the NBA finals this year?" and, "What does NBA stand for?"

I knew my spiritual search was serious, but I also felt it had to be fun, even funny at times. All the spiritual writings I enjoyed most—Hammarskjöld's *Markings*, C. S. Lewis's *Mere Christianity*, G. K. Chesterton, even that sly novelist, Graham Greene—they all had some sense of life's frailty and profundity, but, too, its absurdity and humor. Which is why I felt drawn to it, the idea that life was serious but also real by being funny, which is to say, human.

When I taught Sunday School in college, other things happened. Somehow God became very real to me that autumn of my freshman year. I think God has a lot to do with discomfort, loneliness, and feeling lost. Which occurred in October, 1967, when I went with Roger Adams to a Bible study in the cozy Amherst village home of a woman named Evelyn. I cried, felt loved, and I was sure I'd found God.

It happened again when I left pre-med and became a Fine Arts major, only this watershed moment contained elements of exhilaration, hope, and confidence. I could feel it again, this summer of 1971, flung forth into the world. No summer work. No grad school in the fall. No selling dictionaries with John door to door.

I sat by Old Hickory Lake and drew, but from lakeside looking back up toward the trees, a kind of loose but truthful pen and ink. I read my Bible. I paged through the El Greco book. I sat there and mused, wrote brief notes in my journal.

I wondered about Kathy, was she back in Iowa now? Camp would start this coming week. I missed her, perhaps I'd phone or send off a letter. Mom, too, although I'd never called, after Dad's encouraging words. And, Darlington—how was Carol doing? And my brothers in Michigan, Pennsylvania.

It was my first summer after so many years of education. I was not at home or at a camp or painting houses or mowing lawns. I was sitting here, considering life, this life right here, the sun slowly but graciously, finally breaking through, lighting things up, and, I was daring to call myself an artist. Really? What's that? Lawyers, doctors, businessmen. In my family, we know those men, but an artist?

I loved sitting there, quietly taking this all in. The lake water, as if a little shy, lapping softly. The sun bright now, day heating up, and a kind of warming up, too, of sounds, activities. A wonderful orchestral overture in its way, but, of just what sort of new day?

I was writing in my journal when I heard a clamor of heavy breathing and muted downbeats of footfall: it was John, kicking it in, finishing strong, about 100 feet from me, on that inlet road that split the campsite side from the lake grounds. He pulled up short, then bent down, his hands grabbing at his jog shorts, his mouth open, gulping in the warming air. Slowly he rose, saw me, waved. I waved back. He then lightly jogged off along the orange dirt road but abruptly circled back, easy, gentle, as he headed toward me and the lake.

"Yo!" I said, louder than I wanted.

John toned it down and said, "'Yo' yourself." He began to do post-run stretches, his breathing under control now.

"How was your run?" I asked.

"Good. How was your drawing?"

"Good, too."

"Can I see?"

"Sure." I opened my sketchbook on the concrete tabletop. John continued to stretch each leg, propping them on the picnic table as he leaned close, his eyes taking in the drawing, slowly, carefully, until he nodded. "Nice."

"Are you okay?"

"Fine. Why?"

"You seem a little distant."

"Yeah. Well . . ." John stood, looked out to the lake as he raised both arms, one pulling the other, stretching high up over his head, his whole torso now twisted into a rubbery tree. "I guess I am."

"Did I do something wrong?"

John was now swiveling, twisting right to left, left to right.

"Hey, got news for you, Gar, it's not always about you."

"Really? Oh darn."

"Funny."

"I try."

"Very trying."

"Agh! The story of my young life!"

John began to pull off his sweat-soaked T-shirt. After he sat, he unlaced his jog shoes. "How about a swim?"

"Sure."

"Come on then."

I took off my T-shirt, jog shoes, socks. I already had on my gym shorts so I was good to go. A small motorboat cruised past as I stood and surveyed the still lightly lapping water. It was clear. I could see the sandy bottom, until John took off and dove in, head and arms first. I stood there, watching. The man in the motorboat waved. I waved back. Then, with a whoop, I ran into the water until I finally remembered to dive, too.

It was a strange day, that Sunday. A day of opposites. Once completely immersed and swimming, it felt good. I got energized and said, "Come on, Durl, let's swim to the other side and back!" We were just two heads above water, bobbing, only ten feet from each other. John looked behind him to the far side of the lake which was now all aglow in bright sunlight. More sunlight than details, sparks of sun beamed back from house windows and small, distant boats docked and shimmering. John stared for a moment, then said, "Naw. I'm hungry."

So, we swam briefly. We showered and dressed, then took again the Green Monster. The vinyl seats were hot, the car stuffy. We opened all the windows. Breezes, air, breath, the day at mid-morning was on a tear now. Oh yeah, it was going to be a hottie.

22

Driving along, John was Mr. Chatty, I was quiet. Not sullen, just content to watch, listen, not talk. The hills and landscapes: the big farm fields which lined up, one after another, like big puzzles, checker boards; the big pieces of sky, elongated distances of earth, pastures, groves of trees; the smell, rich and pervasive, of cut grass.

"You okay, Gar?"

"Fine. Why?"

"You seem distant. Quiet."

"Touché," I said and smiled. Then, "Maybe I am."

"Ooh. Well done. So, we're both feeling things, huh, Gar?"

"Guess so." I looked off, felt the tilt of the Green Monster as we left the rows of farms and curved onto the busier two-lane road into town, with houses, shops, and then the assortment of churches: white, boxy, steepled. Groups of people, nicely dressed, were they heading to church or just getting out? Several girls, cute, laughing, held black Bibles in their white-gloved hands. Of course: they were coming out of church. That sort of exuberance, release, finally set free. Now I was very hungry, too.

We returned to the Snack Shack, which was busy. Mostly families coming from church services, pressed and starched, festive. The men, some with ties, most with open collars. Little boys in dark suits or dark slacks, all of them in white short-sleeved shirts and ties, like Dad.

We ordered: John did the traditional fried eggs, bacon, toast, with a side of pancakes. I couldn't decide. I then settled for a bowl of raisin bran with grits, biscuits and a small stack of pancakes. We had a new waitress, not Terri or the older woman but a young plump girl named Frannie, who had red cheeks, big white teeth, always giggling. Sweet. We both sat there watching these families. We didn't talk. We just ate and watched and listened.

I did feel I was now following John's mood more than my own. I noticed how I did this a lot: I always deferred to John, his moods. His desires. His lead. Why? Maybe he was right. Maybe we weren't so good together. Maybe we needed to go our separate ways. But, what about our summer together? Our one final bachelor-bud glory of a summer?

John took a forkful of egg, a piece of bacon, and looked out the window at the parking lot where we'd thrown the Frisbee. It was now packed with cars, pick-ups. I took a piece of biscuit, warm, buttery, lathered some honey on it, took a bite as I looked at all the families, so alive, busy, talking, eating, laughing. "I think I might be a little homesick," I said, still watching the breakfast fanfare.

"Huh," said John, his head down as he poked at his food. "Me, too."

"I feel like I want to go to church . . . it's probably too late, services are all over."

"Maybe not."

"Would you wanna go, too?"

"Naw. You go if you want."

"I dunno."

"I miss Brookie. Maybe I'll call her today."

"Kath starts her camp tomorrow."

I finished my small OJ, then sipped some ice water. Then, "So, Durlie, what're we doing today?"

"Gar."

Uh-oh. That tone. I panicked. "What?"

"Remember what I said last night? About my aunt in South Carolina? And Brookie up North."

"You have an aunt in South Carolina?"

"Yeah, Gar . . ." John paused, put his fork down, and slowly looked at me, as if searching my face, my eyes. He smiled. "You don't remember a thing I said last night, do you?"

"Um . . . something about Rickey Henderson. No, Maury Wills, sliding into . . . um . . ."

"The shooting star, you remember that?"

"Kind of."

"Nothing else?"

"It was a great night sky. We could hear the Opry still playing on the radio. I was sleepy. That's it."

"Okay." John took a sip of his large juice. "I think we have to talk."

"What're we doing now?"

"No, Gar, you know."

Oh dear. I began to take bites of my three-layered blonde pancakes, covered with a nice ooze of dark syrup.

"I'm going to drive to South Carolina today, to visit my aunt."

"Oh." I stopped everything.

"Then, I'll probably just head north, go see Brooke, and then, I'm not sure."

"What about us?"

"That's why we have to talk."

"Okay."

"I love us, you know that. And I think if we had a structure, like selling books, you know, with a real project, a mission together, we'd be fine. We'd make our summer money, and, we'd have one last summer together. But now, I don't know what this is."

"Yeah. I don't really know, either."

"I guess I'm a little confused."

"Me, too." We both poked at our food, ate a few bites. John looked out the window, I looked around at the crowd inside. "God," I said, "so this is it? This is our summer together?"

"I know."

"Oh man, now I'm really confused."

John nodded and sipped the last of his juice as he resumed looking out the window. I felt bad. I felt homesick, missed Kathy, missed Darlington and Huckleberry Lane. I even missed John, the Durl, the Earl of Durl, my best buddy, but he was sitting right here. And then he wasn't. He was going to leave soon. South Carolina. And he wasn't inviting me. But why would I want to go with him, anyway? I didn't know his aunt. No desire to. I was here, down South, on an adventure. Kind of. But. Was this all my fault? I was so adamant about this damn con of selling, wanting no part of it. Books. Personality. Charms. Smiles. Wiles. No thanks. No more. I still felt this but, now what? I didn't know there would be other moral consequences, other than my initial outrage and exhaustion. Sell books? We couldn't go back to that but I felt like it was my fault, I'd blown it somehow.

"Look, Gar. I'm glad. I mean, I'm sorry we can't sell books together but don't ever think it was your fault."

Now he was reading my mind, forgiving me, letting me off the hook: see why we're best buds? See?

"It's just . . . I mean, I was ready deep down to stop it. I'd had enough. But I didn't really know it. Until your reaction, your vision, really, Brown One. You are a wise soul, don't ever forget that."

"Really?"

"Really. You just gotta keep believing in yourself, okay?"

"Okay."

"And then to find out what a rip-off those books were, which I kind of always suspected. But I'd gone along. I almost had to go along, not just for the summer money, but for the things I learned, y'know? About life, people, about hanging in there, especially when things looked so bleak."

"Like now."

Durl slowed, looked at me and smiled. "Yeah, Gar . . . like now."

Why I looked over to the counter, I don't know. But there he was again. On the far side. In a grey flannel suit, bowler hat, talking to someone taller than himself as he leaned in and asked for—what? It was so crowded and noisy, I couldn't hear him or see him that well.

"John, see that man? The other side of the counter, see?" John followed my pointing finger. "Which man?"

"Grey suit, bowler hat. See him, leaning in?"

"Oh yeah."

"You know who that is?"

"Should I?"

"Take a good look."

"It's tough, so crowded." John kept stretching to see.

"Now he's drinking a glass of water, the cashier is giving him his change back, see? Now he's giving it back to her, tipping his hat. See him?"

"Okay. So?"

"That's him! Omigod. Maybe I'm going crazy."

"Maybe so."

"Look, he's leaving! He's holding the door open!"

"Yeah, that happens when you leave places."

"Durl, you don't get it. I gotta go talk to this man."

"Okay, but, Gar . . ."

I got up. I started for the door, then got held up, bumped into Frannie. "Oops!" she giggled, looked at me. "Gosh, I didn't know you were so tall. Be careful. I coulda spilled on ya."

"Sorry."

She was clearing. The chairs were tight, the place so crowded, when I made it to the door and swung out and looked both ways—gone. Elwood P. Dowd and Harvey. A glimpse, then—poof! I slowly weaved my way back to John. He was looking over the check, totaling his portion, as he pulled out his wallet.

"D'you catch him?"

"Yup. Knew it. Jimmy Stewart. He introduced me to Harvey."

"Harvey?" John held several bills in his hand. He looked at them, then at me.

"Yup. Good ol' Harvey."

"Oh, the rabbit!" John licked his thumb, then silently counted the bills.

"Man, that is one tall bunny rabbit, and *big.* Must be six-six, two-forty at least. Very BIG."

"God, Gar, now I know you're off your rocker. Ha!"

I took the green-lined bill, looked it over, pulled out my wallet and added my five dollars to John's. He took the money and bill over to the far counter and the cashier. We slowly worked our way out of the Snack Shack. I continued to marvel at all these energized families, conversations, minglings.

Leaving the cool of the Snack Shack, it was now sun-bright, hot, and humid, too. Yet somehow things weren't so bleak.

"Gar, whaddya say? You wanna?" John made a sliding motion with his right hand, over and over, like cracking a whip, only sideways. I knew immediately.

"Of course."

Even though the dusty parking lot was jam-packed, it didn't matter. The more obstacles, the better: another jerry-rigged gymnastic challenge. Lavender Frisbee in hand, we started close, with small strokes, about ten feet from each other, and then a gradual spreading out, until, among the cars, trucks, John was once again deftly reaching high, lunging left, legging it right, looping, lingering, lifting, lofting, the whole ballet-like arsenal of his agile, versatile, skinny frame. This was no longer the Snack Shack's packed parking lot but rather the signature coda to our elastic friendship, my spill of dusty, rugged frustration and desire combined with John's wily, tender touch of juggling and flight.

After our Frisbee antics, a revival of sorts, and a celebration in its way, of our youth and friendship, John seemed to defer to me and my suggestions, all that afternoon and into the evening. Which made it that much more difficult for me to let him go.

We drove back to the lake. John packed his things. Then we got into our swimsuits, took our towels, as well as our respective notebooks, sketchpads, books, et al. Our beige concrete table beside the lake was available. There were a few families on the slope, and over to our right, lounging on towels, one group had a radio tuned into an Atlanta Braves-Mets baseball game.

John took a nap on his towel next to the table while I did a quick pen and ink that caught the foreground edge of picnic table, John's legs and torso, and then beyond, to spots of sunlight, people on towels, and then the bulk of shade and trees. I liked it: I didn't try to draw everything. Hints. Impressions. It got me excited, a desire to paint. A shape that is a lopsided circle of black ink would become a nice warm blob of sunlight in a painting, a whole bunch of them piercing the violet/blue-black shade might be a little Matisse-decorous but also lush and somehow arousing. Then I napped, too, on the opposite side of John. I lay on my towel, my upper body on the grassy side, my feet warm in the partly sun-dipped sand.

I'm not sure how long I was out but John was at the table, writing in a loose-leaf three-ring notebook, when I woke. He was very intent, absorbed, his tongue involved, too, as he very carefully, as if carving the letters into the paper, wrote his upright, at times child-like, cursive. "I didn't know you kept a journal, D-man."

"I don't." He didn't look up. "This is a letter. To my folks."

"You still gonna phone Brooke?"

"I might."

I slowly stretched, yawned, rose up.

"Or I might write her, too."

I joined him, sitting on the other side of the table, not wanting to crowd him.

"I looked at your drawing."

"You did?"

"You left your pad open."

Almost instantly I wanted to know what he thought of it. I saw how much I wanted his approval. I asked myself, why? John's not an artist. He knows very little, really. But I always want this from him, his nod, his okay, his pat on the back. No. I won't ask. Nope. Not this time.

"Nice, Gar."

"What?"

"The drawing. Think it's your best one yet. I kept thinking it'd be a really neat painting."

"Really?" What do you know?

We spent that Sunday afternoon fairly sedentary. I also wrote a letter—to my folks, long overdue. I told them about our car trip, the hotel in Nashville, the styles of book-selling. I thanked my dad again for his help with Titine. I wrote about Big Jim and our crew of young salesmen, how John was taking good care of me. But I didn't tell them about our escape from Nashville and the Southwest Company, or how I couldn't stomach selling books door to door. Not yet. Maybe the next letter. Or in an eventual phone call. I wrote the truth but from a week ago. Not the present truth, that I had no job, that I was camping out under the stars, that John was soon about to leave me.

For some reason I didn't ponder this present truth all that much. I was saying little prayers, especially as each day began. I was reading my Bible. But I was also just being alive, outdoors, with my best bud, in a new and fascinating culture, Donelson, the South, Old Hickory Lake, Tennessee, or, "Tin Sea," as all the locals called it. I still had a good chunk of money I'd saved up during my senior year. I'd get by. I had my sketchbook, my pens, my watercolors. I hadn't found the art store in town but there had to be one. Or a department store with sketch pads and those children's watercolor sets. They'd do just fine. I wasn't starving. And the people I'd met so far were all very kind, polite.

Even John's leaving was okay. I loved him, but we'd already had a few special summers together: the summer after we graduated from Darlington, when our American History teacher, Dr. Harper, asked us to drive up to Vermont and help him build his dream-house. That was a great summer. Then, the summer after freshman year in college, when a woman from my dad's office in White Plains hired us to drive her red MG all the way across the United States to a small town outside of San Diego. An amazing trip. Granted, the car broke down in the Mojave Desert, just outside Barstow, but still. The people we met, the country we saw, big cities, small towns. We finally dropped off her car, visited one of John's aunts in Los Angeles (how many aunts around America do you have, Durlie?), and then hitched our way up the coast to San Francisco—this was the summer of 1968—where we stayed in a man's apartment in Haight-Ashbury. Oh yeah. The man, handsome, in his forties, had his eye on John, which got a little dicey. But still. Can you imagine? I was even a little jealous that the man was interested in John and not me. Ha. Another in our cavalcade of Life's Greatest Hits. It was in that man's home that Durl took a photo of me asleep, with a window view of a San Francisco church spire in the distance—a peace-making gesture from John to me as we concluded our trip. We'd had an intense ongoing argument about Freud vs. Christ; John was closing in on psychology and becoming a therapist while I was still pre-med but very much on a spiritual quest.

During the summers of our college years, John and I saw less of each other. I was a camp counselor at the Pomfret School one summer, working in a commercial art studio in Westport the next, while John sold his books. I did visit him that one summer in Omaha, Nebraska, when I worked for my dad's company, traveling to various grocery stores, writing up reports on illegal coupon redemption.

Now, here we were, our final summer together as bachelors. It was looking brief, all too brief. But memorable. Maybe it wasn't just circumstances. Maybe it was us, and time, and moving on. Could that really be?

John went to the payphone up by the restrooms to call Brooke. I paged through my El Greco book, watched the few swimmers, and then began a letter to Kathy.

23

By the time we went for a swim (we never did swim across and back), it was later than we thought. Deceptive late afternoon, early evening sky. We swam, showered, dressed, took both our cars into town and had another—this time farewell—meal at that Burger King. We sat outside again, burgers, fries, shakes.

John ate and looked over his Triple-A map of the eastern United States, trying to assess the shortest distance between two points: Donelson, but really Nashville, since Donelson was too small a town to be on this map, to Spartanburg, South Carolina. The highway exit in Donelson, going into Nashville (not in the direction of the County Fair from last night), would take him to the edge of Nashville where he'd join 40 going east, and, but for the Appalachian Trail and the Smokey Mountains, he figured it would be a straight shot into South Carolina.

It was about six-thirty p.m. as we finished our meal, he'd be on the road by seven p.m., drive for two hours, as the sun set, until nine p.m. or so, then maybe a couple more hours in the dark. Stop somewhere for the night, "Or, maybe sleep in the Monster," said John. "Who knows?" And then drive the rest of the way on Monday morning. With any luck, he was pretty sure he'd arrive at his aunt's home by lunch time.

I sat there, looking at the map, listening to Durl plot his route, nodding agreeably, almost complicitly, as if we were doing this together. Inside me, it was suddenly happening much too fast. What's going on? Is this really happening? Not so much panic as a certain kind of restlessness. Okay, fear. My bud, the Durl. We were parting ways again. I didn't like it.

"Let's drive over to the library parking lot, that hillside, Gar, and say good-bye there, okay?" I nodded as John folded up his map.

We pulled in, the library closed, the parking lot empty but for the long shadows, the grove of trees backlit by the sun's brightening descent, the shadows laced with streaks of sun. I parked next to John. We got out of our cars. John leaned against the passenger-side door of the Green Monster. I joined him and leaned, too, against the grey bowler-hat driver's side grey doldrums of Titine.

We faced each other silently for a few moments. John looked down into the village of Donelson, more cars on the four-lane road than people among the mostly closed shops, all of them laid out: the Burger King furthest away, the McDonald's, a video store, the big boxy Shop-A-Lot nearest us, to the right, open twenty-four hours. All of this choreography of steel and concrete and glass draped now in lengthening shadows, brilliant sunlight. "Well," said John.

"Well," I said, then making a joke, "ayeah, that's water, alright!"

John watched me and laughed. It was a reference to our Vermont summer when we worked on Dr. Harper's house and the one day when the backhoe wouldn't work. These two Vermont icons, older men, simple men, tried to figure out what was wrong. Eventually, they both got down on their knees, looked under, and found stuff dripping. First one, then the other dipped fingers and tasted it, and then said, "Ayeah," echoed John, beaming, "that sure is water!" We both laughed.

"So, Durlkins."

"So, Gar-Pear."

"Weird, huh?"

"Kinda, yeah. What about you, Gar, what will you do?"

"I dunno. I'm kind of in shock still, about us. So . . ."

"Yeah . . ." John looked off, the other way, toward the sun, his face suddenly brightened, half of it a burnt orange, on fire. "Well, you got out of selling books and into the Great Outdoors," John offered.

"True. Not how I pictured it."

"Me neither. But like I said, I'm glad and I have you to thank."

"Right."

We both now looked off, back down into the village.

"Say hi to Brookie for me."

"I will. You think you'll see Kathy again this summer?"

"Dunno about this summer. We're still planning for Europe in the fall. Her sister Ellie's wedding in London."

"Right. Your graduation gift. Nice."

"Hope so."

"Well." John was ready to get going. "I'll phone you when I get to my aunt's."

"How?" I asked. John looked at me. "How will you reach me?"

"Oh yeah. Here." He reached in his back pocket, took out a folded piece of notebook paper. "You gotta pen, Gar?"

Always. T-shirt pocket. Handed it to him. John jotted a number and name on the lower half of the paper, after he twisted into position on the Green Monster's rooftop. "This is her phone, her name—Dotty. So, you call me, how about tomorrow afternoon?"

"Okay." I re-pocketed my pen along with the strip of notebook paper. "Durlie, I been missing you all day today. So, you better get going so I can really miss you."

"Right." John twisted back facing me, and then waving both his open palmed hands, he said, "Come on."

"Do we have to?"

"Gar! We have to."

This was a painful ritual of ours, dating back to perhaps our first high school years. Gangs have their finger signs, clubs have their secret handshakes, athletes and sports teams have their high fives and chest bumps and various handshake configurations, most all based on meetings, greetings, and triumphs. Ours was for good-bye. Never for greeting, just good-byes. And I hated it. John loved it. Where did it come from? Sports, sure, but also that child's game of slap-hands, where one set of hands is on top, palms down, the other set of hands is on the bottom, palms up. The hands on the bottom try to catch and slap the hands on the top. If he misses, it's the other's turn. If he catches even a piece, he continues on. So, take the slap-hand motif but we reversed it: the hands on the top come down on the open palms on the bottom. John always liked me to go first.

"Come on, Gar, we can do this."

"I know, Durl, I know." I raised my hands, palms down. I looked at them, looked at John's, palms up, and measured the situation: John always managed to slap my hands so full, so hard—so painful—and his pleasure in this. The last few times, I had hit just off-center, not full on, so never quite the sting that John often triumphed with.

"Gar."

"Okay, okay." My hand with palms down moved into the start position until I stopped. "Durl, can't we just say good-bye?"

"Gar, this IS our good-bye. Come on."

"But, D-man."

"You love this."

"*You* love it."

"You love our ritual."

"Yeah but—"

"*Gar,* you can do it. NOW."

"Oh God." I raised my hands in one fell swoop, up, then swishing, crashing—down—and SHWAPPP! A united slapping sound that surprised both of us—my palms on John's—centered, swift, and that nice full-bodied STING!

"Whoa, Gar—OOH!" John shook his hands, to relieve the stinging heat.

"Huh?" I was pleased. Mine stung, too, but it'd been clean, triumphant.

"Jesus, Gar, that was your best ever."

"I think so."

"Well done." John offered his hands, now with palms facing down, waiting for mine to position, palms up, under his. I slowly maneuvered just below his, then pulled away. "Or, we could quit while we're ahead?" I offered.

"Are you kidding?"

It was competitive now, as it had been all along. By doing as well as I had, John would now have to do that much better. Oh God.

"Gar."

"Alright, Durlie." John watched my hands move into place, his hands and face now bathed in the burnt orange sunlight, brilliant and sad. He swished his tongue, eyed our sets of hands, measuring, watching, all of him waiting for the proper moment, the perfect impulse. As his eyes grew bigger, darker, crossing the mix of sunlight and shadows, he pulled up his arms, palms rigid, like a great maestro, this conductor of our elegiac good-bye orchestrations, and then, leading with his head and shoulders, he dove down, down, bringing both firm palms with him, a climactic joining and stereophonic—THWACHT!

"Oh—WHOA!" I cried.

As my hands sizzled, red, hot, and the smoke drifted off (it felt like that, truly), John slowly lifted both his palms, and eyed them, his face and eyes bright, gleaming, tongue dangling now, until this critical glare came over him.

"I dunno," John said.

"Oh, that was good, Durlie."

"No, no. We've done better."

"D-man."

"No, Gar, yours was solid. Mine was off."

"No way! I have the red palms to prove it!" I held them up, showed him, my palms pulsing, a-tingle (truth be known, it wasn't his best but—).

"Let's do another. That one stunk!"

"NO. D-man. We did it."

"You sure?"

"Positive." We both wrung out our heated palms, our tingling fingers. Oh man. Then we said good-bye. We hugged. We shook hands. We patted each other on the back.

John stopped, eyed me carefully. "One more time, Gar?"

"Ha!" I lightly tapped his left cheek. "Funny, Durl, very funny."

"Well?"

"Yeah, you be well. You go well, D-man. I'll call you late tomorrow."

"Not too late, Gar." John was now pulling keys from his pocket and making his way around to the driver's side.

"Five p.m.?"

"Make it six."

"Six it is!"

"Okay, Gar, have a great summer!" He was in the car.

"You, too, Durl." I bent and spoke through the rolled-down

passenger window.

"You going to be okay, Gar?" John turned the key, the engine coughed once, then hummed.

"Oh sure. Say hi to the Brooker."

"Will do. Hi for me to Kathy." John backed out, wrestled the Green Monster's steering wheel, and then turned and slowly departed the Donelson Library parking lot, his left arm suddenly jutting up, into a wave. I waved back. I kept waving while John paused as two cars passed, then accelerated left into the traffic, and made his way uphill and down and gone.

I just stood there, my arm still raised, my hand no longer waving. Now, just a lone figure with an arm raised, trying to ask a question that might never find an answer.

John's green Plymouth a blur. Faded. Gone. Now it was just me, standing in the Donelson Public Library parking lot. I slowly pulled down my arm. I rubbed my hands together again, examined them. Still red but not quite so stingy. The sunlight, that orangey pink of beginning summer dusk, was on me, all over me, my hands, my shorts, my bare legs, my arms and T-shirt. A Connecticut boy in a Tennessee summer dusk.

I looked back down the hillside into the Donelson village. A few cars moving along. A woman pushing her grocery cart in the Safeway parking lot. Then a grey and white dog appeared at the rear of the Safeway, from behind its grey walls. The dog moved slowly, head down, then abruptly stopped, pulled up and sat, as if he'd come to watch the lady, her plastic black and red purse dangling from her right shoulder, as she slowly continued to push her silvery rack of brown grocery bags. He watched her. I watched him and her.

I walked over to the Donelson Library glass windows. Deep inside its darkened interior, books, so many shelves of books. Maybe tomorrow. They were a comfort. I walked back to my car. The lady was slowly loading the brown bags into the trunk of her car. The dog: I had to look twice, and then all about, a wider view, but he was gone. Like John. I got into Titine, put the key in and turned: the engine was going fine, then I was gone, too.

Funny, how we end up in certain places, not sure why we're there. We go for one reason and end up staying, pulled into our lives, for quite another reason or reasons, which we may not understand at that time, or maybe never. I came to Tennessee to sell books, dictionaries not Bibles, door to door. But now what?

I drove back to the lake to spend the night, alone. My best bud, John D, had gotten me to follow him—literally, my car tracking his—and then he'd left me here. Our last summer as bachelor buddies a bust. We'd had a little over a week together, and, for just the two of us—Friday, Saturday, and most of Sunday. That was our summer that was. It was as if John had picked me up in Connecticut, car and modest belongings and all, and then dropped me in a small, remote town in the United States of America, just outside Nashville, Tennessee, and then said, See ya.

As if to say, "Okay, Wandering Minstrel, deal with it." Yet, there was no blame attached. It wasn't John's fault or the Southwest Company's or anyone's or anything. Maybe not even mine. It was just—life. Now, for the first time ever, it really felt like: oh, that over there, that was growing up and childhood, high school traumas, that elaborate college thing, a Liberal Arts Education. All that was—over there.

But this, right here—my rumbling junk-heap of a car, this small Southern town, this lake, the burgeoning night sky, the owl, the crickets, the sweet earthy night air, and, this loneliness and curiosity, too—this drifting, no plans, no *plan,* but to just keep driving, watching out the car windows, and listening, and for a while, not even being hungry, and the beauty, too, of all this, as the dusk becomes night. This was now the other life, the real one.

I parked the car. I took my sketchbook and watercolors down to the picnic table by the lake. I drew, and then filled in with my watercolors, the bright orange and pink and lavender and blues of the fireworks across the lake, over there. Just over there. I did that watercolor and then another one. Then, one more, for good luck. I sat alone lakeside and watched and painted. Then, I just sat and felt this, all of this, continue to wash over me, fill me, John in his car, well along on the road now.

I walked up the hill, back to my car. Went and did my ablutions. Laid out my sleeping bag. Lay down, arms behind my head. The stars, too, just up there—a nice batch of jewels, glistening, seductive, charming, and they were John's, too. They belonged to both of us now. But this—all of this, slowly, it continued in me. All of this, right here—not over and done with, over there.

All of this right here, upon me, in me—was mine now. Alone. By myself. This, glorious, unfathomable, was my life. Mine. Now.

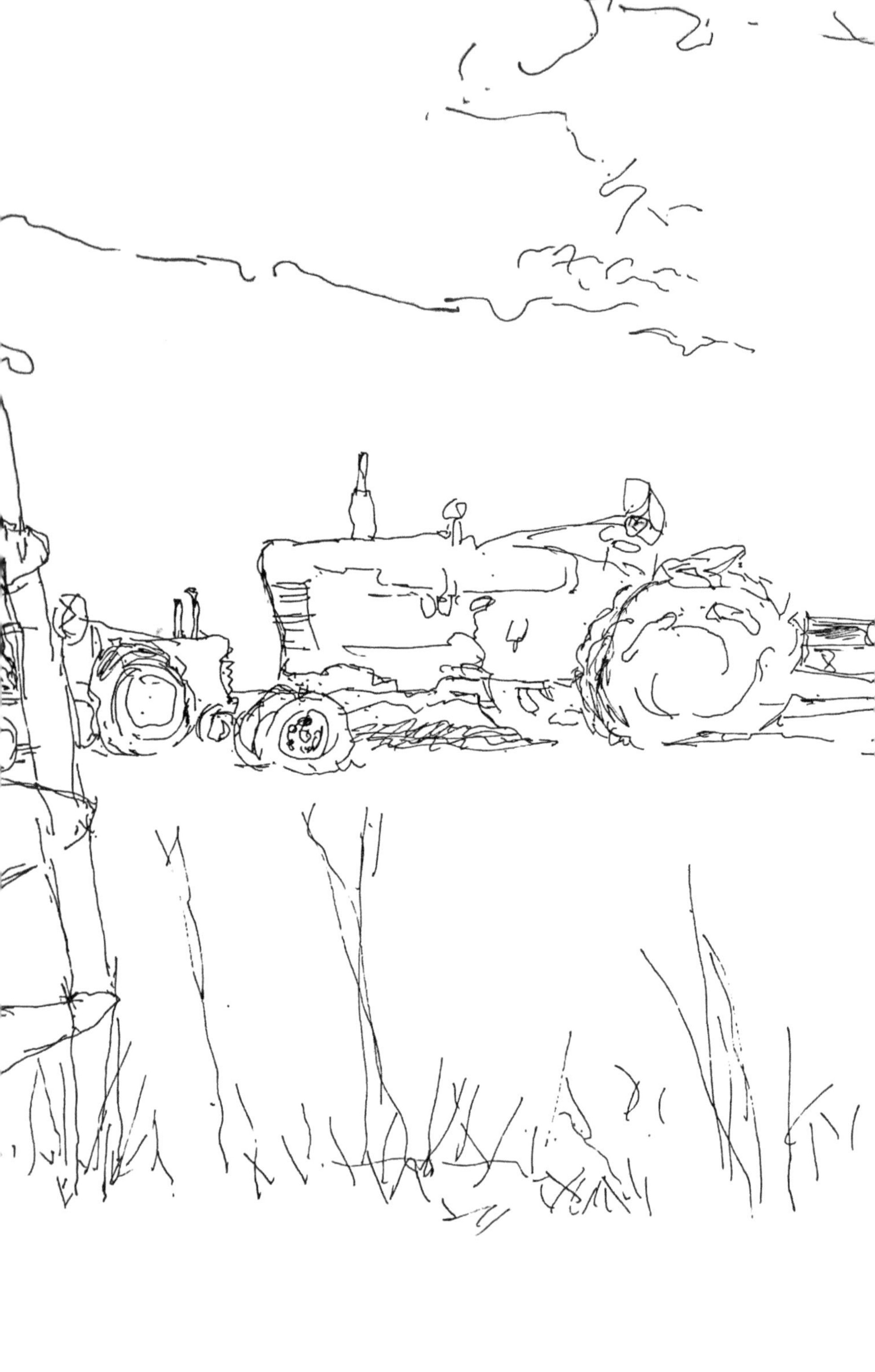

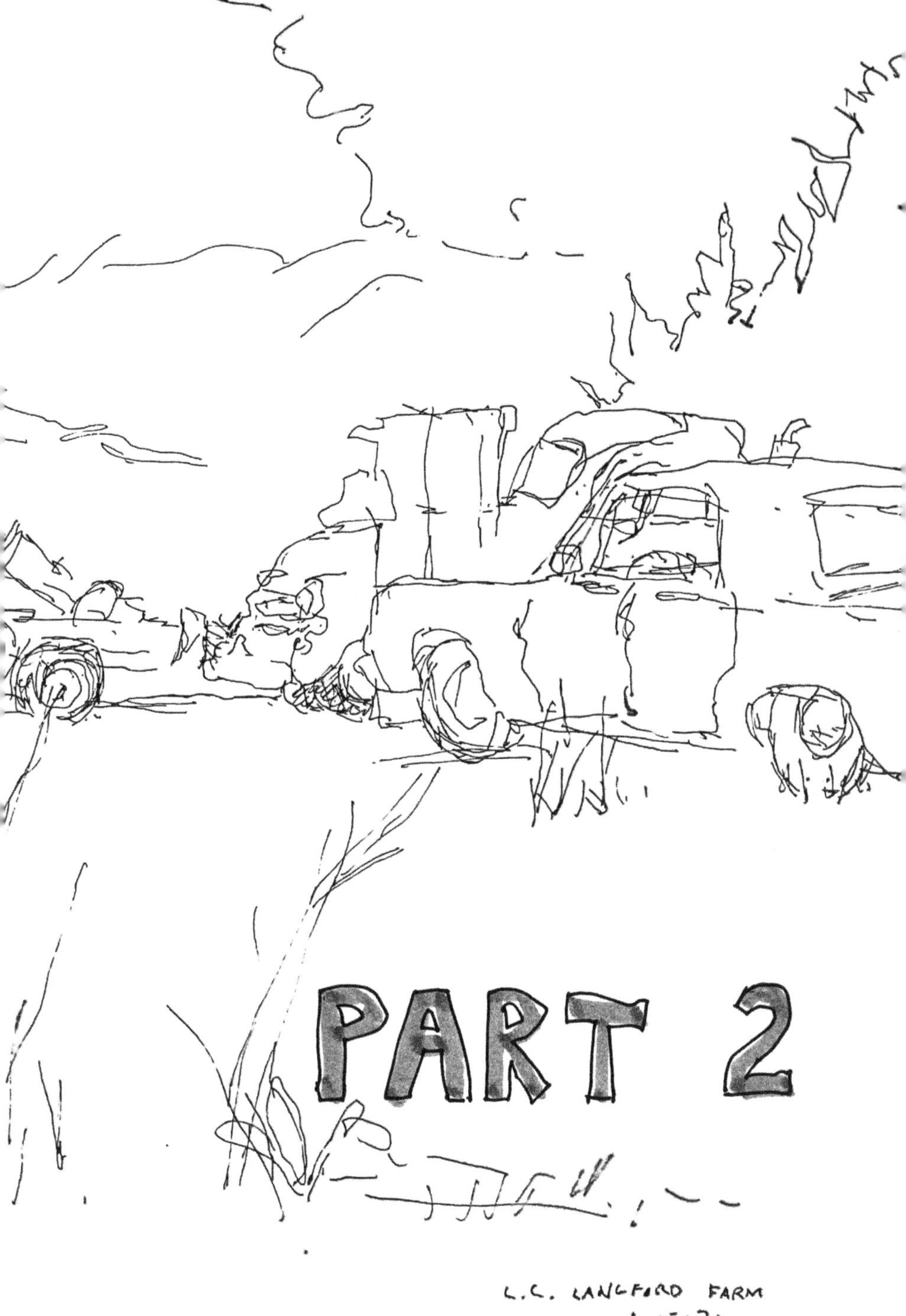

PART 2

L.C. LANGFORD FARM
6.15.71

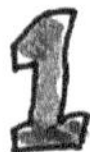

Monday morning, the last Monday in June, that summer of 1971, I woke up hungry. I folded up my sleeping bag, dropped it inside Titine. I didn't feel like a swim or a jog. Maybe later. I washed up, then sat in the car and read my Bible. A passage from Corinthians. I jotted the lines down in my journal, tried to meditate on them (in vain), made a few notes. I reread the incomplete letter to Kathy that I'd begun the day before. Hopefully later, lakeside, I'd finish it, copy it, and send it off on Tuesday morning.

The farms I drove past, I saw men working in the fields. The morning sunlight cast long shadows as they worked. At one farm, there were several trucks parked, a tractor, and a big rack with bales of hay piled on top. Haying. I had a passing thought that this might be work I could do. Eventually, I would need to find some way of making money.

These rustic farms had a great appeal: their open spaces, so many fields of different shapes, greens, straw yellow, and then the distant groves of trees beside farmhouses, barns. They were old songs, tender melodies, but when I merged onto the two-lane road into town, there was that Monday morning buzz, the scratchily upbeat riffs of pop ditties. More traffic now than on the weekend, the town of Donelson was roused, heading to work.

Two cars and one pick-up truck pulled out as I entered the Snack Shack's parking lot. I nodded, thanked the man in the red rusted pick-up as I took his spot. I brought my sketchbook with me into the diner.

The booth by the window where John and I had sat (both times) was vacant. I took it. I wasn't ready to break tradition, John stayed close this way, rumbling as he was, off to South Carolina. He'd probably been up and on the road for a couple hours by now. I do this:

after loved ones or friends have departed, I track them in my imagination. Kathy seated in that plane, looking out her window seat, or John, singing songs out loud as he speeds east in his Green Monster.

I sat, stared out the window. I saw Titine. I saw another car pull out. The diner was clearly finishing its rush hour. It was close to nine. When did the library open? That was the only thing I had planned. That, and perhaps a stroll along sidewalks. Maybe do some pen and inks. Maybe do a pen and ink of this window view. This love of windows, openings into other worlds. The painting rectangle, framed pictures, all are windows before they become an experience, an encounter, sometimes even a kind of mirror . . . hmm. Am I being sophomoric or is that an insight? I took out my small notepad, hadn't jotted in it much. This was a 4 x 6-inch ringed binder, smaller than my three-hole journal notebook. I jotted names, book titles, quotes, sometimes my own musings. I opened it, began writing down this notion of picture, rectangle, frame. The previous entry had been Big Jim's address in Hartsville, 23 Willow Lane. Before that, a quote, a kind of ditty from John Marin, the painter:

> "I am a Small town Gink with a small town disposition
> I'll insist on being an old Fashioned Critter
> but the town must be of my choosing
> the critters in this town of my own choosing too
> and since I cannot bring this about—I don't belong anywhere."
> —*Marin on Marin,* p. 30.

A good quote and, helpful right now. Small town. This feeling, I didn't quite belong, anywhere. Didn't want to go back to Darlington. Or tag along with John to South Carolina. No selling books. So. Did I choose this small town? Not quite. But—

"You ready to order, Sonny Boy?"

I looked up from my jotting and musing. "Terri?"

"That's my name, don't wear it out. You want somethin' to eat or you gonna just keep chewin' on that lil notepad?"

I laughed.

No sign of her husband. She seemed more carefree, looser, clearly a flirt, this was her "theatre of operations." She was a star, sweet, playful, sexy.

"Okay." Terri straightened her skirt, raised her arms, pencil and pad ready. "What'll it be?"

I eyed the menu. I wanted to say something, then got shy.

"Forget how to read?"

"No, no," I chuckled. "Okay: two fried eggs, over easy, bacon, home fries, a large OJ, and a glass of water."

"Very good." She leaned close and took my menu. "That wasn't so hard, was it?"

"You don't remember me, do you?"

"Oh God, there've been so many and it's always dark, the music's so loud." I must've looked startled. "Oh honey, forgive me. That was a lousy, cynical joke. You do look familiar . . . You're not Bill Norton's cousin, who just moved down from up North?"

"I am from up North."

"Okay . . ."

"My best buddy and I were here Friday night . . . there was an electrical storm . . . and, that man, Mr. Steward, walked by?"

"I remember some of that but . . ."

"It's okay."

"Let me put this order in." She waved the pad, winked, and then bolted off. I bowed my head, red-faced. Suddenly, I was very lonely. I missed Johnny D. I missed Kathy. I missed being known and cared about by people who mean something to you. I closed my small notepad. I looked out the window. I felt ready to cry or get angry. Then, the light shifted a little, a pick-up truck pulled in, causing a shadow, a flickering. I began to consider this window view as a drawing, even a potential painting.

Terri appeared with my juice, a water, and straws. "You're the artist, right?" She placed the juice and water and began to bounce up and down. "Of course you are! I'm sorry. I get so busy sometimes and forget things. Please forgive me! Listen, this breakfast is on me, okay? Order anything you want. Hey! Where's your sketchbook?"

"It's here." I pulled it up from beside me.

"Any new drawings?"

I looked at the sketchbook as if it might speak up. "Yeah. A few. Wanna see?"

"Oh dear, yes! Let me check on your food first. What's your name again?"

"Garry."

"And I'm Terri again!" She offered her hand, we shook, she laughed. "Terri and Garry, get it? Nice to really meet you. I won't forget next time. Promise. Be right back."

I watched her dance off, her red and white dress aflutter. She seemed much younger than a woman in her forties. My crush was in full swing.

"Here you go." She was back, bearing gifts. "Brought you a side of hot cakes, for good measure, okay?"

"You didn't have to do that."

"Artists need to eat. Can I see?" She wiped her hands on her apron as she nodded to my sketchbook.

"Sure."

"Scoot over."

I loved making room for her, my side of the booth. I started to open the sketchbook as I moved it toward her.

"No, let me. See if I can find where we left off." Very gracefully, she took the sketchbook. Something was going on in the front of the diner, men's voices, some commotion, as Terri tenderly began to turn pages. "Oh, there's your girlfriend again. So lovely. What's her name?"

"Kathy. Kathleen."

"Kathleen. Lovely. Is she really that, y'know, well endowed?"

I laughed, "Yeah, she really is."

"Lucky you, huh?" And she nudged me, an impish grin, almost as if she were an older brother. This was that tomboy thing. Kathy had it, too, a female relishing the joys of being male, or, what is that? But it's very delightful.

Something I would later learn is actually rare in women but somehow a necessary ingredient in the artist, this equanimity, delight in women, men, things, objects, places, a delight that the world contains gestures, energies, that all feed the spirit of the creative. I was just beginning to learn this, a difficult lesson because it is so easily confused with the raw, lusty sexual. I didn't know yet about Eros and the love of all things, man-made and natural; the love of the flow, that might be a clue to an art that remains unconditionally caring, that seeks the gravity of the heroic, that sneaks up on the eternal. Right now I was just glad to share my drawings with this sweet-smelling attractive older woman.

Until this darkness entered.

"Christ. Here you are!" It was him, black hair, unshaven. He swayed there over us. He had pieces of straw on his torn work-shirt, all over his worn jeans.

Fred, the cook, quickly came over. "Come on, Stan, Terri's working. Come on. Let's go in back."

"She's working alright! Who is this kid? You seeing him?"

Terri moved quickly from the booth and stood. "Jesus, Stan, what're you doing?"

"He fired me. Dumped me. Fucking Floyd Underwood. He *fired* me, d'you understand?" Stan was almost crying and shouting at the same time.

"Oh, Stan, you stink to high heavens. Come on."

"I'm sorry." Stan bowed his head, just stood there.

"Come on, Stan. Let's go," said Terri.

"I don't want to," Stan pouted. "Christ."

"Stannie, it's going to be okay."

"Come on, Stan," said Fred, pulling at his arm. "Come in back. Things are slow. You and Terri can have a little talk. Come on."

Stan wiped his face, his big hand worn, dirty. He opened his mouth wide, like a yawn, then gave out a loud moan. "Aaoowww! Christ. I fucked up. Oh, fucking Christ."

"No, Stannie, it's okay."

"Don't tell me it's fucking 'okay.' I'm the goddamn man, okay?"

"Come on, honey," and Terri now walked off. She nodded to me, mouthed "Thank you," and then back to Stan, "Stan? Fresh coffee, come and get it!"

"Right . . ." Stan spoke to his shoes. Slowly, he lifted his head and began to walk, to follow Terri. Then he stopped, raised his face to the ceiling, said, "Riiiggghhtt." Abruptly he turned back, came to my side of the booth, grabbed my T-shirt and pulled hard and forced me to rise up: "Don't you dare fucking touch my wife, y'hear?" His eyes were black, solid, his breath sour and cloying.

"Yes, sir," I said.

He kept tugging. *"Y'hear?"*

"I do. Yes, sir."

"Stan!" Terri rushed back, grabbed Stan and pulled him away from me. "Stop it! Jesus. That's the artist. He was here Friday night, remember? He's done all these drawings, I was looking at them, okay?"

"Okay." Stan hung there again, now looking off, toward the front of the diner where mid-morning light filled the diner windows.

"Come on!"

"But I want some coffee."

"That's where we're going."

"Oh shit." Stan hung his head again. "I really fucked up."

"Stannie, Fred's got fresh coffee. We can talk things over. Come."

"Okay." Stan slowly moved now as Terri held his left arm and directed him past tables to the counter, then behind, and into the kitchen.

"You like that kid?" Stan asked as he pointed a finger back at me before it began to fiddle with his left ear.

"Just forget it, will you? Come on."

"You don't have to be so mean, was just asking."

The first fantasy I had about Terri and her sinister husband was that Friday night when John and I first met Terri. It went something like this: I'd approach this man, Stan, call him out, and then go out in the parking lot and fight for the honor of loving Terri. Just now, forget my accommodating "Yes, sir." Instead, I would stand up, pull off Stan's big grubby hands, and slug the fucking bastard. Lay him out, right there. Pow! Terri would come running over, screaming, and I'd calmly say to her, "That'll sober him up."

But, big, tall, and athletic as I was, I didn't like violence. I was never a macho kind of guy. There was a bravado to it, a pose, that I abhorred, knew was not really who I was. Though I did envy it somewhat, its vulgarity was so simple: "Don't fuck with my woman,"

"I'll break your f'ing face," or, as my dad would say, while watching the evening news with Walter Cronkite, "Bomb the fuckers back to Kingdom come!"

Would it were that simple. Or was I simply afraid of this dark man? His angry sullen presence, his drunken adolescent rants, reminded me of my dad on a bad night. My dad scared me. Stan scared me. His grabbing me completely shocked me, shut me down.

When Terri finally returned, fifteen minutes later, I told her I was fine. I lied. I was still shaking.

"You're sure? You look a little pale."

"Really. I'm good."

"I am *so* sorry. It's just, Stan's had it rough. Lost his first wife to cancer fifteen years ago. Raised his boys, worked so hard. Then we met and about a year after we married, his business just fell apart. He's been doing odd jobs here and there. He's always been a drinker, but since his business went under, it's gotten really bad. He's not really like this, okay?"

"How long have you been married?"

"Three years the end of this August. My first, his second."

"You like being married?"

"I do. But I waited a long time. All these young punks kept calling but I really wanted to meet a mature man. I'd known Stan when he was married. His wife was so sweet, April, really a doll. Then she died fast, a horrible cancer. Stan was a wreck. He started coming here a lot. We got to talking. I made him laugh, which he appreciated. One night he took me to a really nice dinner over to Nashville. And a movie. I picked it, a funny one. We laughed, we talked, y'know, it was so nice. A few weeks after that, he asked me to marry him. I said yes, didn't even hesitate . . . I'd better go check on him. I told Fred, your breakfast is on the house."

"No, no, I can pay."

"Sure you can but I *insist.* Next time, I want to have a real good look at those drawings, okay?"

"Maybe you'll let me do one of you."

"Me? Ha!" Terri blushed. "Old freckle-faced me. No way!"

"Really."

"Go draw someone really beautiful, like your girlfriend. See ya." Terri leaned in and pecked my left cheek with a tender kiss. She winked and waved as she ran off. I finished my breakfast "on the house." I did do a quick pen and ink of the view out the window into the parking lot. The sun's long shadows, shortening, as we headed into late morning.

2

My first day on my own. It was all just fine. I was anonymous, fine. I was alone, pretty fine, though I could see the nights as being difficult, a little lonely. But, my basic impulse, after my hunger had been satisfied, was to immerse myself in books.

I loved books. And I didn't have very many now. I wanted to be reading, not just art books or about artists. College had almost ripped the love of reading from me, turned it into a labor, a function of discussion and papers and seminars and analysis and showing off. It had lost its privacy and power, its warmth and intimacy. I wanted it to become mine again. I still had this ache for books. I drove straight to the library.

"So how did you like Mr. Greco?" came a loud whisper.

I'd just walked in. "I beg your pardon?"

From behind the main check-out counter, Mrs. Lexie Helms peered over her reading glasses and asked again, "Mr. El Greco, how was he?"

"Oh!" I was headed for the Fiction section when she accosted me. I joined her at the counter. "Fine, thank you. A wonderful painter," I whispered.

"So I hear."

We were both whispering. "And a really nice book. Thanks again. I'll get it back to you by the end of the week."

"No rush. Have you an address yet?"

"Not really. I'm out at Old Hickory Lake, sleeping under the stars."

"Tough to get mail there."

"Yes."

We both laughed.

"May I make a suggestion?"

"Please."

"Hermitage, the small town near there. Very small, really. But I think there's a post office. You could rent a box."

"That's a great idea."

"I thought so."

"Thank you."

"Don't mention it. In the meantime, my library card is your library card."

"Really? I don't want to—"

"Really. Now. Find something you can read, not just look at."

"Thanks. I'll do just that."

She smiled. I smiled. Then, as she took off her glasses and let them fall, the dark blue cord around her neck catching them, she turned and called in a loud whisper, "Rosemary! Come. I want you to meet someone."

I turned, too, and saw him. Lexie Helms called to me again, "Mr. Brown? Yoo-hoo!" She was whispering and I was watching: through the glass doors, a man in a grey suit, it was him. Mr. Steward. If body language reveals truth, I swear to you, he seemed to be with a very tall invisible companion.

"Mr. Brown?"

"Yes . . ." I was still staring, as Mr. Steward nodded to his "companion" and then departed.

"I want you to meet Rosemary."

"Um . . ." There was time. I might catch him. But if I did, what would I say? And, was I going crazy?

"Please, Mr. Brown," Mrs. Helms whispered loudly, "Show your face."

"I'm sorry." I turned. Two women now at the counter. Mrs. Helms and this lovely brunette, in her twenties, porcelain white skin, eyes shadowed by a pair of scholarly black eyeglasses.

"Mr. Brown. I want you to meet—"

"Mrs. Helms, who was that man?"

"What man?"

"See? He just went out the glass doors. See? Walking along in the parking lot. Grey suit. Kind of loping?"

"Oh. Lovely, sweet man, Mr. Steward, right, Rosemary? Rosemary knows him. You know his family, too, right? Say hello to Mr. Brown, our visitor from the North. A Yankee."

"Hi." Rosemary had dimples and a brilliant smile, all white teeth.

"Hi." We shook hands. "Garry . . . Garry Brown."

"Rosemary Blanchard." She blushed, then asked me, "Do you know Mr. Steward?"

"No. I've just noticed him. He looks a lot like Jimmy Stewart, the movie star?"

"I *love* Jimmy Stewart!" said Mrs. Helms.

"I don't think I know Jimmy Stewart." Rosemary blushed.

"What?" Lexie turned to Rosemary. "You must. A charming actor, *It's a Wonderful Life, Mr. Smith Goes to Washington*? Rosemary!"

"I'm sorry . . ." Her white skin a shade of pinkish rose.

"And . . . *Harvey*," I offered.

"Harvey?" Mrs. Helms now turned to me. "Harvey who?"

"Harvey. The movie. With Jimmy Stewart. Harvey the invisible rabbit?"

"I don't know *Harvey* but I do know Jimmy Stewart, and you should, too, Rosemary. Go see a movie. He's such a delight."

Rosemary smiled shyly, a little giggle, too. "Honestly, I'd rather read a good book."

That always appeals to me, particularly when an attractive woman says she'd prefer reading a good book to seeing a movie, or a dinner out, or going to a party. Now, I was more interested in Rosemary than chasing after Mr. Steward.

"He doesn't drive a car," said Rosemary with a shy glance downward. I was staring at Rosemary.

Lexie joined in. "Mr. Steward. Doesn't drive."

"Oh?" I finally managed.

"I knew his brother, Francis. Frank. Who was killed in Vietnam."

I continued to watch Rosemary, her shy gaze, her white skin contrasting with her dark hair, really an auburn, brown and red tints, her full dimpled cheeks.

"She knew his brother, Frank, who was killed in Vietnam. Just a year ago, wasn't it, Rosemary?" said Mrs. Helms, as if translating.

"No," said Rosemary. She pushed on the frames of her black eyeglasses. "Two years ago. It devastated James. People think he's crazy but he's not. He just carries this enormous sadness with him. He misses his younger brother very much."

"He misses his younger brother, Frank, very much," echoed Lexie, as she bore her look into me. Rosemary continued to look down.

"He's a sweet man. Kind of a chameleon. I saw him selling vegetables one day, way out past Hermitage, off the main roads, in this little cul-de-sac. He looked quite happy."

"Really?" asked Lexie.

"Yes." Rosemary now looked up and off, toward the parking lot. "I'm not sure how he does it. One day selling produce from a wagon, the next he's sitting in the bank president's office."

"Well, his family owned that Fidelity Trust of Tennessee, right?"

"Yes. Sometimes, he just sits in overalls on his porch and reads books or the paper. I bump into him everywhere."

"Very private man, isn't he, Rosemary?"

"Very private, and, I think very troubled. Restless."

"Yes," said Mrs. Helms. Both women now stood looking past me, out toward the parking lot. I turned and watched, too. He was gone.

"Why does he always walk around looking up, over his shoulder?" I asked.

"He does?" asked Lexie.

"Yes," confirmed Rosemary. "I always thought it was part of his eccentricity, like a nervous tic, you know?" Then Rosemary looked at me. "How long are you here for, Garry?"

"Yes," chimed in Mrs. Helms, "how long you gonna visit our fine village of Donelson, Tin-sea?"

"Not sure. Just got here. But I like it. Everyone's very friendly."

"Good. And now you know Rosemary, too. So, you got two friends in the library. I'm mentoring Rosemary, aren't I?"

"You are, Mrs. Helms."

"She just got her degree in Library Sciences and then came to us, all the way from Georgia!"

"So, you're new to Donelson, too?" I asked Rosemary.

"Oh no," that pink flush again. "I grew up here, went off to GT, did graduate work there, too, and now I'm back."

"And we're lucky to have her."

"Why, thank you, Lexie Helms!" Now Rosemary perked up. "Well, I'd better get back to it."

"Yes, both of us, lotta librarying to attend to," added Lexie.

"Of course."

"You call on either one of us if you need anything, okay?"

"I will. Thanks."

They went back to work. I turned and headed for the Fiction section. I browsed. I stopped. I went to the windows and looked again for James Steward. Of course, he was long gone. When I turned back and re-entered the shelves, there, leaning among the first stack of books, the A–F section, was a tall white rabbit. He was fingering, or, I should say, pawing, at a book. I asked if I might help him. "Thanks," he said as I reached in and handed him the book.

"No," he said. "It's for you. A must-read. I insist."

"For me?"

"Please," and he pushed the book back into my hands.

I read aloud the title, "*The Great Gatsby.*"

"Fitzgerald. A great book. Perhaps his best."

"Why, thank you," I said and eyed him as I shuffled a few pages.

"Don't mention it."

"Listen, I don't mean to be rude, or, perhaps I'm just going crazy but aren't you—?"

"I am. You recognize me, don't you? You saw my movie?"

"I did! I loved it. You and Jimmy Stewart and—"

"Thank you. My first big role. I'm very proud of that film. The play is very good, too. I did it on Broadway before we made the movie. A big hit. God, I love New York."

"You did it on stage first?"

"Oh yeah. Mary Ellen Chase. What a doll. How she comes up with this stuff, you got me. But I'm forever grateful. Listen, I've gotta meet my buddy Jimmy over at the Old Horseshoe Tavern. Would you care to join us?"

"Oh—what? Now? A bar?"

"A tavern. Pub. Bar. Whatever. Wet the whistle, right?"

"Oh gosh, thanks, I don't really drink but, another time maybe?"

"'Another time maybe' . . . Sure. Hmm. That'd be a good title, wouldn't it? 'Another Time Maybe.' Like it. And yes, of course. You take care. Enjoy this book. A little gem, you'll see. Bye now."

And he was gone. Disappeared.

I borrowed *The Great Gatsby,* thanked Lexie Helms again, waved goodbye to her and Rosemary. Then I drove out to Hermitage, found the post office, just there, next to a hair salon, a few miles beyond my turnoff for the lake. I rented a PO box, number 1277. There was a sandwich shop a little further down where I had lunch. Then, I started back to the lake. Perhaps I'd go for a swim, sunbathe and nap, read, draw, before I'd head back into town for dinner. That's pretty much what I did except for one unexpected and fortuitous detour.

3

What are these impulses or intuitions? How they push us to act, to do something. Was that what this summer was about, to learn to trust them, not question them, but just, essentially, listen to them and follow? For several days now I had passed these big farms, on my way back and forth to the lake. At first with Durl, and now on my own, I kept eyeing them, curious. Acres of fields, rolling hillsides, meadows, too. Way back, off the road, on a small rise, surrounded by trees, would be the farmhouse and other smaller buildings, and a big barn, too, often red, sometimes grey. I would see workers in the fields.

That Monday in June, late afternoon, around five p.m., as I left Old Hickory Lake and headed back into town to find some supper, I saw several men moving slowly out of a field toward a small grouping of farm machinery, trucks and several cars.

What possessed me?

Next to a black and white mailbox, a sign read, "Langford's Farm." I turned on to the long dirt road, a thin dusty aisle between green fields that led to a small bend where these men and machines were gathered. I slowly drove in, pulled over onto a grassy shoulder about thirty feet from where these men stood. Their heads turned. They eyed me.

I was a little nervous but I was buoyant, too, nothing to lose, it can't hurt to ask, can it?

Three men stood there. A big man in overalls, wiping his face with a dirty rag; a shorter man, very tanned, wiry, T-shirt, jeans, a ball-cap on and a few teeth missing; the third was actually a boy, perhaps high school age, red-haired, freckled, a piece of straw in his mouth, who just watched me very carefully. The other two continued to wipe their faces and dust off. I assumed the bigger man in overalls was the man in charge, the one to talk to, "Excuse me . . . Howdy!" I slowly walked toward them.

"Howdy," the big man said and nodded.

"I was wondering if I could hire on, y'know, work for you?"

"You wanna work?"

"Yes, sir."

"This here work?" And the big man slowly spread his big hand over the fields into the blue sky.

"Yes, sir. Whatever you need me to do."

"Uh-huh." The big man eyed me, then looked over at the other two, the boy still staring, the tanned one slapping his dusty jeans legs.

"He should talk to Floyd, right, Hub?" The wiry tanned one looked up from his dusting off.

"Right," said the big man, Hub. "Right, Charlie, that's just what he should do."

"Floyd's not comin' back today," the red-haired boy spoke in a thin whiney Southern drawl.

"I know that," said Hub, looking off across the fields. Then he eyed me again. "Tell you what, young man—"

"Garry . . . Garry Brown, sir." I offered my hand. He looked at it, then slowly pulled his up. We shook hands.

"Herbert. Folks call me Hub. Here's what you do, son. You wanna talk to Floyd. Floyd Underwood. He's the boss, y'see?"

"Yes, sir."

"He is looking to hire on, Hub. I heard him talk." The wiry one, Charlie, offered this.

"That's what I'm tellin' him, Charlie."

"But he ain't gonna be back today, Hub. I know Uncle Floyd. He'd be in town by now."

"Russell, just shut up, will ya? And listen what I tell this young man."

"Yassir," and the red-haired boy, Russell, turned and stretched and took his piece of straw and tossed it.

"So, your best bet . . . you come back here tomorrow mornin', alright? Floyd be here first thing. You talk to him. He'll probably do you right. Okay?"

"Okay. Thanks."

"You betcha."

They continued to clean up. I began to walk back to Titine.

"Oh." I turned. "What time tomorrow morning?"

"What time, Charlie?" Hub asked.

"Best by eight a.m.," said Charlie. "No later. Maybe sooner."

"Eight a.m.," I called back. "Thanks!"

Hub half-waved as he bent down, patted his left leg of weathered, roughened blue denim overalls.

I wanted to hold onto this a moment. These two men and a slippery red-haired boy; me, in a T-shirt and Bermuda shorts, slowly walking back to my car. Now and then I glanced back at them. Perhaps now and then, between their dustings, they watched me. Was I curious to them? This college kid, all eager and not quite tanned yet, getting into—what kinda car is that? Not American, that's for sure.

And those three. The sun beginning to descend, standing there in silhouette, just finishing a good day's work, a regular day for them, but somehow magical, elemental, pivotal for me. I got into Titine but I didn't want to leave just yet. I wanted to hold this moment. Forever. But how? I wanted to watch them, to perhaps draw them, do a pen and ink, a painting, perhaps. I was excited, hopeful.

I was going to work, perhaps, with these men. I was going to join this world. This wasn't a classroom or a book. This wasn't a movie or an adventure story or a TV show. This was my life, out here, among these men, those sun-baked fields. As I turned the key in the ignition, as the car began to mumble and mutter, I kept watching and aching. It was a profound hungry acquisitive inquisitive ache. I didn't want to leave. I slowly pulled the car off the grassy shoulder, turned it around, my eyes on the rear-view and side mirrors. Those, too, would make fine drawings, paintings, these images of sun and men and earth, and my life, too, now.

I tried to watch the long dirt driveway and see the fields on either side, to smell the dry hot earthy aroma of green and dirt and nowhere to go now but turn right, back on to the tarmac, back into town and, perhaps, somehow, tomorrow morning, find work, find this life, my life.

I ate a small meal at the Burger King. Then, I found a public phone and called the number John had given me, his aunt's phone number in South Carolina. The line was busy. I got a refill of soda, sat and watched two boys razz a young attractive girl, then tried again. Still busy. Well. Tomorrow, I'll call tomorrow.

I drove back to the lake, parked Titine in her usual spot, then grabbed my journal, my sketchbook, *The Great Gatsby,* and sat on the cement picnic table nearest the lake. I figured I had about an hour left of daylight. I wrote a little bit, mostly read in the novel: I liked it immediately, the voice of the young man, Nick, not so unlike myself, trying to make sense of things, of his life, of this man Gatsby. About forty-five minutes later I watched as the sun seemed to slowly move toward the far side of the lake and then dip below so quickly. I stayed, and in the afterglow, I did some doodles and sketches and tried to do some boxy cartoon-like drawings from memory: the Donelson Library; Langford's farm; Hub's big hands.

Was it that night or later in the summer that I learned that there's so much more to a sunset once the sun goes down? The afterglow, I learned, lasts a good half-hour past the sun's disappearance. This knowledge felt unique, a discovery, even profound.

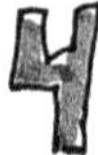

The next morning, a sun-bright and humid Tuesday, I pulled in and parked on that same grassy shoulder. It was 7:45 a.m. Over near the line-up of several cars, a tractor, a long metal mower next to a big green truck with an open wooden platform in back, were Hub and Charlie, just standing there. They watched me approach.

Charlie smoked a cigarette and drank from a white cup of steaming coffee. Hub had a piece of yellow string (I realized later, it was bale string) that he was fiddling with, twisting it among his fingers. As I got closer, way off to the right I saw the red-haired kid, Russell, jogging in place, then starting off until he stopped to jump and shoot an imaginary basketball. Faintly, I could hear him saying words, his own play-by-play, I presumed, as he went through his moves.

"Howdy again!" I gave a small nod and wave. Both men stood there and nodded.

"Howdy," said Hub.

"Hey," said Charlie, who looked off, took another drag, another sip.

I felt a little awkward. I hadn't packed any jeans. John had said selling books door to door was pretty informal, and hot most summer days: so, a few nice shirts and a few pairs of Bermuda shorts would be fine. I was wearing my khaki Bermuda shorts, my grey gym shirt (for jogging), and my white Converse All-Stars.

I stood to the other side of Hub from Charlie. I watched Hub play with his yellow twine. Then I looked over at Russell as he continued to play his imaginary hoops. He had a pretty good jump shot but never went to his left. Neither man spoke to me. I chose to follow their lead. I was nervous but I didn't want to be chatty or overzealous. I just stood and watched and waited. Finally, Hub spoke, not to me but to his fiddling fingers. "You ready to work?"

"Yes, sir," I said.

Hub nodded. A few minutes passed. Then Charlie spoke, "You ever done farm work before?"

"My uncle's farm, upstate New York. One summer."

"Uh-huh," Charlie said, as he continued to smoke, sip his coffee and watch Russell make his jump shots, accompanied by bursts of dust clouds. Normally, I'd launch into conversation, "I grew up in Connecticut, college in Massachusetts . . . ever been up North . . . ?" Instead, I chose to be like them: brief. I liked being laconic. It was kind of a relief, even a freedom.

"Christ, Hub," Charlie dropped his cigarette and rubbed it out with his leather boot toe. "Why does fuckin' Floyd always gotta keep us waitin'?"

"He'll be here." Hub twiddled his twine.

Charlie pulled a pack of cigarettes from his jeans pocket.

"Here he come! I seen him." Russell was now running toward us, pointing toward the far paved road. Both men looked toward the road. I watched Russell run up, then stop, and aim his jump shot toward the road. "See? See, Hub? That's his Caddy! I called it, right?"

"What," said Charlie, "you wanna prize?"

"Sure do. A big prize. Why not?"

They all watched. I watched, too, as this long car turned off the tarmac, onto the Langford Farm drive, and, like a big white fish, made its way toward us. It was a white Cadillac that got bigger as it approached, clouds of dust trailing in its path. The car pulled in, about ten feet from where we all stood. Russell skipped and danced over to the driver's side, tapping the front fender.

"Mornin', Uncle Floyd!"

The sunlight was bright off the windshield, yet it looked dark inside as the car door opened and this husky voice said, "Don't be hittin' my Caddy, Russell, how many times I gotta tell you, huh, boy?"

"Yes, sir, Uncle Floyd. Sorry. Can I have this car some day?"

"You work hard, maybe so." A big man sat on the edge of the driver's seat and looked out. He wore a white suit, light blue shirt with a Texan clasp around his neck. "Gimme a hand, Russell."

"Yes, sir, Uncle Floyd." Russell moved quickly and offered his right hand and forearm. The big man, who had dark circles under both eyes and held a thick half-smoked stump of cigar, grabbed hold with both hands and said, "One-two-three—pull!"

Which Russell did. The big man hardly budged.

"Jesus, Uncle Floyd, you gotta help, too."

"Again," said the big man. "Come on. One-two-three . . ." And before he said "Pull!", the big man was out and up, all on his own. "Ha! Gotcha, didn't I?"

"Uncle Floyd, you did! How'd you do that?"

"I got my ways." He straightened out his white suit jacket, dumped ash from his cigar. "Christ, it got hot again, huh, Hub? Huh, Charles?"

"Yes, sir, Mr. Floyd. Very hot," said Charlie as he downed the last of his coffee.

"Well then," Floyd said. He was big but not tall. "Grab them coffees, will ya, Russell?"

"Yes, sir," said Russell.

"Not for me, Floyd," said Hub, his twiddling fingers at rest by his sides.

"I might have another, Mr. Floyd," said Charlie, who then eyed Hub. "What?" said Charlie to Hub.

"Remember last week?"

"What about last week?"

"That extra coffee."

"Yeah," said Charlie.

"Your stomach problems?"

"Oh, yeah." Charlie looked at the ground, then turned and faced the fat man. "Second thought, Mr. Floyd. No thanks."

"Jesus." Floyd pulled a white kerchief from inside his suit coat and wiped his face. "I mean, I got you boys coffees. You turnin' me down?"

"Sorry, Mr. Floyd," said Charlie, "I'd better not."

"I'll have one, Uncle Floyd." Russell stood up now, with the white cardboard cup holder and three white cups of coffee.

"Russell, coffee's not good for you. You an athlete." Floyd went silent, wiped his face again, took a puff of cigar. Blew out a small greyish cloud. The rest of us just stood and waited. "What about you, son?" Floyd eyed me. "You drink a cup?"

"No, sir. But thanks," I said.

Floyd continued to puff, turned and faced out toward the open distant fields, where he blew his next cloud of cigar smoke. "A lotta good hay in them fields," said Floyd.

"Yes, sir, Uncle Floyd."

"You can put them coffees back in the car, boy."

"Yes, sir." Russell bent and thrust the coffee holder deep into Floyd's Cadillac.

"Hub tells me you wanna work, son, that true?"

"Yes, sir." I nodded.

"You done this here work before?"

"Upstate New York one summer. My Uncle Elmer's farm."

"What kinda farm?"

"Milk cows mostly."

"Alright. Lookee here, Hub, I'm gonna take him this morning—what's your name?"

"Garry, sir. Garry Brown." I offered my hand. Floyd looked at it, put his cigar back in his mouth, then took it. We shook hands.

"I'm Floyd Underwood. This here's my operation. These here are good men. I run a clean business, that right, Charlie?"

"Yes, sir, Mr. Floyd. You do. You really do."

"Good to meet you, sir." We released hands.

"Fine. That's fine. We got good weather next week or so, Hub."

"That's what they're saying. Uh-huh," nodded Hub.

"Hate to lose a man, Hub."

"We had differences, that's all," said Hub.

"He was an asshole, Hub. And you know it. A holier-than-thou bastard."

"Charles," said Floyd.

"I'm sorry, Mr. Floyd, but it's true. In the military, they'd shoot that sum bitch."

"Ha!" Floyd began to laugh. He pulled out his cigar as his big middle rose up, shook and shivered.

"Friendly fire they call that, right, Charlie?" said Russell.

"Not so friendly with that sum bitch."

"Okay, Charlie. The man's gone. Don't need him. Right, Hub?"

"Didn't say that, Floyd."

"Today, you a three-man crew. Lotta Langford's still to do. Do whatcha can. I'll pick y'all up . . ." it looked as if Floyd took the cigar from his mouth and the cigar had disappeared up his left sleeve, "say, around noon. Get you boys some lunch . . . You—" Floyd gestured with his ashen cigar. "You, son, come with me."

I nodded, waited.

"Alright, Uncle Floyd, we'll see ya then," said Russell, jogging off, then pulling up to hit another jump shot.

"Hub, you good?" asked Floyd.

"Yes, sir. 'Til noon." Hub turned, pocketed his twine, and did a slow march off.

"Alright, Mr. Floyd, we'll see ya around noon," said Charlie.

"Charles, those really your dog tags?"

"These here, sir?" Charlie pulled on a pair of small metal plates that hung around his neck, on a small chain necklace. He lifted them and let them fall. "They're mine, Mr. Floyd. Damn straight. Phnom Penh. Mekong Delta. Shit yeah, Mr. Floyd. They my lifeline, sir." He grinned.

"That's good, Charles. Don't you ever forget what you fought for, son."

"Yes, sir." Charlie nodded, turned. Then turned back. "What's that, Mr. Floyd?"

Floyd pulled at his cigar, then looked at him. "This here, boy, look! This here land. This here work. This here all-American life, son! We thank you. You know that? Those faggots in Washington and New York, all them big cities, they may not get it. They may forget, but not me, son. No real American will ever forget what you done."

Charlie bowed his head a moment. His boot kicked at the dirt and gravel. Hub and Russell were already at the far rusted green truck with the big platform on back. The dust at Charlie's feet curled in small wisps.

"Thanks, Mr. Floyd. Thank ya," Charlie's eyes welled up, reddened. He tried to catch his breath as he went from nodding to just looking down, the dust settling. Floyd watched him, then turned away, a puff on his cigar, as he again looked off and blew smoke across the broad mown field. Still looking off, Floyd said very quietly, "You done real good, son . . ."

"Thank you, sir." Charlie quietly collected himself, turned and walked off toward Hub and Russell. His dog tags made a light jingle-jangle sound.

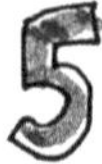

Floyd Underwood told me to get in his Cadillac, which I did, and we drove off. It felt a little weird at first. I'd left my car, my sketchbook, all my belongings, really, and just departed, not sure where I was going or what I'd do. I was in the land of few words and little or no explanation.

I watched for a bit out the window, which I opened to get a breeze. Saw the dust swirls as we cruised along Langford's drive, saw the men hop up onto that truck and platform (called a "hayrack," I learned later). Then, I just watched fields, felt the gentle, welcome breezes, and now and then sneaked glimpses of Mr. Floyd Underwood as he and his mouth maneuvered that shrinking stump of cigar.

About fifteen minutes later, we drove along a dirt road to where a small two-acre field spread out, edged by a small growth of trees, dotted with a number of full-grown trees. The field was all clumps of dark brownish orange earth, a lot of it looked dried and hard. A few days before a tractor had turned it over, Floyd told me, "Now, it needs seed, y'understand, son?"

"Yes, sir."

We got out of his big white boat of a car. I almost bumped my head as Floyd got out first and the car suddenly lifted, bounced up and down.

"You ever seed before, son?" Floyd pulled out his cigar and looked at it.

"No, sir. I've mucked stalls and mown lawns."

"'Mown lawns'?" Floyd gave me a concerned look.

"Y'know, lawns. In front of and back of houses. With a lawn mower?"

"Oh," he chuckled. "That faggot suburban shit. That ain't work, son. That's cosmetics."

"Yes, sir."

"You wait here. I got to talk to one of my men."

"Yes, sir."

I stood there in the still-morning sun. It wasn't hot. Not yet. Almost cool, unless it was just me and my nerves. Floyd had walked up to a small white house which had beside it a big dirt area leading to a barn, and, behind the barn, a fenced area that looked muddy. Behind that and another section of fence were what looked like small wood houses like coops for chickens.

Slowly, sounds began to filter in, step up: squawking, a rooster's crow, and the grunts, quick, staccato, of a lot of small men with deep, dark muted voices, or were they? Later, Floyd would explain that this was his cousin Roy's pig farm, "which I now got a controlling interest in, y'understand, son?" I continued to watch and wait. Then, a brief moment of panic: what was I doing here? Anything could happen to me. Who was this man, Floyd Underwood? Did he really have good intentions? Was I really going to work and earn some money? I returned to just taking it all in, breathing the earthy, pungent morning air, delighting in the fine, full blue sky

Floyd and a man in denim overalls came from the far barn. Floyd pointed toward me as they talked. The man scratched his bald pate, watched me, and nodded. Floyd pulled out his cigar, looked at it, as he kept talking, then dropped the cigar and slowly, still talking, swiveled his right foot, which became his whole white-suited body, swaying over his mushed and, by now, muddied and extinguished cigar.

The bald man was holding a big brown paper bag. It looked weighty. He handed it to Floyd, who nodded, looked into the bag, nodded again, said some last words over his shoulder as he slowly walked toward me. The bald man watched as Floyd trudged off, looked at me again, swatted his own head (flies, I supposed) and turned and walked back into the barn.

"That's Roy, he my cousin, good man. He keep an eye on you. You need somethin', you go knock his door or call to the barn. He'll come to ye."

"Yes, sir."

"Here." Floyd handed me the brown bag, solid, and oh yeah, pretty heavy.

"You got it?"

"Yes, sir."

"This here's seed. That there's the field you gonna seed, y'understand?"

"Yes, sir. Um . . ." I looked over at the expanse of orange/brown earth.

"What, son?"

"So, I just place a seed in the ground, then pat dirt on top of it?"

Floyd watched me mime my notion of seeding, and then, all of his big white suit heaved and jiggled as he reared his head and laughed, "Ha-ha-ha! You never seed before?"

"No."

"Bring that bag. I show you." Floyd pulled out a cigar from inside his jacket. He unwrapped the clear plastic and tossed the wrapping. He kept walking. "Come on, over t'here." Now fingering the cigar, smelling it, then putting it in his mouth, he swiveled the cigar, almost licking it, like it was a popsicle or a lollipop.

"Start right here, y'see?"

"Yes, sir."

Floyd bent down, touched the orange-brown clumps of earth.

"It's pretty good, not too hard. Here, gimme some o' them seeds, a handful."

I held out the brown bag.

"Grab a handful, and as you walk, you toss it—over here, over there. Not too fast, not too slow, y'understand?"

I nodded.

"Here. Take a handful, you try it."

I dug into the brown bag, got a handful, put the bag down, and copied Floyd: a slow walk, toss the seed right, toss it left.

"Good, thass good, but, here." Floyd handed me the solid brown bag of seed. "You gots to keep holding the bag as you walk. So you can refill and keep going, y'understand?"

"Right." I took the bag from Floyd.

"Fine. You seed this here field, row by row. I'll come get you for lunch."

"This whole field?" I held the bag toward it. "All of it?"

"Whatsa matter?"

"Nothing but—"

"You run out o' seed, you go knock on Roy's door. He fill you up again, awright?"

"Yes, sir."

"Good." Floyd pulled matches from his suit pants pocket, stopped to light his cigar, flicked the match in the air as he continued to walk over to his big white Caddy.

I turned and looked out over this expanse of brown and dark furrowed earth. The sun was much hotter now. From the slight breeze, the air had a musty dark smell to it. A sweet and sour mix. I grabbed another handful of seed and began a steady, regulated walk. Toss right, toss left. Toss right, toss left. Floyd's white Caddy sent a swirling smoke signal of good-bye as it stirred and drove off.

I was alone again as I saw Floyd's white Caddy disappear. I looked over to the white house and barn. No one seemed to be around now. Just me, this bag of seed and the stiff, churned-up dark earth. Which was brown and even black in spots compared to the earth, and dirt roads, over by Old Hickory Lake, which had that pekoe tea complexion. Why was that? No matter. Mine was not to reason why—mine was just to seed, not cry. Or die. Or say, Fie! Though after a couple hours, I might want to since it was getting so hot. I was excited. I was going to work. It was simple, it was repetitious, it was monotonous and it was satisfying.

I was outdoors. No mind needed, no words, no difficult terms to understand. No quiz later, no grades. I was walking, I was tossing. I held the seeds in my hand, they were not small, not big, black with yellow streaks. I didn't even know what I was planting. Corn? Cotton? It didn't matter. I held the seeds, felt their grainy dry texture, shook a bunch in my hand, and then tossed—left, right, slow walk—right, left. I'd vary it, mix up the tossings, or, in some rows, I tried to stay as mechanical and identically rhythmic as possible.

Throughout this enlivened no-mind physical process, I remembered Van Gogh's *The Sower.* His version, Millet's version. Then Van Gogh's version of Millet's version. My arm and hand would swish and deliver and I'd flash on these paintings. And then, Francis Bacon's version of Van Gogh out walking that looked like a version of his sower. I wasn't just sowing seeds, planting these fields. Somehow, I had joined history, or, at least, art history, and paintings—two of my all-time favorite painters, Vincent Van Gogh and Francis Bacon. I'd joined their mushy, gloppy, painterly oils.

I'd joined the work force, the weather, this hot day, these rapturous aching muscles. They, too, the painters, had been in the sun. I became these paintings for a few hours, a glimpse, and perhaps, this was a hint of things to come. A premonition, not only of good, hard work but more, of paintings and painters, figures in a landscape.

A little under three hours later, I finished up. After, I sat in the fragmented shade of one of the perimeter's tall trees, the brown bag emptied but for a thin layer on the bottom. I'd had enough seeds. I'd finished my task. I sat and waited.

A door slammed. The man called Roy, quite intent, didn't see me but headed out of his white house into the barn. The grunts of the "little men" now made me laugh. I tried to hear the pigs' oinks as if they were small men, grunting, but no, they were pigs now. Plus, the squawk of chickens, with now and then the caw of crow, and in the trees, birds chirping. Then there'd be quiet and the heat, nearing midday. The sun, high, in full blaze. No more clouds. Blue sky not so much blue as a hazy pasty mirage of blue. The shade helped. My body warm, sweat trickled down my forehead along my face. A good workout but only the beginning, I was sure.

As I sat in the shade musing, I dreamt and pondered and started tossing bits of earth, pebbles, scraps of wood. I was doing this when Floyd's big Caddy crunched its way back in and parked close to the barn. He ignored me. Out of the car, into the barn. He reappeared with Roy. They stood talking. Floyd no longer had his cigar but was now wiping his face with his white kerchief. He nodded to Roy as he walked off, headed for his Caddy. Finally, he looked my way, waved me over, calling, "Come on, son. We're done here, gots to get some lunch!"

"Yes, sir!" I called as I headed for Floyd's Caddy.

"Hustle up. Got to meet the others."

"Yes, sir."

We got in and drove off. He didn't check my work. He didn't look at the fields. "Whatcha got there?" Floyd eyed my two hands.

"The leftover seed?"

"Gimme that. That's done now."

I gave Floyd the worn and wrinkled brown bag. He tossed it in the back of his car.

I waited for Floyd to ask how it went. Nothing. We drove in quiet. Then, wiping his face, the white kerchief looking extra-large, he said, "Got to hurry it up, get to the Ranch House Market. Don't want to keep them boys waiting."

"Yes, sir."

Floyd looked at me as if I'd said something rude or contradictory. Then he nodded, wiped his face some more, and stepped on the gas.

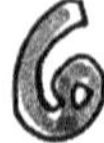

The Ranch House Market was a shack as grocery store with one gas pump out front. Inside, there were three rows of stocked items, several refrigerators with beverages and one low freezer with cones, ice cream sandwiches and next to it, a low bin of pre-made packaged sandwiches: ham and cheese, tuna salad, roast beef, egg salad, pork roast, BBQ. For the next two weeks, the last phase of haying season, this is where Floyd would take us, or join us, and buy our lunch. There were days when Floyd would arrive late, but not this day. Floyd and I pulled in next to the gas pump before the others.

"Go on in and git yourself somethin' to eat. Sandwich. Sodie. Go on."

"Yes, sir."

Floyd went to the pump. He took the hose, pulled the metal chrome lever and filled his big white Caddy. I went inside but wasn't quite sure how this worked. I was looking at the bin of sandwiches when Russell, first his red hair, then his lanky legs, skipped into the store. "Gimme one of them shaved ices, Bennie!"

A man with hairy black forearms, missing both front teeth, his bald pate covered with five black hairs, wearing a blood-smeared white apron, stood at the counter and said, "What flavor?"

"You always ask me that, Bennie. You know."

"Just makin' sure. So?"

"Strawberry o' course." Russell seemed to waltz through the store, picking out a bag of chips, some candy, until he stopped next to me at the bin of sandwiches. It was as if I was invisible. He dipped in the bin, came up empty. "Dontcha got no more meat loaf sandwiches, Bennie?"

"What's there is what we got."

"Aw, shit. That ain't—okay!" He popped up with one of the pork BBQ sandwiches. Still ignoring me, he did a slip-slide dance over to the counter.

"That it? What about a sodie?"

"Oh right. Well . . ." Russell opened one of the big glass doors, grabbed a large Coke, put it on the counter next to his small pile.

"And what about you, son?" Bennie stood there, unshakable, calling to me. I stood by the sandwich bin, startled, indecisive. Then, as Charlie and Hub shuffled in, followed by Floyd, Russell, on tiptoes, spoke to me for the first time, "Come on, pick out what you want. Put it here. My uncle Floyd'll pay for it."

"Damn straight," Floyd muttered as he finished wiping his face with his white kerchief and began to fold it. "Ain't that right, Hub?" Floyd continued.

"What's that, Floyd?"

"I pay for everything, don't I?"

"Yes, sir," said Hub, coming over to the sandwich bin. "Except for the green grass, the blue sky and the hot sun, everythin' else is pretty much outta your pocket."

"That right. Russell, y'hear?"

"Yessir," said Russell, taking a can opener and popping the top of his Coke. Bennie handed him his snow cone which he began sucking on.

"Christ, Russell, where you gonna put all that?"

"I got places, Uncle Floyd. I'm hungry."

Floyd was at the counter, opening his billfold, "Come on, boys, let's move it. Gotta eat and run. Add six gallons of gas, too, Bennie."

"Ain't you hungry, Uncle Floyd?"

"Grab me a Coke, Russell, will ya?"

"Yessir."

Outside, toward the road, among a tree, some shade, and a rough patch of dried grass, there was an old knotty wood picnic table. Charlie and Floyd sat on one side; Russell seemed to dance off one edge across from them and next to me, at the other far edge; Hub leaned on the tree.

We ate in silence except for Russell, who kept fidgeting, now and then doing little tap riffs with whatever fingers weren't holding his food. I quietly ate my egg salad on white bread which actually had a sweet mustardy taste that reminded me of my mom's deviled eggs. A wave of homesickness came and passed. I watched Russell and wondered about these men. Floyd sat with his back against the table edge. He looked to the road and the small field just across it, sipping his Coke. Charlie ate a BBQ sandwich, sipped a lemonade and kept stealing chips from Russell, who, when he caught him, would swat at Charlie's hand. When he finished, Charlie pulled out his cigarettes, shook the pack of unfiltered smokes, drew one out, popped it in his mouth, found a pack of matches, lit up and sat there smoking, watching Russell, chuckling, and now and then intentionally blowing smoke toward Russell's face.

"Quit, Charlie."

"What."

"Blowin' smoke."

"At least I ain't blowin' smoke up your ass, like you, you dumb fuck."

"Watch yer mouth, Charles," said Floyd.

"Yes, sir, Mr. Floyd."

Hub was the real quiet one. Floyd's quiet had that sullen boss-like complexity. Hub's quiet was more like a deep, soulful privacy, maybe something painful had occurred. Hub leaned against the tree, quietly ate his roast beef sandwich, sipped a Coke, wiped his mouth, finished up. He faced the picnic table so he wasn't looking off or far away, but he never really looked at any of us. He threw away his Coke bottle, wrappings and napkin, returned, and continued to lean there. He was tanned, a solid, sturdy man, perhaps my dad's age—as old as Floyd, maybe older. All three men—my dad, Floyd, and Hub—were in their fifties. All men I somehow longed to respect and even know. I wanted all three men to appreciate me, know me, see me, respect me. I don't think I could've said this then but now, I'm pretty sure that's what was going on, what so intrigued me.

That summer I was devoted to striking out, adventuring into the world, to become an artist. Also, that summer, I was hungrily trying to become a man. That afternoon, I was also determined to work hard, keep up, and make some money, even though I still had no idea how any of this worked.

That was the last time I'd ride in Floyd's Caddy. After lunch, Floyd told me "to hop on the hayrack and head back to Langford's with the men." Which I did.

Russell ran to the truck cab, calling, "Shotgun!" Charlie drove. I sat on the hayrack wood platform, the opposite side from where Hub sat. About a fifteen-minute ride back to Langford's, the mid-afternoon was in full swing: stark blue sky, a few loungey white clouds, and hot. No bird song but lots of crickets. And, very shortly, the hardest work I'd ever do. Those two weeks and, perhaps, ever since.

The front drive into Langford's farm was the showy façade. We passed our parked cars and continued along the dirt drive, curling past a farmhouse, a stone wall, a barn, other smaller wood houses, down a small hill. Then, leaving the dirt road, through a wire and wood fence, we entered the first field, with a glimpse of fields that continued and spread out for what seemed for miles. Miles, acres—oceans—of fields, wide open sky, an elaborate brace of parcels: rolling greens and woods, small hills, big long loping hills. From a civilized cosmetic suburban version of earth and grass into a realm of rustic and untamed that I'd had no knowledge of—until now. And heat: hot sun and sweat, dripping, pouring from my face, arms, legs.

Row on row of dried green and yellow coffin-like bales. Fifty to sixty pounds each. Taut, prickly bale string. Burns. Lashes. Cuts. And, the wrestling of these bales, as if each were a big steer—grabbed, leaned into, lifted and heaved—up onto the hayrack ledge, for Hub to grab and begin to design his house of brick-like bales, his tower of hay-dom.

Here we were in Langford's fields: a truck with a hayrack platform slowly moving through rows of bales on either side, with Russell on the left, myself on the right; Charlie driving and shouting at Russell; Hub on the platform placing each bale in such a way that the load remained balanced and steady. Russell liked being on the driver's side of the hayrack, so he could shout back at Charlie as he drove, continuing their constant banter. Hub stayed atop the platform, slowly building his straw castle.

I roamed the right, passenger side of the hayrack, hustling to get to the next bale and bend into it. The straw, with its small chitty bites, would graze my bare knees (no jeans, just my foolish Bermuda shorts). With both hands, I'd try to grab deep into and under the taut blonde strings, left and right. Then, with a full bend and hearty lift, swivel and turn just as the hayrack was a few feet within reach. With one last push up, using my knee and thigh, my hands pushing, too, the bale would suddenly fly onto the hayrack ledge. Sometimes the bale would just hover there, not solidly on or not yet claimed by Hub so I'd stumble back and give it a firm push, insurance it wouldn't fall off. Then, I'd turn and hustle over to the next bale, looming there, not a seat or a chair but a boxy ship in this sea of grass.

This was the procedure: row on row of bales, grabbed by two competitive young men, either side, a high school punk and a rookie college grad—grab, lift, deliver; from flat grass cut and molded into boxy bales now gathered onto a hayrack and built into a looming temple. Then, with Hub's command to Charlie, "Charlie! That's it!", the hayrack, five rows high and eight rows deep, would slowly rumble and cough its way back downhill, across fields, back to dirt road, onto pavement, and twenty minutes later—oh, a brief and welcome reprieve—we'd arrive at a big red barn, behind an old abandoned stone wall, near an empty stone house.

There, Charlie, with Russell again riding shotgun, would back into the big mouth of open barn doors while Hub and I sat atop those prickly straw bales, somehow magically interlocked by Hub's fleet maneuvering. We did not fall, though as we bumped along, I had worried about it. Now, arrived, I followed Hub's lead: slowly I fingered and footed my way down and off once the truck had finally stopped inside the barn.

That summer, during the final two weeks of haying season that I worked, we delivered to three different barns. We were collecting hay bales from two farms, Langford's and one other. Monday to Saturday, weather permitting, with only Sundays off. Two weeks, which felt like two years. The hardest, most demanding physical labor I'd ever done in my life. I remember thinking: hey, this isn't so bad. I can do this.

7

Until we entered that first barn. "How hot is it in here, Hub?" It was Russell's voice, as he and Charlie climbed out of the truck cab.

"Hundred easy," nodded Hub. Hub and I were now standing near the back end of the truck. Hub told Charlie, "You might could back it in a few more feet." As he got back in the truck, Charlie called out, "I'll bet it's more like a hundred ten, Hubber." Hub nodded, watching the truck edge further in, "Don't much matter when hot is this hot."

Hot, steamy, suffocating. Just standing there, not even moving, perspiration began to drip from my forehead, along my arms, my legs.

Off to the side was a narrow stairwell ladder. Hub climbed it to reach the hay loft. Dark and stuffy, but for the open barn doors, the cracked fissures of roof and sides sent grainy paths of sunlight across us, thin swords that contained bugs, flying pieces of straw and dirt and the radiant hot of mid-afternoon. The humidity was like a thick liquid quicksand.

"That's it, Charlie! Far enough!" called Hub.

"This okay?" Charlie looked out and up.

"Thass what I'm sayin'. GOOD!"

Charlie killed the engine and got out. Hub pulled out his white kerchief, wiped his face and forehead as he sized things up. Then, "Charlie, you come on up here. Russell, you and the young man, get atop them bales and swing 'em over to me and Charlie."

"Yassir!" called Russell, who then completely ignored me as he bolted onto the end of the hayrack, grabbed straw and bale strings, and hoisted himself atop as if we were racing one another. I made my way steadily from the other side. Though I am afraid of heights—atop those bales, it was pretty high, maybe fifteen feet—I wasn't really scared or even concerned. Being peeved at Russell's constant ignoring of me and competing helped.

In the unloading, the trick was keeping your balance as we took turns swinging one bale after another over to Charlie, who then fed Hub, who now built a new set of rows inside the barn loft. We were a human conveyor belt. Charlie watched as a bale landed near his feet, then bent and lifted and lugged it over to Hub. Hub took it sometimes in mid-air and placed it in its appointed slot. The loft was not that steep, maybe ten feet high, and arched. Hub would start building, get two or three bales high, then throw down a new row of bales which he then stepped on as he built the preceding row higher. Again, this was not just stacking. There was some real art to it, a kind of brick wall style of overlap, so that the rows stayed sturdy, well-built. We found a good rhythm.

There would be hiccups: Charlie and Russell continued to joke with one another, which always seemed to end with Charlie getting Russell upset and Russell calling Charlie names. Hub would tell Charlie to knock it off, Charlie'd say, "Right, Hubber," make faces at Russell, and our conveyor-belt rhythm would resume.

I stayed silent, observant. Which was different for me. I liked it. Plus, I was getting tired, my back ached, my legs and knees were streaked and sore with red scratches, all those pieces of bale straw biting and pawing. I was thirsty, too. There were moments when I couldn't catch my breath, it was so stifling in there. Then, it was over. All those bales loaded in.

I walked out of the barn and it was like I was swimming in Old Hickory Lake, it was that cool, that refreshing, that much cooler and breezier than the sweatbox of that barn. It was still ninety degrees in the shade, but such balmy, lush freedom—and air to breathe again! Hub wiped his brow, looked at his watch. "That should do it for today. Let's head back to Langford's."

"Really, Hub?" asked Charlie.

"After five. Really."

"Okay," shouted Russell, "I got shotgun!" Russell ran around to the passenger side, hopped in. Charlie put the truck in gear as Hub and I took seats on either end of the empty hayrack. Then, sweetness and light. This was the delicious part: the ride back, an empty hayrack, our work done, and the waft and waves of cool

breezes, like drinking, like swimming.

I could see again—everything brighter, clearer: the fields just off the paved roads, the long shadows, the patches of sunlight, the sun lower now in the sky, not quite so overbearing; Hub's steady gaze; Russell's antics with Charlie in the truck cab. I couldn't make out their conversation but there was a looseness now, some whistles, Russell's annoying bark of a laugh. Even that pleased me.

That late afternoon, I returned to the lake. The beach and woods deserted, I walked to the lake's edge with my towel, undressed at the picnic table, my sweaty clothes slung onto the concrete top, myself, thrust into the cool dark waters. A few lights were coming on in houses across the lake, the sun still setting, probably an hour to go.

My body refreshed, I emerged, glistening in the slivers of dimming sun, and felt just how achy and sore I really was. This was only Tuesday: I had four more days to go before a day off. My hands hurt, my forearms, too, and my lower back. Both legs lit up with the hiss of stingy scratches. I dried off, wrapped my towel around my waist, and just sat there, staring, savoring the cool breezes and fading light. Way across the lake, a man on a dock was bending over his motorboat, readying to go for an early evening cruise.

I missed Kathy. I wondered about the Durlando. I'd copied out my letter to Kathy but hadn't mailed it yet. I wanted to paint this lake scene. I wanted to draw. I also wanted to sit quietly and read my books. But mostly, I realized I was starving.

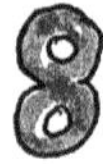

I took a quick shower, then drove back into Donelson. It was moving into dusk, a Tuesday night, late June, shops were closing. I thought I'd just eat at McDonald's or the new Burger King. Instead, I found a different diner, not the Snack Shack. It was called The Spot, near another laundromat, which was open, too, fluorescent lights ablaze.

Why didn't I go to the Snack Shack if I was so lonely? I knew a few people there, at least. I was lonely and homesick, but I was also still exploring. Perhaps it was my physical exhaustion taking over: just eat a simple meal, read one of my books, and then get back to the lake and sleep. Which is what I did. Almost.

As I read *The Great Gatsby,* I sipped—actually, guzzled—my iced tea and lemon. Had a turkey club, lots of mayo, and a piece of apple pie a la mode. The waitress, Mel, was fair-haired, had a thick Southern twang and a bored look. She was fine. The food was okay. I was tired. The restaurant was empty but for myself in a booth and an older man nursing a coffee at the counter. It seemed like there were many more people in the brightly lit laundromat next door, where moths and flies buzzed about its grey outdoor lamp.

I finished up, paid my check, and slowly drove through town. The pinks and oranges of the far western sky, just beyond the bank and hardware store, were going dim, into dark. It was nighttime and I got very sad. I pulled over on Main Street, pretty much empty but for a red and white delivery truck on the opposite side. I sat there, inside Titine, bowed my head over the steering wheel, and began to cry. Little gasps that became bigger ones, with gobs of wet from my eyes, down my cheeks.

What was going on? This was crazy. I shook the steering wheel. I got angry. I wanted to yell but couldn't. I just kept clenching the steering wheel until I made fists and began to punch it and the dashboard until, oh God, I wailed. My hands were already sore enough. Jesus.

I stopped, rubbed both hands together, then looked up to see if anyone had noticed my moribund antics. No. Except: just ahead, under the streetlamp, a man in shadows. A dark suit, a hat, it was him again! James Steward, Elwood P. Dowd, whoever—it was him! And I was going to catch up with him this time.

I started Titine, pulled out, and cruised along Main Street. He was fifty yards ahead of me. I would just troll along, following him, until the time was right to pull over and call to him. As I got closer, he turned, gave me a direct look. Then, I swear he actually tipped his hat to me, winked, turned, and ran up about twenty steps into this brick church.

I pulled over and got out. The lit sign out front said, "United Methodist Church—Come one, Come all—Sundays, 10 a.m. Choir Rehearsal, Come Join Us, Tuesday nights, 7 p.m." Then, further below, "Rev. Bill Abernathy Officiating—Paul Small, Asst. Minister." Below that, a quote, "God's blind eye is bigger and better than your best two."

The church looked dark, closed. But the big wood doors were open. Choir rehearsal, I thought. I love choirs. That sort of song, voices joined, a kind of communion. I'd been in freshman choir in college. Bruce McInnes, the natty, keen-eyed choir director. I was terrified of singing alone, but I did it for him when I auditioned. I think he took pity on me, knew I was an athlete, felt my eagerness and enthusiasm. Probably just needed more baritones.

Once inside, straight ahead, dimly lit, I could make out the rows of wood pews, all painted white. A light was coming from above but the portal I stood beneath was dark. "Hello? Mr. Steward? You in here?" Silence. I called again, a little bolder, "Hello! Anybody home?" Then an older man's voice, weakly, ". . . Hello . . . ?" Was this him finally?

"Where are you?" I asked.

"Upstairs," the man replied. "There's a stairwell to the left of the entry door." Sure enough. I'd overshot it. I backed up, entered and ascended. Finally, I would meet this enigmatic Mr. Steward, my doppelganger Dowd.

The upstairs opened into a brightly lit balcony of similarly white pews, four of them, with about eight people variously seated there, three men, five women. An older man stood in the front row, balcony pew, looked at me, nodded. I completely forgot about Elwood P., who seemed to have disappeared, and blurted out, "Is this the choir? Do you need any more choir members?" There was a noticeable gasp. The older man also reacted, looked at the others, then caught his breath and answered my question with a question, "Excuse me, young man, but you'd really like to sing in our choir?"

"Well, sure."

He paused. His face reddened, he looked again at the group. Were they upset that I had just barged in? "Forgive me," he began. He continued to look at the others before he raised his head and spoke to me, "I think we're all a little awestruck." Two of the women nodded. One of the men actually laughed. Another pause. He had small eyeglasses, thinning hair, a wrinkled brow, a worried face but tanned. Perhaps a teacher or academic. He had a very slight Southern accent, "You see . . . we haven't even sung yet tonight. There's been a drop off in our numbers. Folks take vacation and all, but. Well. We were discussing whether we should just simply discontinue the choir since there seems so little interest. Not an easy discussion since those of us who are here are so devoted. We all love to sing these hymns. So. We then, just now, prayed together about this, and, of course, hoped God might give us some indication of how to proceed." Again, he paused, looked at the group, wiped his brow with a small white kerchief, smiled and said, "And then you appeared."

"Oh," I said.

Everyone laughed. There were nods, looks and words among themselves, like a great sigh of relief. "I think we got our answer. Please, please join us. My name is Dr. William Stillman. I teach at a small college nearby and have had the pleasure of directing this choir for the past eleven years. And you are?"

"Hi, Dr. Stillman, and all, I'm Garry. Garry Brown. Baritone. From Connecticut. Down here for the summer. And, thank you. Nice to meet you all." I stood there, nodding, smiling.

"No, no. Thank *you,* and, I suppose we can thank God, too."

Everyone laughed again. I nodded, smiled, and sat down. A grey-haired woman handed me a blue hymnal. I thanked her.

"Well," said Dr. Stillman, "how about we turn to page one hundred and sixty, 'A Mighty Fortress Is Our God'? We'll work on this and two others while the night's still young. And, Garry, why don't you sit over here with Bob and Ralph? You baritones and bass fellows need to stick together, especially when you're up against these lovely altos and sopranos, right, Judy?"

A plump, red-faced woman, in a yellow blouse, blushed and nodded. "That's right, Dr. Bill!"

So, we sang. This motley Methodist choir. We rehearsed. Bob, Ralph, a man named Tim, myself, and the five women: that grey-haired woman, Joan, and Judy, two young housewives, and an auburn-haired beauty named Sarah who seemed a bit stuck-up. We sang a cappella, over and over. Once each section had been learned, Dr. Bill moved to the center area where a small bench and full organ was built into the balcony, floor to ceiling. He'd sit there, play the organ, and still raise a hand to direct us or note the downbeats. Each song, in turn, came together, played in full.

Around nine-thirty p.m., the rehearsal finished up. Everyone slowly descended the stairwell, and a conversation began among the three young mothers. Each person there that night came over, shook my hand, thanked me or welcomed me. Except for Sarah, who stood talking to Dr. Stillman, then gave me a slight nod and walked off. She was tall, thin, quite attractive, a real Southern belle, maybe in her twenties.

Dr. Stillman laughed. He still couldn't believe it. I was a prayer answered. "I have a feeling this is going to be a very interesting summer," he said, patting my arm. "Oh, by the way, Garry, how tall are you? What's your suit size? We need to get you a white gown for Sunday's service, which is every Sunday, ten a.m. We like to meet around nine, nine fifteen, do a warm up, get ready, okay? If any problems come up or you're going to be late, here's my phone number, okay?" He wrote his number on a piece of notebook paper. I told him I was six feet, four inches, 44 Long.

"Fine. We'll see you Sunday."

We were on the steps, dimly lit by the near streetlight. Which reminded me, "Dr. Stillman, do you know a man in town named James Steward?"

"James Stewart, the actor?"

"No, no. He's a local man who looks like Jimmy Stewart, actually, but his last name is 'Steward,' with a 'd'?"

"Don't believe I do. A friend of yours?"

"Not really. Thought he might've been in your choir."

"No. Nobody named Steward."

"Okay. Well, g'night!"

We walked off in opposite directions.

I just sat in Titine for a while. The moths danced about the streetlight. I watched the now dim, shadowy brick church. I was tired. And still kind of sad but also grateful; I felt as if I belonged, even though I still barely knew anyone in this sleepy little Southern town. But I had joined the choir. It was a thrill and a comfort to hear the organ, our voices rising and falling, as the night got slow again and quiet. I drove back to the lake, said g'night to the starry sky, curled up in my sleeping bag and slept, a deep, sound sleep.

The next morning was a scorcher, hot and humid from the get-go. I awoke sweaty in my sleeping bag, left it atop Titine's trunk to dry out, took a quick swim and shower, ate a banana and managed to show up for my second day of work right on time. Hub was there, pacing. Russell was throwing stones at one of the Langford farm dogs. No sign of Charlie. Apparently, Charlie's car wouldn't start. Floyd had picked him up. Soon after I got there, they arrived.

The morning went well. We continued to load bales off Langford's fields. My blisters had dried up, were a little cracked and hard at first. But with a good sweat, they softened, along with my achy lower back and forearms; once I was in a good rhythm, everything seemed okay, not as painful, as if I'd gotten some kind of miraculous second wind. Or was I just getting back in shape? Even the scratches on my legs seemed less annoying, as if my body had accepted these conditions and was now compliant. We worked steadily and hard, broke for lunch. I hoped that, by late afternoon, there'd be a few breezes. But there were no breezes and, no let-up in the steamy heat.

Our routine came to a halt when we arrived at Slocum's barn with a packed hayrack. This was a big old grey barn, taller and longer than Langford's or Tatum's barns. It was next to a grove of big old trees that spread a kind of mossy cover along the barn's sides and probably in back. As we pulled in, I saw parked nearby a lemon-yellow Mercedes. One of the big barn doors was half open.

The lemon Mercedes struck a note. I had an instant of, Is that my dad's car? Is Dad here, did he come to surprise me? It was a four-door, 220SL, just like my dad's unless, didn't I know someone else who had a car like this one?

Hub went into the barn. Charlie and Russell stayed inside the hayrack cab. I was over by the Mercedes, admiring it as it glistened in the cool shade. I could hear shouting coming from inside the barn, no clear words but definitely a man's voice. Hub returned, shaking his head. He walked over to where Charlie leaned out from the driver's side window. I walked over and listened in. "It's no good. Man in there, sitting on a crate. Nice suit on. Holds up a black pistol, starts screaming at me to get out. Says he's gonna shoot the rabbit. 'Get out,' he says. Waves the gun. There's a rabbit in there, too."

"What?" said Charlie.

"I dunno," said Hub.

"What about these bales, Hub?" asked Russell.

"I *says* I dunno." Hub pulled out his white kerchief, wiped his brow. Still standing there, near Hub, it hits me. That Mercedes, not my dad's but—

"Hub, can I go in there and talk to the man?"

"I wouldn't do that, son. He's wantin' to be private."

"I know him, Hub." I started toward the barn doors.

"Whaddya mean you 'know him'?" called Charlie.

"He was one of the first people I met when I arrived in Nashville."

"You be careful," said Hub.

"Yes, sir." I nodded, then pushed on the big barn door. Inside, it was stifling hot. Also bright, due to hayloft windows that were streaming with sunlight. Specks of straw, dust, bugs filled the columns of angled light. I stood there, trying to adjust my eyes. Beyond, deeper in the barn, next to an empty stall, sat a figure in shadows. "Big Jim?" I softly said his name.

"I said to get the hell outta here! Load your hay some other day. Get the fuck *out*!"

"It's me, Big Jim. Garry Brown. John Durland's buddy, remember?"

"Who? Who's there—John Durland?"

"His friend, Garry Brown, remember? I'm the artist guy who couldn't sell books door to door?"

"Garry Brown? Come over here, let me see you."

I walked through the steeped rows of sunlight, along the straw-strewn floor, into the dim shadows where I could see, yes, Big Jim. He sat on a wood crate, in one of his creamy blue suits with one of his Southwest Company blazing red ties, a black gun on his lap, his back leaning against the scarred wood stall. I stood near him now, looking down. "Hey," I timidly waved.

"Hay is right. Jesus." He leaned his head back, closed his eyes, sweat pouring from his ruddy plump face.

"Are you okay?"

"Not really," said Big Jim, his eyes still closed.

"Sorry to interrupt. Want me to leave?"

"No, no. What the hell you doin' here, anyway? Thought you were off followin' your dream . . . paintin' landscapes and pretty girls."

"I still plan to. Just, I needed some money. So, I joined this haying crew."

"You're with these guys—haying?"

"Yes, sir."

"Oh."

I stood there, maybe five feet from where Big Jim sat. He was clearly tired, slow, with none of his normal Rah-Rah peppiness. He seemed sad. I wanted to say something to make him feel better but I just stood there. I hadn't noticed the rabbit. Not at first. It was about ten feet across from Big Jim, facing him, nibbling on a carrot, watching the two of us.

"Christ! What a fuck-up . . . Can't even shoot myself. Got a great deal on this gun, too." With one hand, he tapped it, gently. "Buddy of mine sold it to me. Even went to a practice range a few times, so there wouldn't be any surprises. That's when I remembered this barn. Slocum's. Spent a summer out this way years ago. Loved these woods. Used to ride horses when I wasn't mucking out stalls on my uncle's farm. My uncle and Slocum were old buddies. World War II. I used to ride horses with my uncle, my cousins, through the woods, come to this barn. A great old barn. He had cows in here for a time. Nice herd. Used to help milk 'em, drink fresh raw milk—the best!"

Big Jim paused a moment. His head still tilted back, his eyes were now open, squinting, thin streams of perspiration running down his temples and cheeks. "Christ . . . I'm tired . . ." I was going to say something dumb about how hot it was when he started up again.

"Everything's fucked up . . . can't do anything right. Left Kelly *two* notes, can you believe it? One at the house, smack dab on the kitchen counter with a bouquet of flowers. The other on the dash of my Mercedes. Pretty good notes, too. Shit. All set to go. Drove out here, nobody around, completely deserted. Found my spot. Then, started thinking about Slocum and my uncle. Uncle Johnny, a good man. Heavy drinker. Big joker. He and Slocum'd take me and my cousins to this great ol' swimming hole after our farm work. Shit. All ready to off myself and then I start reminiscing. I start laughing. Crying. I'm a fuckin' middle-aged wuss. So, I pull myself together, more or less. Cock the gun. Ready to go. Say a few prayers. Mostly about Kelly and how sorry I am . . . about our life, our little boy, my daughter from my first marriage . . . I'm trying to sort things out . . . make my fuckin' peace . . . and *this* guy appears . . ." Big Jim lifted the gun and pointed with it. "See him? The rabbit. Do you believe this? What are the odds? Just like the one I pulled out of our swimming pool . . . and we kept him as a pet and all, Kelly loved the little bugger. One day he got out of his cage. No idea how. Kelly thinks it was the cleaning lady but, I dunno . . . Now . . . Jesus, he shows up here. *If* it's him. Looks identical, crouches there just like the other. See? Like he is now. Eyeing me. Won't take his eyes off me. So. Okay, smart ass . . . I decide I'll shoot him first and then myself . . . then there's this rumbling outside, the barn doors open, this leather-faced farmer tells me he's got to unload his hayrack . . . Then you waltz in. Christ! Totally broke the spell. All my good planning—poof!"

"Sorry."

"No, no. Look. I don't really believe in God but if there is one, He's sure having a hay-day with me. Pun intended."

I nod, slowly.

"Get it? 'Hay-day'?"

"Got it. Good one, Big Jim."

"Thanks. So. Alright. Go get your buddies. Tell them they can unload their bales. Hell, maybe I'll help."

"Really?"

"Really. Go on." As Big Jim slowly rose up, dusted himself off, I hustled out the barn doors. Told Hub and Sammy we were good to go.

Hub looked at me. "You sure?"

"Yes, sir, and, Hub," I caught him before he began signaling Sammy, "could my friend, Big Jim, help us?"

"Sure." Hub watched me. "Why not?"

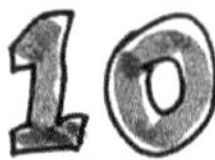

There were no introductions. Big Jim came out the barn doors. "Just a sec," he told us, as he carried that brown and white rabbit curled up in his arms. He put him in his car, cracked a couple of windows. Then he undressed, the gun must've been in his cream blue jacket. He undid his tie, took off his white shirt, put everything in his car and came back to us, bare-chested, rubbing his arms. Charlie had already begun backing the hayrack in as Hub called out, "Left! Left! Charlie, I said *'Left,'* y'hear?"

"Sorry, Hub. I'm dyslexic or something, always confuse my left for my right. Sorry."

"Keep comin' . . . more LEFT . . . yeah, okay!"

Big Jim climbed up in the hayloft with Hub. He was pretty agile, still sweating, his meaty midsection heaving and shining. I was pretty sure I saw a smile on his face. He just joined in, like one of the guys, calling out to Charlie, "Come on, man, hit me with another!" Going after Russell, too, "Come on, Red, tote that bale, pull that barge. Come on!"

Russell got all worked up. "Name's Russell, Mister," between gasps for air, "*Russell*—not Red, y'hear?"

Big Jim laughed. "Hey, kid, I don't care what your name is. You got to step it up. Come on, bring it to me—*come on*!" Big Jim worked all three of us. Hub watched it all as he steadily packed bale on bale, the heat steamy, all of us breathing hard and heavy. Man, did that barn fill up fast. Later, Hub told me, no question, in all the summers he'd been working the farms, that was the fastest he'd ever seen a barn fill up with hay.

Though only a few clouds were rolling in, Hub said it just wasn't right, this late in the day, to fill up another hayrack and then just leave it. The bales were better off in the fields. They'd dry faster in the next day's sun.

Charlie disagreed. Better to fill a hayrack and then put a tarp over it if we didn't have time to get them in a barn. I tended to agree with Charlie. Russell, of course, was all for knocking off early. I was, too, but no way was I going to let on. Rain, I learned, however it came, was a haying crew's worst enemy. Great for growing and much needed, but not good for harvesting, baling, and putting up in barns. It didn't rain that afternoon, and we did lay off about an hour earlier than usual. Big Jim said he'd drive me back while Hub and the guys drove off.

Big Jim finished buttoning his shirt, put his tie back on, loosely knotted. The rabbit was nestled in among his suit jacket and the black gun in the back seat. I rode shotgun as we drove back to Langford's farm.

"God, that's hard work. I'd just about forgot," said Big Jim

"See my blisters?" I showed him both of my red, welted hands.

"Oh yeah, I gotta few comin' that way, but, man, it sure felt good!"

"Doesn't it? Think it's the hardest work I've ever done in my life!"

"You bet. Haying, mucking stalls, too, back-breakers, and they got to be done. Hell, farm work is *hard* work. Nobody gets that. Kills your back."

"And your knees."

"Right."

"And hands."

"Hands, oh yeah. Fucks up your whole damned torso, but, Lord, how your spirits soar!"

"The good earth."

Big Jim nodded. "Yessir . . . the good earth." We drove a mile or so in silence. Big Jim watched the road. I watched the clouds move in, shifting patterns of light and dark along the road, in among the fields.

"Whaddya hear from Johnny D?" I asked Big Jim.

"Funny, I was just about to ask you."

"Well, we parted last Sunday, he said he was going to South Carolina first, to visit an aunt, then head north to see Brooke."

"Sounds about right."

"I miss him."

"Yeah. Hell of a good salesman, and a real good guy." We approached Langford's farm. I pointed Big Jim down the long dirt drive. "Jesus, this is a nice lookin' farm."

"Yeah. See down there? That's Old Hickory Lake, where I stay."

"I know Old Hickory. Some great fishing in there."

"Really?"

"Oh yeah." We pulled up next to Titine. I hopped out. Big Jim got out, too. We stood next to Titine and said our good-byes.

"What about Ed and Chuck and those guys, how're they doing?"

"Ed's doing pretty good, he's in a town not far from here. Brad and he stuck together at first, think they've split up since. Chuck is hanging in but Monroe, well, that boy's religion gets in the way or somethin'."

"How so?"

"He's strugglin' a bit. Happens when all your ideals bump into real people. We'll see."

"You gonna be okay, Big Jim?"

"Sure thing. Hey. It's been a rough time, y'know, a rough few years. Sometimes I take it all too personal."

"Maybe that's good."

"I dunno."

"Not killing yourself but, maybe something's telling you to change or do something different?"

"Maybe. I'm not a big thinker. Just go with the flow but then the flow didn't seem to go anymore. I got confused, I guess."

"We may not agree about this book-selling stuff but I think you're a good guy, and Kelly really loves you."

"You think? Really?"

"Of course!"

"Thanks, man. Speaking of which, I'd better high-tail it before she calls the cops!" He started for his car. I called to him, "Good luck!"

"Thanks, and hey, maybe I'll come track you down and take you for some real good Tennessee barbeque one of these days, okay?"

"I'd like that."

Big Jim revved his shiny lemonade Mercedes and kicked up a good cloud of farm dust as he trailed off down Langford's drive. He honked a few times as he turned onto the tarmac, headed toward town. Hub and the others had already come and gone. I was all alone now, the sun still burning hot, but lowering. It felt good to just stand there, survey the fields, the trees beyond, the rise of hills, dotted with houses, the great open space and distances. I was tired but not lonely.

Just beyond the fence were the tractors, the baler, the hayrack, and not far behind them was Titine, happy to be among all that machinery. I didn't feel like rushing into town or back to the lake for a swim. I didn't want to rush anything. As I slowly walked to Titine, I surveyed the sheared fields before me, something about the light mixed with the perspective near the fence excited me. I decided to do a pen and ink, see if I could catch a glimpse of all this. I grabbed my Rapidograph pen, the big 18 x 24-inch sketchpad, and found a spot not far from the wire and fence post. Slowly, steadily, I began to draw, called it, "L.C. Langford Farm 6.15.71." That's my Peugeot, Titine, on the far right, if you ever see this drawing.

After that first week, as the sun set on Saturday afternoon, atop one of Langford's hillsides, Floyd sat us all down, gave a little speech on how we'd worked hard and good. After explaining how he'd made his calculations, we got paid. Cash. He licked his thick thumb, counted out tens, fives, and singles. Twenty-four dollars for the week's work. Hard-earned. Well-earned. Sweat labor. And I was grateful. Excited. Even elated. Why did I feel like a wealthy man? The kid complained, "Are you sure, Uncle Floyd? Seems like it should be more than that."

"What'd I tell ya, boy, about *greed*?"

"Yes, sir but—"

"Butts are from cigarettes."

"But, Uncle Floyd—"

"You want this good money or not?"

"I want it, Uncle Floyd. I just think there should be more of it."

"Hub, Charlie, you feel I'm cheatin' you?"

"Uncle Floyd, I didn't say you were cheatin' us."

"No? Sounds like some kind o' pettiness. Hub? Charlie?"

"I'm good, Mr. Floyd, real good. Thank y' kindly," said Charlie.

"Hub?"

"Buy the boy a sod'r."

"That what you want, Russell? Sod'r and candy and stuff?"

"No, I just—"

"Hub, you okay?"

"Thanks, Floyd. See y'all Monday."

"Thass right. Y'see, Russell, these are gentlemen. Y'see that?"

"Yes, sir. Jesus."

"What you say, boy? You watch your mouth. *Jesus*? After all I do for you—*Jesus*!?"

These haying days continued. I was there by eight every morning. We had our lunches, paid for by Floyd. The kid and I continued to race each other for those bales; Hub continued to stack; Charlie maneuvered that hayrack among the cut grass, pock-marked earth, angled along rolling hills, over dirt and paved roads, and into barns. It never did rain. End of each day, I swam, washed up, got dinner and slept hard and deep in the penetrating pitch-black starry nights. I didn't get to visit the library or stroll through town. But I did sing in the Methodist choir the first Sunday after that fateful Tuesday night rehearsal.

11

That Sunday, this was my mind, "at play in the fields of the Lord." John was in South Carolina, or maybe he'd already arrived up North. We still hadn't talked. My last phone call home had been when I talked to my dad after Titine's repairs in Nashville. It hadn't been that long ago, not even two weeks but it felt longer. I still needed to either phone Mom or write her a decent letter.

I kept my brothers and my sister in my thoughts, but I wasn't in touch with them either. Chris was in Meadville, Pennsylvania, teaching summer school and hopefully not drinking too much. Brother Sandy and his wife Judy were in Kalamazoo, solidifying his surgical practice. My sister Carol was shaky at best, after her most recent hospitalization for her continued mental instability. She and Dick and their three kids lived near my folks in Darlington and it was time I mailed them a postcard or something.

I still hadn't neatly copied my letter to Kathy. How was she going to write me if I didn't write her first?

All of this hit me on Sunday as things slowed down. I wasn't toting bales. I wasn't painting or writing or lounging by Old Hickory Lake, reading. I was in church, the ten o'clock service, pretending I knew these hymns after only one rehearsal.

There we were, nine of us, in our white smocks, mock-angels, up in the balcony, smiled at and doted upon by our choir director, Dr. William Stillman, Dr. Bill. With his silvery wire-rimmed glasses, there was a little shine from his thinning grey pate. Throughout, he gave us a series of benevolent grins, surprised eyes or then glares, as he weighed in with arms, hands, waving and fingering the air, leading us through the Valleys of the Shadows of Death and into the Mighty Fortresses of Our Gods.

Through the service, there was a fair amount of standing up, but a lot less than the Episcopal church I went to growing up in Darlington. I enjoyed just sitting there, watching the congregation below. That is, when I wasn't caught up in my list of worries and epistolary chores, or wondering about Kathy (and Kink).

I liked the sermon a lot. The minister's name was Reverend William Abernathy. Everyone called him Reverend Bill. Dr. Bill and Reverend Bill. He was a little younger than Dr. Bill, early fifties, white haired, tanned, a heavily wrinkled brow, dark eyes that were bright, attentive, constantly vigilant when he was in the pulpit. He didn't have a heavy Southern accent, was well spoken, and seemed truly to believe that humility was at the core of knowing God. Humility, modesty, listening, and pitching in. Humility, he said, was next to, not Godliness, but broken-ness. A great striving and then falling, failing, suffering. In that suffering, he went on, "as Jesus our God so suffered on the Cross, there is His broken-ness." A man crucified. Not a big success. No TV cameras or news clippings. No medals or awards. No big pay-day. Plain, simple, exposed: a fallen man. In that pure and inviolable humility, at its most mysterious, there is God.

A good sermon. I wanted to tell him so. When the service was over, after the altar boys and ministers marched along below—we sang them out—there was an organ postlude played by Dr. Bill. After a final prayer from the doorway by Reverend Bill, there was this great whoosh, as if a huge window had opened, this rush of breezes, bodies, clopping shoes, a great rustling as the church rose up and emptied. The nine of us plus Dr. Bill were the last ones out.

Emerging from the cool church into the bright sunlight, it was hard to see at first. I looked among the numerous groups gathered on church steps, among diagonally parked cars, and over along the patch of lawn off to the right.

With all my fervent glancing about, I completely missed Reverend Bill. He was almost lost in a small line-up of people, shuffling past him, shaking hands, on the steps just below me. I walked down and joined the "receiving line."

"Well, Dr. Bill told me to expect a tall, Northern gentleman.

Welcome!"

"Thank you, Reverend Abernathy."

"Reverend Bill, please. How do you like our Southern life?"

"I like it."

"How long will you be with us then?"

"Not sure exactly. I was going to sell dictionaries but—"

"Is that your calling? Business? Sales?"

"Oh no. I was pre-med in college but then took this art class. I want to be an artist, Reverend Bill, a painter."

"Really?" Reverend Bill stopped his line of questions, took a real look at me.

"Yes, sir."

"Well. That's *powerful.* You must come talk to me one day, have a chat. That's an enormous gift, to create art. Enormous."

"Yes, sir. I think so."

"So good to meet you, Garry, is that right?"

"Yes, sir. Garry Brown."

"Garry Brown . . . even have some color in your name!"

"Yes, well, but, Reverend Bill—"

He had turned to greet the next person in line, an older woman, who leaned in, kissed his cheek. She wore a black hat, called him "Bill," said, "Thank you, dear, such lovely words." As I moved down the steps, I watched them, his gentle smile in return, her tender, even melancholic words. I decided, not now. I'd tell him another time. Then I had a moment of panic: watching everyone mingle and then disperse, I didn't want to be standing there alone on the church steps. Suddenly, I missed my mom, my dad—Dad didn't enjoy church the way Mom did, but he still joined her every Sunday. Kathy and I, in a similar domestic moment, now and then, during our last two years of college, would go to church some Sundays. Was Kathy going to church with Kink, who was also, if not religious, probably spiritual? With the sun beating down, my brow perspiring, and the crowd now almost gone, I decided to head for Titine, as if I, too, had things to do.

"Garry! Hello? Garry?" A man's voice. I stopped, turned, looked about.

"Up here!" Atop the steps was Dr. Bill, waving, smiling. "Come up here, want you to meet some friends."

I skipped up the steps, joined Dr. Bill and a young couple in their thirties. The woman seemed very sweet, smiled, nodded. The man had dark black combed hair. He immediately offered me his hand. "Hi, Garry. I'm Tom Gottshalk, my wife Tillie."

"Hi . . . Tom . . . Tillie . . ." Hers was a delicate handshake.

"Tom is a fine musician. Had him in school, taught him all he knows, right, Tommy?"

"Yes sir, Dr. Bill, indeed you did."

"He's choir director now for a big public high school the next town over and Tillie teaches art there."

"Wow," I said, smiling, nodding, "you two must have your hands full!"

"Oh sure," said Tom. "But say, you guys sounded very good this morning. I know Dr. Bill is real excited you joined the choir."

"Me, too. It was kind of a strange convergence."

"Dr. Bill told us. God and his mysterious ways, right?"

"I think so!"

Then Dr. Bill chimed in, "Listen, Garry, I'm having Tom and Tillie and a few others over later this afternoon for drinks and snacks and hopefully some rousing music, would you care to join us?"

"Really? Gosh, but I have no nice clothes."

"These are nice. It's casual. Your shorts, a decent shirt. Whaddya say?"

"I say, yes, and thank you."

Dr. Bill jotted down directions, not from the lake but from the center of town (it was complicated from the lake, he said). As I climbed into my hot and steamy car, I decided I would treat myself to a nice brunch. Big crowd or not, I'd head over to the Snack Shack.

12

The Snack Shack wasn't crowded. It was packed. I waved to Terri, called, "Hey!" She nodded, looked about and then waved me over, pointing to a small table in the rear, no window but a view back into the packed eatery.

"Where ya been, Picasso? Sorry no booth. Is this okay?"

"Perfect."

"Know whatcha want?"

I knew: pancakes, a cheeseburger, medium rare, with fries, a large OJ, and a sweet iced tea with lemon.

"You sure that's enough?" Terri winked.

"Okay. A small garden salad, too." I winked back.

The Snack Shack was noisy, the kind of steady, unceasing buzz that becomes white noise. So, I pulled out *The Great Gatsby,* to read a little and finally, try to catch up. Of course, all these people, bits of conversations, glimpses of families bickering and joking, were hard to ignore. I kept wondering if there wasn't a drawing or painting among all this Sunday rabble-rouse. I was torn: to read or to draw? I wanted to do both. Okay: read until the food comes, draw after.

I'd read almost two pages when my attention was pulled from the book by some sort of ruckus. Voices, deep as well as high-pitched, began to dominate the crowd drone, rise above it and finally take center stage.

Stan, Terri's husband, staggered near the front counter. He was dully, loudly, saying slow, dark words to Terri, who was shrilly telling him to shut up, to stop. But he kept at it, now pounding his fist on the counter, his eyes slowly blinking and pointing in my direction. As I watched him, I wondered how he stood there without falling over. He reminded me of my drunken dad.

Then it went quiet. That is, the crowd drone of a busy diner returned. I resumed reading: Nick had found a house by the water out on Long Island. I liked his modesty, how he appreciated his summer environs, and, his being a bit of a loner.

"You like haying, boy?"

I looked up. It was Stan, unshaven, the sour smell of too much alcohol, eyes slowly blinking.

"I beg your pardon?"

"Don't be all fussy-polite with me, college boy. Come down South, steal work from hard-workin' folk. You heard me! Or, should I spell it out . . . YOU . . . LIKE . . . HAY-IN' . . . ? Hear that?"

I nodded. "Yes, sir. It's hard work but I like it."

"Is that right?" Stan swayed there, wiped his mouth, watching me. I didn't know what to say. It felt like any words would light his very short fuse. Then Terri appeared with my food. "Stannie, what you doin'? Go see Fred, he's got fresh coffee and biscuits. Leave this young man alone. Let him eat in peace." Terri said this as she lightly nudged Stan. He didn't move. She had both arms full of my order: hotcakes, cheeseburger and fries, a small salad bowl, and a large sweet tea with lemon.

"I don't want no biscuits."

"There's fresh coffee, go get you some fresh. Go on now."

"No."

"You never told me what salad dressing you want, Picasso."

"Thousand Island, Terri, thanks."

"Be right back. Stan, it's rude to hover. Come with me."

"No. This kid. 'Picasso' you call him? He stole my job."

"No, Stan. I talked to Floyd. You fucked up. It was your own damn fault."

"Did not."

"Floyd said you did."

"Floyd's full o' hog shit, all those fuckin' pigs o' his."

"Stannie, watch your mouth."

"He's workin' my job, this kid. Ask him. Go on."

"Stannie." She eyed Stan. He tried to eye her as he swayed. "Okay. Fine. Excuse me, Picasso, you hayin' for Floyd Underwood?"

"Yes, ma'am. Just started on Tuesday."

"Really? That's why we haven't seen you. It's hard work, isn't it?"

"Hardest work around. Damn straight," muttered Stan.

"It is, it really is," I agreed with Stan and looked from him to Terri.

"So, you're really workin' with Floyd's crew."

I watched Terri's face: her eyes, too, blinked more slowly, as if this new information was slowing everything down.

"Dint I tell ya, Miss Smarty Pants?"

"You did, Stan. I apologize for doubting you, but you still fucked up. It's not this boy. Floyd coulda hired anyone."

"It ain't right . . . it ain't fair."

"Stannie, come get some fresh coffee. I'll be right back with your Thousand Island." Terri winked at me and took off.

Stan called to her, "No. Told you, no biscuits, no coffee. Shit." Stan stood there, watching as Terri departed. I began eating, pancakes first, a bite of cheeseburger, a sip of sweet tea. I was starved. Still looming but for a little wavering and slow eye-blinking, Stan kept his dark eyes on me.

"How much f'ing Floyd payin' you, Picasso?"

"Um . . ." Stan leaned down, over my food. I looked up. "Twenty-four dollars?"

"Twenty-four?" He stood and looked off. "Not bad." Then he bumped the table as he suddenly jerked back down into my face. "That's my fuckin' money, college boy!" I just watched him. "Y'hear? Thass mine, you lil pissant!" Now he grabbed the table and shook it, three times, very fast. "Come on, you lil fucker, let's go outside. Come on!"

It was one of those moments when everything slowed down, faces, gestures, all went into slow motion. A moment when all sorts of thoughts ran together. This man had scared me the first time I saw him. I knew then he was not a good man. Maybe he'd been one once but now, no. He was troubled, infantile, rageful, vulgar. I didn't like him. I didn't like how he carried on, and I certainly didn't like how he treated Terri. I wanted to save Terri from this man. I wanted to be a hero. I wanted to knock this bully for a loop. I wanted to kick the shit out of him and defend my pride.

Yes, I was a college kid. Yes, he scared me. But I'd been a college athlete and gotten into fights and tumbles and knew I could hold my own. This man was practically a staggering drunk, and thus, in some respects, helpless, even harmless.

I weighed my options: walk outside with this man. He was a man, I was a kid, but I was also as tall as he was, maybe taller. Let him throw punches, step aside, and he'd drunkenly spill to the earth, or . . . stand my ground, take his punches so I'd be justified in socking him a few solid blows—to the face—and then a big punch to his gut. He'd double over, gasping, and collapse to the ground. But would this really prove anything? I didn't need to impress Terri. She belonged to this man. She'd be saddened, hurt, dismayed. She might even lose respect for me since she already knew her Stannie wasn't operating with a full deck.

And, I didn't feel like fighting. I was hungry. And, I wasn't that scared of Stan anymore.

"Come on, you smart-ass punk! Y'heard me, let's go!"

So, I stood, half-heartedly, a little confused.

"Thass right, Picasso, time to get your ass whupped."

Which is when I saw him again—Elwood or James Steward or whoever he was. He came right up to the Snack Shack windows, off to my right, cupped his hands over his eyes and moved his face flat against the window. No one saw him but I did. He searched the insides of the diner and then got very still. He looked straight over at me. It was almost as if he'd been looking for me, and this is the strange part—he winked at me.

Then he nodded, pulled away from the window as he waved toward me and walked off.

"Hey, let's go, pansy ass. I'm going to kick your—"

"Stan."

"What?"

"I'm very hungry. Do you mind if I finish my brunch and then we have our fight?"

"Wha—?"

"I'm really starved. Been singing all morning in the Methodist church choir. You hungry?"

"Naw." Stan stood there, quiet now, not only drunk but a little dazed. "You sing, too?"

"Church choir, the Methodist Church. Over on Main?"

"The double Bills."

"The 'double—'?"

"Reverend Bill and Doctor Bill."

"You know that church?"

"Used to go there Sundays with my first wife. Liked it. Damn good choir. That Rev' Bill's a pretty good preacher." Stan still loomed, more sad than drunk, his shoulders hunched now as he looked down.

"Stan, you wanna join me?"

"Naw. I'm good."

"Please." I got up and pulled out the other chair. "Come. Sit. How 'bout a cup of coffee?"

"Well . . ." Stan galumphed into the chair. "Those hot cakes look pretty good."

"Stay right here." I found Terri over near the counter pulling a few receipts, asked her for another order of hotcakes and a fresh cup of Fred's coffee.

"You drink coffee, Picasso?"

"No. For Stan."

"Oh?"

13

When I returned, Stan was slumped in his chair. He'd nodded off. I didn't wake him. I watched him. I ate my pancakes, a bite of cheeseburger, a little salad, some toast, some fries. I alternated among all my delicious food groups. Stan slept quietly. I pulled out my sketchbook.

Here's a funny thing about observation, which does get to the moral crisis of making art. Is it adjacent to the moral dilemma of journalism? There's a fire, a house is burning down. It's quite ravishing, the leaping flames, sparks against a night sky. It's a great photo, a great article, a wild painting.

But it's a house burning, someone's home. People are still inside, who didn't get out in time. It's a tragedy and it's a poignant piece of writing or a Pulitzer-winning photo or the basis for a heroic painting. When am I an artist? When am I a man?

Here's Stan. A tyrant of sorts. Some might say, a bad guy, an evil bastard. Yet, in repose and closely observed, what an interesting face. Is this the face of evil or is it an intriguing pen and ink? Or, not either/or, but both?

Someone asks: how can you get close to that? Stay away. It's evil, he's evil. How can you? Is evil outside of me or is it in me, too? Could I have become a Stan or some narcissistic tyrant? Perhaps. Given our personalities and our circumstances, who knows how I might have evolved or disintegrated or gotten bigger than myself, miswielded my power, taken to drink, and turned into a feckless, reckless, soulless son of a bitch?

I slowed my eating as I began to draw Stan. His body leaned in the chair, both hands limp on his lap, his head drooped to his left. The wrinkles in his forehead, his jowls, cheeks all sagging to the left as well. In repose, his black brows, so often narrowed and intent, were now drawn up in openness, even innocence. His eyes, deep in their sockets, were no longer edgy but had become shaped flickering ovals; they seemed to swivel behind his closed lids, perhaps tracking some dream.

I drew his slumped body, his drooped face as it caved into his sagging shoulders. I wanted to capture, too, the tender almost dainty care-freedom of his two big leathery hands as they lay atop his grey work-pant thighs.

"Here you go," said Terri, who quickly stopped speaking as I put my finger and pen to my mouth, shushing her. As she placed the hotcakes and coffee in front of Stan, she whispered, "See? Isn't he a sweetie?" She kissed the side of his head, then looked over at me. "Whatcha doin', Picasso?" She came and stood next to me, another whisper, "You doin' a picture of my Stannie? Aww . . ."

I kept drawing. It was almost finished. A smaller pen and ink like this I could usually do in about fifteen minutes. The ones in the bigger pad (14 x 17 inches) took longer, about a half hour. Terri kept looking over my shoulder. "Wow. I mean, you are good. That really looks like him. Let me get Fred." Terri scuttled off.

I put in the final details: the rounded piece of chair back, edge of the table, crack of shadow and light through the diner window just off and behind Stan's drooping head.

I thought how nice it'd be to do a sketch of Stan awake, sitting there, his solemn, dark, tainted Lincolnesque face. Maybe one day I could do a double portrait, Terri and Stan.

I finished, then propped the drawing up against the ketchup bottle, chrome napkin dispenser, and the clear glass sugar jar. I liked it. A fairly good likeness, it was also an interesting drawing.

Terri returned with Fred, who kept wiping his hands on his apron. He was laughing as they approached and Terri kept slapping at him and shushing him. "Fred, hush now! And just look."

"At what? That sleepin' drunk?"

"Fred, stop now."

"Girl, I got food orders to fill."

"Take just a minute, Freddie. Now look."

"Where?"

"There. See? On the table."

"That a drawing? Lemme see." Fred started to reach for it. Terri stopped him. "Can we pick it up, Picasso? Have a look?" she whispered.

"Please." I helped Fred take hold of it. Terri looked over Fred's shoulder as they both slowly eyed it. Fred kept squinting.

"That's Stan, isn't it?" said Fred.

"Ain't it a good likeness?"

"Surely is. You did this, son?"

"Yes, sir." I nodded, ate some pancakes.

"Did what?" a dark voice grumbled. "Christ." Stan wiped at his face, he was waking up. "These for me?" Stan eyed me, then the hotcakes.

"All yours," I said.

"I guess I am hungry." Stan poured syrup then sipped at his coffee. "Jesus, Ter, this coffee's cold!"

"Cuz you were asleep, Stannie. I'll get ya fresh."

"Asleep?"

Terri rushed off with his cold cup. "Whatcha lookin' at, Fred?" He cut into his hotcakes and watched Fred.

"I'm lookin' at you, Stan."

"These are pretty good, Freddie." Stan solemnly chewed each mouthful.

"Thanks, Stan . . . sleepin' like a baby, ha!"

"Whatcha talkin' about?"

"See?"

"See what?" Stan bowed into each forkful of hotcakes; he used his fork as a knife, edged off a section, swirled it in the lake of syrup, then bowed again toward the raised fork, as if his mouth had to search for food.

"This, Stan. You. See?" Fred placed the drawing where I'd leaned it but now so that it faced Stan. Stan stopped eating. His fork hovered. He finished chewing his last bite, swallowed, and his mouth fell open. He stared, cold, unflinching. "Jesus Christ," he whispered.

"I gotta get back to the kitchen," said Fred, but before leaving, he looked back at me. "Nice work, Picasso."

"Thanks."

"When you gonna do one o' me?"

"Really?"

"Why not? You're willing to do his ugly mug, why not mine?"

"Sure."

"We'll talk. Gotta go feed the hungry multitude."

Stan continued to stare, not eating. "Jesus . . . F'ing . . . Christ . . ." Oh-oh. I didn't know how to read Stan's reaction. Stan was frozen, not eating, not moving. Just this blank stare into the leaning sketchpad. "You did this?"

"Yes, sir."

"When?"

"While you dozed."

"I was *asleep*?"

"For a bit."

"How long?"

"Fifteen to twenty minutes."

"You did this then?" Stan's questions were like an attack. He'd sobered up. He seemed angry. I was reactive, even defensive, "Well, yes. But . . ."

"This is really *good.* This is—has Terri seen this? *Shit,* man." I sat there, my turn to stare gape-mouthed. "Hey, Ter. Hey, doll!" Stan stood, waved, called.

"I'm comin', Stan. Fred made fresh, be right there!"

"Forget the coffee. Get over here!"

Terri waved, disappeared into the kitchen, and a few moments later, joined us.

"Pot hadn't even finished brewing but try this, Stannie." She placed the cup in front of Stan.

"Why, thank you, darlin', you are so kind."

"Remember who loves you, you big lug."

"Let me taste." Stan picked up the cup as if he'd become royalty, his little finger pointed up and out. "Oh my. Oh yes. Very good."

"Alright?"

"But this is even better." Before Terri could speak, his big thick fingers waved to the drawing and then grabbed it and pulled it closer.

"You like it?" asked Terri.

"Kind of an eye opener."

"Now, can't you be nice to this boy?"

Stan looked over at me as he wrapped Terri in his free arm and held the drawing in the other. "I dunno. We got a fight planned out in the parking lot, right, Picasso?"

"That's true," I was finishing my cheeseburger.

"O' course, I might hurt him bad."

"Oh Stan."

"If I swell up his eyes, bloody his hands, I mean, what if I broke his drawing hand? That wouldn't be good."

"True, Stannie."

"What're we fightin' about again, Picasso?"

For a moment I couldn't remember. "Oh. Work. I took your job."

"Thass right. Shit."

"You were drunk, Stannie. Admit it. Floyd was fed up."

Stan kept his eyes on the pen and ink. "Yeah . . . I had it coming."

"Aw, Stannie." Terri pulled his head to her.

"I'm a dumb shit, a dumb drunken shit. Have a look. It's all right here in this drawing."

"Stop that, Stan. I gotta go."

"Yeah. Me, too."

Terri turned back. "Where you goin'?"

"Home. Lawn needs mowin'."

"Okay. Don't forget to leave a nice tip for the waitress." Terri smiled as she moved off.

Stan stood. "Did you buy them hotcakes for me?"

"Yes, sir."

"And you did my drawing, too? My red-letter day. Here." Stan reached in his pocket, pulled out a small wad of bills. "A couple bucks toward the tip."

"Oh."

"Thanks, Picasso. Enjoy the haying."

That was it. My run-in with Stan. No white horse, no cloud of dust, no punches thrown. I didn't get the girl, either. I was not a hero. No applause. No write-up in the local paper. Terri didn't come over and give me a big hug or a big wet one on the smacker. She did say this as I was leaving: "See you around, Picasso. Maybe one day you'll do a drawing of me?"

I grinned. "I'd like that." If I'd had a cowboy hat on, I would've tipped it.

Fred came from the kitchen. "I heard that. Oh no, I got first dibs, right, Picasso?"

"Yes, sir. That's true."

Terri swatted Fred's shoulder with her receipt book. "So it's age before beauty, is that it?"

"Hey now!" Fred ran off. Just as I turned to go, Terri waved me back. I joined her at the counter. She waved me closer. "Thanks, Picasso, for being so good to my Stan. It means a lot to me. Thank ye." She took her fingers and kissed them. Then she placed those kissed fingers on my right cheek. They were damp, cool. I got on my horse and rode out of town.

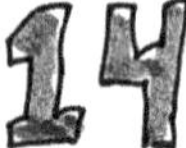

I drove Titine up to the empty library parking lot, where seven days ago, John and I had said our good-byes. I parked in a nice shady spot. It was afternoon now, the day thick with heat and hot sun. A thin black and white cat slinked across the grassy periphery of the parking lot. It slowly sauntered toward the library. It was an indifferent stroll until the cat looked back. At me? Then it picked up speed and darted past the far edge of library, out of sight.

I lay back in my driver's seat and closed my eyes. I could've turned on the radio. I still hadn't found *the* radio station yet but I didn't want to hear music. I listened to the low drone of cars passing on the main road through Donelson. There was birdsong, a car door slamming and, in the distance, the steady whir of a lawn mower.

What was I doing with my life? What was I doing here?

I remembered an op-ed article from *The New York Times* by the poet W. H. Auden. He said that his greatest gift as an artist was that "he always knew what to do next." Sure, he implied, there is a Big Picture, but even with the best intentions, we're not always privy to such "insider information." But, what's next? Which becomes, what do you want to do *now?* That's an attainable piece of the puzzle. This was some comfort. I nodded off.

When I awoke, my face was hot, sweaty, my shirt damp. Titine was heating up, the shady spot had moved. I got out and walked over to the shade. I stood there, looking at the big grocery store below. The big, long, and high beige Shop-A-Lot. It looked like an A&P, or, up in Connecticut, a Grand Union. I kept watching: a car pulled in. Another car pulled out. Several people, a man, woman, child, and an older woman, as if following them, pushed carts slowly through the parking lot.

I retrieved my 14 x 17 sketchbook from Titine. Slowly, I walked down from the library, through a row of trees, and joined a dirt path, among the low growth. I walked over to the rear edge of the boxy building: big crates leaned against the rear wall. Thick piping and a heating unit leaned out from the wall. All of these jousting rectangles began to excite me. I stood there and did a fairly quick drawing.

Once done, I jogged up the path, got in my steamy Titine, and headed back to the lake. Time for a swim. Also, I wanted to rewrite my letter to Kathy, do some reading, maybe do some more sketches lakeside. Wait: Dr. Bill's invitation, music and drinks, four p.m. What time was it? A glance at my watch: already past two.

The roads were mostly empty, only a few cars and, fortunately, no Sunday drivers. Once I neared the lake, I stopped, pulled over in front of Langford's farm. Crazy. I'd be there again bright and early. But. The long gravel and grass drive, fields on either side. A gaggle of machinery, dormant at the bend in the drive, the big rise of hillside and fields beyond that. Far up, to the right, the big white house next to a grove of shade trees. I continued to gaze, muse, when a side door opened: a woman wearing a pink apron emerged with a big laundry basket. She marched quickly to the clothesline strung between two of the bigger trees. I was tempted to drive up and introduce myself.

"Hi. I'm Garry Brown from Connecticut. I'm haying your fields and I'm glad to be here. It's the hardest work I've ever done in my life. Can I do a pen and ink drawing of you?" The woman, attractive, with that rustic country beauty like Terri's, would pull a clothes pin from her mouth, look at me, and laugh. Or, invite me in for a cold drink and laugh some more. The two of us in her spic-and-span kitchen, aglow with afternoon light.

Until Mr. Langford himself would come into the kitchen, surprised, What in hell's going on? Introductions. Oh, so you're the new guy, the kid they've been talking about. They have? What're you going to do when the haying season's over, in a week or so? Well. I'm an artist. I'll draw. I'll paint. I'll carry on. An artist? Prove it. Well . . . I go to Titine. I bring in my sketchbook. Mr. Langford begins paging through it, Mrs. Langford looks on, leaning close to him. They're a married couple in their fifties. They still love each other. He nods, Not bad. She thinks they're wonderful. Could you do a drawing of my husband? Not me, he says, Her. Could you do her? Or the two of us, she asks, like a double portrait? Sure, I tell them, Sure.

She bends each time, moves the basket along the ground as she keeps placing clothes upon the taut rope line. I watch her. I watch the fields and the dirt drive and the big house beside her. I watch how the clothes, mostly whites, yellows, some pinks and blues—shirts, jeans, undergarments, socks—all gently waft and flap, a slight breeze kicking up. What are these days? Who are these people? What is this place?

After my swim, I just sat at the concrete picnic table and stared off across the shimmery water. I watched two little girls—sisters?—having a water fight. Another family, they looked Hispanic, lay on their big towel, the mom and dad nuzzling faces, the little boy scooping sand into a yellow pail.

I wanted to read *Gatsby,* I wanted to take a nap. I just wanted to slow it all down. Perhaps this late-afternoon gathering at Dr. Bill's felt like my busy, planned life up North, another scheduled event, another demand. That was my reluctance. But I was also lonely.

15

After a quick shower, I put on the cleanest shirt I had, a pair of jeans, and drove into town. From there, I followed Dr. Bill's directions. The drive began among lots of houses, small streets, then stretched out into patches of trees, hillsides, now and then glimpses of distant fields. Dr. Bill's home was higher up, nestled on the upside of a small lake.

"Well, this isn't really Donelson anymore. Now it's Covington," Dr. Bill said.

"Oh?"

"Same county, different town. Closer to the college where I teach."

"What college is that, Dr. Bill?"

"College of Billington. Not Bennington. Billington . . . Come, Garry, have something to drink." Dr. Bill and I had moved through his quaint antiques-laden living room out onto his patio. He walked me over to a small outdoor bar where a young man named Todd was serving drinks. "Todd, this is Garry Brown, my new lyric baritone."

"Oh yeah, man, nice to meet you. Heard you really saved the day."

"Oh?"

"Want some tequila, man?"

"Todd, behave."

"Ha! Just jokin', Dr. Bill. Garry knows I'm just kiddin', but, hey, do ya? Got some fine stuff, man."

"Todd. Stop. Garry, what'll you have?"

"Ginger ale?"

"Wait," said Dr. Bill. "Try my fruit punch, has just a touch of rum."

"Or, I could lace it with tequila?"

"Give him a cup of punch, Todd. As is. Please."

Todd nodded, fixed my cup of punch. He was a little strange, unexpected. Dr. Bill had a slight Southern accent but Todd had none.

He reminded me of guys in college. Really bright guys who were always high on something, kind of spacey and irreverent.

"Here you go, man. Bottoms up!"

"Thanks." I took the cup of purplish punch, toasted Todd, who gave a thumbs up as Dr. Bill pulled me away. "Come, Garry. I want you to meet some folks . . . Don't mind Todd. He's a drug-head from Florida by way of Chicago by way of outer space, but he's a very gifted musician, as you'll see. Come."

The sun was getting lower and leaving long strips of shadow on Dr. Bill's flagstone patio and back lawn. It was a much larger gathering than I'd expected. I'd thought five, maybe ten people, but this looked more like fifty, maybe more. All nicely dressed, all chatting, drinking. An older crowd, mostly couples in their forties and fifties. Dr. Bill escorted me around and seemed to delight in introducing me as his "prayer answered." Most everyone had Southern accents. The men nodded, drank; the women asked questions about my coming down South from Connecticut of all places.

Earlier, by the lake, I'd felt tired, but now, I perked up. Dr. Bill finished our tour of introductions and dropped me off with the young couple I'd met at church: Tillie and Tom Gottshalk. "Hiya, Garry, you made it."

"Yes. Nice to see you again." We shook hands. Dr. Bill started off, "Keep an eye on this young man, won't you?"

"Sure thing. Say, Dr. Bill, when are we going to stir things up, you reckon?"

"Pretty soon. You in a hurry?"

"Not at all. Just that Tillie has a few butterflies and—"

"Tom, stop." She quickly love-tapped Tom's shoulder. "I do not."

"Okay but—"

"I'm just waiting on a few more folks. Some dear friends from Knoxville. Once they're here, we'll get started."

"We're fine, Dr. Bill, don't mind Thomas," said Tillie in a gentle whisper.

"Oh, but I do." Dr. Bill paused. "I mind him and I heart him, too. Both of you."

"Oh, Dr. Bill, you're so sweet."

Dr. Bill blew a kiss, then waved as he hurried off.

"We've been standing here, looking at that lake," said Tom.

"Isn't it so pretty?" added Tillie, her eyes brightening.

"Then we wondered, how does Dr. Bill get to the lake? You see a gate or path? I don't." The three of us stood at the edge of the patio, where it touched the lawn, as if we were on a dock or at the edge of a pier. I searched the far outline of where the lawn rounded into hedgerow and trees. There was no gate or indentation in the growth.

"And then," said Tom, the three of us still eyeing the party and the puzzling lake, "we thought for sure that man over there, sitting on that lounger, being fussed over by those two ladies. See? We keep thinking, that's got to be Jimmy Stewart. See him?"

I suddenly lit up, as if startled awake. "Where?"

"See, just in the shadows there?"

Far off the patio and on the lawn but into the far bend, in a shadow created by the hedgerow and overhanging trees, there he was. A creamy dinner jacket, a pinkish bow tie, beige slacks, loafers. Mr. Steward . . . Elwood. One woman seated on the edge of the lounger next to him, another, tall, thin, stood there, bending to listen, as he nursed what looked like a martini. He made a remark. Both women laughed.

"Well?" asked Tom.

"Yes." I kept watching him.

"Right? Jimmy Stewart? *Mr. Smith Goes to*—Nashville?"

"It's a Wonderful Life," said Tillie.

"Yes, but 'A Wonderful Life' in . . . Donelson, or Covington?"

"You think Dr. Bill knows Jimmy Stewart, Tom?" Tillie asked.

"Maybe they're old college buddies, or maybe he's making a movie in Nashville," Tom offered.

"Shall we go over and say hi?" I asked.

"Oh gosh." Tillie blushed, put her hand to her mouth, giggled.

"No. You know, a person, even a big star, likes his privacy," said Tom.

"Thomas?" It was Dr. Bill.

The three of us still peered from the patio's edge. I felt caught, as if we'd been doing something wrong. Dr. Bill came over and quietly said, "I'm sorry to intrude but could you and Tillie come help me? We're going to start soon, okay?"

"Sure, Dr. Bill. No problem." Tom took a long last gulp of his drink. Tillie carried her empty glass and nodded. The three of them walked off, Tom looking left and right for a place to put his empty glass.

Here was my chance. Finally. I was nervous, some butterflies, a light buzz. But dammit, enough already. I needed to know. Slowly, I edged off the patio flagstones onto the soft, lush lawn, all the while keeping my eyes on him, like a man with a gun aimed, slowly moving closer. As I moved from the sunlit places into the shadows, I was being careful. I didn't want to miss this opportunity. As I got closer, he remained oblivious. Both women were talking. He nodded, smiled, sipped his martini, and watched both women intently, his eyes mostly on the one seated beside him. Then, all three of them laughed. I continued my slow-motion walk, closer, closer. The sunlight flickered, or what was that? Then he turned, just enough to see, over the seated woman's shoulder, my approach. He saw me, kept his eyes on me. I continued to watch him as I walked gently, slowly, closer still. He smiled, nodded, then raised his nearly empty martini glass in a mock salute, I was only ten paces from him now. He said, "What's up, Doc?" I nodded, smiled. Then—all hell broke loose.

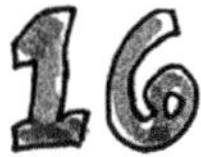

“It’s time, everyone!” Dr. Bill’s voice called out. He stood center stage on the patio, just in front of the glass doors that opened out onto the expansive patio where most of us circulated among patio and backyard and the lake below. We all turned to look back toward Dr. Bill and his home, while behind him, Tom, Tillie, the bar-man Todd, and another dark-haired young woman were positioning themselves among instruments, chairs, and music stands.

“Please, everyone, gather ’round. Bring your chairs, bench, loungers, whatever you’re sitting on, and if you don’t have a seat, get one. Or sit on the lawn, wherever is comfortable. And, enjoy this modest mid-summer night’s—okay, early evening’s—dream of a concert!”

I saw Elwood start to stand. Then Dr. Bill called to him, “Stew? No. You’re fine, you and the ladies.” And ‘Stew’—Stewart? Steward? Who was this man?—turned toward Dr. Bill, waved, and reseated himself, the ladies joining him, one on either side.

I thought I’d find a spot close to Stew and the ladies but already, in this flurry of seating, a group had brought chairs, a small wood bench, and even a blanket they spread on the grass. As I was nudged aside by this onslaught, a lovely young girl of about fifteen, looked up from her big blanket and said, “We have room on this blanket . . .”

“Oh. Thanks.” I nodded and slowly alternated looks toward Stew, the blanket, and the girl, as I made my descent.

As Stew and the ladies re-positioned themselves—I was nearer the patio, to their left—I saw Stew grow concerned, his brow wrinkled as he quickly surveyed the various groups in the audience, their seating travails, until he finally found me. His face relaxed, he looked at me, nodded, raised his glass and—winked. I blushed. I turned away. I was embarrassed, confused, flustered.

Dr. Bill, the impresario, returned. The chamber group, behind him, at the ready, he cleared his throat and spoke, "Again, welcome. All of you. From near, and you, James and Bertie, from afar. So glad you all could join us. It means much to me to share this summer interlude, these fleeting days of our lives, gratefully contradicted by something that sometimes feels like forever, such a gift, the joy of great music! This first piece is a divertimento by Mozart, followed by some Faure, a Schubert sonata, and finally, a hallowed American piece by Aaron Copland . . . You know Thomas, at the piano—we somehow trudged it out here, this overworked upright!" Dr. Bill leaned back and tapped it, ". . . his lovely wife, Tillie, on cello; Todd, from our Billington U, on violin, and Jennifer on clarinet. With a bit of luck, I'll join with my cranky old violin. But please, welcome these gifted artists, and first—Mozart!"

There was a huge burst of applause, a few whoops, and immediately, the music began. The violin and the clarinet led off joined by the cello and then a series of flourishes from the piano.

They must have played for almost two hours, without a break. Dr. Bill did join them, on the Faure, the Schubert, and on the finale Copland piece. At first it seemed that Dr. Bill, as he joined in, was nodding to us, but no, it was his way of playing. His head bobbed, he eyed chamber mates and seemed to see us but really not, more as if eyes were watching the notes as they joined the summer dusk.

All of them were a contrast to their more affable social selves: Tom was now close to the piano keys, head bowed, and then with a head turn, pulling away, clearly immersed and ferocious; Tillie, who seemed a bit nervous and giggly earlier was now cradling this big bold cello, feathering its dark tones, her brow furrowed, serious, at once angry and elated; Jennifer, on the clarinet, was tall, willowy, her black hair sifting the air as she seemed to blend her lovely tilt of body with the fingerings and mouthing of this dark wood and its singing.

The wildest head-turner was Todd, who had seemed so spaced out and weird at the bar. Once he began to slowly saw and brush those violin strings, a completely new man emerged. His posture was strangely straight and strong in contrast to his almost schlumpy drug-bum pose at the bar. His eyes were sharp and focused, completely present: he would nod and feel the notes as if sharing with just his fellow chamber-mates. Each stroke strong, sure and what flourishes there were, never showy or prolonged. There was humor, too, as he and Dr. Bill seemed to banter with their violins throughout the penultimate Schubert sonata.

The highlight for me was the final piece, this chamber orchestra version of Aaron Copland's *Appalachian Spring*.

Several summers previous, after Kathy and I had been dating for a year or so, on my cross-country travels (my visit to Durl when he was selling dictionaries in Nebraska), I stopped in Davenport, Iowa to visit Kathy and her family. Toward the end of my four-day stay, one evening after everyone else had gone to bed, Kathy and I curled up on the den sofa and sat there listening to Copland's homage to America and the Shakers.

I'd never heard the piece. Kathy had just finished a double-semester course in "Listening to Music and The Classics."

"This, Gar, I think you're really going to love." I'd listen to anything with her, the lovesick state I was in. Maybe now I'd have to say that's "our song." Some have Frank Sinatra. My mom and dad had Peggy Lee. My brother Sandy and wife Judy had The Freshmen. Brother Christopher, think he and his Judy had Elvis, maybe The Four Tops. Durland and Brookie were hooked by Frankie Valli. But Kathy and I, for me, it will always be *Appalachian Spring*.

As the shadows lengthened in Dr. Bill's backyard, I thought this version was the most heartbreaking rendition I'd ever heard, probably because I was missing Kathy so much. When it finished, I was flushed, red-faced. I wiped my moist eyes, cheeks, and then, with everyone else, rose up clapping, as people hooted, whistled, cried out, Bravo!

The musicians looked at each other and, instantly, on Tom's piano downbeat, they recommenced: a tantalizingly light, cheery epilogue. Otterino Resphigi's *Ancient Airs and Dances* (learned this later). It was a bright melodic send-off, especially as the Tennessee late afternoon had become summer evening, the pink and orange blending into blues, greys, and a charcoal-like darkening.

Time had passed. Then I remembered James Steward. I looked over to his group. The two women, now standing, were talking to Dr. Bill. People were coming off the lawn, crossing onto the patio. I kept looking but—where was Elwood?

"Did you enjoy that?" It was the young girl whose blanket I'd shared.

"Oh yes! Thanks again for letting me join you and your folks."

"Not at all. Would you like something to drink?"

I watched this young girl: dark shoulder-length hair, a white summery dress, so poised, so polite, so bold, really. I was mystified.

"Um. No thanks."

"Really? Dr. Bill's punch is *so* good!"

"What's your name?"

"Patricia. What's yours?"

"Garry. Garry Brown."

"I'm Patricia Willard." She actually curtsied as she offered me her hand. I thought, does she want me to kiss it? I shook it.

"My folks, see? That's them talking to Dr. Bill?"

"Yes." I had nodded to them when I'd sat down. Now, they had just walked over and joined Dr. Bill and the two women. Still no sign of 'Stew.'

"They teach in the music department with Dr. Bill. Actually, my daddy just became head of that department."

"How about that."

"Are you a musician, too?" Patricia asked.

"No."

"I play piano, violin, and cello. I love all three. But piano really is my favorite."

"You must be very gifted. Well, Patricia—"

"I guess, but, really, it's that I have a very deep love for music, all kinds."

"I bet. Well, Miss Willard—"

"No, I liked it when you called me 'Patricia.' You have a funny accent."

"Oh?"

"Is that English, like from London?"

"No, it's American, like from Connecticut."

"You're from up North? I love New England. Boston, New York. Those are wonderful cities. So much energy and culture."

"Quite true."

"I'm going to perform in Carnegie Hall one day, I just know it!"

"You're very confident, aren't you?"

"I think that's all an artist really has, finally, a belief in oneself. Don't you?"

"I do. But a lot of doubts do creep in."

"Oh, they're just little hobgoblins, little trolls under the bridge that try to scare and distract us."

"Well put. Patricia, do you know how to get to Carnegie Hall?"

"Oh gee, it's in New York City. Guess we'd take 40 East to I-95 North to—"

"Practice."

"I beg your pardon?"

"Ask me."

"Oh, you mean . . . Right! Um, how do you get to Carnegie Hall?"

We both said, "Practice."

I laughed, she didn't.

"That's what I'm doing. Every day."

"That was like a joke."

"But it's true. I try to put in at least five hours a day."

"Really? When?"

"Before school, two hours. After school, two hours, and if I can, an hour before bed. That's when things really sink in, the unconscious meets the creative."

"How do you know all this? You're so young."

"Not so young. Fifteen in August."

"You're fourteen?"

"Fifteen in August. Soon."

"Okay but—"

"I know these things because I *feel* them, in my hands and arms, in my whole body, and, in my heart, my soul."

"I'd love to hear you play some time."

"When?"

"No, I mean. Oh. Let me catch Dr. Bill before he runs off."

"Okay. I'm going to get more punch. Then we can talk about you coming to one of my concerts, okay?"

"Right," and before I could leave, "It was very enjoyable talking to you." Again, she curtsied, gave an impish smile, then skipped away, toward Todd and the outdoor bar.

Patricia and I never did talk again that evening. It would be Lexie Helms, the librarian, who would reconnect us. I never did catch up with Stew. The two women had stood, Stew stood, in fact, everyone had been standing, clapping, and then the mingling. And then, his somehow slipping away. I meant to ask Dr. Bill about this enigmatic man, but just as I was about to, Tillie and Tom came over. I started to gush over their wonderful playing. Then, tired and hungry, it was time for me to leave.

A dark, warm summer night. I made only one wrong turn, finally got back on track, made my way into a Sunday-solemn and deserted Donelson. The Burger King was still open, brightly lit as the night sky held one last pink crease, like something leftover, a scrap. I bought a strawberry shake, a burger and fries. I snacked on the fries as I returned to Old Hickory Lake. It had been a wonderful afternoon and evening, a good weekend. I was more homesick than ever.

17

The next week was the final push of haying season. I don't think I knew this at the time. I was a soldier, pure and simple. I showed up. I obeyed orders. I worked. Hard. Almost as if it were a code of honor, to defy this "college boy" label, which in the South—the North, too—translated as lazy, entitled, spoiled. Not me. I was determined to be otherwise.

Walking the dried grassy earth, lifting bales, bending, twisting, grabbing taut strings, without gloves, one's whole body a slick sweaty muscle, more and more tanned, more and more muscular, I became a silent warrior. This was my surrogate battleground. This was my sweat, tears, bloody, raw hands. Not death defying but certainly, for me, it was fraught; it was my first real passage among men. Not college boys but men who worked hard, who made their living among these elements, who had no other life, and, apparently, no other choices.

For me, it was a hellhole. A strange new world—dark, hot, not spoken of, removed from the world of cars, offices, nice homes, "good jobs." It was a basketball scrimmage in a gym with closed doors, closed windows, no referees, few time-outs, and no scorekeeping; a football scrimmage, play after play, down a long grassy field that had no end, football field after football field, day after day; a baseball game from dawn to dusk, and running bases: running, running, running, around and around, without the crack of a bat, without a game-ending catch in deep left center. Because deep left center was just over the next hill. Once there, just beyond the ridge there, see? Then across that brook, through that row of trees, and up that next hillside. World, haying world, without end. Amen.

That next week, Monday and Tuesday were long days, the sun bright, strong, hot. Two of the hardest days we worked. Floyd met us at lunchtime, bought our meals, sat with us, smoked his cigar, rarely ate, and instructed Hub. Both days we started at eight a.m. and finished around seven p.m.

After work, I'd go into town, grab a Burger King meal, drive to the lake, take a swim, shower, sit by the lake, try to read or draw. Only briefly, since it was already close to nine p.m. and getting dark. If I wasn't too tired, I'd sit in Titine, doors open, and read by the car light. Both nights, though, I barely read a few pages. Soon enough, I'd set up my sleeping bag. I hardly lay down and I was lights out—no prayers, no musings, no nod to the starry night sky.

Wednesday, though, was different. Hub didn't show up. It was just Charlie, Russell, and me. Still the blazing sun, still Floyd as our luncheon chaperone. Now the instructions went to Charlie, who enjoyed being the leader. We worked hard that afternoon until Floyd came around at four p.m., told us we could call it a day. Which I greatly appreciated, three men doing the work of four was not easy.

That day, after lunch, Charlie had mentioned how Hub had a drinking problem. "Hub's a boozer," said Charlie.

"It's true," said Russell, "Uncle Floyd saw Hub before you got here. Man, he was hung over like a stump-broke cow. Floyd told him to go back home."

"He's probably gone fishin'. Hub loves to fish," said Charlie.

"Does he have family?" I asked.

"Dunno," said Russell.

"He's got family, sure. Hazel. Real good cook. Married thirty-six years."

"You married, Charlie?" I asked.

"Four years now. Met in high school. Married in Texas, after I got back from 'Nam. Worked there, then Arkansas, Oklahoma, Kentucky. Now Tennessee."

"Any kids?"

"Nope."

"I ain't married," offered Russell. "Never gonna be. Goin' to college on a basketball scholarship."

"How do you know?" I asked.

"Just know."

"He's *good*!" said Charlie. "I seen Russell play once. Plus, he's got all kinds o' clippins'."

"'Clippins'?" I asked. "What's 'clippins'?"

"You know, from the papers, photos and writin'. All about me, right, Charlie?"

"Thass right. He's got—how many colleges come lookin' for you, Russell?"

"Was twelve, now only three cuz I don't want but one school, and how'm I gonna decide?"

"What three?" I asked.

"UT, UT Knoxville, and Southern Illinois."

"Gee, those are all good basketball schools."

"I know."

"When do you have to decide?"

"This year's my senior year, then we'll see. But . . ."

"What?"

"I just don't like leavin' home. Wanna stay close."

"So, UT then. Right?"

"Yeah, but Southern Illinois's a real basketball school, and I really like the coach."

"So go there."

"I dunno . . ."

"What?"

"I get homesick real easy . . . and . . . people in Tennessee, they'll be upset if I leave the state. It's complicated. Which is why I'm not gettin' married either."

"Cuz it's complicated?" asked Charlie.

"Basketball isn't but women are, real complicated. Thass not for me, no thanks."

Funny, to be just now getting all this new information about all three of the men I'd been working with. I hadn't pictured Hub as being married but more of a loner, independent. And Charlie, with his dark good looks, broken front tooth, slick muscular arms and tattoos, I pictured as a rebel, a ladies' man, and probably a drinker. Russell, too, with all his whining, fawning over his Uncle Floyd, he seemed more like a brat-boy, favored and spoiled. I knew he was competitive from the way he'd race me to the next set of bales. And, his constant running about, shooting phantom hoops—into what I imagined was a farmyard basket—not some orange-painted metal rim against a glass backboard as they have on those big luminous college courts. All his carrying on I just saw as some kid's dreamy nervous tic, not a potential hoops star in the making. The rest of the week, I looked at each of them a little differently.

But this was still Wednesday, a hot one. We'd finished early, four p.m. Time enough to get into town, visit the library, get a decent sit-down meal at the Snack Shack, and get to choir rehearsal on time.

I left Langford's, went for a brief, refreshing swim at the lake, put on a clean T-shirt and shorts (I'd done laundry on Saturday), then headed for town. This time I had my letter to Kathy, the one I'd finally recopied, which included a few funny cartoon-like faces on the back. Sealed it and, at the post office in Hermitage, I bought stamps and mailed it.

I passed by the duck pond. I passed the father and daughter and their big grey cart with huge metal-rimmed wheels, full of vegetables and fruit. I almost stopped but I wanted some time at the library before it closed, and I didn't want to rush dinner.

Terri wasn't at the Snack Shack. I had a quiet meal, reading a bit more of *The Great Gatsby.* Choir rehearsal went well. Three good old church songs, which gave me a pang of heartache for my folks, especially my mom, who loves church so much, and church music. Then, I had a nice chat with Dr. Bill, thanked him again for his Sunday "soiree," and completely forgot to ask about "Stew." Probably because Reverend Bill popped in to say hi and thank us all for our service to God and the Church, and for our "lovely voices, which fortunately drown out my off-key sorry excuse for a baritone."

We all laughed. When he finished consulting with Dr. Bill, the Reverend came over to me, leaned close and whispered, "I'm serious now, come by one day, late morning's the best time, and we'll have a chat. It's rare I get a chance to talk to a bona fide artist. God's gifts must be appreciated. Come by, okay?" I told him I would and thanked him.

I walked into the balmy night air, looked up, greeted the bright white spray of stars, strolled over to Titine, and headed for the lake and a much-needed good night's sleep.

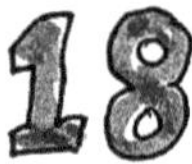

It was on the drive back to the lake that I happily replayed the highlight of the day: my visit to the Donelson Library. I didn't need another novel. *Gatsby* was going great, I was maybe a third of the way in and savoring it, so filled with summer light and sadness. But I did need another art book. I browsed the Art section: Edward Hopper, Van Gogh, Rembrandt, Matisse, a few old thick museum collections, the Metropolitan, the Prado. I pulled out the Matisse, the Rembrandt, and then I spotted a tall thin book of Giacometti drawings and paintings. I took all three over to a neighboring table and paged through them. Only one would go back to the lake with me: the Rembrandt.

After the art books, I began to doodle some ideas in my sketchbook, the nine by twelve, scenes from the past couple of days out among Langford's fields. I'd make small rectangular boxes, maybe six to a page, and then try to recall with a few lines, blocks of shading or cross-hatching, the various shapes of the earth—trees, roll of hills, droopy lengths of shadows—all in black ink, with scribbled notes on colors for the several that excited me as potential oil paintings.

I had my head bowed over the sketches, oblivious to everything else, my mind's eye and senses back among mown hay, sunlight, and the great swoops of Tennessee earth when a whispered voice, and then another, broke in, "Hi." "Excuse us, Mr. Brown from Connecticut . . ." I looked up. It was Mrs. Lexie Helms, eyeing me over her tortoiseshell reading glasses. Beside her was shy bespectacled Rosemary.

I smiled and said, "Hello."

"How're your books?"

"Good. Real good. Thanks."

"How come you haven't visited us? Rosemary and I thought maybe you'd fallen off the face of the earth, or gone back to Connecticut. Have you found another library? You don't like us anymore? Were you sick and bed-ridden? Locked in your car lo' these many days? A, B, C, All of the Above, None of the Above? Stop me when you hear something resembling the truth. I can go on, you know. After all, I am a librarian. I reside among vivid imaginations."

"I've been haying. Still am. See?" I showed them my callused hands.

"Oh," said Rosemary.

"Oh my," said Lexie. "No wonder you're so tanned. It's hard work, isn't it?"

"Hardest work I've ever done . . . and I love it."

"Do you? I got some windows need washing. How 'bout it?"

"Sure. I am no longer afraid of hard work."

"Were you ever?"

"Well, no."

"Say, this isn't Floyd Underwood's operation, is it?"

"In fact, it is."

"Now there's a character for you. I've heard he's got some big ol' pig farm, plus there's talk he's got an interest in several houses of ill repute in downtown Nashville."

"Really?"

"I heard that, too," said Rosemary. "But he's a sweet man. I met him once. He came in here looking for his nephew."

"Russell?"

"Believe that's him. He's got a bunch of family . . . the boy who's so good at basketball?"

"That's Russell. He's on my haying crew."

"*Your* haying crew? You running things now, Mr. Brown?"

I blushed. "No, I just mean—"

"I know. Be careful with all that. He's a very powerful man."

"Floyd Underwood?"

"So I'm told."

"Yeah," Rosemary nodded, several times quickly. "A few years back, Floyd Underwood was brought up on racketeering charges and prostitution, and there was some suspicion that he was connected to some murder."

"No!"

"Oh yes." Rosemary was excited. "But the grand jury couldn't find anything. All the charges were dropped."

"Wow." I looked out toward the darkening sky. "He buys our lunch every day."

"Just watch your backside, Mr. Brown." Lexie turned. Someone was calling.

"Okay, Sabrina," Lexie whispered back. "Rosemary dear, could you go take care of that? It's Mr. Steward on the phone. He's probably wondering about that book about the Easter Islands. Go talk to him, would you?"

"Sure, Lexie. Bye, Mr. Brown. Please don't be strange anymore."

"She means, 'Don't be a stranger.'"

"Oops. I do. Thanks, Lexie. Bye!" Rosemary's eyes blinked brightly as she waved and scooted off.

"Sweet girl but shy around young men. Now then . . ."

"Yes?"

"I don't mean to pry but this isn't the first time I've noticed. Is this a sketchbook?"

"Yes, ma'am."

"You an artist or something?"

"I am an artist or something."

"Which is it?"

"An artist."

"Come on. For real?"

"Yes, ma'am."

"Don't 'yes, ma'am' me. Can I see?"

"Please, have a look."

She did. I offered her the seat next to me. She almost sat, thought better of it, and then just stood, turning pages. "Oh my . . . I like that one . . . and that . . . and—good God, these are very good . . . You're really an artist, aren't you?"

"I want to be one, yes."

"No, my dear boy, you are one. These are as good as anything I've seen in our museums around here . . . Oh, I like that. Is that Old Hickory Lake? Very nice. Oh, I know him. That's, what's his name? Sound asleep. You know."

"Stan. His name's Stan."

"Yes! A rough kind of man. Been through a lot. His first wife died very sudden. He took it hard. Hasn't been the same. I do think he's very lucky to have that Terri, she's a real sweetie."

"You know everyone in Donelson, Mrs. Helms?"

"Just about. Listen. These are good drawings. You're a very fine artist. I got two sons. Mike's thirteen and Samuel's your age, a little older, going to be a dentist. Why don't you come have dinner with us one night, would you like that?"

"I'd love it. Thank you."

"Which night?"

"Oh."

"How about next Monday night, before the week gets away from us? This one's just about done."

"Alright. What time?"

"How about a half hour after the library closes, say, six-thirty? Is that good?"

"Great. Thank you."

"Could you do a pen and ink of my boy Mikey? I'd pay you for it."

"Oh no."

"Oh yes, and maybe on big paper?"

"I have a fourteen-by-seventeen-inch sketchbook."

"As big as that, could you?"

"I could."

Then Lexie waved over to the check-out counter, and in a loud whisper, "Rosemary! Come have a look! Is that okay, Mr. Brown, artist from up North in Connecticut, can she come look?"

"Of course."

Rosemary came over, said she'd taken care of things with Mr. Steward, ooh'd and ah'd as Mrs. Helms showed her the sketches as if she'd done them herself.

It wasn't until I was remembering and savoring all this, cruising along to the lake, the moon out now, that I realized they'd been talking about Mr. Steward. Enigmatic, shadowy, and so far, an evanescent and slippery phantom figure that had me shaking my head, kicking myself.

Why didn't I think to ask about him? As I pulled into my parking slot beside the small, grassy knoll. I kept laughing as I brushed my teeth and readied for bed. I looked into the restroom mirror, nodded to my dimly lit face, shrugged, said to mirrored self, "C'est la vie." That's life. And, so far, this was my life.

19

The next morning I woke up tired and dragged through the day. My eyes felt heavy, my head in a dull fog. I didn't really shift gears until we gathered the first load, when I broke into my first real sweat. It has to be said again: summer in the South is a constant swelter, a great giant maw of hot breath, like a quicksand of heat. No place to hide. The brief cool-off at lunch was the only respite. That, and with the hayrack emptied, the ride back to the fields, or even better, that final ride of the day when the body eases up, slows, knows it won't be asked to do any more.

It was good to have Hub back, captaining the hayrack. He seemed in good spirits. No mention was made of his absence except when I overheard him proudly tell Charlie that he'd "caught three rainbows. That lil lake is a trout goldmine. It's real good fishin'."

With Hub in fine form, our work rhythm was fully restored. We were once again "a well-oiled machine," the sweat pouring from us like spilled motor oil.

At the end of this second week, I remained an observer and listener. I hardly ever initiated a conversation except to ask questions about haying or, sometimes, just where were we exactly? I never asked what kind of hay this was, a fine sweet grass. Alfalfa? Still don't know. Except that by the time it had dried, was baled, and we were lifting those sixty-pound blocks, it was a heavy, stiff straw, that could prick you, stick you, bite you if in any way you handled it without enormous strength and respect.

While I remained reserved, my college-boy glibness put on hold, I appreciated that each of these men had begun to loosen up and reveal parts of himself. How Russell was so afraid of those "complicated women" although you could tell he really wanted a girlfriend. Charlie's big beef was his wife. "She's always talkin' about babies and family and how she's goin' to gimme a big bright shinin' boy but she don't get pregnant, Hubber, and that makes no sense to me, y'know?"

Charlie never spoke about Vietnam or fighting or killing. You could tell he had a very dark, perhaps even violent side to him. But he had a tenderness, too. When Russell mentioned an older cousin of his who had been killed in 'Nam, Charlie nodded and got real quiet, said he'd heard about Russell's cousin. "He had a reputation among the Marines. He'd been a brave soldier, a steady and good man, who fought well, and, I don't care what most folks say about 'Nam, he did not die in vain."

There was never really any in-depth talk about things, just these asides, more like anecdotes or told as jokes, especially in regard to women, work, or money. Even Vietnam was never really talked about, though it did stay in my thoughts. Once, Hub joined in, spoke of his service in World War II. Also, how Floyd had never fought in Korea but during WWII, he'd been part of the military police in the local Nashville Reserve.

"He had that 'MP' patch on his arm all the time," said Hub.

"But he never fired his gun, right, Hub?" asked Russell.

"Dunno."

"Cuz he used to show it to folks, he told me," continued Russell, "and laugh. He even admitted he hoped he'd never have to fire it cuz he didn't really know how to."

"I don't believe that," said Charlie.

"Thass what he said, right, Hubber?"

"Might've. Floyd's clever that way. Relaxes folks by makin' jokes on hisself."

Both Hub and Charlie kept harping on Russell to finish his education, go play basketball in college. Don't go to war, don't be a fool.

"But you fought, Charlie."

"I had no choice. Besides, I got lucky. You, you got a real opportunity, Russell."

"But I ain't no sissy. I believe in my country."

"War isn't about being a man, Russell," said Hub. "Coward or hero, you can still be a fool."

"But Charlie was no fool."

"I'm not sayin' Charlie's a fool."

"Hub's right, Russell. I'd've been a fool if I knew what I know now and what you know and had the opportunity you have," said Charlie.

"It's one thing to fight a man who slaughters Jews. It's another thing to fight poor farmers in a far-away country who done nothin' to me or my kin. If you love fightin' and killin', go. But you don't need war to make you a man. Just tryin' to live a good, decent life'll do that. It's hard enough," said Hub.

Talk of military service always made me nervous. I was glad they never asked me. I'm sure they assumed that, because I'd gone to college, I was less likely to be drafted. Although, my last two years, they'd reinstalled the draft, and I'd drawn a low number—51. And yes, I wrote my CO papers; yes, I didn't believe in organized killing; and then yes, my acne got me declared 4F. Still. I did feel somewhat guilty. Among these men, including Floyd, I did question my manhood, even though I agreed with Hub, "Going to war is not how you become a man." Or how you prove you're a man. Still, I also felt I was abandoning a good number of the young men of my generation. That summer and the three summers before, since 1967, really, my big question was: why was I given this particular life, this destiny?

Why was I Garry Brown, sitting by a lake, making pen and inks, baling hay, and not Charlie, say, or my friend, Joe Pantalone, who did join the Marines and died, not in battle but, of all things, while he was taking a long overdue R and R in the Far East?

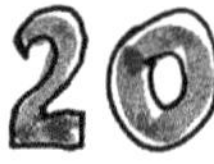

At Friday's lunch, Floyd was waiting for us as we pulled into the Ranch House Market. Charlie parked the hayrack truck in the shade. We clambered into the deli, Russell, as ever, leading the way. I changed things up with a BBQ sandwich, a bag of chips, a large peppermint patty, and a root beer.

Outside, even Hub sat with us at the picnic table. Russell and Charlie did most of the talking. As usual, Floyd paid, then slowly strolled over to our small party and stood nearby. He smoked a cigarette instead of his cigar while he sipped a cream soda and looked off. I watched and listened as Russell taunted Charlie. Hub sat on my side, looking out toward the two-lane road, a cornfield just beyond that. There was the hum of cicadas, electric wires popping and clicking now and then. I smelled gas fumes from the nearby fuel pumps. The air conditioner kept up a steady clattering and whir.

I'd finished my BBQ and chips, was half done with my root beer, and started to unwrap my peppermint patty when Floyd flicked his cigarette butt into the grass and said, "Slide in, wouldcha?"

"Sure, Mr. Underwood." I was now seated between Hub, to my left, and Mr. Underwood, to my right. "You can call me Floyd, son."

"Yes, sir." I ate small bites of the patty. The sweetness of the mint and its small sting combined with the crumbling, melted chocolate darkness tasted very good.

"'Bout to finish up here," said Floyd.

"Yes, sir."

Floyd looked off to the cornfield, as he spoke in a low, hushed tone. He folded his hands before him and leaned on the table with both elbows. Not once did he look my way, but his mouth seemed to twist in my direction. I knew they were completely different men and yet, Floyd still reminded me of my dad. "You like this work?" asked Floyd.

"Yes, sir. I do."

"You done real good. One of my best workers."

"Thank you, sir."

"I'm not just blowin' hot air. I mean what I say."

"Yes, sir. I appreciate that." And I did. The college kid in me was thumping his chest and beaming. I'd done it. I'd held my own.

"Whatcha gonna do when we finish up here?"

"Well, I'm not really sure yet." I wasn't. I thought I'd sit by Old Hickory Lake, draw pictures, go to the library. Find another job. Try to make a few more bucks. I didn't need much money. This summer was about other things, still being discovered.

"Well, I got some ideas."

"Oh?"

"Good ideas, you might be interested in. I know these ideas are interested in you. Wanna hear?"

"Yes. Please." I now looked at Floyd as he kept facing toward the road. Three crows had landed in among the second row back of those six-foot-high corn stalks. A thin line of perspiration trailed down Floyd's left temple, toward the white collar of his short-sleeve linen shirt. The crows in the cornfield began to caw. A truck backfired as it pulled to a stop in front of the first gas pump. All of us, except Floyd, looked over as the truck gave a shimmy and rattled before the engine fully turned off.

"Well," began Floyd. He pulled out a pack of cigarettes, took one and began tapping it on the picnic table, just the way my dad did. He put the pack away, pulled out a boxy silver lighter, flicked its top open, the lighter's flame flashed. Floyd held it to his cigarette, flipped the top closed, put the lighter back in his pocket. Then, just like my dad, with his fingers he carefully picked out a few bits of tobacco off his tongue. He sat there, slowly dragging on his cigarette as he continued to watch the cornfields and the crows. "I got this pig farm."

"Yes, sir?"

"I don't got a lotta pigs. Not yet. But it's a good bidness. Pigs. Lotta people don't understand or know that. But it is. Pigs are good.

They eat all kinds o' garbage and shit. They don't need a lotta grooming or nothin' but you get yourself a good crowd o' pigs, they get good and big, you got yourself some good hard cash. Bacon, pork loins, y'know, tenderloins, good for barbeque. Y'see? Barbeque is real big in the South, y'see?"

"Yes, sir."

"Well . . ." Floyd took a nice slow draw on his cigarette and just as slowly blew a big shaft of smoke up toward the tree limbs above us, rounding off toward the road and cornfields. Then, "I wanna expand my bidness. Get more pigs, a lotta pigs, really get things going. And. I need a man. A strong, smart young man, like yourself. I pay good money. A lot better'n this haying crap. A whole helluva lot better." Floyd took another short drag, blew it out quickly, then turned, looked at me for the first time, which was startling, almost intimidating, and asked, "Does this interest you?"

I watched his eyes as they focused on me. I turned away, as if to fend off this invasion. "Well, Mr. Underwood—Floyd."

"Yeah? Whaddya think?"

"Well . . ."

"Yeah?"

"You mean, I'd be like the foreman of your pig farm?"

"Thass right! Precisely. Couldn't think o' the word. Thass it. Foreman. Be my right hand. The lead guy, my *foreman.* Whaddya think?"

"I dunno. I like haying and all."

"Go on. Tell me your thoughts."

I didn't know my thoughts. My gut feeling was: No. A pig farm? Are you kidding? I was flattered, in a way, even kind of touched. This seemingly cold, indifferent and powerful man thought enough of me, my work ethic, my athletic strength, and, without any more words between us (this was our first real conversation) than a "hello," also presumed I was intelligent. Which I appreciated. But. Foreman of Floyd Underwood's pig farm? It would be a job, a program, an agenda, a steady, daily demand. But no, I thought. I can't do it. Certainly not after thirteen years of education: schedules, assignments, bells ringing, alarm clocks, basketball practices, basketball games, numbers, letters, dates, papers—demands, constant and unremitting, even at times, unforgiving. This was finally my time. I wanted to be careful and wise as to how I used it. Spend it. I wanted to be an artist, a painter, which takes a lot of time. A different kind of time. I couldn't tell Floyd this, though. That'd be like telling him, "Mr. Floyd, you see, I'm an alien from Outer Space and I gotta get back to Mars." Also, Kathy and I still had plans to go to Europe in the fall. Floyd didn't need to hear about that, either. That'd be like saying, "This summer here in Donelson is just a lark, a What-I-Did-Last-Summer experience." Which, at first, perhaps, it was. But now it wasn't. It had changed. I was looking forward to sleeping in. I'd have enough money to keep me going for a while. There must be other work I could do. A foreman of anything, be it pig farm or hay crew, meant commitment, daily showing up, hard work, and demands. Which, if I said yes, I'd be hidebound to honor. But I didn't want to say simply no, outright. I didn't want to hurt Floyd Underwood's feelings. And when I told him no, I wanted to give a decent explanation without any college-boy glibness. Oh, I'm off to Europe. Oh, I'm just here to taste life, see another part of the world before I go back North and do my real life. What I'd been doing was a few weeks of good, hard work so that I could have more time to not work—at all—and just draw, paint, read, and write some, too.

Floyd smoked, sipped his cream soda, both of us still looking out at the cornfields and those noisy crows.

"Well, Mr. Underwood—Floyd."

"Lookee here. We got lots o' work to do now. You think about it, sleep on it. We'll talk end o' the day tomorrow, y'hear?"

"Yes, sir. Fine. Thank you."

Floyd slowly rose up, flicked his cigarette off the grass and called, "Okay, men. Let's go." Before he moved on, Floyd leaned back toward me and said, "But I do believe you'd make one hell of a pig farmer. I really do. But you think on't."

"Right. Thank you."

As Floyd walked away, the spell now broken, I realized that things had quieted. Hub had just been sitting there, picking at his teeth with a toothpick. Charlie and Russell, on the other side of the table, though seated with their backs to us, had stopped their feisty banter. As we dropped our wrappings, napkins and soda bottles into the big outdoor trash bin, it occurred to me that all three of them had been listening to this intimate discussion, privy somehow to my inner thoughts as well. A flush of embarrassment raced through me, that I seemed to be chosen, as if I were "more" and they were "less," this invader from the North.

That afternoon was long and hard. No one made remarks or commented. I was left alone with my thoughts. I considered Floyd Underwood's proposal as if it were a real consideration, but I knew it wasn't. I knew in my heart of hearts I had no real interest in pig farming. I was flattered, and I appreciated having the rest of this day, the night, and most of the next day to appear to consider it. But it was only that, an impression of serious consideration. At least I could give Floyd Underwood that.

21

Saturday evening, close to seven p.m., we finished filling up Benson's barn with the final load. The end of a long hard day, end of a long hard week. End of the haying season, too. I asked Hub as we hopped onto the hayrack, heading back to Langford's farm, if it was really over?

"It's over," said Hub as he nestled into his corner. Before he ducked into the front cab with Charlie, Russell called out, "Don't think so, Hubber. Floyd says he's got some other work, west side o' Nashville."

"Maybe so but these farms be done," Hub spoke toward the cab window where I could see Russell silently shaking his head, smiling back at us, wagging a scolding finger, No, No, No.

My body still ached. I held tight to the wooden rack and enjoyed the ride.

It was a nice long ride, maybe five miles. Lumpy fields, bumpy dirt roads, long curves, a few twists, one old wooden bridge over a low trickling thinned-out river that sparkled and wove bright bracelets of water and light before we joined the paved roads.

Evening birds were making their runs from barns to trees and back. Evening calls, evening rounds. The cicadas were now less hysterical, their mid-day, hot-day histrionics slowed to a steady, gentler kvetching. All the smells, too, and all the final flashes of sunlight.

The smell of hay, cut grass, was still dominant, but the earth, that pekoe tea-colored earth, that earth-smell mixed with certain summer flowers. I didn't know their names. Were they roses, hyacinths, hibiscus? The smell of hot tar, too, melted by the hot sun, or had a crew been out patching pieces of the State Road?

Floyd, his bulky silhouette, stood on the hillside among the nearest of Langford's fields. He was smoking one of his cigars, stayed facing away from us as we pulled in. He looked out across the rows below of checkerboard fields, a few fallow but most of them trimmed, now turned a tattered dried yellow.

Charlie parked in among the other machinery and our parked cars. The four of us left the hayrack as it coughed once before the engine finally cut off. We made our lumbering shuffle over to where Floyd looked ready to raise a baton and orchestrate the final notes of the setting sun's brilliant red-orange chorus.

"Have a seat, gents," said Floyd, puffing smoke, as he pulled out his cigar, looked at it, tapped off some ash.

A low wood-paneled flatbed was propped near us. It'd be used to eventually haul the baler off to the next work site, if there was to be one this summer. For now, it became a bench for me, Hub, and Charlie. Russell sat on the grass between Charlie and his uncle Floyd. I watched Hub's face as Floyd began to talk, pulling from his linen shirt pocket the thick folded bills of our money.

Herbert known as Hub. His darkly tanned face, neck, forearms. His short-sleeved white shirt, mussed, grass and dirt-stained, under his blue bib overalls. His big thick dark leather boots, mud-cracked, worn but not stiff. Hub's dull stare toward Floyd, or was he looking beyond, at the shift of light and clouds as the sun set? What would become of this man, married thirty-six years, and did he have children? Grown kids by now. For a few weeks we were fellow workers, almost brothers, though either Floyd or Hub could have been my father. Same age, late fifties.

But Hub never tried to father me. He watched me, he listened to me the few times I'd speak up. He'd join with all of us now and then. One afternoon, on a water break, he took a string, wrapped it around an old red brick and showed us how a brick could twirl and dance. What did this man think? Did he love his life? Did he hate it? Charlie claimed he was a drinker, but I saw no torment in him, no discontent. Yet, there was melancholy. A man, who perhaps had hoped to do other, bigger things with his life, had surrendered, settled for this simple work life.

Charlie sat there hunched over, his left arm propping up his head as his right reached for pieces of grass, straw, that he'd flick toward the back of Russell's red hair.

Charlie with his Vietnam past, his young wife, their nomadic travels, tracking work. Where would they end up? The tattoos on his left bicep, right forearm: a voluptuous woman on the left with the name "Margie" under it. On the right, a long thin arrow, a big black arrowhead point, a feathered end. It ran parallel with his forearm, the word "Scout" printed along its middle. It must have had something to do with his role as a Marine. He was one of the men who went ahead, into those Vietcong tunnels, preparing the way. If he survived, he'd report back. He was one of the few who always reported back. Scout. Now he worked the farms through mostly the Southern states of America. A hired hand. For now, like a pestering big brother to the lanky red-headed Russell.

Russell, sitting Indian-style, kept his eyes on Floyd and the slow unfolding of crisp bills. Russell, always playing up to whomever was in authority. Be it his uncle Floyd or Hub. With Charlie, he could be prankish and silly as well as the idolizing little brother; he had great respect for Charlie, his having been a vet, a warrior, a real man of the world. I think he would've remained indifferent to me had he not seen me one afternoon, our haying work finished, seated in the grass near the machinery doing a pen and ink. Russell came over, saw the drawing and seemed mystified, even dumbstruck. "What is that?"

"It's a pen and ink drawing," I said, not looking at him but staying focused on the scene before me.

"But . . . that's these fields, right? That's Floyd's backhoe there," Russell bent and pointed at it in the drawing, "right?"

"Yup."

"But . . . you did this?"

"Well yeah, I'm doing it."

"You mean, like an artist or something?"

"Or something. Yeah."

"But . . . it's just . . . you're doing this right now, right? That's not from a picture book or nothin', right?"

"Right."

"It's like . . . real."

"Pretty real. Except it's a drawing."

"No. This is real. I see it. I see the fields and the trucks and the baler, too, and then I look down and, man, it's just black ink that . . . it like keeps coming from that pen, right? And . . . but you're doing it. And it's real. I see it."

"I hope so."

"How'd you learn that?"

"Good question. When I was young, I used to draw cartoons like from Superman comics and then I just kept doing it. I stopped when I was in high school but then I started again in college."

"You can stop and start like that?"

"It seems."

"But what makes you do it?"

"What makes you shoot hoops?"

"Hoops? I just like the feel of it."

"Same thing here."

"But . . . how does it come out like that?"

"How does the ball go in the basket?"

"Okay. It's something you do and don't do . . . it's a feeling and then everything else just takes over."

"Yeah, Russell, that's it."

After that afternoon, Russell and I both looked at each other a little differently. We were still very competitive while we were working, but sometimes he'd suddenly turn to me, right in the middle of a row of hay bales, look out across the fields below and say, "That's a nice view, isn't it?" Or, "What about doing a picture in colors, like those fields and clouds and sky and such?" Also, he began to watch me at the end of a workday. Everyone packing up, getting in their cars, he'd call out, "You think you might make another picture?" I'd look over at him. It was a sincere question. I'd nod and smile, go pull out my sketchbook and wave it. And Russell would wave back as he and his Uncle Floyd drove off.

22

Floyd showed us his penciled pieces of paper, his stick figure calculations, which he then pocketed. He placed his cigar on the left edge of his mouth, tilting his head away from the spray of grey smoke, as he tried to eye the packets of bills he'd finally, neatly formed. "Alright then," Floyd began, fingering the folded packets, in front of him, as if his large middle were a kind of table. The sun was low in the big expanse of sky. Shadows were long, with bright tufts of cut grass catching in bright flickers, like flames, the last sunlight. "Alright, Hubber, you done good work. You know I appreciate your steady leadership. I put in a little extra, for you and Hazel."

"Thank ye, Floyd. Much obliged."

Then to all of us, "So, fellas, I'm sorry but we gots no more work for a spell."

"But, Uncle Floyd, you said last week—"

"Russell, hush. Last week is a long time ago in farming. Here, take your money."

"But—"

"Here."

"Thank ye."

"You're welcome. Charlie?"

"Yes, sir, Mr. Floyd."

"You done real good, too. Wish I could find a way to keep you on. Right now there's not much. But, before you move on, whyn't you check back with me over't' The Florence. Okay?"

"Yes, sir. Thank you." Charlie took the folded bills from Floyd. I found out later, The Florence is a hotel not too far from downtown Nashville. Supposedly, one of the flophouses Floyd is part owner of.

"And, son . . ." I must have looked at Floyd rather quizzically because he continued with, "Yes, I'm talking to you. Here you go." Floyd waved the folded bills. "You done real good and, I think we need to talk, am I right?"

"Yes, sir. Thank you."

"Alright then. Thank ye, men, thank you real much." Floyd came toward me with my money in one hand, his cigar in the other. I stood. Hub nodded toward me, began to walk off. Russell swatted at Charlie's head, then dashed away. Charlie stood, stretched. As Russell circled back, Charlie gave a sudden shoulder shift, as if he were about to give chase. Again, Russell ran off, with a little whoop. Charlie slowly strolled toward Floyd's white Caddy where Russell now hovered. Floyd and I were about to meet but I felt as if I wanted to catch Hub before he got away. I watched Hub, all alone, steadily make his way toward his pick-up.

"Well then," Floyd said as he got near. Hub was in his truck now. I wanted to call his name or stop him. I could see him turn his head as he began to back out. "Here's your money, son. Good work."

"Thank you, Mr. Floyd."

Hub's truck was on the dirt drive out of Langford's, dust kicking up as he slowly shifted gears. Good-bye, Hub, I said to myself. Why was this upsetting me so much? Hub was gone. Would I ever see him again? Floyd stood before me, cigar in his mouth. He then turned away, gave a puff as he pulled out the cigar and called, "Russell! Be there in a minute, got some bidness to attend to."

"Okay, Uncle Floyd." Russell and Charlie were shadow-boxing next to Floyd's white Caddy.

"Ain't that right, son. We got bidness, don't we?"

"Well, Mr. Floyd . . ."

"Say now, I don't like that tone. Not at all."

"I know. Look, sir. First, I'm very flattered and I really appreciate your asking me to work your pig farm."

"Not work it. Be my *foreman,* remember?"

"Right. I thank you for considering me, for asking me but—"

"It'll pay much better'n this. I can help you with housing, find you an apartment or house."

"Thank you, Mr. Floyd."

"This is a real good offer I'm making."

"I know, sir. I mean no offense."

"No offense taken."

We both stood there. Floyd looked at me as I darted a look toward him, then began to eye the ground. Floyd looked off, across the shadowy fields.

"So, 'no thanks' you're tellin' me?"

"Yes, sir."

"Alright then. You take care." Floyd put his cigar in his mouth. We quickly shook hands. He hardly looked at me as he abruptly finished our handshake, grabbed his white kerchief from his back pocket, wiped his face and back of neck, turned and quite sturdily trudged over to his car. Russell was next to Floyd's Caddy, jumping up and down, repeatedly shooting one, then another, of his phantom jump shots. Charlie leaned on the passenger-side door, between Russell and the car, smoking a cigarette, looking off, as if completely unaware of the imaginary basketball game in progress.

I stood for another moment and watched the hay fields among the lengthening shadows. When I turned to slowly follow Floyd's path, and then head over to where Titine sat quiet in the shade, I saw Russell get in the driver's side and begin to pretend-drive while Floyd and Charlie, both smoking, talked intently face to face. I couldn't catch all they were talking about but I did hear Charlie's voice get excited and the words "pig farm."

I wasn't sure what I'd do that evening. I bent over Titine, looked into her grey, white, and black interior. I was also very tired. No energy. No desire. Then I heard my name, "Hey! Hey, Garry! Yo!" I pulled away from Titine, stood up, and looked over toward Floyd's white Caddy, all pink now in the fading sunlight. It was Russell. Charlie was walking off, headed for his banged-up Chevy Impala. Floyd had just started up his Caddy. Russell stood by the passenger side, had been about to get in when he'd called to me, first time I'd ever heard him say my name. "Sure is a beautiful night. You gonna make a picture?"

"Maybe so, Russell," I called back, "maybe so!" I reached into the back seat of Titine and pulled out my big sketchbook, the one he'd seen me drawing in before. I raised it high overhead and waved it.

"AWRIGHT!!!" He laughed and waved back, then descended into Floyd's white Caddy. Floyd reached out his window, flicked cigar ash, then turned away as he backed out, lined up the Caddy in the dirt drive. Suddenly, explosively, spitting gravel and dust, they roared off. Charlie moved his shiny blue Impala into the long dirt drive and followed. Both autos steadily crunched through gravel and dirt, trailing whirls of small brown clouds, until they reached the thin strip of tarmac, glistening a shimmery blue in the fading sunlight.

The hills were getting cool, dampening. Dusk was beginning to catch up with dimmed sky. How was I going to do a drawing in this light? And, did I really want to?

I felt a sudden emptiness. I could see the sky becoming bruised, a much darker blacker blue and, a first star. Way off below was an answering blue, away from the hillsides of farm, fields, down to the gradually lit-up homes surrounding the mirroring waters of Old Hickory Lake.

I could stand there, try to figure out once more where in that distance was the small hillside and curb where I nightly parked Titine, my sleepy pasture. I could listen as the small birds began their free-for-all, chattering and skitting about, joined by bats, making their runs among trees and barns. A dog's bark way off, a bit of a howl. A pick-up's steady thrum as it moved past Langford's, its lights on now, indifferent to me, this figure in a hayfield.

I missed these men already. I missed Durl. I missed Kathy. I missed my folks back up in Connecticut. And then, I didn't. I felt a buoyant night-time freedom. I was in the world, and of it, and not. I was here, just here in this dampening ripe-sweet earth of hay field, and then, I wasn't. I was everywhere, among those small lit houses below, along the blue streak of road leading to other roads, leading to town, the town of Donelson, leading to other towns, leading where? Just where was all this taking me?

An owl. I heard an owl. I began to cry. I was a child, a lost child, and, I was a man, almost a man. And I was lost, so lost.

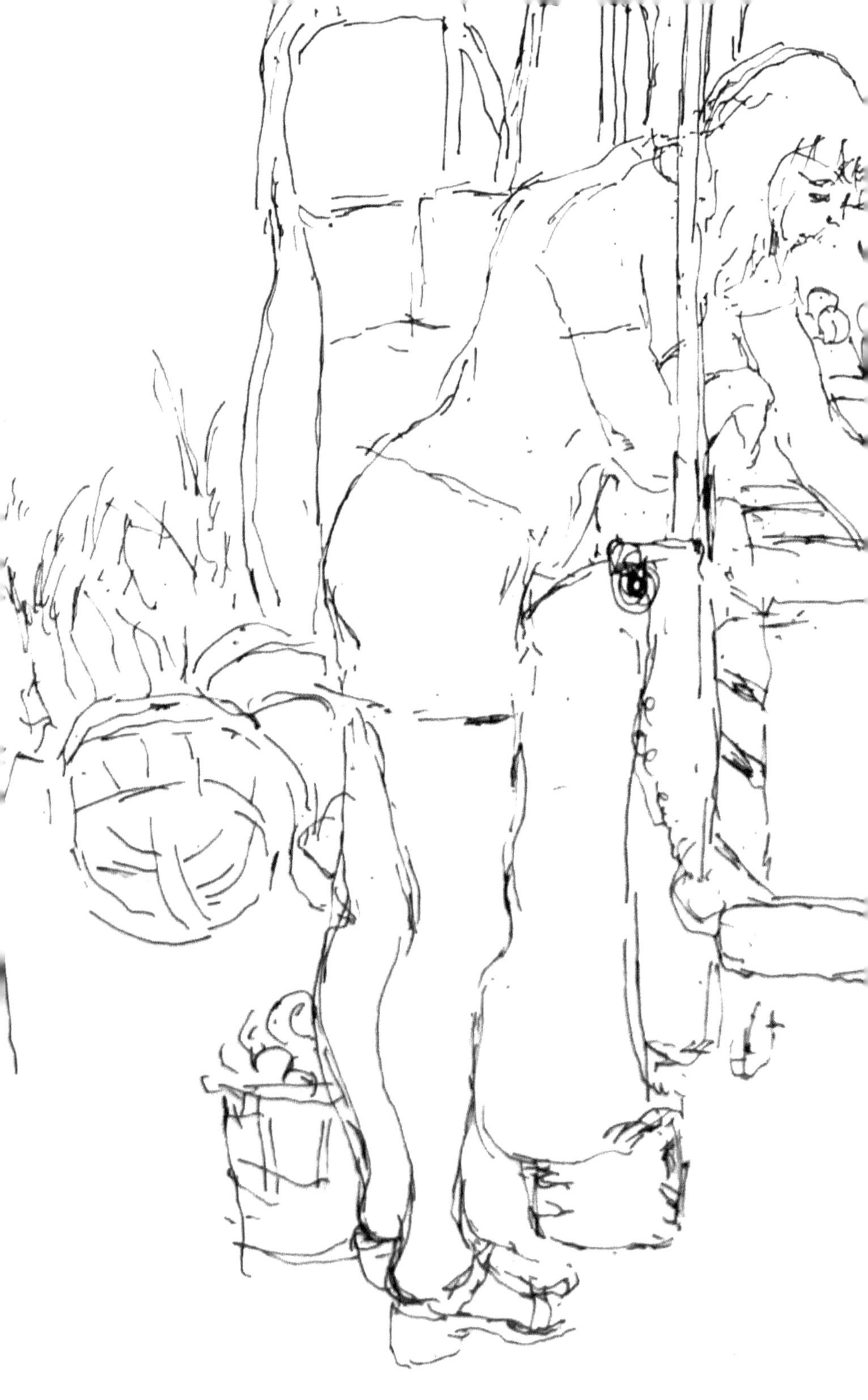

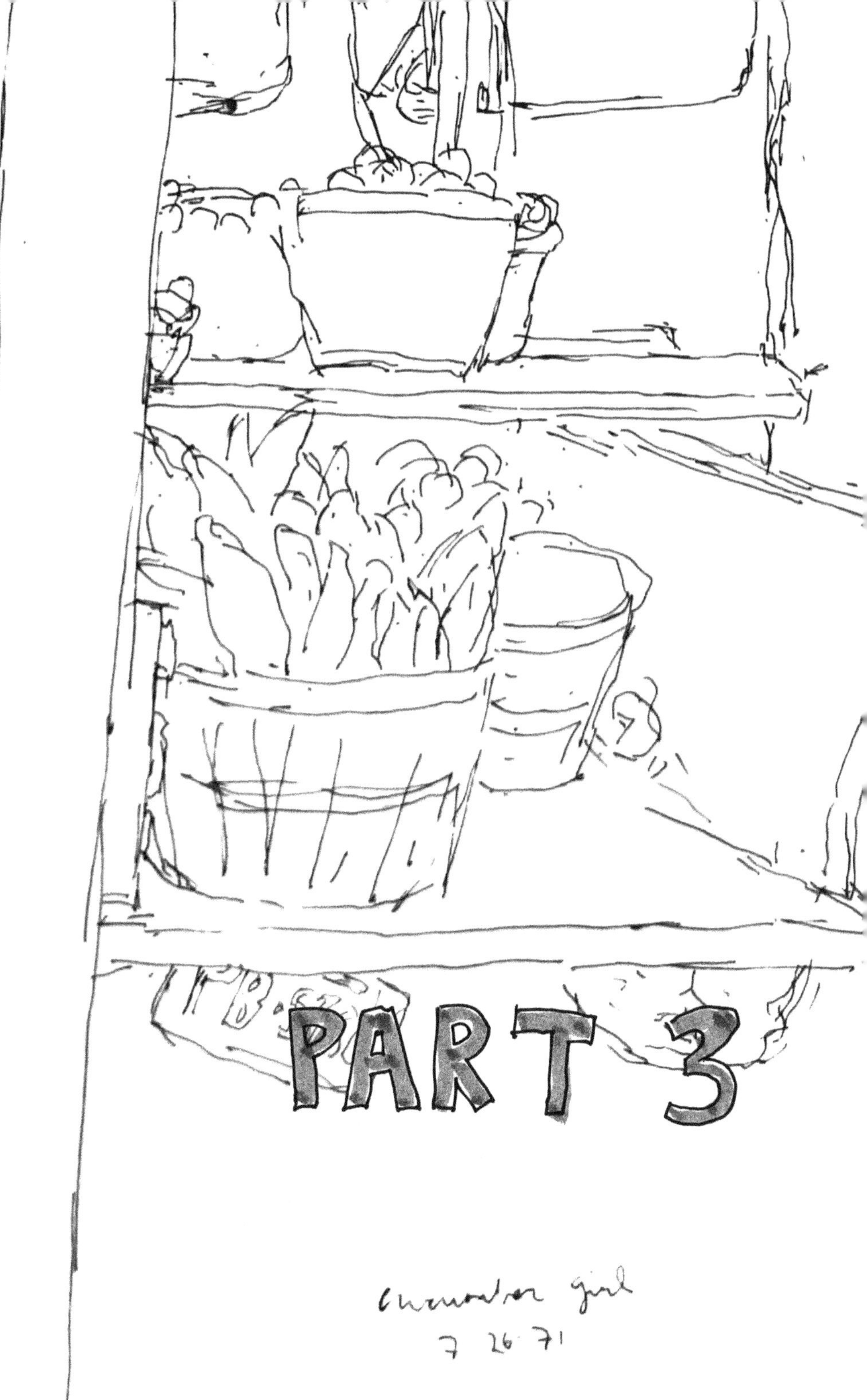
PART 3
girl
7 26 71

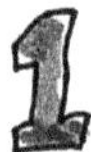

It was Mrs. Lexie Helms, the librarian, who had suggested I get a PO box and where. It was she who'd said, "Open a bank account. You'll need it." She recommended First Bank of Nashville, "Good folk work there. Talk to Bobbie, she'll take care of you."

So, I did that, too. In fact, I opened that account with the cash (almost fifty dollars) I made working the hayfields. I did that late Monday afternoon, before I returned a few art books to the library. Where I browsed some; borrowed a tall, thin book on Matisse, and then followed Mrs. Lexie Helms around to the back of the library, past the parking lot, across an imaginary border where her lawn and a few bushes edged into the library tarmac, and marched up the back stairs into Mrs. Lexie Helms's home.

And, it was in Lexie Helms's home that same Monday, early evening, the summer of 1971, in Donelson, Tennessee, that I had my first home-cooked meal since leaving Connecticut. She seemed to soften a little bit in her own home. A softer voice, a gentler tone, an attentive homey ease.

It was a real home. A two-story house with a big yard that backed into the library parking lot, the afore-mentioned bushes, a couple of tall trees, and then, off the small front yard, her driveway with a two-car garage. Her kitchen had that warm, steamy intimation of cooking while through the open window, I caught hints of fresh-cut grass. I looked out, saw that it had been recently mowed.

"Have a seat," Lexie said as she pulled on an apron. "My oldest, Sammy, is upstairs studying. He'll be down in a minute. Mikey's in the garage, putting the mower away. He knows I'm home. He doesn't ever miss a meal. You wanna soda?"

"Sure. Thanks."

She opened the fridge. "I got Fanta, 7-Up, Coke, ice tea,

lemonade. Name your poison."

"Or, we got beer, too, Ma. Offer'm one of my Buds." A young man leaned into the kitchen.

"Now, Sammy, he's not quite your age yet. Don't wanna corrupt him."

"Ma, come on. Hey, I'm Sam. nice meetin' ya."

I liked Sam immediately. He wore a short-sleeve shirt, khakis. He was tanned, open-faced, smiling. We shook hands, I said hi. Sammy pulled a beer from the fridge. I had the Fanta orange. We'd just started sipping our drinks when Mike clumped into the kitchen.

"God, Mikey, don't you know how to walk like a regular human being?" said Sam.

"Look who's talkin'," said Mikey. "Mom, do I have time to wash up?"

"I expect so. Don't dawdle."

Lexie was in the shadows, moving among oven, stove top, crockery, and plates. A few bowls had been pulled from the fridge and placed in the oven. She began to chop carrots on a cutting board as she talked. "Hope you like chicken, Brown."

"Oh yes," I said.

"Barbeque version, Ma? That's her finest." Sammy nodded to me.

"You'll see. And, you'll eat it happily. I hope."

"Your mom said you were upstairs studying," I said to Sammy. "I thought school everywhere was pretty much over, or is this summer school?"

"Naw. Exams. I'm done with my studies. Going to be a dentist, and this is the big exam that'll get me my degree and allow me to finally become a Doctor of Dental Medicine."

"When do you take it?"

"In ten days."

"Is it hard?"

"Not really."

"Sammy's bright. He'll do well. Although he gets nervous whenever he has to take a test. Any kind."

"I do not."

"Sammy. Remember your SATs?"

"Oh God, Ma, that was years ago."

"And, senior year of college, you got all worked up during finals."

"Well . . . this won't be a breeze, but I love dental medicine, so, you know, I think I'll do alright."

"You'll do fine," said Lexie. "Where's Mikey?"

Lexie wiped her hands on her apron, quickly exited the kitchen and called out, "Michael? Dinner is being served. Come now, please!"

From upstairs, through halls and walls, in muted tones came Mikey's "Okay, Mom, be right there!"

It was a great meal, so good it made me homesick. Barbeque chicken done in a casserole pot in the oven, Lexie's own homemade French fries, peas with tiny white onions, corn on the cob and a wonderful fresh salad with carrots, big hunks of tomatoes, and small pieces of toasted bread and Thousand Island dressing.

We three guys did very little talking, mostly just ate. And ate. And ate some more.

Lexie ate slowly, quietly, asked a few questions, and seemed pleased as she watched us devour her meal. The final triumphant touch was dessert. Lexie placed before us a freshly baked blueberry pie. Each slice was served warm, with creamy vanilla ice cream on top. As we finished our desserts, Lexie began to talk to her sons about my artistic gifts.

"You mean you just make drawings?" asked Mikey.

"Paintings, too," I said.

"Not *just* drawings, Mikey," said Lexie. "It's quite something to be able to draw a likeness. Make a person feel another person, not just their face but, like you could hear them or know them."

"That's a true art, a real gift," added Sam, nodding and watching me.

"Where's your sketchbook, Brown?" asked Lexie.

"In Titine."

"Titine?" asked Mikey.

"My Peugeot. My car."

"Could you go run and get it? Show these boys instead of all this talking?"

"Sure."

"Don't worry," called Lexie as I departed and hustled down the back-door steps. "We'll save your seat. Maybe even some more blueberry pie, too!" I waved back as I crossed the dusk-lit lawn. Titine sat quite alone in the library's front parking lot. I grabbed both the medium and larger sketchbooks and jogged back. I could see the boys' faces in the window and the shadow of Lexie hovering as she cleared the table. I knocked on the back door.

"Don't knock. Just come in, Brown," called Lexie.

As I placed the sketchbooks on the table, I wondered where Mr. Helms was but didn't think it polite to ask.

"No, Mikey. Stop!" said Lexie, pulling the smaller sketchbook away from his curious, eager pagings. "You can't just rush through his drawings like that."

"It's disrespectful," added Sammy.

"That's right. Really look. It's not television. This is art, real art," admonished Lexie.

So, Sammy led, slowly, the big sketchbook first. Mikey got up and came around and watched beside his mom. I resumed my seat and watched from the side. All three remained quiet, slowly paging, now and then, Lexie would point, Sammy nodded while Mikey would look at the drawings and then kind of quizzically look at me. Very little was spoken.

"God, wouldn't your daddy love these?" They continued to page on through. I wished I'd had another sketchbook so I could make a drawing of them, a mother and her two sons.

"He's probably in Memphis by now," said Lexie.

"Who? Daddy?" asked Michael.

"Who do you think, knucklehead?" Lexie gently swatted Mikey's brown crew-cut hair.

"I dunno." Mikey had Sammy turn back a page as they both lingered on the pen and ink of Stan asleep.

"Their daddy's a railroad man, Brown. An engineer. Some kids dream of trains, he actually went and did it. From here to Memphis or then to Knoxville. All over the South. A good man but he's gone a lot."

"Too much," said Mikey.

"But he loves his work, which makes him good at his work," said

Sammy as he finally turned the page. "And a happy man."

"A lucky man," added Lexie.

"And lucky for us," said Sammy, who moved Mikey's hand so he could continue to turn the next page. "Except that we miss him."

"A lot," said Mikey pushing Sammy's hand away.

"So, Brown, what if you did a pen and ink portrait of Mikey?" asked Lexie.

"Sure," I said, carefully balancing some ice cream with a generous spoonful of pie.

"How much you charge me?"

"Oh, nothing."

"No, really. What would it cost? Haying's over, right? You can't live off thin air. How much?"

"No idea."

"Brown, it's time. It's your gift. Thirty dollars? Fifty?"

"I really don't know what to ask."

Sammy spoke, was very intense, leaning toward me, shaking the sketchbook, "I don't mean to butt in. This is Mom's thing. But, you're a professional."

"I hope to be."

"You need to ask a good price. Just like when I become a dentist. People are paying you for your abilities and experience."

I looked at Sammy, then to Lexie, then Mikey. "How does twenty-five dollars sound?" I was a little squeamish. Was I asking too much, seeming ungrateful?

"Sounds good. When can you start?"

2

I started. And finished—that next afternoon. Mikey had summer camp. Lexie said he usually got home around three p.m. I popped into the library, said hi to Lexie and thanked her again for the wonderful dinner. She quietly smiled, officiously nodded, eyed the big clock where we stood at the main counter and said, "It's after three. Michael should be home. You gonna go now?"

"Yes, ma'am, if that's okay?"

"By all means."

"Great. Thanks again, and for this, too." I waved my ink pen and nonchalantly headed out the glass doors.

"Wait. Where's your drawing book?"

I turned, nodded to the parking lot. "In Titine, all ready to go."

"Okay. Good luck!" We both waved and I was off.

Mikey was playing catch with a friend on the Helms' lawn. It was sunny with a nice gentle breeze. Mikey caught the ball in his glove, then held the ball in his right hand, fingering it, then juggling it as he called to me, "We gonna do it now?"

"If that's okay with you."

"I guess. This is my friend, Perry. Can he watch?"

"Sure. Perry can watch. Where you wanna sit?"

"At the picnic table?"

"Great. What picnic table?"

Both boys looked at me as I looked over the length of the empty yard, and then both laughed.

"Around the side, over there, is the picnic table. Come on. Come on, Perry, he said you can watch."

"I dunno." Perry stood there, suddenly shy.

"He said it's okay."

"Yeah. But."

"It's just a drawing, Perry."

"I dunno." Perry watched Mikey, then looked down. He wouldn't look at me.

"Perry, you want to see some of my drawings?" I held out my sketchbook toward him.

"Well . . ."

"Oh yeah, I wanna see, too," said Mikey, running over.

"Okay," said Perry, "I'll look."

"Why don't we sit at the picnic table and look at them?" I suggested.

"Okay," said Mikey. "Come on, Perry."

"Okay." Perry slowly followed Mikey over to the far side of the house. He still kept his head bowed down as he dragged his baseball mitt along with him. His shyness looked kind of mopey.

The picnic table was in the small side-yard just off the side of house and two-car garage. We were paging through when Lexie appeared. "How's it going, boys?"

"Pretty good," said Mikey.

"I'm on a short break. I'll get you boys some drinks. Lemonade sound good?"

"Very good, Mrs. Helms," said Perry.

"Some cookies, too?"

"Yes, thank you, Mrs. Helms," said Perry.

"Good. Be right back."

Perry watched as Mikey continued to turn pages. I sat opposite and watched them, every now and then pulling away to consider what might be a natural pose for Mikey, a positioning that was both comfortable for him to hold for twenty minutes, and that said a little about who he was. A person's physical posture can tell a lot.

"Here you go." Lexie had a tray, with drinks. "Don't eat all the cookies, Michael. Let your guests have some. Besides, I have a nice dinner planned."

"Yes, ma'am."

"Well, I'll leave you boys to it. Do a good drawing, Brown. Bye!"

I sat watching Mikey, as if staring but, now with my sketchbook opened to a new page, I was looking at Mikey and picturing how his figure might fill the white space. I'd look down at the blank page, then back up to Mikey and how he sat there.

"Are you doing it now?" Mikey leaned forward and put both forearms on the red-stained picnic table.

"Can you hold that, Mikey?"

"Hold what?"

"Are you comfortable?"

"I guess. Hold what?"

"That position, just like you are?"

"Okay. Can I scratch my nose?"

"Sure."

Mikey rubbed his nose, then returned his right hand and folded it back into his left, interlacing the fingers.

"Great. That's great. Hold that, okay?"

"Okay."

I started with Mikey's hair, the outline of his head. I would do his head, hairline, outline of his ears, down along both sides of his neck, even outline where his neck moved into the wrinkled seam of his navy-blue T-shirt, down his short sleeves into his forearms, then outline the hands folded in front. Then, I went back and began Mikey's face, his brow, eyebrows, that spacing, into the nose and mouth, and then, the most challenging part—his eyes. (Or, anyone's eyes. Get them right and all else can be forgiven.) The eyes went pretty well.

Perry was now sitting at the picnic table, next to Mikey, leaning in, his head resting on his raised right arm, like a person thinking. Only, he'd keep watching Mikey, then look down at my hand moving atop the page, pen and ink flowing, slowing, then moving. Perry was an inquisitive mirroring of my process of drawing: intent watching, then back to the page, drawing, intent gaze, back to the drawing, and so on.

Mikey, too, would look down and watch his image slowly emerge.

"Mikey?"

"Did I move?"

"It's okay. Just for a few minutes, I need you to keep your head up, your eyes on me, okay?"

"Okay . . . does it look good so far?"

"Pretty good."

I put the last bit of ink in Mikey's eyes: they were big, brown, with wonderful sparks of light that gave Mikey his youth and his kind of wry, indifferent sense of humor.

Perry got up from the picnic table. He stood to my left and watched. "Where's the house?" he asked. He pointed to the white space surrounding Mikey's figure. "I see Mikey but where's the house behind and the yard, right?"

"Right." Slowly, I filled in each section, to Mikey's right, over his head, and on the left, just hints, bits and pieces, of lawn, shadows, house shingles, door-stoop, rosebush.

Perry placed his hand on my shoulder and said, "That's enough."

"Enough?"

"Now it makes sense."

"Thanks, Perry."

Perry kept looking at the drawing, then over to Mikey, until very gently, he leaned over it and said, "This is very good." He touched its edges and watched it, as if he had said the words to the drawing.

"Can I look now?" asked Mikey.

"Sure . . ." I started to stand with the pad but Perry scooped in. "Let me help, okay?" He carried the pad as if it was a platter of delicate glassware, slowly marched around the table, and laid it in front of Mikey. "I look like that?" asked Mikey. "I smirk like that?"

"Yeah, you do that little smirk smile. It's really you. It's a very good likeness. Really!" said Perry.

"Okay, Perry!"

"You don't have to get mad, Mikey."

"I'm not mad. Okay?" They both stared at each other. Perry fingered the drawing. Mikey swatted at Perry's hand. "Don't, you'll get it dirty."

"I just like it. It's a nice drawing."

"It's my drawing. Get your own."

"Maybe I will."

"Good."

"Fine.

I retrieved the pad, reviewed the drawing, added a few more lines to the shingled shadows of the house, the lawn. I signed it in the lower left corner, parallel to the planes of the red picnic table, "G.M. Brown" and printed next to it, "Michael Helms" and the date, "6.30.71."

Not long after, Sammy came home, driving a small metallic green compact. "Hey, Brown, or should I call you Rembrandt?" Mikey and Perry fought over showing Sammy the drawing. Sammy looked at it, smiled, nodded, as if he knew it would be very good. We got to talking. He lived at home to save money while he studied and worked at a hardware store: "Hardware biz, good—dental work'd be better." He didn't like it. But it helped him pay his grad school bills and car payments.

Then Lexie returned after closing the library, loved the drawing, and talked me into staying for dinner, said she had an idea. Seems she had several ideas, one of them concerning Sammy's girlfriend, Courtney, "When're you gonna marry that girl?" Mikey and Perry giggled and joked with Sammy about "Courtney and Sammy up in a tree—K-I-S-S-I-N-G." Sammy just shrugged.

Perry's mother phoned. Perry had permission to spend the night and go to day-camp with Mikey in the morning.

"And," said Lexie, "think we're going to get you another commission, Brown," nodding to Perry. "But first, how much for an oil painting of my Michael?"

"What about me?" joked Sammy.

"All in good time, Sam. First, I wanna see how Brown does with oils. How much?"

There was a bit of haggling, back and forth. Not with me. Between Lexie and Sammy. Money and arguments: $175, said Sam. Professional. Respect. Don't sell yourself short. Or, $150, continued Sam. Too much and folks around here won't go for it, said Lexie. A reputation. Worth, said Sam, and again . . . Respect. $100.

"Seventy-five seems fair to me," I finally joined in.

"Brown," said Sammy.

"I don't need a lot of money."

"Sammy's right. You can't sell yourself short. But."

We all sat for a moment staring at our empty plates (Tennessee BBQ or what we call Sloppy Joes up North, all gone. Delicious).

"Can we have dessert, Mom?" asked Mikey.

"Sure, boys, sure." Dessert was ice cream and homemade chocolate chip cookies.

Finally, agreed: $75 for an oil portrait of Michael Helms.

"How big, Brown? Bigger than the pen-and-ink?"

"I was thinking twenty-four inches by thirty-six inches."

"That big? Really?"

"Sure."

"When can you start?"

3

We started that Thursday, worked some on Friday, too. Mr. Helms came home that Friday night, so we took the weekend off. Michael sat for almost a week.

The days, and nights, too, were now different. The intensity and complete immersion in the haying work was now over. I now had my days, and, of course, the nights, too, were mine again. I did not go to sleep so exhausted, though I was still a little lonely. Living beside Old Hickory Lake, and sleeping under the stars, were a comfort. The days had small routines but no overall plan or organization. I'd go to the library, say hi to Lexie on my way to spend those afternoons, after Mikey got home from camp, painting. It felt good to mix oils again—pigments, linseed oil, turpentine. I've always loved the mixed smells of oil paints, turp, linseed oil, and the faint whiff of grass and earth, a ripe octane mix which enabled me, in my idolatrous and inflated way, to feel close to Van Gogh, Pissarro and, of course, the great Monet as well as Corot, all of whom loved to paint outdoors.

I'd also been receiving mail in my Old Hickory PO box. Durland. Kathy. Mom.

I was curious about Reverend Bill's invitation to come visit and talk. It was also during these new mid-summer days that I met Thomas, the Donelson Library custodian, as well as the attractive would-be writer Sheila.

Funny, how you hope for mail, something every day, and then you get a bunch of letters all at once: Durland sent a postcard with a photo of Niagara Falls. He'd visited his aunt in South Carolina, stayed a week in Darlington, but was now looking for a job in East Aurora so he could be near Brooke while she took some summer school classes in science, "and I might have to stay in a furnished room!" Which made me laugh and remember all we went through before we ended up sleeping under the stars.

My mom sent a long, newsy two-page letter with a crisp ten-dollar bill folded inside. Everything was fine. They went for a weekend cruise on Herb Cleaves's forty-two-foot "yacht," as she called it, over to Long Island. Grandma Gertrude (her mom) was in a nursing home in Danbury, near my Aunt Roberta and doing fine. Sandy and Judy were going to drive East in August for Dad's birthday on the twenty-second—"Could you come home then, too? We miss you and love you. Your dad is out mowing the lawn, so he *really* misses you. Love ya, Mom." Everyone in our family, even Dad when he rarely wrote, signed off with "Love ya."

It was Kathy's letter that sent me from the post office into the late morning with a light step and a hopeful, dreamy heart: she had a summer break from camp, two weekends from now, could she fly into Nashville and come stay a few days? *What? Are you kidding me?* I started skipping around, blew kisses to the big heavy-set post-mistress, Emmy, and then in the car, I started crying. Then, I reread the letter:

> *I love camp this summer, Gar. I have more responsibility than I've ever had but that's okay, maybe even good. I can't be a flake like I often am. I have to set some rules and follow them. I love these kids. They're, all of them, so full of life and funny. Our counselors are a fun bunch, too. A few nights ago, we had a big campfire for the kids and counselors. We all made s'mores and sat around telling ghost stories. I have to say, I was very surprised when Kink (Greg Kinkel, you know) told this really scary ghost story. He's always so shy. I didn't know he had it in him. Anyway, also that night, a bunch of us counselors all went into town after, which was fun, just to get away. And be silly. And goofy. A few got a little tipsy but mostly, it was nice to get away and not have to be the adults for a change. Are you sleeping beneath the stars? And what have you heard from John? I hope you have made lots of drawings and paintings and I hope I get to see you real soon. I have a summer break coming up in two weeks. Could I fly into Nashville and stay for a few days? Save me a cozy spot under that big dark Tennessee night sky, okay? I'm blowing you kisses, Kathy.*

I sat there in Titine, picturing Kathy and Kink and the big campfire and the trip into town. A moment ago I was so happy. Now, I was suddenly confused and kind of glum. A big plump hand opened the post office glass door. It was Emmy, peeking out. She spotted me and called, "Hey, Garry, you okay?"

"Oh yeah."

"You were so happy a minute ago."

"Yeah, well, I just started thinking about some things."

"Oh my, you mustn't do that." Emmy closed the post office door, went back inside.

I continued to sit there. Picked up the letter. "I'm blowing you kisses, Kathy."

She had never said, "I love you," or signed a letter, "With love, Kath." No heart shape. No Xs and Os. None of that. And now just, "I'm blowing you kisses, Kathy."

But she'd written a four-page letter (both sides of two sheets of Camp Agawam stationery), which meant she cared. She was thinking of me. Other guys seem to not want so much, remain cool, indifferent. I didn't know how to do that. I loved her so much. I wanted her to love me just as much in return. It was uneven. Unequal. It hurt. But. She wanted to come visit. She was coming. In two weeks. And, that's where I finally landed and rested. I started the ignition. I'd be okay.

4

I wanted to drop by the Methodist Church, see if I could finally have a visit with Reverend Bill. The First Methodist Church on a Monday morning looked different, even strange. The church parking lot was deserted but for two cars parked at the far end, nearest the back entry. I parked near them and went looking for the church office. It was a few doors down a quiet, shadowy hallway on the left. To the right, in a row, were a small church library, a few classrooms, and then a big room with tables, chairs, and a long sill shelf beneath a row of windows that looked out on grass, a small grey wall and then, houses, trees and yards beyond.

I'd brought from Titine's trunk my almost-forgotten and stowed away Olivetti portable typewriter, thinking I might find a spot to type up some letters—to Mom and Dad, Durlie, Kathy. Maybe Grandma Gertrude, too. And, my sister Carol, who I always worried about a little. That big room with such a nice inviting row of windows and so much light would be ideal. I was also considering one of the picnic tables over at the duck pond, or maybe I'd just wait and do it at my concrete picnic table back at the lake.

But it was hot outside now, steamy, and this big room was so cool, quiet, inviting. When I heard a woman's voice calling, "Reverend Bill? He's on the phone now," I stopped my exploring.

I went back across the darkened hall. The linoleum floors gleamed. The door to the church office was open. Inside was a bright mix of office fluorescent and sunlight. A woman sat at an L-shaped desk. She listened for a moment on a phone which she then very carefully hung up, slowly placing it down. She then swiveled to face me as she fluffed her dark black hair. "Howdy, I'm Marlene. What can I do you for?"

We shook hands.

"Nice to meet you, Marlene. I was hoping I might visit with

Reverend Bill."

"Is he expecting you?"

"Not really. We spoke last Sunday. He urged me to come by and have a talk. So . . ."

"Okay. Look. He's on an important phone call just now. You mind waitin' a minute?" She pointed to three wood chairs and a small plastic pink and white loveseat nestled in the corner across from her desk.

"Sure."

"Want some water?"

"No thanks. I'm good." I started to sit, then had a thought. "Could I go browse in the church library while I wait for Reverend Bill?"

"The church library?"

"Across the hall. All the religious books?"

"We got a library?"

"I think so."

"Show me." Marlene came around from her desk.

We were at the door. "Which way?"

"To the right. That door down the hall on the left."

"Oh, that's the children's library."

"Okay. Maybe I'll go have a look while I'm waiting?"

"Sure. But, well, let me see, too." As she entered the library, she flicked on the light switch, then led the way, going to the first bookshelf on the left.

"I think this is a library for adults. Coulda fooled me."

Then, from down the hall, "Marlene? What's going on?" Marlene grabbed my arm, gave a squeal. "Oh, Reverend Bill!" Reverend Bill's tanned face and full head of white hair poked in at the doorway. He wore a black shirt, black slacks, and a white collar.

"I'm sorry, but I couldn't find you. Heard voices and, who's this? Mr. Brown, our resident artist?"

"Hi, Reverend Bill." I went to him, we shook hands.

"Marlene, you can't leave like that without letting me know, remember?"

"I know, Reverend Bill." She flounced her hair as she slipped by us and started down the hall. "It won't happen again, but hey," then she paused to pull down her blue skirt, "I didn't realize we had such a sophisticated church library. Pretty impressive!" She pulled at her blouse and continued down the hall.

Reverend Bill muttered, "This library's always been here, don't know what she's saying." Then he turned back to me, still holding my hand with both of his, in a gentle but firm handshake.

"So, you've finally come for a visit." He continued to hold my hand and with his other, now moved it up to my shoulder. "Good, good. Shall we sit and talk a moment?"

Still holding my hand in our now frozen and somewhat uncomfortable handshake, he took the other from my shoulder and pointed over to the wood chairs by the windows.

"Sure," I said, carefully slipping my hand out of his. "Thanks."

Once we both sat, I expected we'd have a fairly lengthy visit. But, not so.

"Oh wheee," Reverend Bill let out a big gasp of air. "Feels good to get away from that office and the phone ringing nonstop."

"Busy day?"

"Mondays are. I've been here seventeen years and, people who care about God and worship and the affairs of the Soul and the Word of God, always have a reaction to my sermons."

"I like your sermons."

"Do you?"

"I like how you mix the Bible passages for that Sunday with things that are concrete and real in our daily lives."

"Well, thank you, Garry. Now then, how are you gettin' on?"

"Pretty good, thanks."

"You're a long way from home. Where in Connecticut?"

"Darlington. Southern Connecticut, about an hour train ride from New York City."

"Ah, the Connecticut suburbs."

"Yes, sir."

"I grew up in the Chicago suburbs, went to college in Knoxville, did my seminary in North Carolina. Was a kind of nomadic substitute minister for a long time until I was offered this church seventeen years ago."

"So you know the North."

"Don't miss those Chicago winters."

There was a pause. Reverend Bill eyed his watch. Then, we both looked to the doorway. We could hear the clopping of brisk heels on linoleum. Marlene leaned in at the door. "It's Mary Wolfson, Reverend. Shall I take a message?"

"Oh gosh, she called earlier, told her I'd call back and forgot. I'd better take it. Tell her I'll be right there. Thank you, Marlene."

"Yes, sir." Marlene smiled, sculpted her hair with her right hand as she pushed off from the doorway with her left and clopped back down the hall. Both Reverend Bill and I stood up.

"I'm sorry. Mary Wolfson's in her eighties now, a wonderful spitfire of a woman, one of God's sturdy souls, and I do need to talk to her. But, don't rush away. Browse our little library if you like. Perhaps not as sophisticated as Marlene thinks but a few classics, a few of the latest faddish Rah-Rah religious propaganda, too, but you might find something. Please."

"Thank you, Reverend."

"Another time we'll get into things, alright? Art and philosophy and such . . . later in the week is sometimes better. I write my sermons on Wednesdays. I do hospital visits on Thursdays. Things are often slower on Fridays and Saturdays."

"Okay."

"Ministering and being an artist, I've always felt they are kindred callings. Look at Van Gogh, right?"

"Yes?"

"How he wanted to be of service, to serve something Greater, right?"

"I suppose so, yes."

"I'm curious about your journey, the quest you're on. So, we must really talk some time, okay?"

"Definitely."

"Good." Reverend Bill came over and again took my hand in both of his. "God bless you and keep you, Garry. And keep singing in our choir! We need your good strong voice!" He started out the door.

"Oh, Reverend Bill?"

"Yes?" His face turned very serious. He didn't like his exit or last lines to be interrupted.

"Might I ask a favor? That long room down the hall, with the tables and chairs? I have a portable typewriter and was wondering if I could sit in there and write a few letters?"

"The big room? With the long row of windows?"

"Yes, sir."

"I don't know why not. Help yourself. If you need anything, typing paper and such, just ask Marlene."

"Great. Thank you."

He started off, waved and called over his shoulder, "The Lord be with you, and your letter writing!"

I stayed in the church library for about twenty minutes. I was surprised to see *The Courage to Be* by Paul Tillich: it was a worn, rough-edged paperback with the same criss-crossed orange and grey cover, much like the copy my mother had in among her books of religion and Dickens and the red volumes of Jules Verne that my dad's family had passed on to us. There were a bunch of children's books on God and the life of Jesus as well as a hard cover version of Keith Miller's *Taste of New Wine,* which had made such a strong impression on me when I read it the spring of my freshman year at Amherst. I paused a moment, paging through it, as I considered whether I might want to reread it. Then, no, I was almost done with *Gatsby.* I wanted another novel, perhaps Thomas Wolfe's *Look Homeward, Angel,* plus the art books and my daily Bible readings were keeping me pretty well-read. I put the book back, went out to Titine and grabbed my typewriter and small sketchbook.

In the cool shade of the long church room, I opened one of the six big windows, the one nearest me, about a foot. I set up my typewriter. A nice warm breeze wafted over me as I reread my mail. Probably should write Mom and Dad first. Or, maybe Durl. I'd save Kathy for last, maybe even wait and think about all I want to tell her. I was homesick and lovesick. Then, after typing letters to my folks, Grandma Gertrude, and Durlando, I was very hungry. I went to find some lunch. Snack Shack or Burger King or a new place?

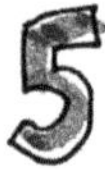

I had a BLT and a strawberry shake at a small diner within walking distance of the church. I was tired. I thought it'd be nice to nap out by the lake, take a swim, too, but to do all that and make it back in time to meet Mikey by three p.m., and resume his portrait, would make everything rushed. So, I drove up to the Donelson Library: if I was lucky, I'd be able to park Titine in the far corner of the front lot where there would be shade. I was lucky. One car parked nearest the street, the other shady portion still vacant. I pulled in, it was just two p.m., turned off the ignition, opened all the windows, tilted back my seat and took a nap. Well, I started to, then I decided to reread Kathy's letter. Then I looked at Durl's postcard again. Finally, I reread my mother's letter. Then I napped. I slept longer than usual.

I had first started taking cat naps in college. Depending on the season, I'd go to football or basketball practice, eat a big dinner and then head to the Frost Library to study. I'd find a carrel, fold arms, lower head and doze off for eleven minutes. The patented eleven-minute refresher nap. Pretty uncanny. I could then study for a pretty solid four hours. Now, I was doing it on these slow summer afternoons, a short revival of energies but, the eleven minutes often became fifteen minutes, and today it was almost a half hour.

When I awoke, I looked out the driver's side window, my eyes still blurry. I could see blue and grey, the look of water—but that couldn't be the lake, I was at the library. Then it all moved. It became Thomas's janitorial uniform. His dark face leaned in my window, and, in a deep bass voice, "She be askin' for you, Mr. Garry."

This was Thomas, the Donelson Library custodian. I first met Thomas about a week after I began hanging out at the Donelson Library. He was pulling a trash basket out toward the trash bins in the lower parking lot. I asked him if I might do his portrait.

He looked at me, said, "I don't think so," and shrugged. I wasn't sure he understood. "Thomas—you know what a portrait is?" He shrugged. "No, suh." It bothered me that he was twice my age and called me "Sir."

"Thomas, you ever see me in the library with my pen?"

"Your pin? Tough to find a pin in a haystack, Mr. Garry, let alone the liberry."

"You got that right."

We both laughed.

"Look . . ." I showed him my 11 x 14 sketchbook.

"Uh-huh."

I paged through it and slowly showed him the pen and inks.

"Dat's a nice book, Mr. Garry. The liberry gots this or you bought it?"

"No, Thomas, see?" I showed him the last twenty to thirty pages, which were blank.

"Oh. Dey cheated you, Mr. Garry. They dint print all of it. Too bad."

"No, no. Thomas, this is a sketchbook, see? I did this drawing . . ." I pulled out my Rapidograph pen. "With this pen, see?" Then, on the next blank page, I started to draw the front end of Thomas's big black work shoes, thick-soled, scuffed, the right one.

"See, Thomas?"

"What dat, Mr. Garry?"

"Your right shoe, see?"

He leaned in, I turned the page toward him. "Dat's my shoe?" He took a moment, watched it very carefully, then, "Why, shore 'nuff, Mr. Garry. I get it. That's my big right foot! Ain't dat somefin?!" With that, Thomas broke into a big shoulder-shaking laugh, with rich bass tones. I joined him, we laughed together.

"You an artist, dat it?"

"Well yeah, I want to be."

"No, suh. You is. You really is!"

"Thank you, Thomas. So, here's my question. Could we sit down one day and I draw your face, your portrait?"

"A pitcher o' me, Mr. Garry?"

"Like this one." I showed him Mikey's pen and ink.

"I knows him! Dat's Mikey, Mrs. Lexie's young son. Dat's good, real good!"

"Thanks, Thomas. Can I do a drawing like that of you?"

"No, suh. I don't think so, but thank ya." Thomas resumed pulling the trash basket over to the outdoor bins.

"It doesn't have to be today. Another day. When you're not working so hard. When things are slow, okay?"

"I dunno, Mr. Garry."

"Please?"

"Why you want me, Mr. Garry?"

"Your face, Thomas. You have character."

"Character? Dat's a person in a book, Mr. Garry. Not me."

"Thomas, I think you're being humble."

"I try to, Mr. Garry. Yes, I do." Thomas continued to wrestle the trash bins.

I walked away somewhat puzzled and defeated. Most everyone I met was interested, or at least curious to have me draw their picture. But not Thomas. This impressed me. I liked him all the more for his shyness, his modesty, his resistance.

Then it became a running joke. Whenever I'd see Thomas at the library, out front near the bushes, out back near the bins, or as he'd briskly walk past the stacks to the stairwell that led to the big downstairs room, I'd call to him, "Hey, Thomas, later today?" "I don't think so, Mr. Garry, but thank ya."

This called to mind a story I'd heard about Leonardo Da Vinci. There were days Leonardo would leave his studio, walk the cobbled streets of Florence and stop people, right there in the street, and hold them at arm's length, to survey this man's face, that woman's profile. Hold them silently, watch them carefully, seeing things: how the nose turned up, the shift of light in their eyes. Did they know him as a great artist? Was it his reputation, his fame? But he'd pick a person and lead this soul, who knew him or not, back to his studio where he or she would sit for the great artist. But why that man or woman? Why that particular face? Why Thomas?

Thomas was a sturdy Black man, not well educated but his face had such depth, even pain, perhaps. His eyes were clear, wary, a slight heavy-lidded-ness to them but not an indication of slowness as much as weariness. His dark brown skin always glistened; there were pock-marks from perhaps a severe case of acne growing up; his ear lobes were big, thick, but his ears were close to his head; his hair was black, a few flecks of grey along the sides, and a thick fine wiry texture of medium growth. A handsome face, rugged, careworn. When his eyes caught the light, his mouth in a shy curl, there was this wonderful impish grin, rare but always lurking. So, now, Thomas's big hand loomed. A woman, asking for me? "Mrs. Helms is asking for me, Thomas?"

"No suh, I mean this young lady over heres." Thomas swiveled away from me, his big hand slowly leading as if making a broad, flowing introduction.

There, curled up on the grassy edge of the parking lot, near the bushes and the path to the Shop-A-Lot, was a young woman in a white blouse and pleated navy skirt, her legs curled up under her as she leaned over a three-hole notebook, intently scratching a ballpoint pen across the midsection of a white page.

"Dat right, Mr. Garry."

"She knew my name?"

"She say to me, 'I lookin' for Garry, the artist, you seed him?' So I showed her your car and then we both seed you asleep. So she sat downs to wait. Then, I see youse startin' to lick your lips, blinkin' your eyes, rubbin' your face, so I come over to make introductions, y'see?"

"I see. I don't think I know her."

"Me neither, Mr. Garry. Mrs. Lexie say she from up North, too, and so sent her to meets you."

"Ah, good ol' Mrs. Lexie."

"Yes, suh. She's a fine lady."

"So . . . now what?"

"I don't knows. I'm just pointin' her out, Mr. Garry. I better gets back to it."

"Thanks, Thomas."

"Yes, suh, Mr. Garry." Thomas slowly moved off. The girl on the grass looked up at Thomas, called, in a sweet light voice, "Thank you,

Mr. Thomas." Thomas nodded, gave her a salute, and said, "Yes'm." The girl turned her look toward me. I nodded, smiled. Thomas was halfway across the parking lot. I called to him, "Hey, Thomas, you wanna sit for me later today?"

He stopped, turned and stood there, looking at me. I had Mikey to paint later today. What was I thinking? What if he said yes, called my bluff? In an impish drawl, Thomas called to me, "I don't think so, Mr. Garry." He turned and continued walking as he waved. "But, thank ye."

I finally emerged from Titine, strolled over to where the young woman sat, scribbling. She saw me and stood up to greet me. She was tall, thin, wore a flowery (reds, blues, greens) dress, which she straightened as she stood. She had dark eyes, almost black hair that hung to her shoulders, naturally red lips and freckles. The freckles helped soften what immediately felt like a sharpness in her.

"Hi. I'm Sheila Swift. Mrs. Helms said I should talk to you."

"Okay. Well," I offered my hand, "I'm Garry Brown."

"I know. Ooh. Your hand is rough."

"Really?" We both looked at my right hand as we released our handshake.

"You have some blisters. See?"

"Wow . . . I do."

"I thought you were an artist."

"I am but I just spent the last two weeks working on this haying crew."

"That sounds cool."

"It was. It was also hard work. I'd forgotten how roughed up my hands had gotten. Sorry." I shrugged and shook both hands as if they were wet and I'd gotten her wet and I needed to dry them out.

"No, it's okay. I like men who work hard."

I nodded. She quietly stared at my hands. Was she attracted to me? Why did Lexie want us to meet? She kept staring, now into the short distance, toward the cars in the parking lot. Well, mine and the other one, which the sunlight had begun to edge into. "I'm going to be a writer," Sheila said, still staring off.

"Oh?"

"I've wanted to be a writer ever since I was a little girl. Five or so."

"Wow. So, you've been writing for a long time."

"It really kicked in my last year of high school."

"Okay."

"Now, I'm over a year out of college and I still want it very badly."

"Right."

"I'm on vacation, visiting my aunt. I live in Baltimore, where I'm a paralegal. Well, an intern, really. My dad's law firm. Everybody either wants me to have a decent job or meet a decent man. My aunt lives here now, and she's the one person in our family who's always loved my stories and always encouraged me, and, I just felt I needed to see her again. I'm glad I came."

"I bet."

"Then my aunt introduced me to Lexie Helms. What a great lady."

"Isn't she?"

"When she asked what I was doing with my life, I told her that I'm working in a law firm but that I really want to write. Immediately she said, 'Oh, you should meet our resident artist, Garry Brown, also from up North.'"

"She said that? 'Resident artist'?"

"She did. She's quite fond of you."

"She's very sweet. She and her family have been very kind to me. Oh God! Which reminds me. I'm sorry. I've got to meet her son, Mikey . . ." I saw my watch, ". . . as of about fifteen minutes ago, to paint his portrait. Shit!"

"Oh. Okay."

"Nice to meet you, Sheila."

"But we need to talk. Don't you see? This is Kismet!"

I grabbed my sketchpad from Titine and began to walk. Sheila followed.

"Kismet?"

"Well, you know, meeting you. A real artist. How confused I've been and then meeting you, a person my age who is really doing it, you know?"

"I think so."

She stood at the top of the parking lot as I began my descent along the right side of the library, down to the lower lot and then across to the Helms'.

"So, how do I reach you? Do you have a phone number?"

I stopped and watched her. She was a little drooped now, deflated I guess, and loomed in silhouette above me as I called back to her, "I live out at Old Hickory Lake. No phone. But I always drop by the library. Leave a message there, okay?"

"When can we talk?"

"Oh gosh."

"I'm only here for a few more days."

"Oh. Soon then."

"Tonight?"

"I have choir rehearsal tonight. Maybe tomorrow?"

"Okay. I'll leave a note. In the library . . . with Lexie . . . with my phone number, okay?"

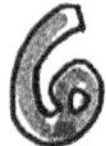

Once I turned and began to jog across the parking lot onto the Helms' lawn, I realized it: I'd just lied to Sheila. It wasn't a conscious lie. I really did think it was Tuesday, choir rehearsal night. But the words just spilled out. Why'd I do that? It was Monday, not Tuesday. Not a big lie but it was a lie. I didn't like lying. Dear God, what to do? I stopped part way across the Helms' lawn. I turned and jogged back to the parking lot and looked up. She was gone. I turned around and went looking for Mikey. No sign of life in the backyard. The back door to the kitchen was open. I called through the screen door, "Mikey?"

"Yeah? We're in the living room." He and Perry were like imitations of one another, both slouched on the big green plaid sofa watching TV.

"We thought you forgot."

"Sorry. But I'm here now."

"Do we have to do this?"

"Watch TV?"

"No! This portrait thing. We're tired."

"But it's not done."

"Can't you do it without me?"

"Well . . ." I paused. Oh God. Mikey's always been so willing. Then Perry popped up, said, "I'll do it!"

"Well . . ." I stood there thinking. That might actually work: I had Mikey's face painted in, almost done.

"You're not me, okay? It's *my* picture, dummy."

"Mikey, I'm not a dummy. I'm not."

Mikey looked at Perry, realized he was hurt.

"Perry, I'm just joking. Come on." Mikey slowly unloosed from the sofa. "We can do my painting now."

"Mikey, wait," I said.

"What?" They both sat up, looking at me.

"Go ahead and rest a little longer. I've got a small errand I need to run, over at the library, okay?"

"Okay."

"Be back in ten minutes or so and then we'll do the painting. Alright?"

They were both back eyeing the TV. "Alright."

When I walked in, no one was at the main desk. No sign of Lexie or the other librarians. I looked in on both sides of the library, in among the stacks, in among the magazines and sitting area, and then every nook and cranny where there were chairs, tables, displays. No one. No sign of Sheila Swift either. Maybe outside, on the grass, where I met her. Nope. I returned inside, to the main desk. Still no sign of Lexie but Rosemary was there. "Do you like that girl?"

"I'm sorry?"

"That Sheila girl, she left you a note. Do you like her?" Rosemary held out her pale white hand: between her two first fingers was a finely folded piece of notebook paper.

"She seems nice enough."

"I thought you had a girlfriend. In Iowa."

"I do."

"Then why are you fooling around with *her*?" Rosemary pointed to the note, adjusted her thick, black eyeglasses and wriggled her nose as if dealing with a bad smell.

"Rosemary."

"Yes?" Now she was all bright eyes.

"Um . . ." I was going to say how I didn't know this "Sheila girl" but why should I explain my life to peevish Rosemary?

"I didn't think you knew my name," Rosemary said, beaming.

"Of course."

"Yes?" Now she was a little too eager.

"Never mind. Do you know when she left this note?"

"I don't like her."

"Rosemary."

"Ten minutes ago. You just missed her. She takes herself much too seriously. She's ambitious. I have a feeling she eats young men and spits them out."

"Are you a writer, Rosemary?"

"Oh God . . ." She began to blush. "Please don't tell a soul. I write poetry. It's my passion. Only Mrs. Helms knows but she's sworn to secrecy. You must promise, too, okay?"

"Sure." I took a moment to look at her. Rosemary had a slight Southern accent but then she pronounced "privacy," not with a long "I" but with a short one, the English way of saying it. Normally I'd ask, is that an English accent I detect? But Rosemary was a little too eager to divulge that she didn't want to divulge, so I backed off.

"What?" she said.

"Your secret's safe with me."

"Oh, thank you! I knew you'd understand, being as you're such a gifted artist yourself."

"Why, thanks, Rosemary."

"Remember I saw your sketchbook that day you showed Mrs. Helms? Then, last week she showed all the librarians the pen and ink you did of Mikey."

"Oh?"

"Such a sensitive rendering. But . . ." She was making a face of such concern, her nose scrunched up, her brow moving into a frown.

"What?" I asked.

"It's just, I looked very closely . . . I couldn't find the pencil marks before you went over it in ink. You must erase very cleanly."

"I don't do a pencil sketch."

"You just do it in ink on your first try?"

"If I'm lucky, yeah."

"Omigosh. You really are good!"

"Thanks. I do make mistakes, but usually I can incorporate them into the picture. Also, around critical areas, like the eyes, I use smaller, almost pointillist strokes, so I can absorb little miscues more easily."

"Interesting. I'm not sure I understand. Maybe you could show me some time?"

"Oh sure. Which reminds me, right now I'm working on Mikey's oil portrait and he's waiting. I'd better go."

"Okay. Aren't you going to read your note? I'd keep an eye on her."

"Right. Thanks." I waved good-bye with the note. I was feeling a little overwhelmed, even exasperated, maybe even flattered, too. Rosemary's mother-hen boldness, that was a first; Sheila wanting to talk about writing and being an artist; Rosemary wanting to talk about not wanting to talk about *her* writing, yet so curious about my pen and inks; Mikey not wanting to sit for me today. Then a wave hit me of missing Kathy. I wished I could just go out to the lake, take a swim and sit for a while reading, and just do nothing. But the note. It was folded in quarters. Just as I reached the back stairs, I stopped and opened it:

> *Dear Garry, it was so nice to meet you.*
> *My aunt's name is Cynthia Hickson, her phone is 453-6603. I will be there tonight, tomorrow morning through lunch but will drop by the library by late afternoon. Maybe we could go for a walk or get a bite to eat tomorrow evening? If you don't call, I'll look for a note from you tomorrow at the library. Sheila.*

I didn't leave a note. I didn't phone either. I wasn't sure what to do. Mikey and Perry were in the Helms' driveway playing catch. Eventually, with Perry looking on, Mikey sat and I painted for a little more than an hour. I picked up a sandwich and soda on my way out to the lake. I sat at the picnic table, watched the sun set, and had my modest dinner. The place was deserted. The sun, in a great flamed burst, dipped out of sight and then the afterglow loomed for another good half-hour. I sat watching. Felt lonely. Waited for the stars to begin piercing the dusky cloak, the moon to appear.

Later, I sat in Titine and finished *The Great Gatsby,* hoping the car's small center ceiling lamp would not drain my battery. Then, across the damp night grass, I laid my sleeping bag in place and almost forgot to watch the night sky, I was so sleepy. But I did watch, and saw one star speed out of formation and, like a match lit and blown out, smear across the sky and fall. I took this as a sign of luck, good faith, and comfort.

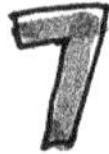

The next day, Mikey had asked if we could meet earlier than usual. He and Perry were going on a field trip with their camp into Nashville that afternoon, something to do with the Grand Ole Opry. So that morning, I took what I thought would be a shortcut. The road from Old Hickory Lake was a fairly straight line to the main road. Left to Hermitage. Right to Donelson. But there was a big bend in this fairly straight line where another road crossed it. By taking a right there, I was sure I could cut out a few minutes and come out on the other side of the library, near the road that cuts past the Helms' driveway and swoops out next to the other side of the Shop-A-Lot.

This "shortcut" swooped and cut and swung by alright but then it passed a few farms, a small creek, a good-sized and lovely tree-enclosed lake, and brought me to another bend in the road where a lone vegetable stand was nestled. It was an old, weathered, once green-painted wagon, stocked with tomatoes, potatoes, green peppers, carrots, corn, and fresh strawberries. No cars passed by at all. It began to feel as if the route had gotten much longer, not shorter. I was worried I was now going to be late meeting Mikey. There was a gentleman standing behind the vegetable wagon waving at me and smiling. It was Mr. James Steward himself.

Or Elwood. Or whoever it was, it was him. And he knew me. I pulled over, stopped, got out and walked slowly over to get a closer look. "What took you so long?" he said in that slow crackly Jimmy Stewart drawl.

"I'm sorry?"

"You. Yourself. Your—selves. Where you been?"

I had no words.

"You know, you're a very elusive young man. Which is a good thing, I suppose. It's the luxurious privilege of youth. But it makes for a difficult time trying to catch up with you."

"You've been looking for me?"

"Well, you sure haven't been looking for me!"

"But I have, or—I was."

"Oh?"

"Then, I gave up. I stopped. I finally just settled in here. Gosh. I think I might've even forgotten you for a while."

"That's okay. That's a good thing. That's when things finally happen."

"I'm not sure I understand."

"Oh, just some kooky law of the Universe. You gotta try real hard for a long time and then, some do it in despair, some take it personally. Some are just plain exhausted but, finally, you give up."

"Okay . . ."

"Yes. Some even say, 'I deserve better, I'm not putting up with this. Let it, or that or them, come to me!' But whatever style it is, you got to finally quit. Enough. No mas. Y'see?"

"Um . . ."

"Then . . . Time, Destiny, God, the forces that be—what have you—no longer your will but the Great Big Will takes over and, like this, we finally meet!"

"Right." I watched his cheery presence. I remained somewhat mystified: it was really him! I'd finally caught up with him. But I couldn't think. I was so excited, pleased, and—confused. He was so interested in me. Was this Jimmy Stewart? My mom'd go crazy if she knew. Was this Elwood P. Dowd? If so, then, where was Harvey? Or was this really the village idiot known as James Steward or . . . ? Who was this man?

"So," he held out his hand to me. It was a bit weathered, tanned, and had a tough, leathery feel as I shook it. "Nice to finally meet you."

"Same here."

"Now, you've got one on me. You know who I am but I'm forgetting your name?"

"Garry. Garry Brown."

"Right! Garry. From the name 'Garrett'—an 'honest warrior,' if I recall my etymology correctly."

"Really?"

"How's Harvey doing?"

"Harvey?"

"My good buddy. He's been traveling around with you, right?"

"Has he?"

"Oh, there he is, leaning against your car. Hi, Harvey!"

We both looked over at Titine. I didn't see anything but my car.

"Things are okay?" He continued to talk to Harvey. "Good, good. Getting enough to eat, are ya? Oh? Well, of course . . ."

Elwood, I guess—I still wasn't sure who he was—began to place a bunch of carrots in a paper bag. I returned to looking at Titine. I didn't see anything. Maybe a vague feeling of something hovering. A tree shadow. A curious, hungry feeling. I wanted to see Harvey, but I couldn't.

"Don't try so hard. That scares him off. Just relax and trust." Elwood was speaking as if into the paper bag, which was now filled with carrots. It was as if he were whispering to me, in private. Then, in a much louder voice, "How about some corn, too. Huh? And strawberries, sure, Harvey." Then to me, "You must try these strawberries."

As he gathered corn in one bag and a carton of strawberries in another, he again spoke softly, into his working hands and the paper bags but it was to me, he was advising me, "He's with you now. But you can't force it. He'll appear when he feels safe and ready. You just have to believe, over and over . . . There'll be some difficult days ahead, believe me. But Harvey'll be there . . . it's you, you're the one who'll try to leave or disappear. Don't. If you can help it. Hang on. Be patient. Trust. Find a way to relax . . . and don't try to be clever or cute or think there's some gimmick . . . You. Just more and more of you, that's what Harvey loves . . . You. Me. Us . . . in all our perfect fallible risible dumb glorious incorruptible ineluctable inevitable imperfection . . . he thrives on that . . . and one day, you will, too, okay?"

"Okay."

"Here. Have a taste." He stuck a strawberry in my mouth. I pulled off the green stem and ate, chewed, swallowed. A lovely sting of sweetness. "Oh God, that's delicious!"

"Alright. Harvey'll be happy with these. You boys take good care. Nice to finally catch up. You better get going. It's almost eleven."

"But—"

"No, no, it's on the house. Skedaddle or you'll be late."

"Okay, but I have things to say—"

"That's right, and you'll say them. In time. It's a wonderful life and—you can't take it with you. So, relish the moments. These are the best years of our lives. Right here, right now. Okay?"

"Okay."

"I'm so glad you and Harvey have become friends. I can tell he's really quite fond of you."

"Really?"

"Really. What, Harvey? I know, I know." Then to me, "He's getting worried. He likes Mikey Helms and doesn't want to keep him waiting."

"Oh Jesus! That's right. Listen, Sir, this has been a real honor. I've admired your work through the years. Really. Thank you."

"Good. I've appreciated your good work, too."

"You have?"

He started to walk with me toward Titine, then stopped. "You know what people always seem to forget? We're all peers here. We're all equals. The young and the old are closer to the Source, perhaps, which leaves that big crowd in the middle. They get so confused. But, bless them all, they're the ones that keep the trains running, maybe not always on time but they try. Oh God, they're very trying! But they do their best . . . Patience and forgiveness seem to be the keys, huh? See, you got me rattling on again. Go on! Hurry up! And you both take good care."

As I started to walk off toward Titine, I called, "But, sir, will I see you again?"

"I hope so. Bye, Harvey! I love you, too. So long!"

I jogged back to Titine. I looked over to the passenger side. A clear view through car window into dark brush with a dash of sunlight in among the grouped trees beyond. The passenger-side door didn't open and close on its own either. But, after turning the key in the ignition, I was glad to look back at the vegetable stand and see that Mr. Steward, or whoever he really was, was still standing there. As I edged out onto the road, Mr. Steward began to frantically wave, directing me to drive over toward him, which I did.

"Don't forget Harvey," he said. "We had to have a little good-bye chat . . . he also wanted another carton of these strawberries. Shall I put them in the back seat?"

"Sure."

He placed a small paper bag in the backseat next to the three other bags and shut the door. Then, he opened the front passenger-side door, "No, no. Allow me, Harvey . . . There you go." He closed the door, then leaned in its window. "Alright, guess you boys better hustle. What? Thanks, Harvey, you take care, too. Good to finally meet you, Mr. Brown. Drive safe."

"Thanks again," I called as we pulled away. He waved. I waved. I assumed Harvey waved. After a few more wrong turns and some more rerouting, I pulled into the Helms' driveway, wondering just how late I really was.

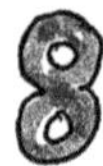

Mikey and Perry met me at the front door. "Gaw, you're early," said Mikey.

"Early? No, no. I got lost and—" I looked at my watch. It was seven minutes to eleven. "Yeah, I guess I am."

"Who's that in your car?" asked Perry.

"What?"

"With the big ears. See?" All three of us looked out at Titine. The car looked empty to me.

"See, Mikey?" Perry pointed.

"Oh yeah. Who is that anyway? He can come in if he wants."

"Thanks. That's my friend, uh, Harvey but—"

"We better get started," said Mikey. I looked again out the door. Nope. I saw an empty passenger seat. But they'd seen him. They'd caught a glimpse. I went through the motions. I called out the door, "Hey, Harvey? Come on in if you want!"

"I don't think he heard you," said Perry. "He's still sitting there . . . must be shy." Perry cupped his hands around his mouth and called, "It's okay. Come on in! We won't bite you!" He dropped his hands and giggled.

"Perry," said Mikey, "leave the guy alone. Can we start?"

"Sure, Mikey," I said, still checking Titine, ". . . to the basement we shall go."

Mikey sat. Perry looked on for a bit, until he stepped away, took a small whiffle ball from his pocket and shot hoops into the waste basket over by the woodworking bench. The basement smelled of wood shavings, a sweet piney smell.

I hated being in the bright fluorescent lights of this low-ceilinged cellar but it was the best setup for controlling the biggest variable, the light source. Outdoors the sun moved through the sky and we weren't always consistent with which time of day we'd get together to paint. Plus, the American flag on its pole, dangling next to Mikey. Once we'd found this spot, it was good to stick with it.

If Harvey was there with us, neither of the boys mentioned it. The painting was going well. I finally felt pretty good about Mikey's eyes. And his slight, diffident smirk.

Almost two hours in, there was a rumbling upstairs, which included a door slam.

"Hello! Anybody home?" Lexie called.

"Down here, Mom!" Mikey shouted back.

"You and Perry down there?"

"Yeah, with Garry. Painting."

"Oh?" Of course, Lexie knew this. "Can I come down?"

Still holding his pose, Mikey called, "I dunno."

"Sure, Mrs. Helms, come on down!" I called to her.

"Okay. Here goes." There was a rat-tat-tat clopping noise on the wood stairs. "Can I take a look?"

"I thought you had to wait. For the official unveiling," said Mikey.

"Just a peek?"

"It's okay, Mikey," I said.

"Go ahead, Mom. Gaw."

She slowly drifted over and stood to my left. I was on a stool, the canvas was upright on the easel. Just beyond, in a metal folding chair, sat Mikey.

"Oh my," said Lexie, watching the painting, then leaning to look at Mikey. "But where's your Boy Scout uniform?"

"Whaddya mean?" I asked, looking at the painting.

"Mikey! You're just wearing shorts and a tee. You're supposed to be in your uniform!"

"No, see?" I pointed her back to the painting. "I've finished painting in the uniform, see? Today, I wanted to rework his eyes and face."

"Oh. Right. Okay . . . Oh my."

"'Oh my' what, Mom?"

"Oh my, this is really something."

"'Oh my really something' good or 'Oh my really something' bad?"

I appreciated Mikey's concern.

"Oh, Mikey, so many questions. And . . ."

"And?"

Lexie paused, put her hands to her face as if to scream but instead, in an intimate whisper, she said, "Oh dear God . . . I *love* it!"

"Oh," said Mikey.

"Oh good," I said.

Then Lexie tapped my shoulder. "Not 'oh good,' this is 'oh GREAT'! Wait'll Sammy sees this. And your dad. This is so exciting. Don't you love it?" She tapped my shoulder again.

"Yeah. I'm pleased."

"'Pleased'? I can't believe it. 'Pleased'? This is *great!* And it's done, right? This is it, right?"

"Pretty much."

"Really?" asked Mikey.

"Well, no. We're almost there. Two more sittings."

"But why?" Mikey was not happy. "I'm tired of sitting for this."

"I'll sit!" offered Perry.

"Boys, slow down. Garry knows what he's doing. If it's not done, then it's not done."

"Oh gaw," said Mikey.

"Just some final touches, Mikey. Maybe only one more sitting, but I want you to really love it. We're very close, Mikey, okay?"

"O . . . kay . . ." Mikey hung his head. "I'm hungry."

"Me, too," said Perry.

"Me, three," I added.

"I'm so impressed. Okay. Let me fix you boys some well-earned sandwiches. Oh, and, Mr. Brown, there was a phone call for you, I jotted down the message. Here you go."

Lexie handed me a folded piece of white paper. Then she bustled upstairs.

Mikey came over and asked if he could look at the painting.

"Sure," I said.

"Can I look, too?" asked Perry.

"Why not?" I was opening the paper note. Both boys stood at the side of the easel, just a few inches behind the canvas. I looked up, hadn't read the note yet. Mikey watched my face, eyed the painting from the side still, put a finger to his chin and then said, "Naw. I'll wait." Perry completely duplicated Mikey's gesture, said, "Me, too." They both ran upstairs. Mikey called from the stairwell, "But only one more sitting, right?"

"Hope so!" I called back. They disappeared. I forgot the note for a moment. I just sat there, looking at the canvas, into the basement's harsh light and shadows, mixed with creases of sunlight that began strong at the several small aperture windows but then paled, blended, once inside the basement proper. What kind of day was it? It had been hot in the morning, humid, too. The basement was cool, a darkened chill refuge. I had gotten lost for a couple of hours, immersed in this mix of hand and eye, of oil paints and shapes and drawing and small flicks of a brush that turned color and line into this simulacrum life. Magical.

That's when I saw Harvey. Felt him, really. He was behind me, looking on. I heard a sweet, gentle voice say, with a slight Midwestern slowness to it, "I like it. I like it a lot."

"Thanks," I said. "Thanks—a lot."

"It's an amazing world, isn't it?"

"Yes," I said. I wanted to turn and see him, but I didn't. "It really is." Then, silence. But I still felt his presence. Then, "I'll wait for you in the car."

"Okay. But, aren't you hungry?"

"Take your time. Enjoy lunch. I've got a feeling Lexie's a good cook."

"She is."

"I'll wait for you."

"Okay." I was afraid to turn back but I did, slowly. I was sure I caught a glimpse of him on the stairs. Then a voice from the stairwell, "Don't forget to read your note!"

"Right," I called back. "Thanks!" Harvey was gone. I kept staring all about the basement. Was I going crazy or, was I clearer than I'd ever been? More connected, more attuned. How to explain this exhilaration

I'd felt? Then Lexie called from upstairs, "Lunch is ready. Come and get it!"

"Be right there!" I replied. I still had to wash brushes, put things in order. I didn't cover the painting but placed it, still on the easel, over in the far corner, to the right of the workbench, facing the wall. If Lexie or Sam, or anyone, wanted to look at it, they could, but it made it a little less accessible.

"Hurry please, or we'll have to start without you!"

"Okay. Coming!" Brushes, lunch, note. I opened the note. It was short:

I'll be at the library after lunch. Want to go for a walk?
Hope so. Sheila.

I raced upstairs. "I still have to wash these brushes—"

"Come join us, Brown. Please."

I placed the brushes on a paper towel. I sat. We all bowed our heads.

"Mikey."

"But, Mom."

"Please."

"Dear Lord, bless this food, bless this day. Thank you, Lord, in every way. Amen."

"Thank you. Was that so hard?"

"No, ma'am."

At the center of the table there was a big plate piled three layers high with halves of sandwiches, some matched, others not: peanut butter and jelly, baloney and cheese, meat loaf, tomato and cheese, and a few with barbeque.

After eating half of a barbeque sandwich, I mixed things up, with a PB and J. Hadn't had one of those in years. It got me homesick, a small distant pang.

"Your father comes home this weekend, Michael."

"Yes, ma'am."

"You excited?"

"Yes, ma'am. What's he look like again?"

I looked at Mikey. He smirked.

"Very funny, young man." Then Lexie turned to me. "You having a nice summer, Brown?"

"I am. In large part thanks to you, Mrs. Helms. Lexie."

"Oh pshaw! By the way, think I got you another portrait commission."

"Really?"

"After you finish Mikey, you'll do Sammy, right? Then, this one's a lovely young girl, daughter of a couple of teachers who frequent our book stalls. Nice, very bright. You'll like her."

"Wow. Thank you!"

"Don't mention it. You read your note?"

"Yes, thanks."

"A nice note?"

"Yeah."

"Not sure about that one. You be careful. Might've been a mistake to send her your way."

"Whaddya mean?"

"She's a little snaky. Slippery. Not sure what she's really up to."

"Rosemary was concerned, too."

"Oh God! Rosemary detests her! Of course, Rosemary's so very shy and you're so big and open and friendly. Now, she's got a crush on you."

"No!"

"Brown, are you blind?"

I looked at her. I was surprised at Lexie's outburst.

"Mrs. Helms," began Perry, pretty sure he was going to ask for something else to eat. "I don't think Garry is blind. Look at that painting he made of Mikey."

"That's sweet, Perry," said Lexie. "No. Mr. Brown's not blind, Perry. In fact, he sees really well. Some things. Some other things, maybe not." Lexie looked at me and winked.

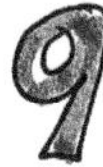

Just as we finished lunch, Perry's mom was in the Helms' driveway honking. I offered to wash dishes while Lexie ran out and talked to Perry's mother, who would be one of the chaperones for their field trip to the Opry.

Briefly, I left the kitchen to look out the door: saw the two women talking. Couldn't see Harvey or anyone or anything near or in my car. I was still standing by the front door as the boys came noisily clopping down the stairs with their backpacks and, after a brief barrage of goodbyes, hustled out the door. Mikey asked if I was coming tomorrow after camp. I said yes, and they were gone.

I went back into the kitchen and finished the dishes. Afterward, Lexie and I made a speedy beeline for the library. We didn't say much. I kept pondering some of the things we'd discussed at lunch, the big question being when I thought I'd head back North.

I was often lonely. I was in and out of being homesick, but going home, going North, I really hadn't thought about much. Lexie made it clear that "Rosemary, the boys, you know, a lot of us would like you to stay as long as possible." They liked having me around, "But," she sighed, "we all know, all good things must come to an end."

But this felt more like a beginning. Kathy would be coming in another ten days or so. I had Mikey's painting almost finished. Sammy's would be next and then the portrait of the young woman Lexie mentioned. I was reading good books. I'd returned *Gatsby* and was about to start on *Jane Eyre.* I had art books I reveled looking through. John Marin's book was a constant companion. My lakeside life had become a comforting refuge. I missed the men and the haying, but I had the library, my choir rehearsals and Sunday services, along with Reverend Bill's church library as a place to type letters and muse, reflect. No, this was still just unfolding. I wasn't ready to leave, although it was July now and Dad's birthday (August 22) wasn't that far away. I didn't have a plan.

This was just life now, and more and more, *my* life.

Which meant just being here and observing and tasting, wondering, and then drawing, painting, and writing—my journal, my letters home and to Durl, Kathy, Gramma Gertrude, even some lame attempts to write poems and stories. So, no, no plan and, no thoughts about leaving.

Sheila stood outside the library's glass doors, dangling the leather strap of her small red vinyl purse. "I was afraid you wouldn't show," she said.

"No, no. I got your note."

Lexie greeted Sheila, said good-bye and left us to stand there, looking at our feet.

This was not a date and yet, we were both—young woman, young man—unsure and so it had the unfortunate setup for or appearance of just that. Through the glass doors, I saw Lexie move swiftly to the main counter where she was joined by Rosemary. They spoke. Lexie went toward the rear office as Rosemary began to make angry faces and wave her hands at me, a kind of mock-jealous mime show. I smiled, nodded, and made a simple, modest hand-wave back, as if to say, Calm down, we're just going to have a little talk.

"What're you doing?" asked Sheila.

"What?"

"Who're you waving to?"

"Oh. Rosemary. Inside. See?" Rosemary had walked away.

"The librarian?"

"She's an assistant but yeah, she was just being silly."

Sheila looked through the glass doors. "Why?"

"Just bored, I guess."

"Oh."

We stood there, a fairly uncomfortable pause. Then, "You want to go for a walk? I'd like to talk over some things with you." This sounded much too serious for a lovely, almost balmy and not-so-humid summer afternoon.

"Sure. Where to?"

"Down past the Shop-A-Lot, go for a soda or something?"

"Okay."

We walked. Sheila was tall and thin, willowy. She was wearing a shimmery white dress with big clusters of dark blue, dark red, and black. She smelled sweet. As we walked and talked, mostly in the sunlight, I began to perspire, even though I had on my khaki shorts and a loose T-shirt. She got sweeter smelling. I just got hotter.

"You like my dress? I call it my 'moo-cow.' Don't I look like a cow? These big spots?"

"It's a nice dress. Summery."

"Thanks. I see you brought your sketchbook."

"I see you brought your notebook."

"And my purse. This is my treat."

"No!"

"I insist. I invited you."

"But you're visiting."

"No discussion. About art and being an artist, writing, painting, yes. About who's treating, no."

"Those the ground rules?"

"Yes. Agreed?" I looked at Sheila. "Agreed?"

"Sure. Thank you."

"Thank *you.* I know you had to rearrange your day to make this work."

"Not really. Mikey had this field trip."

"Anyway, thanks."

We passed the Shop-A-Lot. We passed the two gas stations, the upscale Mobil, the rundown Sunoco. And then the long row of dental office, thrift store, used book shop, a small Woolworth's and, instead of going another block to the Snack Shack, we crossed the street and landed at the still spiffy Burger King, where a tinge of sadness hit me: the last time I was here was when Durl and I had our farewell dinner.

"I think I'll have a chocolate shake instead of a soda," said Sheila, opening her red purse.

"Sounds good. I'll have a strawberry shake."

We sat outside at a small circular table in the sun, not far from where John and I had sat. The shakes were very thick. Several times I tried to sip through the straw. Nothing moved. Frustrated, I tried to drink it. Nothing. Now, I was getting thirsty.

"These are really thick, aren't they?" Sheila said as she poked at hers with her straw.

"I'm going to get a spoon. You want one?"

"No. The less I have of this the better."

Our discussion and our shakes both took a while to loosen up and get going. The spoon did help. I was flattered and a little self-conscious, too, when Sheila placed her notebook on the tabletop, clicked her ballpoint and said, "I want to write that down, okay?" Probably a quote from Marin or a paraphrase from my mentor, Fairfield Porter, who once told me that "one's art" was like a small child, to be protected, nurtured, and not thrust out in the world too quickly or desperately.

I told her about growing up in Connecticut, being pre-med in college, and seeing the movie, *Harvey.* She also jotted that down. I didn't tell her about my vision or my rapturous encounter with Jimmy Stewart or Elwood, or whoever he was. Certainly nothing about my partial glimpsing of Harvey. I was possessed, no doubt, immersed in drawing and painting and this yearning to be a great artist. But I wasn't going to let on that I might be off my rocker, too. She wanted to see my sketches, so I showed them to her.

It pleased me, how she took her time, looking at each drawing carefully, fingering them, pointing things out, talking less, looking more. Also, her words were related to the drawings, or triggered ideas, which brought her back to the drawings. They had become important to her, as if she were getting to know and appreciate me, which she was. Not that we didn't talk about her. We did. I asked a lot of questions. But the exchange was equal, neither one of us dominated. She loved her mom and dad. She had a younger sister. Her brother was the youngest. She'd been born outside Boston. Then, due to her father's work (medical supplies), they moved to the Baltimore area. She went to Johns Hopkins, came home, lived at home, worked as a paralegal, and was about to get her own apartment when she decided to visit her Aunt Cynthia, here in Donelson. She was the only one in her family who really seemed to believe in and support Sheila's creative gifts, her writing.

She'd written stories as a little girl, won a prize in junior high, edited the literary magazine in high school. She then backed off from writing and anything literary during college until Tillie Olsen came to Johns Hopkins and gave a talk. That did it. She'd read *Tell Me a Riddle,* a collection of three short stories and a novella. But this woman, her talk, her easygoing manner, her sense of humor, her abiding belief and passion in the magic of the creative in an often cynical, ambitious and technically advanced world, it moved her: that a woman, sitting at a table with pen and notebook, or typewriter, could somehow transform her ordinary world. But Olsen spoke, too, about the challenges, as a woman, finding the time and place to write and the silences that can intrude, the silences of just making a living, making a life that lets you make your art.

"I couldn't agree more," I said, draining my cup.

"Really?"

"Really."

"Okay. So, here's my burning question . . ." Sheila leaned in and eyed me carefully.

I leaned in, too, and said, "Shoot."

"How does one do it? How did *you* do it? Leave everything and pursue your art?"

"Have I left everything?"

"Seems like you're far from home, your parents, your siblings. Even your best buddy, you said, has gone back up North. Your girlfriend's in Iowa."

"How'd you know that?"

"That little dark-haired girl in the library."

"Rosemary?"

"That's her name? Kind of a busybody. I think she's afraid I'm going to run off with you."

I laughed.

"What?"

"Rosemary's sweet."

"Yeah. She made sure I knew you had a girlfriend. You miss her?

What's her name?"

"Kathy. Miss her a lot."

"What does she think of your being an artist?"

"Not sure. She admires and respects my gift . . . I think she's a little afraid of what I'm doing . . . because she's afraid for herself. She's still unsure about what she wants to do with her life."

"I know. I am, too. What about money and a career and marriage and family and all?"

"Whoa! Slow down."

"See, there's a lot to be scared about."

"But you can't look at it all at once." I put my empty cup down and went on, "In college, it hit me, this all-American sequence. I even jotted it down: 'college, work, marriage, kids, family and work, retirement, death' . . . and I thought, Oh no. Does it have to be that way? I really didn't want that predictable route."

"Fine." Sheila stirred her milkshake dregs. "But," she looked up at me quickly, "what about money? Surviving?"

"Good question. My dad worked hard, we lived well. I shined shoes, had a paper route, mowed lawns, painted houses. I like working. But I've never been obsessed with money or material things. So. I dunno."

"You don't know?"

"This may sound weird but . . ." I wasn't sure I wanted to divulge this fairly private part of who I was.

"But . . . what?"

"I pray. I believe in God. I feel like I'm being taken care of or guided or—and sometimes, I don't at all. I get lonely, homesick—"

"I believe in God, too. But—"

"This summer, maybe that's it. This summer is really putting my faith, the little bit that I have, to a pretty huge test."

"Really?"

"Here's the strange part. The longer the odds, the greater my faith has become. Does that make sense?"

"I think so."

"You wanna walk back?" I asked.

"Sure. I mean, no, not really. I feel like I could talk to you forever.

But I guess we should."

We got up. I took Sheila's empty cup and straw and with mine, dumped them in the trash bin near the back edge of the patio. We slowly strolled down the sloped parking lot and walked back along the near sidewalk. Late afternoon was now moving toward evening. It was cooler, the air gentler, mild. A beautiful summer day slowly winding down. Cars continued going by in both directions, shops still open, but the light was changing. The sounds were different, too. More of them, in contrast to the hotter part of the afternoon when fewer people were out and about and air conditioners created a kind of dull, sodden drone. Now, amid the chirping of birds, homebound traffic, a revived energy was palpable. Sheila and I continued to talk and walk, walk and talk.

To discuss art and its mysteries, life, philosophies, faith and survival, how to get on in the world, mixed with the longing to paint and/or write, to create, and, to share this with a bright, attractive young woman, well, I admit I was not only spiritually but even a little (okay, a lot) physically turned on. I think Sheila was, too. Because there we were. It was past six, the library was closed, and, on the small hill, that strip of grass lined with trees at the top edge of the parking lot where, in fact, I'd said good-bye to Durland, there we were, rolling around on that grass, kissing and hugging, hugging and kissing. Without guilt. Without shame. With a lot of creative ardor, you might say.

And then we stopped. We laughed. Sheila straightened her dress. I wondered what just happened. We were both a little embarrassed. But we both agreed, it had been a nice, even lovely, even invigorating afternoon. As we got ready to part, I said to Sheila, "Do you want to read to me from your notebook, what you've been writing?"

"Oh." She was surprised. "Well," she blushed, "no. Not yet. I'm just kind of fooling around. Some sketches. One idea for a short story. I think it's a short story. I don't think I'm ready to share any of it just yet. But, thanks."

"Sure."

"I wish I could see the painting of Mrs. Helms's son."

"When do you leave?"

"Friday morning."

"Meet me here tomorrow at three p.m. You can walk over with me and see it."

"I might go to Nashville with Aunt Cynthia but, if we don't, I'll be here."

"Sounds good."

Sheila looked off and said, "Thanks for today."

"Sure . . . thank you . . ." It was getting awkward again. "You need a ride to your aunt's house?"

"No. It's a nice walk . . . Bye."

"Bye."

I hadn't really seen Sheila walk before. I'd talked to her, walked beside her, but it was startling to see her, that lively dark spotted dress shimmy and sashay across the parking lot. One of those revelations, you suddenly realize, gee, she's an attractive young woman and, what am I doing heading out to Old Hickory Lake, all alone, when the night was just beginning, was still very young? And so were we? She turned at the end of the parking lot, just before she joined the sidewalk. Her purse and notebook in one hand, she gave a little wave with her left, then blew a kiss. As I waved back, she turned and walked on, those shimmery hips flouncing as she got smaller and smaller in the distance.

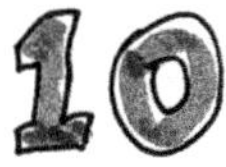

I stood there, thinking. Sheila was now a small jot well along Main Street. The sun, a brilliant orange, tinted the trees and grass and all the shapes near and far in a wilting orange glow. My lanky frame made a dark shadow across the parking lot. Wait. Where was Titine? No cars were parked in the library lot. Had I parked in back, down below? As I jogged toward the rear, I spotted the Helms' backyard and remembered that I'd left Titine (and Harvey, too?) in the Helms' driveway. The edge of the Helms' house was lit in orange. There were lights already on inside. Just as I reached Titine, a voice near the house said, "Hey, Picasso." I looked toward the side-door. There was a bluish cloud and a small point of glowing light as if the brilliant orange sun had suddenly been miniaturized. Once my eyes adjusted, there was Sammy, sitting on the steps, having a smoke. "Hey, Sammy."

"Gonna do some painting?"

"Naw. We did earlier. Mikey back from his field trip?"

"They called from Nashville. They're on their way."

"Well, have a good night."

"You, too." He stamped out his cigarette. I opened the car door. Then Sammy called to me, "Let me ask you. Whaddya think of marriage?"

"No thanks. I gotta girlfriend."

"Very funny. I'm serious. Life is short, right?"

"Right." He wanted to talk. I closed the car door and strolled over.

"I'm not keeping you, am I?"

"No, no. What's going on?"

"My girlfriend. You wanna smoke?"

"No thanks."

"You mind if I?" He pulled out another cigarette. Newport Lights.

"Please, go ahead."

"You don't smoke. You don't drink. No vices, huh?"

"They're just not obvious."

"Guess you are human."

"All too human."

"How about women. Girls. Have you figured them out yet?"

"Honestly? No. But I enjoy the exploration process."

"That's just it. I think I want to keep exploring."

"Good. Do it. We're young. There's time, right?"

"Not according to Courtney. She's putting the squeeze on."

"What's your mom say?"

"She thinks I'm a fool. She likes Courtney but she thinks I should slow down, enjoy life . . . She didn't want me to go to dental school, not right away. She thought I should get out, see the world. But what's to see? I got lots of world right here. Nashville, Knoxville, Memphis. I've traveled."

"New York? Boston? California? Europe?" I asked.

"Naw. Not really interested."

"Do you love her?"

"Sure. She's great. But why can't we just keep doing what we're doing? I don't want to lose her. It's just, y'know?"

"She's on a different timetable, sounds like."

"Exactly." Sammy took a long drag, then gave a deep slow exhalation. The blue-grey smoke came out in a thick gush that ended in small rings as Sammy made his mouth into a big O.

"Smoke rings. Nice," I commented.

"Thanks. So, how about you?"

"What about . . . me?"

"Artists do it real different, right? Picasso, all those Europeans. Wives, mistresses, sexy models, right? Must be confusing."

"Yeah, I like keeping a harem. Never get lonely."

"Ha! You have some girl in Iowa, right?"

"Yeah. We met in college, freshman year . . . dated off and on all four years. She's a counselor at a Y camp in Iowa this summer."

"Nice. You love her?"

"I do."

"She loves you?"

"Well. That's the big question."
"Oh?"
"There's this other guy."
"Where's he? In Iowa?"
"A counselor at the same Y camp."
"Uh-oh."
"Yeah."
"Have you proposed?"
"No."
"Why not?"
"Long story. If it's meant to be, I don't want to force it."
"Why not?"
"Because . . . it's got to be real. True. Right?"
"Right. God!"
"What?"

Sammy flicked ash off his cigarette, then took another elaborate drag. "You're no help at all. You're just as confused as I am."

"Really?"

"Sounds like." Sammy slowly swiveled his shoe on his dropped cigarette butt, then picked it up. "Mom doesn't like me leaving butts around. You had dinner yet? Want to join us?"

"Thanks, but I have choir rehearsal."

"Jesus, you're an artist AND you sing in a church choir? Man, they broke the mold with you."

I laughed, "Guess so." I wasn't sure if Sammy was lauding or razzing me.

"Come on, I know you're hungry."

"Really, thanks."

Sammy walked over to the small woodshed by the side of the house where he opened doors, leaned in, and deposited his small handful of cigarette butts. "You sure? Fried chicken."

"Don't tempt me. You and your mom and Mikey are really swell but I don't want to take advantage."

"We like you, dummy! Come on!" Sammy was very persuasive. Then the side door slammed open. "Sammy, five minutes 'til dinner!"

"Thanks, Mom."

"Who you talkin' to?"
"Have a look."
"Can't see, it's gettin' dark. That you, Brown?"
"Hi, Mrs. Helms. Lexie."
"Five minutes, both o' you, go and wash up!" She was gone.
"Well, Brown, it's dinner time. Ha!"

The fried chicken was delicious. I had seconds. Lexie kept hinting and hoping and urging me to finish the painting so Mr. Helms could see it when he got home in two days. I assured her that it would be done. After they looked at it, if they didn't like it, or, saw things that needed changing, I could do that next week.

Mikey got home from Nashville just as we finished up. He'd really liked the trip to Nashville, a lot more than going backstage at the Grand Ole Opry, which he said was boring. I asked Mikey if this girl, Sheila, could come over tomorrow and look at his painting. He shrugged. "Doesn't matter to me." The mention of Sheila got Lexie going. Sammy, too. Both of them curious. Sammy was surprised since I told him I loved Kathy.

I blushed, got a little confused, but finally reassured them that my friendship with Sheila was about the arts, not romance.

Choir rehearsal went well, was even fun. Three people were missing, so it was a smaller, cozier group. Dr. Bill told a few off-color gossipy stories. We had some good laughs. One song really got to me, made me homesick, a little teary. We only worked on it for fifteen minutes or so. I could've kept singing it all night. "A Mighty Fortress Is Our God." It reminded me of our Episcopal church back in Darlington. My mom loved that song, even Dad would join in, light up a little when we sang it.

It was a quiet drive back out to Old Hickory Lake. I readied my sleeping bag. A cool, damp night. I tried to read a little in Titine but I was really tired. I lay there and thought about Harvey and Elwood and the mysteries of families and girlfriends and just how do people become writers and artists and librarians and—dentists?

I watched again the great cobweb of stars and galaxies, thought about Kathy. Was she already asleep? It was an hour earlier in Iowa, and would she think about me or was I just "old reliable"? Was Kink the exciting one, the adventure?

11

The next afternoon, I finished Mikey's painting. Sheila never showed up. I acted indifferent when Mikey, then Sammy, and then Mrs. Helms, too, asked about her. Don't know what happened to her, I told them. Said she might be going to Nashville with her aunt. No big deal. But it was. I was disappointed. Not because I had any romantic designs but because I wanted her to see a real painting of mine. Not just a sketchbook full of drawings and unfinished watercolors. Okay: I wanted to impress her a little.

But I guess I impressed Mr. Helms. After the weekend, I saw Lexie at the library. She was very excited. "Doyle loves the painting, Brown! Say's you're real talented, which we all knew. Everyone's real happy with it, even Mikey!"

"Really? Mikey likes it?"

"Might be 'cause Perry likes it so much."

"Of course."

"Perry's bringing his mom over to see it. See if she'll let him get his portrait done. Who knows, Brown, you might never be able to leave this lil ol' portrait-hungry town. Ha!"

"Ha."

"My Sammy's up next, right?"

"When?"

"You say the word."

"Tomorrow?"

"Fine. But after he's home from summer school. Five p.m.?"

"Yes, ma'am. Thanks again, Mrs. Helms." She gave me a cold stare. "Lexie. Thanks."

"Don't mention it, Brown. Plan to stay for dinner."

"Oh no."

"Oh yes. Art needs good food and energy."

The next day, and the rest of that week, except for Wednesday night's choir rehearsal, I worked on Sammy's painting. We'd begin around five and go until it got dark, around eight. It made a dent in the Helms' dinner hour but Lexie didn't mind. Only Mikey complained; often he'd eat earlier, alone.

Sammy was a really good sitter, not too talkative, attentive, patient. It seemed to go faster than Mikey's had. The first night Sammy and I sat in the backyard. He sat at the picnic table, I sat across from him. He did most of the talking while I did several sketches of him. A couple with pencil and then, as we got close to the desired pose, I did a more detailed pen and ink.

It was a beautiful night, not hot or humid, a little breezy. There were lovely swaths of last sunlight filling in behind Sammy, gentle streaks of dark and light greens, which I wanted to include, maybe even some of the night sky. I asked Sammy if he'd mind sitting in the aluminum cross-hatched summer chair.

"I don't mind. You're the artist. You call the shots."

"Thanks." I wasn't used to so much respect from a man who was older than I was. So much of college life, you're an underclassman, and, in or out of college, I guess I was trying to prove myself. Sammy didn't really know that much about me except that, to him, I was an artist. That gave me a certain kind of cache, which I would never abuse. But then, how could I, since I didn't believe in myself as much as Sammy did? I had doubts.

Sammy wore a button-down turquoise short-sleeve shirt, which was fairly worn—once a formal short-sleeve become a kick-around comfy stand-by—with khaki Bermuda shorts and a pair of beat-up white top-siders. I asked him if he liked what he was wearing.

"These? Yeah. Casual. Comfortable."

"It's a great look. If you're okay with it, well, you'll have to keep wearing this combo each time we work on the painting."

"Sure. No big deal."

"Great. Could you cross your legs again?"

"Like this?" He placed his left leg over his right.

"Actually, the other way."

"I did it right over left before?"

"Yeah."

"Okay." Instantly, right leg over left.

"Comfortable?"

"For a little while, sure."

"Just let me get an outline sketched in, the composition, and then you can rest."

"Great."

The sketches helped. I sat on the far side, on the picnic table's worn wood bench.

Sammy looked comfortable. He rested his elbows on the aluminum chair arms. With his tanned face full on, his shirt unbuttoned—three holes from the top—and strips of sunlight against the shadowy grass with hints of dark blue night sky beyond, that was it. We had our composition.

For starters, with a No. 6 brush, some turpentine and burnt sienna, a loose wash, I sketched in shapes, no details. Just like the pen and ink, areas next to areas, a kind of looser paint-by-number diagram. No colors yet. I wanted to begin filling in his face: a series of light washes, highlights and shadows, or, at least, light washes of the grass, sky, chair, his legs, shirt. But, no. We'd already worked over two hours. I didn't want Sammy to burn out. "Okay. That should do it for tonight."

"That's it?"

"For tonight."

"Oh man, I was just getting going."

"Me, too. But, don't want to wear you out."

"Not a chance. I'm psyched. This is fun."

"Great. Same time tomorrow?"

"You got it, Brown. Leave the chair in this same spot?"

"Sure. But, if it's moved, I've got enough reference points from the sketches."

"Can I see?"

"Sure."

Sammy tapped the aluminum chair, then sauntered over, like a guy trying to look at, but not stare at a pretty girl. Behind me now, he looked back at where he sat, then back to the painting. Quietly, he said, "Huh." I watched him as I put away pencils, brushes, paints, and closed up sketchbooks. "So, this is how it starts, huh?"

"Not much to look at right now."

"I think I get it. It's so blotchy, all shapes. When does it become a painting?"

"Great question . . . it's gradual. Today, the shapes and colors look this way. Tomorrow, or the next day, I may keep the major outlines and basic composition . . ." I was next to Sammy, pointing at the sketched-in areas, "but I may paint over colors, lighten them, darken, change tones as one area brightens or goes dull, which then affects another area. The whole picture is a constantly changing pattern until we finally get to a blend of shapes and colors that seem to work, that are lively and exciting, lifelike, not rigid, or, you know, stale-looking."

"Yeah. God forbid I get 'stale-looking.' Courtney'd have a fit."

"How're you guys doing?"

"Pretty good. We talked. She wants to slow things down."

"That's great."

"Yeah. Except now, that worries me. I start thinking, Is there another guy? Is she getting cold feet? Does she really love me? You know?"

"Oh boy, I do know."

"Think I liked it better when she was pressuring me."

"Really?"

"You mind if I smoke?"

"Go ahead."

Then, Lexie's voice, through the screen, from the open kitchen door, "Sammy! Brown! You boys done? You hungry?"

"Yeah, Ma, in a minute."

Then, "Can I come look?"

Sammy looked at me. "Can she?"

"I don't mind if you don't."

Sammy called to her, "Sure, Mom!"

The screen door slammed. Through the slips of house lights and evening dusk, Lexie emerged, undoing her apron. "I left food on the table and in the fridge. Mikey's watching something on TV. I'm going to bed."

"Where's Dad?"

"He's already in bed. He leaves tomorrow early, remember?"

"That's right." Sammy took a deep inhale, then stepped away to slowly blow out a great bluish grey cloud.

"God, Sammy, I wish you'd stop that." Lexie had her hands on her hips, the white apron not quite folded, drooped from her right hand. "An ugly habit. Dirty. Smelly. They're already saying it's a cause of cancer."

"So?"

"I just hate it. This it?" Lexie pointed to the canvas, which still glistened like the flap of an envelope after it's been licked.

"This is my Sammy?"

"Well—"

"No, Brown, I'm joking. I know. It's a *process* . . . did you see this, Sammy?"

"Yeah." Sammy took another drag. "It's neat."

"Neat? More like blotchy, not neat."

"Reminds me of those finger paints Mikey used to do," said Sammy.

"Oh yeah," said Lexie, "Brown, you're not using your fingers, are you?"

"Not yet." I was all packed up. The three of us now stood looking at wet paint.

"It'll be recognizable like Mikey's, right?" asked Lexie.

"Think I know now why folks aren't supposed to look at a painting until it's finished," I began.

"Why?" asked Lexie.

"Because," Sammy jumped in, "it's not what it'll be yet. It's not a crown, it's still a busted piece of tooth."

Lexie looked at Sammy. "What?"

Sammy laughed as he scrunched out his cigarette in the heel of his hand.

"Oh God, you guys. Come on, time to eat."

"Lexie, I don't want to impose."

"Impose? It's fixed and waiting. Do what you want. I'm going to bed. 'Night." Lexie marched off. The screen door slammed shut.

12

Kathy's flight was due in around noon at the Nashville airport. The night before, during dinner with Sammy, I'd checked with him about directions: I'd taken Kathy to the airport from Nashville, but coming from Donelson, I wasn't sure, the route might have some new wrinkles.

I had a nice slow morning by the lake: some quiet time, a short jog up past Langford's farm and back, a good swim, a shower and shave, and the last of my clean laundry in which to "dress up." That is, I wore my light blue short-sleeved shirt and my khaki Bermuda shorts, my brown loafers, no socks. Only problem: By then, I was hungry, and I was running out of time. So, before I got on the first highway, route 40, I stopped at the gas station/deli where Floyd always took us for lunch. I filled Titine, got a blueberry muffin, a banana, and an OJ. And got going, eating and drinking as I went.

Only a few back roads, then one highway that led to the main highway and the airport exit. Friday, mid-morning, the traffic light, I made it in forty-five minutes. I parked close to the American Airlines section of the modest bivalve airport terminal, and ate my banana and watched as Kathy's plane landed.

When I got inside, I checked the monitors and saw that her flight was due to arrive at Gate 6 in fifteen minutes. I made my way to the gate and waited for her plane to pull in. First, I watched a plane rise up from the distant horizon and gradually ascend. Slowly, the front end of an American Airlines plane appeared. Then, its mid-length belly, the wings, and finally its slivery back end. I was watching and waiting for it to make that slow turn into Gate 6 when my eyes went dark: my upper face got warm, moist; a thin female voice whispered near my left ear, warm, breathy, "Guess who, Gar?"

I didn't speak right away. Her warm hands felt so good on my face, my eyes still covered. And, her voice, that little girl's mischievous joy. I choked up, then spit out, "Kathleen?" She released her hands, I turned, and there she was. "Hi, Gar!"

"Oh God!"

We hugged. We kissed, nothing big or mushy but pretty nice. Well, maybe semi-mushy. My cheeks were wet. I wanted to hold her forever.

"Oh, Gar, are you crying? You silly boy!" Kathy wiped my cheeks and watched me and laughed. Then, leaning in close, she quietly asked, "You okay?"

"Yeah. I've just missed you, that's all."

"Me, too." She kept watching me as she pulled off a big green canvas backpack.

She had on a sleeveless pink T-shirt that stretched tight across her breasts as she reached back to untwist the metal and canvas straps. She wore blue jeans and blue sneakers. "There." She put down the backpack. "It's not that full but it was getting heavy. Now, let me give you a real hug."

We hugged again. This, for me, was pretty sexy. I could feel her warm breasts against my chest and then there was her sweet smell. I wasn't crying. I was very horny.

"You big galoomph."

We stopped hugging, pulled apart and looked at each other.

"Hi, Kath."

"Hi, Gar."

"Whaddya doing here? I'm waiting for your plane, see? Think that's it. Gate six. See? Now, all those people are going to come marching off and—wait. Where are you? Kath? There's the airline ticket guy, Excuse me, Sir, my girlfriend, Kathleen, was supposed to be on that plane but—"

"Well, sir, she got an earlier connection, or—oh, Gar, I dunno."

We laughed. We looked at each other.

"So, wait. When'd you get here then?"

"A few minutes ago. Gate eleven. Surprise!" Kathy laughed, jumped up and down and clapped her hands.

"You're really here."

"I'm really here. I came back."

"You brought a backpack. Going hiking?"

"Want to?"

"Not really but."

"I just bought it. Isn't it great? For our trip to Europe in September."

"Really? You still want to do that?"

"Silly. Of course. Besides, I have to be in my sister's wedding, remember?"

"Ellie. Marrying Sir John Humpty-Dump. Westminster Church. London."

"Not quite a Sir but he is a very handsome surgeon, John Hampton-Scott. And, it's Christ Church, London. But not bad, Gar. Nice try."

"Yeah. I'm very trying."

"I'll say."

"Oh man, what's a guy to do?"

"Hmm. Take a girl to lunch?"

"You wanna?"

"I wanna. I'm starving."

"Me, too. Let's go."

I grabbed her backpack. "No suitcase?

"Nope. This is it."

"It's not that heavy."

"Yeah, but you're big and strong. Not small and frail like me."

"Ha!" I watched her flushed face turn into an impish grin, the way her breasts bounced as she turned to jauntily follow me, hands in her pockets. She tapped my arm,

"Oh Gar, this is Tennessee again!"

"Yup."

"It's nice to be back."

"I'll say!"

We waltzed through the airport. Youthful and loving, the sky was the limit. People stared. We were happy. A Friday in mid-July, late morning, planes soared overhead as we continued to dance along the sidewalks out to the short-term parking lot. The blast of humid hot air didn't slow our pace or thwart our sense of adventure. Instead, it became the sweet, heated embrace of tropical buoyancy that young romantic love is often inflated with until the bubble bursts. But it didn't burst. Not this weekend. We had a big chunk of Friday, all of Saturday, and into the late afternoon of Sunday. Not unlike our former college weekends. We were going to make the most of it.

And we did.

13

We had no plans except life itself. I wanted to show Kathy everything, my "Tin Sea" world. But where to start? We had lunch at the Snack Shack. A slow lunch. Terri was there and acted jealous and joked and told Kathy how lucky she was to have a guy like me, "So talented, a real artist." By the end of lunch, she was telling me how lucky *I* was, what a lovely girl Kathy was and, "You treat her right, okay? Or, I'll come and find you, y'heah?" I promised I would.

After lunch, we parked in the front lot of the library. We sat inside Titine, talking. I pointed to the Shop-A-Lot and the ragged path, through trees and shrubs, that led there. I showed her that behind us, in that sunlit patch of crescent grass and trees, was where Durl and I had said our good-byes.

"What do you hear from Mister Durland?"

"Not much. He made it back North. To Connecticut and then to East Aurora, to be near Brooke. Which reminds me. I want to show you my local branch of the post office, my PO box, where Emmy, the PO Mistress, informs me if a letter from you has come."

"Really?"

"Really."

"That's sweet, Gar."

"Yeah. Like you."

It went on and on like this. Love's indulgences. The bounteous eternity of Only Now. Kathy followed me as we made our way toward the library entrance. Thomas, lumbering and dark, was sweeping the modest library stoop. "Thomas, hi!"

"Mista Garry, yassaw!"

"This is Kathy, my girlfriend, all the way from Iowa."

"Nice to meetcha, Missus." Thomas nodded, almost into a bow.

Kathy nodded and bowed in reply. "Hi, Thomas." She offered her hand. Thomas looked at it, then kept sweeping. "Nice to meetcha, Thomas," said Kathy, quietly, pulling her hand back.

"Thank you, Missus."

As we walked through the library's glass doors, I explained, "He wasn't being rude. He's just very shy." Kathy watched him, nodded, followed, "That's what I thought. He seems sweet. And—shy."

"Sweet and shy," I nodded, "That's our Thomas." I also sensed even then, 1971, with all the civil unrest, that a Black man in the South was not only being courteous and perhaps shy but also very cautious.

Inside the library, we stopped just past the entry way. "And this is the Donelson Public Library—ta da! Kind of my home away from home, when I'm not at the lake."

"Oh Gar, this is nice. Bright, cheery, lots of books."

"That's Rosemary." I nodded toward the main counter. "And I want you to meet Lexie. Come on." Rosemary's dark hair was all we could see. She was bent over a piece of writing, her pen moving slowly, steadily.

"Hi, Rosemary."

She looked up. "Hi, Garry." She put the pen and paper aside.

"I want you to meet a friend of mine. This is Kathy."

"Not *the* Kathy?" She pushed her dark glasses up on her nose as she stood.

"Yup."

"Really? Oh WOW." She offered her hand to Kathy. "It's so very nice to meet you. You really do exist."

Kathy laughed, shook Rosemary's hand. "I do. Exist. Nice to meet you, Rosemary."

"Oh my. Let me go get Mrs. Helms. Oh wow."

We stood there side by side, waiting. "Have you been talking about me, Gar?"

"All the time."

Then, a rustling, a breeze, Rosemary returned. "She'll be right out. She's on the phone but I know she wants to meet you."

"Thanks, Rosemary."

"Sure. So, Iowa? I've never been to Iowa. Is it nice?"

"It is. If you like corn and lots of sky."

"Really?"

"But," I threw in, "at least Davenport has the big ol' Mississip', which makes things interesting."

"True," nodded Kathy.

Then Lexie appeared. "Rosemary, that's Mildred again. She says she ordered that book, you know, on great American myths, remember? Over two weeks ago. Will you talk to her?"

"Sure." Rosemary nodded to us and then walked into Lexie's office.

"Is this the famous Kathy from Iowa?"

"I guess so. Hi." They shook hands. Kathy blushed.

"We've all heard so much about you, and I don't mean to embarrass you, but we sure have been looking forward to finally meeting you."

"Thank you, Mrs. Helms."

"Please, call me Lexie."

"I, too, Lexie, have heard lots about you, this wonderful library and your two boys."

"Really?" I was surprised to see Lexie blush. "You've seen Mr. Brown's pictures of them?"

"Not yet."

"You're gonna show her, aren't you?"

"I want to, yes."

"Whyn't you go over now? Mikey's home."

"You sure?"

"Of course. She probably won't make it back for your art show."

"What art show?" I asked.

"Didn't I tell you? I had this grand idea."

"Oh?"

"Yeah. It just hit me. See, we've got this big room downstairs, you know, for used book sales or sometimes an author will come to town, give a reading and draw a crowd. We set him up downstairs. It's a great space. Wanna see?"

I looked at Kathy. She shrugged. I smiled and shrugged and said, "Sure."

I'd seen Thomas go through this door, way over in the Adult

Fiction section, near the rear windows. I'd thought at first it was an exit door or a janitor's closet. But then, he'd never come back out. A slim stairway led to the lower level where there was a whole other section of library, glass-enclosed cases and closed-up file cases. "These are the few 'rare books' we have," said Lexie. Around the corner from this hall vestibule was a big plain empty room, maybe 50 by 100 feet.

"See? One time we had an exhibit of framed book covers from the 1950s, which gave me the idea." Lexie was walking through the space, waving, pointing. "See all this wide-open space? Wouldn't a nice showing of your pen and inks and watercolors, and, maybe I'd loan you my boys' paintings, too—wouldn't they look good up on these walls?"

"You mean, a real art exhibition . . . of my art?"

"Oh Gar!" said Kathy.

"Yeah. Can't you just picture it?"

I stood there, looking. I looked at all four walls. No windows. The fluorescent lights were not bright but they were bright enough. My paintings. My drawings. Really?

"Oh my," I said.

Lexie looked at me. "You don't like the idea?"

"No, no. Just—wow—the idea excites me."

"Oh good."

"This is a really nice space, isn't it, Gar?"

"It is. It's amazing."

"Well, tuck it in your cap. Don't mention it to a soul. I need to check with the powers that be before we get ahead of ourselves. But, might be fun, huh?"

I nodded, still wide-eyed, still picturing the drawings and watercolors. Maybe I'd do some other oil paintings, too. Then I realized: they'll have to be framed.

"When were you thinking, Lexie?"

"Sometime before you leave. End of the summer."

"When are you leaving, Gar?"

"Probably in time for my dad's birthday on August twenty-second."

"Okay," said Lexie, "there's a date to work back from. This is almost mid-July. Let's say, mid-August, okay? A month from now."

"Wow, Gar, that's not a lot of time, is it?"

"No, but this summer, time has played some weird tricks."

Kathy gave me a puzzled look.

"Just, y'know, days feel like weeks, or a week feels like a month, or then a week is suddenly really short. These three days with you, I know they're going to feel like only a few seconds and then you'll be gone again."

"Really?"

"Really."

Which was true.

The parts of the summer that were scary or boring, like the trip South and the Southwest Company indoctrination, seemed to take forever. The pleasurable parts—me and Durl at the lake, going for a run, swimming in the lake, or when I was painting by the lake, or reading—all that went by quickly. The two weeks working the hay fields, so intense, so demanding, seemed like a month or even more.

We walked down to the Helms' place and I showed Kathy Mikey's portrait. leaning against the Helms' fireplace, just below where it would hang above the mantel, eventually joined by Sammy's. I took her to the basement and showed her Sammy's picture, too. Mikey and Perry were having snacks in the kitchen. Once they met Kathy, they followed us around and even showed off for her, pointing out colors and objects and unseen things in both paintings, things I hadn't even considered even though I painted them. Like the worn patch of grass behind Sammy's head that wasn't due to the sun's setting but because of where Mikey and Perry had once placed "home plate" and so the grass had gotten worn there. Or, in Mikey's painting, the American flag as it draped beside Mikey, its discoloration was not a shadow but where the flag had caught fire during the Helms' barbeque one Fourth of July. Kathy and I were impressed.

14

Kathy liked seeing the oil portraits but we both wanted to get out to Old Hickory Lake. I wanted to go for a swim. Kathy just wanted to see it. On the way, we stopped at Langford's farm. We drove down the long dirt drive. As usual, no one was around. At least not where we pulled in, about 100 yards before the turn up to the main house.

I parked, grabbed my big sketchbook, and Kathy and I held hands as I walked her over to the field's edge, where it opened up into endless sky and then descended into a distant roll of more fields. Kathy smiled and said, "Gee, we don't have this in Iowa."

"Okay, okay."

She tapped my arm and laughed.

"How about this then?" I offered as I pulled up my sketchbook. I paged through it, flipped it open full, and then slowly, gently laid it on the grass before us. It was a pen and ink diptych of the same view.

"Oh, Gar. That's it, isn't it? That's really beautiful."

"Thanks." Heads together, we looked down at the drawing, then up at the actual landscape, back and forth, comparing the two.

"What's that over there?" Kathy had turned almost 180 degrees and pointed to a triangular piece of shimmery blue, in the actual landscape.

"That's a little corner piece of Old Hickory, the lake."

"It's that close?"

"Oh yeah. Come. Look . . ." We walked up the dirt drive about thirty paces. I pointed her to beyond the big field and distant row of trees to where there was another drop-off.

There it was. A great big shimmering blue, surrounded by houses, big overhanging trees, a few docks, some nearby fields, and even a few boats and one sailboat, full white sail.

"Oh Gar, that's your lake!"

"Thar she blows! Come on, let's go for a swim!"

I showed Kathy where I always parked Titine. Told her how we would open up and spread my sleeping bag. I'd bought a big blue sheet, queen size, to cover us, and sleep right there under the stars.

"Really?"

"Best sleep in God's green Kingdom!"

I showed her the restrooms. Then I walked her, very dramatically, up and over the crest of hill, down the forested slope, with its rocks and flowers—again, sketchbook in hand and opened, showing her my pen and inks of all this—as we approached the small lakeside beach area: the grassy knoll mixed with sandy beach and the assorted picnic tables. Showed her my favorite table, and more lakeside pen and inks.

We both tested the lake water. A few teenagers, three boys, two girls, were around the bend, splashing, shouting. We went for a swim.

Kathy did a few of her synchronized swimming moves. Her legs rose up out of the water, swiveled, jack-knifed, so beautiful. I mocked her and did my own clumsy version of water ballet, mostly running from the beach into the water, concocting silly flying pirouettes as I slapped and collapsed in the shallow depths. Kathy laughed and splashed me. I swatted surface spray back at her, then went underwater to surprise her, grab her, and then we embraced: we shared our first real passionate kiss of the visit.

"Silly boy," Kathy gasped as we broke from kissing.

We both swam slowly, steadily out to the deeper, colder portion of lake where we stretched out on our backs and floated and watched the sky and spotted wrens and chickadees. Kathy pointed those out, named them. I pointed out the two lumbering crows, with their bullying caws, and what was definitely a scarlet tanager.

"No, Gar," Kathy said as we still floated, "I'm pretty sure that was a cardinal."

"No way!"

"This is the South. Tanagers are mostly in the Northeast."

"Oh? What if they went on a road trip, to sell dictionaries in Tennessee or maybe visit artist friends or become artists, and not stay safe at home? What about those birds, who aren't always where you think they'll be?"

"Those are brave birds but not tanagers."

I quietly slipped under water, swam to her like a submarine whose "up periscope" were my searching hands and tickling fingers.

It was Kathy's idea to lay out our towels on the mix of grass and sand, near the lake water's edge, and just lie there, dry off, take in the sun, dawdle and talk, and ease our slow, gentle way into early evening. I'd never done this before. For all my swims and visits here at this little beach, I'd always either rushed off into town, or sat at the picnic table and sketched, read my books, or wrote in my journal.

But to lie on a towel and doze and muse? No. And, it was delicious. Of course, this had to do with Kathy finally being here in my little summer kingdom. Only loving her and doing my art seemed able to slow me down and, even, in their way, to stop time, too.

I watched her lie there on her back, knees bent, staring up into the deep summer sky.

"It's lovely here, Gar. I like your lake."

"Yeah, it's pretty special." I lay on my stomach, watching her, watching the lake water. "You really think I'm brave, Kath?"

"Brave?"

"You know, the tanager. Birds that go to unexpected places."

"Oh, those brave birds. Like you. Yes."

"Really?"

"Brave or foolish, or both."

"Yeah . . ."

"Look, Gar." She sat up. "Most guys, like Durland and your other buddies, are headed for grad school. For real, or to avoid the war, but you," she paused and stared off, across the lake, "you've chosen a very different path. Kind of scary, I think. I admire you for it. You're so committed. And, since you dropped the pre-med, you seem so happy, and I know it scares you a lot, but I guess it's your faith, too, in God, but also how you really believe in yourself, your talent. You seem really content. Excited."

"I guess I am. It doesn't feel brave though."

"What does it feel like?"

"I do worry. I know I smile a lot, but I do get confused and scared.

And I try to trust God, about my art, but about you, too, and us."

"Me?"

"I think maybe sometimes I love you too much. I come on too strong."

"Oh no, Gar. not *you*!"

"See?"

"You silly boy."

We were both sitting up now, playing with the sand, looking out at the lake water, as we talked.

"The art just feels so right for me, it excites me, fills me. And I know I'll have to take care of it, find work to support it, but I'm willing to do that."

"Like the haying?"

"Whatever. I know it's going to take time. Boy, after that Southwest Company book-selling brainwashing, I just see how everyone's selling something—dictionaries, deodorants, cars, cereal and shoddy Bibles, too."

"What about being a doctor? That's not selling, and you would've been such a good doctor. You're so good with people."

"I think it was the romance of being a doctor that appealed to me. I might have had bedside charm, but I didn't have the academic perseverance."

"But that's just memorizing things, a means to an end. The gift is applying facts and theories to really seeing people and their difficulties, their diseases, which you'd have been great at."

"You think?"

"Oh yeah. Because, well, because you *are* an artist. You see things. And you care so much about things, and about people."

"Really?"

"Oh Gar. don't play dumb. You know this."

"Yeah, but I didn't know you did."

"Omigod, you conceited brat-boy!" She threw sand at me. She pushed me. She tickled me. We wrestled. We kissed. "I missed you, Kathleen."

"I've missed you, too, Garrett Mills."

Then we slowed, settled back, watched the lake.

"What about you, Miss P., and your life in medicine?"

"Oh Gar. Oh God. It's much more fun to talk about you. I'm so lost and confused. It's so boring to talk about. Yuck."

"Come on, you don't get off that easy."

"Are we really allowed to kiss and snuggle and talk about the fate of our lives all at the same time?"

"If *we* don't, who will?"

"I'm hungry and look, Gar, I think the sun wants to set." Kathy pointed. We both eyed the far lake horizon, its trees and house tops and, just above those, a line-up of white clouds turning pink, and, just above those, as if nestled in pink pillows, a glaring orange sun. "Naw. That's a half hour from now."

"How can you tell? Looks pretty imminent to me."

"'Imminent,' huh? Where'd you get that expensive word?"

"Hey, I'm a college girl."

"Oh?"

"Very bright, very savvy."

"I bet. You major in 'changing the subject'?"

She slapped me. I pulled at her. We wrestled again, and kissed some more.

Then Kathy stopped, sat up. "Maybe that's my life's theme: change the subject."

"Yeah?"

"Remember how I loved Art History? Then that classical music class I took."

"But you always majored in Biology."

"Yes, I did. I think now in deference to dear ol' dad."

"It's the 'family business,' right? Carol and her anesthesiologist . . . Ellie and the surgeon, Dr. Hump Dee Dump."

"Hampton-Scott, Gar! You better learn that because when we go to England and we're at their wedding—"

"I wasn't invited."

"You weren't? You will be."

"If I were still headed for med school, perhaps. But now, a scruffy ne'er-do-well artist? I don't think so. Nuh-uh."

"You really think that?"

"Well . . ." I fiddled with a handful of sand plus a few broken slivers of grass. "It also occurred to me," I went on, "my not being a doctor is why, well . . ."

"What? Why what?"

I looked at Kathy and then turned to the lake water. "That maybe you're not sure about me."

"Not sure of you? Oh, Gar, no. It's me, I'm the one I'm not sure about. You've found your path. It's me who's really confused." Kathy's face reddened as if she might cry.

"Okay, Kath, but you love medicine, the sciences, all that. You know that world."

"True. But these kids, Gar. I really love these kids. They're so interesting and shy, like I used to be. Like I still am. But they're so troubled and needy. I think sometimes I could really help, you know?"

"You're great with kids."

"But, is that really a viable choice, given my folks' expectations? And. You know."

"Are they pressuring you?"

"A little. Chrissie hears it more because she's home this summer. But yeah, in subtle ways. My mom. Not Dad."

"Your mom. She's a powerhouse."

"She is, isn't she?"

"A veritable Iowa mother hen, that Winnie, and quite sophisticated."

"Yeah, quite a mix."

"Look, you wanna please your parents, but Kath—"

"I know, I know, but I'm not strong like you. I'm not good at standing up for myself."

"I'm strong? No, I'm just possessed. You, you're shy and you're figuring things out, which takes time. But finally, whose life do you want to live, right?"

"Right."

Kathy let sand sift through her right hand as she leaned on her left arm. In this position her breasts also leaned, close and full, their tilt, their cleavage. This, too, was part of her shyness or restraint, that she was sexy without really knowing it. It was innate; it was, in the simplest of gestures, always there.

We both sat staring at the lake as the water shimmered with the orangey glow of sun, blue sky, pink clouds, and hints of the coming dusk. All the world, as so many of our elders were ready to tell us, lay before us. Yet how difficult it was sometimes to savor it and join with it—to enter with delight and trust, unabashed, full speed ahead. This was 1971, not far off from the late '60s. Rebellion was still in the air. Our "wise elders" were being shown up as out of step, myopic, materialistic, their lives empty. They were no longer the final word, for some of us. Kathy would have to find her way. I loved her family but her mother could be demanding and controlling. And Kathy was quiet, unsure, and easily outmaneuvered by her demonstrative and outspoken mother.

Dr. Pheteplace, like Kathy, was quiet, watchful. He let his wife Winnie do the "dirty work." I was determined that I'd be Kathy's advocate. Maybe not her knight on a white horse but, as best I could, her painterly rebel in arms.

After a long silence, sifting sand, staring at lake water, I said, almost off-hand, "What about combining kids and medicine? Is that a possibility?"

Kathy looked at me. A strange look.

"Did you hear me, Kath?"

She looked out to the pinkish waters. "Kids and medicine. Yeah. I heard you, Gar." Then she violently threw down her partial handful of sand. "And I'm still hungry, you big doofus the Goofus."

"Oh yeah?"

"Yeah! I'll race you, last swim. Come on!"

"Whoa!"

She was up and off to the white-edged waters. I followed, barely, my right foot had fallen asleep. I limped and made it finally. We swam. Her crawl to my laggard (prickly, awakening right foot) dog paddle. Then her breaststroke to my rousing, more sudsy Sturm und Drang than distance and grace, braggadocio of a butterfly. Until finally we both twisted and swiveled (Kathy swiveled smoothly, with style) into a pair of fluent, steady backstrokes. Out to where the waters were dark, deeper, colder.

15

That Friday night we ate hamburgers and good ol' "Tin Sea" barbeque. Too late to eat by the lake, we sat outside at The BBQ Roadhouse, at an orange-painted wood picnic table. We watched teenagers, families, a sweet warm summer night, all the radios blasting, loud with the Grand Ole Opry program.

Then, we drove to the lake, set up the sleeping bag on the not-yet-dewy hillside. We lay on our backs under the blue queen-size sheet and talked some more. We watched the dark starry night sky, the Grand Ole Opry still resounding from several of the RV trailers parked a hundred yards away, on the edge of the woods. We slept like babies.

Saturday, we got up slowly. Folks from the RVs, and a few campers from tents, started to walk by us, on their way to the showers. I went for a run. Kathy wanted to come, too. I told her she was welcome, but then she decided to take my El Greco book and the Bible down to the picnic table by the lake. I finished my run, kicking it in strong, just where the bridge joins the lake area, and then jogged gently, quietly, and tried to sneak up on Kathy. But she saw me. "Hi, Gar. Nice run?"

It was. The day already steaming, hot sun, clear strong blue sky, we went for a swim together, then showered, and eventually had pancakes at the Snack Shack.

After that, of course, there was nothing to do but make our way to the county fairgrounds, about a twenty-minute car ride away. It wasn't even noon yet and already the place was packed. There was cotton candy, homemade ice cream, pies, all kinds of jams on display, lots of stands with different versions of BBQ. There were games with basketballs, tennis balls, hand balls, and even guns, rifle-air guns and BB guns.

There was a roller coaster, a bit weathered and loud, like huge rattling teeth as it shuddered by, and that cranking noise as it slowly ascended. Then the roar of metal on metal as it swung through its loops, finally slowing its clattering as it made its final descent and pulled into the grey wood slatted platform. We could hear it from far off as we drifted among games and booths. Once we found it, I was ready to hop on board. Kathy was not.

We watched it shudder by us at least twice before Kathy was persuaded it was safe, and after a number of frowns, finally acquiesced. And then she loved it so much that we did it twice. She wanted to go a third time. It was me, I began to feel nauseous and begged off.

We bought some cotton candy and slowly made our exit, bearing prizes: Kathy clasped cotton candy and a big pink teddy bear I'd won making five baskets in a row. I sucked my cotton candy while holding another pink bear and a big fuzzy orange elephant, won by throwing rings and shooting a BB gun, respectively.

It took awhile to figure out which direction the parking lot was in. As we neared it, Kathy spotted the fairgrounds water slide, and I wanted some of that soft ice cream. What to do? The day wouldn't end. That was fine with me. We had our swimsuits drying out in Titine's rear window shelf. Why not? We'd have soft ice cream later.

We went to the car, put our "trophies" in the trunk, retrieved our swimsuits, changed in the car, which was kind of humorous (the necessary contortions in the front seat of a 1965 Peugeot!) and erotic, too (Kathy's naked body, voluptuous and innocently seductive). As we locked up Titine and shuffled back through the huge parking lot, the row upon row look of a used car lot, I saw two young men waving books at people, calling out greetings. At first, I thought they were calling to us. Kathy turned to me as I stopped and watched.

"What, Gar?"

"Are those guys calling to us?"

"Don't think so. Come on. It's too hot to just stand here. Please?"

"Wait, Kath. I know those guys."

"Those guys?" She looked their way again. "They look like Jehovah's Witnesses with their white shirts and dark slacks. Gar, I'm boiling."

"Okay but—wait! That's Eddie and Chuck!"

"Eddie and Chuck?"

"You know, from the Southwest Company! Omigod."

"The dictionary thing?"

"Right! I'm sure it's them. Come on!"

"But, Gar."

"We'll keep moving, say hi and then hit the water slide, okay?" I was already heading off in their direction.

A heavy-set man and a thinner woman with two plump kids, all in Bermuda shorts, were getting out of their station wagon. Both Chuck and Eddie stood nearby, flashing their smiles and Southwest dictionaries.

"As good a book as the Bible," said Chuck.

"And made by the same company that makes great Bibles, too," said Ed.

"The Southwest Company, that's right," said Chuck, nodding.

The man nodded, the wife gave an uneasy grin as she pushed the kids along. The little boy and the girl, too, were both quite content to stand and watch this tag-team approach.

"And, what's just about as important as God and the Bible?"

"Your education!" said Eddie, now zeroing in on the kids.

"Truly," said Chuck. "You buy this dictionary and the world of words, all kinds of words, opens up to you."

"An education, a *good* education," added Ed.

"Learn words, good words, lots of words, and all kinds of doors open up to you," said Chuck, nodding some more. It looked pretty hopeless, even ridiculous. Kathy and I slowed our approach and watched. The kids were mesmerized.

"Come on, kids, let's scoot along," said the mom, pale-skinned and cautious.

"How much?" asked the beer-belly dad.

"Just ten dollars, sir," said Ed.

"Ten?"

"Eighteen bucks if you buy two," added Eddie. "One for your daughter and one for your boy."

"Eighteen, huh?"

"Yes, sir."

"Dale," said the mom, "what're yer doin'?"

Dale was reaching into his pocket. "This young man's right, Sal. This is the time for our kids to learn things. Words. Get a vocabulary, right, Mary Sue?"

"Yes, Daddy."

"Right, Jake?"

"I dunno. I guess."

"But, Dale—"

"Look, Sal, eighteen bucks is a steal, believe me."

"Okay, if you say so."

"Here," Dale held out a twenty. "Keep all of it."

"Omigod, really?" said Eddie.

"No. No, sir. We said eighteen. A deal's a deal," said Chuck. "Here's two bucks change, and, Ed, could you grab those books from the trunk?"

Eddie briskly skipped over about three cars away, leaned into a half-open trunk, slowly eased the trunk lid back down, making sure not to close it, and ran back with two Southwest black leather (Bible look-a-like) dictionaries. He smiled as he bent and gave one to each of them. "Here you go, Mary Sue . . . and you, too, Jake. Enjoy!"

"What do you say, Jake?" The mom pressed her son's crew haircut.

"I dunno."

"Mary Sue?"

"Thank you, sir."

"Jake?" asked the dad.

"What, Dad?"

"You heard your sister. What do you say to these two young men?"

"Um, I wanted to know how old you got to be to sell books like these?"

Everyone laughed.

"First things first, Jake. Say 'thank you.'"

"Thank you, Mister."

"Jake," said his dad, "you want to sell books? I thought you wanted to work at the distillery with your daddy."

"I dunno."

Then Chuck saw us. Eddie, too.

"You got a real nice family, sir, and thank you very much for your business," said Chuck.

"Sure, boys, good luck with it."

Everyone nodded, smiled, waved as they parted. Chuck and Eddie called out, "Thanks again! Have a great day! Enjoy the fairgrounds!" Then, just before Chuck and Ed turned to us, they both smiled at each other and shook hands.

"Hey, Chuck. Hey, Eddie, you book-selling guys!" I called to them as Kathy and I approached.

"Garry! Hi, Kathy!" called Ed. Chuck nodded, waved.

We all shook hands.

"Wow," I said. "You guys sure make selling books look easy."

"It's our new strategy, right, Ed? Think it's starting to work," said Chuck, nodding, until he gave us a good look. "What, you guys going swimming?"

"Water slide," said Kathy and pointed back to the far length of the parking lot.

"Nice," said Ed. "Wouldn't mind a swim right now. This Tennessee heat's killing me."

"It's the humidity I can't bear," said Chuck.

"That, too," said Ed.

"Come on. Join us," said Kathy. "You got swimsuits?"

"We do," said Chuck, looking at Eddie. "But, we gotta keep at this. We got a late start. That was only our fifth sale. We're hoping we might knock off maybe thirty sales, right, Ed? Before we call it a day."

Ed nodded, now surprisingly serious. "Thirty sales or dusk, whichever comes first."

"Jeez." I watched them. "You guys are really ambitious, really working hard. You wanna have dinner with us later?"

"That could work," said Chuck.

"Dinner, great! Where should we meet?" asked Ed.

We agreed to meet at the Snack Shack a little after eight p.m.

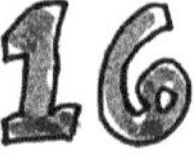

Kathy and I did do the water slide. With too many little kids, it was still a refreshing relief from the heat. I ate my soft ice cream (spoiling my dinner) as we drove away from the fairgrounds. Ed and Chuck were still hard at it, with our directions to the Snack Shack in hand.

Kathy and I took another, quieter swim, at the lake, then showered. As the sun began to spill an orange wash across Old Hickory Lake, we drove back into town. When we walked into the Snack Shack, Terri gave us a shout, "Hey, Picasso, and hello again, Miss Iowa!" She waved us over to a booth. "Is Iowa as hot as it is here?" Terri handed us our menus as we sat.

"Pretty hot," said Kathy. "But not into the evening like this."

"Yeah, this just started a few weeks ago. Not fun, but it beats the alternative."

"Which is?" I asked. Terri stopped, looked at me. "I dunno. Snow?" We laughed. We ordered sodas and decided to wait for Ed and Chuck before ordering.

We were sipping our sodas as Ed and Chuck, still in their ties, white shirts, and dark slacks, found their way to our big table on the rear patio about 8:15 p.m. The two salesmen bumped along and joined us; they were exhausted and starving, they said. Very quickly, I assaulted them with my list of Twenty Questions: What happened to your sidekicks? How'd you end up in Donelson? (They were actually in a town about five miles further north and east.) Have you heard from Durland? Are you making any money? Have you seen any others from our "graduating class" of the Southwest Company convention? Are you having any fun? And so on. All of which, in time, they answered. But the big piece of news concerned Big Jim. "He had a heart attack," said Chuck.

"What?" I was open mouthed.

"Truly," said Ed. "It's very sad. Very depressing."

"Wait. Is he okay? Is he alive? What happened?"

Chuck and Ed looked at each other. Then Chuck explained, "We only heard about it two or three weeks ago. I was working over near Memphis and Eddie—"

"I was stationed near Knoxville."

"Eddie and I stayed in touch, and neither of us had heard from Big Jim for a few weeks. We'd always call him, to check in, then he'd call us back, right, Ed?"

"Right. Then, for a week or so, nothing. I mentioned this to Chuck when we talked. We started checking in at the end of each week."

"Wait. I'm sorry. Is Big Jim okay? Is he alive?" I was scared.

"No, he's alive."

"Barely," added Ed.

"Come on, Ed, it's not that bad."

"It's pretty bad."

I was confused.

"Look," said Chuck, "we finally reached his secretary at Southwest. She said he'd been out of town, visiting this farm where he grew up."

"No way!" I jumped in.

"Yes! It's near here, in fact," said Eddie.

"Anyway," Chuck continued, "he was driving home and he started to lose his breath. He couldn't talk or move his face, but he'd just pulled into his driveway when he had it."

"So, his wife found him," Ed continued. "She'd just gotten home. Heard him pull in but he never came into the house. He was in his car, unconscious."

"Paramedics came. They rushed him to the hospital. He survived. He's okay." Chuck nodded.

Ed shook his head. "He's not 'okay.' He's in bed in a hospital."

"Where?" I asked.

"Not far from here. St. Ann's Mercy. Between here and Nashville. Maybe a half-hour from here. But he's supposed to go home pretty soon," added Chuck.

"No, I don't think so, Chuck."

"Jesus, Ed, you're such a pessimist."

"Realist. He's in bad shape."

"Look," Chuck started with Ed, then tried to explain to Kathy and me, "he's a very big man. He's maybe forty, if that. He's lucky. It was one of those warnings. A wake-up call. He's down but he's not out. And it wasn't a stroke, Eddie. He can talk, he can move."

"Barely."

"What room number?" I asked. "Does he have a phone?"

"Yeah. It's room 305. The phone number is . . ." Chuck checked his pants pocket then his shirt pocket. "I left it in our room. If you have a phone number, I can call you with it."

"No phone. Well. You could call the Donelson Public Library and leave a message for me there."

"What? You live at the library?" asked Eddie, laughing.

"No, no."

"Just about." Kathy nudged my shoulder.

Then both of them wanted to know about me, about us. Was I really living at the library, and had Kathy decided to stay in Tennessee for the summer? It was confusing at first. Terri took our orders. Drinks came. Food came. We ate, we drank, we cleared things up. Kathy was just here for the weekend. I lived out at Old Hickory Lake. The last time I saw Big Jim was while I was still haying, and, he was seriously thinking of killing himself. Probably the same day, ironically, he had his heart attack. I'd wondered why I'd never heard from him again. I told them about the library, Mrs. Helms and her boys, the series of portraits I'd been painting.

Then, once we shared what news we had of Durland (not a lot), they explained how they'd lost their partners, shifted territories so they could stay closer to Big Jim, and also found a big furnished room in a boardinghouse where, by sharing a room, they could save money.

"That Durland, man!" said Eddie, as he chewed ice from his soda.

"I know," Chuck laughed. "Gets us all psyched to sell dictionaries and then skips town."

"I only came on this joyride 'cause of him," said Ed.

"We all did, Eddie. But, hey, we were curious, and I do think we've made some pretty good money."

"But that's why we lost Brad and Monroe."

"Because of John, or because of his leaving? I mean, Brad was a Johnny-clone. I watched him. But what about Monroe?"

"The Christian thing got to Monroe," said Chuck.

"What 'Christian thing'?" Kathy asked.

They both laughed and looked at each other. Then Eddie waved his hand to Chuck as if to say, Take it, Chuck. "Monroe was a born-again Christian, or so he thought. Until he started going door-to-door."

"Oh man, oh yeah," said Eddie.

"What happened?" I asked.

"Well, Monroe was so euphoric about God and His people and being in the Bible Belt, the 'sacred heart of American Christianity.' I think he was surprised when people, all sorts, but probably a lot of them Christians, just closed the door. Even slammed it in his face."

Eddie fingered the dewy rim of his soda. "He thought he could be a Christian among Christians, but he forgot that you have to be a human first. That people, really, basically, are whoever they are, wherever you go, you know?"

"So, with John not there to cheer him on—"

"And cheer him up—"

"He called it quits. Left about two weeks ago," said Chuck.

"Which is when Brad-boy departed," nodded Ed.

"So, Big Jim, propped up in his hospital bed, among tubes and monitors, said, 'Why don't you two partner up?'" continued Chuck.

"So, we did." Eddie drained the last of his soda.

"A marriage made in—Tennessee," laughed Chuck.

"Actually, it hasn't been all that bad," said Eddie, waving to Terri.

We continued to talk and trade summer tales. I persuaded everyone to try the pecan pie a la mode. Kathy told us about her Y camp, the nights of campfires and ghost stories (I tried not to picture shy and vulnerable Greg Kinkel).

Eddie joked that he was falling in love with Chuck, who was such a good roommate, so neat, so disciplined, quiet and thoughtful. Chuck blushed. He, in turn, admitted that he had a bit of a crush on the boardinghouse lady's daughter, who'd recently lost her husband in the

Vietnam War, a widow at twenty-nine, no kids. She'd come to live with her folks and help out cleaning rooms and fixing meals.

"She's not college educated but I dunno, she's really sweet, has a curious mind . . . we've had these pretty deep, almost profound, talks."

"So that's what you're doing," said Ed.

"What?"

"I see you out in the backyard after supper. At the picnic table, all alone reading, and then, I look again. She's seated across from you, smoking one cigarette after another."

"So?"

"She's a smoker, Chuck."

"I know."

"I thought you hated girls who smoke."

"I do but—"

"But?"

"This girl—woman, really—is different."

"She sounds like she's got some depth," Kathy said. "Like she's been through quite a lot."

"She has," said Chuck. "She really has . . ." Chuck looked down at his half-finished pecan pie, dragged a fork through the now soupy white sauce of melted ice cream. Then, in a whisper, his eyes moistening, he almost hissed, "This damn war. I really hate it. Our country. Jesus . . . and all these kids, these young guys—dying for what? The damage it leaves in all these towns, all over America, and for what?"

"You're thinking of your kid brother," Eddie quietly broke in.

"Yeah . . . but this woman, Betsy Sue, I think of her, too. She really loved her husband. They'd only been together a few years. He enlisted, came home after one tour. They got married, he went back, did another tour. Came back. This last tour was when he was killed, and get this: they're not sure, it was a night march, but he might've been killed by friendly fire. Can you believe it?"

We all hung our heads as if on cue. I looked up, looked over at Chuck. He continued to move his fork in among his pie's soggy dregs. "What about your brother, Chuck?" I asked.

"What about him?"

"Is he over there now?"

"Just graduated high school. Kid's a jerk. Had a scholarship to this small school in Pennsylvania. He's a jock, football. But, nope, he went and enlisted. The Marine Corps. Jesus. Can you believe it?"

"Oh man."

"I think it's about proving he's a man. My dad was in the military. Dad finally got one of his boys to 'be a man.' My older brother, Jack, took off for technical school, became a mechanic. But Tommy . . ."

"It's scary," said Kathy.

"But a lot of young people are coming to their senses," said Eddie.

"I do feel a little guilty," I admitted.

"Guilty?" said Chuck.

"This is us, our generation, 'our war,' you could say, and I'm glad to be 4F but I was prepared to be a CO."

"But, Gar." Kathy leaned into me. "You *are* a conscientious objector. You're not a killer."

"True."

"Do you think you're less of a man?" asked Chuck.

"Maybe so. Maybe that's it."

"See?" said Chuck. "See how messed up that is?"

"Yeah," said Eddie. "And I considered going because I'd get to see all those naked men but nope, a high number blew it for me!"

Kathy and Chuck both looked at Eddie. I laughed. Eddie made jokes like this. He was never openly homosexual, and he still gave lip service to dating girls, but it was pretty obvious, Eddie was not straight.

That's how our evening concluded. We were all glad that we'd run into each other. We promised to stay in touch the rest of the summer. Chuck and Ed decided to return to their boardinghouse. Kathy and I drove back to the lake.

17

Our second and final night together under the stars. As we lay on our backs, I kept hoping we'd see a shooting star. It'd be a sign for us, a good omen. No such luck. We talked and cuddled and kissed and talked. My rival, Kink, seemed to lie there with us, on the other side of Kathy, silent, as if alternately she'd hush him, and other times, I'd lean over to kiss her, look his way, and put a finger to my mouth. I didn't want to hear from him, not then, not ever. And then we slept.

Sunday morning, I took Kathy to my Methodist Church. I sang in the choir, she looked up from below, gave a smile, a shy wave. I introduced her afterward to Dr. Bill and Reverend Bill. Everyone made a fuss. I beamed and Kathy blushed.

The Snack Shack was packed but Terri was there, spotted me, waved us to a table for two in the far corner. We weren't very chatty, the gloom of departure had descended, so it helped that the place was noisy with church-goers, kids, families.

Terri kept an eye on us, refilling our drinks, and eventually, on one of her brief visits, she got Kathy to talk about her camp and the kids and how a little loving can change a child's whole outlook and behavior.

"Not just kid-kids either, honey. I gotta grown kid-man and I see the same thing. A little lovin' goes a long way," Terri laughed as she ripped our check from her pad, placed it in front of me, winked, and departed.

After I paid, we slowly zig-zagged our way past the frenzy of diners out to the dusty parking lot. With a certain deliberate slowness, we got into Titine and began the drive to the airport.

I watched Kathy as she stared out the passenger window. We had our windows open. Breezes kicked up and there was a slight coolness in among the waves of humid heat, as if the weather itself were foreshadowing the autumn to come. An autumn I still wasn't sure Kathy really wanted to share with me, her sister's wedding in London, then backpacking through Europe. But we didn't talk about that. We didn't talk much at all. I gave up being the charming entertainer. I was already aching with missing her, the impending return to loneliness.

And yet, it's what we'd done for almost four years, a pattern begun and continued through our college years: these bright, shining hours of a Friday, Saturday into Sunday, begun with such glee and fanfare, concluded with the hollow thump of exhaustion and sadness, something I figured was pretty close to the death of a loved one. And then we parted.

The airport wasn't crowded at all. Her plane sat there, waiting. In those days, I was able to walk her to the gate. We hugged. I looked into her sweet soft summer sky blue eyes. She touched my dimple. "Don't be sad, Gar. Imagine. You're getting paid to paint pictures, and you've made so many wonderful new friends."

"Yeah but—"

"I'll try to be better about writing. I promise."

"Okay."

"Will you sing me a lullaby tonight when you lie down under all those stars?"

"Oh great, you had to say that."

"What?"

"I miss you already."

"I do, too, Gar, but . . ."

"But what?"

She paused a moment. She looked at me with a brightness, a twinkle in her eyes.

This is where I hoped she'd say it first, "I love you." But no. And why didn't I say it? It was so obvious that I adored her. But I wanted to be less demonstrative, more like shy-guy, Greg Kinkel, Kink. I didn't want to come on so strong, to overwhelm her.

"Gar?"

"Yeah?"

"You're such a silly boy."

"That makes you a silly girl, I guess."

"Perhaps. But, Gar, don't you see? You're having a great summer."

"Really?"

"You are . . . I'm so glad I got to visit, to be with you and your very special world . . . Now, go love being an artist, you goof!"

"Thanks, Kath."

We hugged, kissed quickly, and she walked off. "Hey!" I called, "You go love being a camp counselor, okay?" She waved. "And love those kids!" I called again. We both continued to wave.

As she turned, joined the line, and then was swallowed by the boarding tunnel's mouth, I whispered under my breath, "Just don't love that Greg Kinkel, please?" Which then became a prayer, "Oh God, I don't care. Let her love whoever she has to . . . Just bless her and keep her and take good care of her." That's where I got a little choked up. I went to the big windows and looked out, watched the plane as it slowly backed out of the gate and nimbly turned. I could swear I saw a hand and face up against the small O of window, waving, smiling. I wasn't sure. But I was pretty sure.

That Sunday night was not easy. I didn't sing a lullaby to Kathy exactly. I lay on my sleeping bag and moved my hand around, feeling for her. I didn't find her. I wondered about her flight back to Iowa. Kathy back at camp. Durland back up North. My folks in Darlington. Chris in Pennsylvania, a wife, two young boys. Sandy and Judy and their two kiddos in Michigan.

A letter from my mom said they'd be driving east for Dad's birthday in August, that I should get in touch with them. Chris was coming, too, alone. Mom said that he might be leaving teaching. And, Carol, a ten-minute car ride from my folks, her lawyer husband and their three kids. She seemed better, Mom said, since the hospitalization. I'd even had a letter from Mom's mom, Grandma Gertrude.

So, I lay there thinking of old and young, and Kathy, mostly, and what was I doing all alone under all these stars, deep in the heart of the Bible-Belt South? On a piece of the earth named Tennessee, which always sounded like "Tin Sea" when they spoke of it around here?

18

Monday morning was pretty rough, too. I woke early from an antsy, restless sleep. I went for a slow, early dawn jog. Saw a stray dog. Saw a farmer walking to the barns. Saw cows. Saw the sun burn off low clouds. Felt the heat. Got up a good sweat. Took a nice swim, showered, dressed, and ate an apple as I sat by the lake. Read my Bible. Wrote in my journal (not even a page). I prayed. I pondered.

So. I'd visit the library. I'd go to the church, write some letters. I'd do my laundry, and by late afternoon, I'd arrive at the Helms', find Sammy outside having a smoke, and we'd resume work on his portrait. By the end of that next week, Sammy's portrait was finished. There were still some minor touch-ups I wanted to do, but basically it was all there: a sun-tanned Sammy in his short-sleeve shirt and Bermuda shorts, sitting in the aluminum chair, with his handsome face, keen blue eyes firmly looking at you, assured, low-key, ready to take on the world. With lovely shafts of setting sun's light breaking up the deep shadows on the lush green lawn behind him. I liked this painting.

Placed next to Mikey's, they made quite a pair. As distinct as paintings as the two brothers were different, but brothers. Stylistically, the paintings looked similar, although I could see how my handling of the paint was not sloppy but less assured with Mikey's. Also, the skin tones added to this shift: Mikey's indoor lighting gave him a lumpy, pasty tone, whereas Sammy, outdoors and tanned, looked so much stronger, clearer.

Lexie, buoyant, supportive fan that she was, after a few quibbles with Sammy's nose and the wrinkles in his shirt, good notes and adjustments easily made, became ecstatic and overjoyed. She invited me for a delicious celebratory dinner. Sammy, his girlfriend Courtney, Mikey and Perry, Lexie, and me. Still no sign of the train-traveling father.

It was an outdoor barbeque that Friday night. Sammy kept trying to get me to drink a beer. I kept begging off. Courtney kept defending me, even lauding me. "Not all guys have to get drunk, Sam." Sammy looked at her, then at me, then back to her. "You saying I'm a drunk, Court?"

"No. I am saying you like to drink. I'm also saying it's nice to meet guys who don't care about drinking that much. It's refreshing."

"Oh," said Sammy.

"I think I'm just compensating," I offered. "My dad, my two brothers, my brother-in-law, they're all drinkers. Being the youngest, I saw a lot of stupidity around booze and all. So. I'd rather not."

"Oh," said Courtney. "That's too bad."

"I wish I liked drinking. I just have no taste for it."

"That'll change, Picasso. Just you wait," as Sammy toasted his Bud to me.

"Can I have a Bud, Samuel?" asked Courtney.

"Oh, so now you wanna drink, Miss Prudie Panties."

"Sammy, stop! I'm not a prudie-panties. I'm thirsty, okay?"

It was a nice evening. Sammy and Courtney continued to flirt and then bicker. Lexie kept bringing out different side dishes and desserts, too. Mikey and Perry, juggling their leather mitts, threw a new white hard ball, back and forth, on the bright lawn just beyond the grill. I sat at the picnic table and watched all this. Sammy manned the grill: hot dogs, burgers, BBQ.

I asked Lexie what I could do to help.

"You're the guest of honor, Brown. Enjoy it. These events don't come along every day."

True. I nodded, smiled. I missed Kathy. Oh, also a pang of missing my brothers, my sister, Mom, Dad, family. Now and then, I'd turn to look at the two paintings of Mikey and Sam. Lexie, in her enthusiasm and pride, had set them on a wood bench in such a way that the canvases tilted just slightly as they both leaned against the side shingles of the house. Nice. It was fun to see them there. I felt good about them.

She'd already paid me the seventy-five dollars for Mikey's. Another seventy-five was coming tomorrow, she assured me, after she went to the bank. That seventy-five plus Mikey's made one hundred and fifty dollars, plus about thirty dollars left over from the haying work. I was a rich man!

I'd have almost two hundred dollars in the bank, no rent to pay (the campsite and lake and starry nights, so far, were rent-free!), minimal food costs, the weekly laundering, and the promise, according to Lexie, of more painting work to come. Plus, a show of my drawings and paintings to follow in mid-August. Life was good and full and, okay, a little bit lonely, too.

After the meal, I continued to just sit there and watch. Lexie and Courtney were razzing Sammy. Perry and Mikey kept pestering Lexie: they wanted to go in and watch TV. As I nursed my ginger ale and mild depression, a pink VW bus pulled into Lexie's driveway. Out popped Rosemary, from the library, with a young dark-haired girlfriend.

Rosemary called to Lexie as they came over to the picnic table, "Are we in time for dessert?" Then Rosemary turned to me and said, "Hi, Garry. Congratulations on your paintings, your portraits. Can we see them?" I nodded and started to point to the side of the house. The dark-haired girl looked familiar for some reason.

"Pecan pie, with or without ice cream, Rosemary, and, aren't you going to introduce your friend?"

"I'm sorry. This is Patricia. Patty, you know Mrs. Helms."

"Lexie, please, and this is my oldest, Sam, his girlfriend, Courtney. That's my Mikey, his friend Perry. Say hi, boys!"

"Hi," said Mikey who elbowed Perry, who said, "Hi," with a dirty look toward Mikey.

"Can we go watch TV now, Mom?"

"I suppose. If you want dessert, you eat it out here. It's not going into the living room."

"Oh, Ma!"

"Michael, you know the rules."

"Fine. You want dessert, Perry?"

"Naw," said Perry, eyes on Patricia.

"Good. Let's go." They departed.

Lexie finished the introductions. "And this is our Guest of Honor,

Mr. Garry 'Picasso' Brown."

"We know," said Rosemary.

"But Patricia doesn't."

"Oh, I do, Mrs. Helms. I met Garry earlier this summer at Dr. Bill's. Remember, Garry?"

"We did?" I watched her white skin, red lips, bright eyes, long dark hair. Of course, the precocious musician. "I thought you looked familiar. Patricia, right?"

"Yes. And I'm going to be your next painting."

"You are?"

"His next victim, you mean," said Rosemary, nudging Patricia. Both girls shared a look and laughed.

"I don't understand." I looked at them and Lexie. Sammy shrugged, nonplussed.

"This is your next portrait commission, Brown," explained Lexie.

"Right," said Patricia, jumping in, "Mrs. Helms talked about it with Rosemary, who knows me. My mom called Mrs. Helms and it's all arranged. When do you want to start? Tomorrow?"

"Gosh . . ." Did I really want to start another portrait that soon?

"Oh, look, Pats. See?" Rosemary spotted the two portraits. The girls moved to the side of the house. "Oh wow," Patricia said quietly. "Gee, Garry," Rosemary kept eyeing the paintings as she spoke, "I had no idea . . . these are superb . . . don't you think, Pats?" "I'm amazed." Patricia stood there wide-eyed.

"Really?" I smiled. When I looked over to Sammy, cuddling with Courtney, he gave me a big thumbs-up.

"Really."

"Yeah," said Rosemary, now standing next to the paintings, bending closer and eyeing them. "I had no idea they'd be so realistic. So polished. So professional." Patricia joined Rosemary, the two leaning and looking.

"He's the real deal, alright," said Lexie, as she spooned vanilla ice cream onto two separate portions of pecan pie. "Come, girls, sit and have some pie and visit with the artist. Please."

"Oh, why not?" Rosemary reached for her pie a la mode. "Eat, drink, for tomorrow we—diet."

19

In fact, the next day, Saturday, we started. I had thought I was going to have a lazy day by the lake—read, draw, write in my journal, go for a cooling swim or two. Instead, after a late breakfast at the Snack Shack, I met Patricia at the Donelson Library around noon. She wanted to know what she should wear. I said not to worry, that we'd just talk. I'd do some sketches of her face, and we'd figure out a pose all while we visited. She said she'd have directions for me on how to find her house when we officially met the following week. She understood that the library visit was just an informal warm-up. She already knew where she wanted me to paint her—on their screened-in porch. Which I told her sounded great. We met for about an hour.

Lexie said, "Why don't you guys go over and sit at my picnic table? It's in the shade, not quite so busy and populated like this place—with Rosemary looking over your shoulder every other minute!"

Rosemary made a face. "Aw, don't leave." But we did.

Lexie's home was deserted. No sign of Sammy, perhaps off doing errands with Courtney, or taking her to lunch. And Mikey, maybe for a change, was in Perry's backyard playing catch. It felt strange to have it so quiet. Except it wasn't.

Patricia was an avid talker. It helped and it didn't. It helped because it meant I didn't have to talk at all, to put her at ease. No need. She was fully at ease. It annoyed me because a lot of it was just chatter, gossip, or a kind of showing off. Especially when she went on about her music or comparing classical music to the great works of painters like Rembrandt, or a writer like Shakespeare. I'm sure there's a place for this type of discussion, but not when I'm drawing, trying to capture a likeness. Also, she kept trying to have a real conversation, asking me questions. It probably was better when she went off on one of her precocious academic riffs.

"Am I talking too much, Garry?"

"No, no. Keep going. I'll just watch you and draw."

"Don't you like to talk?"

"I do but—"

"A lot of men I meet aren't very verbal. My mother thinks I scare them off."

"Oh?"

"Do you think that?"

"How do you mean?"

"Do I put you off? Because I'm so bright and articulate?"

"Oh. Uh." I was annoyed, sure, but I was also impressed with the degree of her self-confidence. Rare, I thought, in a teenager, and especially rare that she's so able to verbalize it. But because I wasn't responding, I could see that under this bravado was real insecurity: Patricia almost seemed about to cry.

"My dad says I need to be patient. That high school and this town, this area, might not be the place to find like-minded, articulate souls. What do you think?"

"You mean like creative types?"

"Yes!"

"Your dad's probably right."

"Really?"

"Well, I think it's rare. Not just here but all over America."

"Not just Tennessee?"

"Oh no. The Arts are very underappreciated."

"Guess you're right. My mom and dad have said as much. Dr. Bill, too."

"You'll find your tribe," the twenty-three-year-old counseled the seventeen-year-old whiz kid.

"Thanks. How's it looking?"

"Pretty good." Not good at all. She was a lovely young woman, fair skin, high cheekbones, dark eyes, dark hair. But for some reason, I could not grasp even the slightest likeness. Why? Was it her talking so much? Was it that her face was so beautiful? Not a small nose, not a big nose.

And her eyes—I just could not piece together her eyes. Long eyelashes, yes, but what was it? By now I'd done several pencil sketches. Maybe I needed to use the ink pen, the Rapidograph, make it a little riskier. Sometimes pencil becomes too casual, I don't quite focus. The ink pen, it's do or die. One false move, it's pretty much over, difficult to reverse or readjust. So.

"Can I see?"

"Not just yet. Let me try one more in pencil, and then a last one in ink."

"Really?"

"Is that okay? Are you tired?"

"Gosh, no. I could sit here all day. It's so lovely here, isn't it?"

"Yes." The pencil one bombed.

"This is my first time."

"First time?"

"Having my portrait done."

"No! An attractive girl like you?" Although you'd hardly know from these abortive attempts. Oh man. Okay, let's try it in black ink.

"You really think I'm attractive?"

If you don't look at these sketches, yes. "Oh God, your dad must have a well-used shotgun."

"What's that supposed to mean? My dad hates guns and violence of any kind."

"No, no. It was a joke." The ink version wasn't going very well either. "You know, a shotgun. To keep all the boys away."

"Away? From what?"

"You." And these drawings. Yuck. Shit. Piss. Fuck.

We finished up. Patricia wanted to see the drawings. I really didn't want to show them to her.

"Don't be modest. Please show me?"

Oh God. "They're really very rough."

"Please."

"Okay. Here's the pen and ink, but—"

"Oh. I like this. Wow."

"Really?" We both stood over the opened sketchbook, as if fallen in defeat, on the picnic table.

"Is this the pose you like?" Patricia asked, now fingering it.

"Not necessarily. We'll know more once we set up on your screened porch."

"Right. Gosh, I almost look pretty here."

"'Almost'? Because the drawing stinks or you're being modest?"

She laughed. "Because the drawing's great, and I think I'm really a witch, but, not according to this."

"A witch? No way!"

"Boys don't like me and, oh gosh. I'm sorry." Patricia began to cry. She turned away. I had no idea what to do.

"Hey, you wanna a real laugh? Look at the pencil drawings." It was all I could think of. So, I pulled out the five pencil sketches. Patricia wiped her eyes. She laughed.

"You're really a very gifted artist," she said in a very solemn tone, and wiped her eyes some more.

I was getting depressed. I walked her back to the library, where Rosemary took her under wing. We agreed that I'd come to her house after lunch Monday afternoon, around two p.m. I wished her and Rosemary a good weekend. Lexie came out just as I was leaving. "So, Picasso, how'd do? You capture Beauty and Truth?"

I laughed, "Well—"

"He captured something," said Patricia. "And I had a meltdown. Sorry, Garry."

"What? No. Don't be sorry. Hey, it's our artistic temperaments, right?"

"Right. Thanks."

"Two o'clock Monday." I was reading from the flower-design notepaper that I'd grabbed from my shirt pocket. "Greenbriar Way . . . Number, uh . . . 4711."

"That's it," Patricia nodded.

"I may come and watch," grinned Rosemary.

"Don't you dare!" Patricia swatted Rosemary's shoulder.

"We both might," said Lexie. "Us librarians need a little excitement now and then."

"Stop. Both of you, right, Garry? They can't watch, can they?"

"Not at first. Maybe once the painting's really going. Maybe then."

"In a few days then?" asked Rosemary.

"It's up to the sitter."

"Pats, can we?"

"Gosh. Guess we'll just have to see."

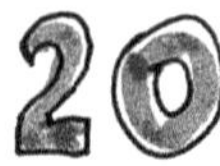

Sunday morning was overcast and hot. I went into town for church. I sang, but my heart was not in it. Don't know why but I got teary when I heard the reading about the prodigal son from Luke:

". . . 'And bring the fattened calf and kill it, and let us eat and celebrate. For this my son was dead, and is alive again; he was lost, and is found.' And they began to celebrate . . ."

Sunshine broke through by the time the service had ended. Everyone strolled from the church and gathered in their groups. I waved at folks, nodded, fake smiled. I had no desire to stop and visit. I almost got away before Dr. Bill called to me, "Garry! Wait a moment. Garry?" I stopped and looked back. Dr. Bill adjusted his bifocals, excused himself from the family he was talking to and came over. "Hey, how ya doin'?"

"Hi, Dr. Bill. Good, thanks."

"How's the lake life?"

"Pretty good."

"I hear you hooked up with my star musician, Patricia?"

"Yes."

"So?"

"Well, it's not romantic, if that's what you mean."

"No, no. She called me, all excited that you're going to paint her picture. Maybe I should have mine done one of these days, what do you think?"

"I'd like that."

"How much do you charge?"

"Oh gosh, whatever you feel is fair."

"Well, what's the going rate?"

"Well, for Mrs. Helms's sons, y'know, Lexie Helms, the librarian?"

"Oh sure. Married to the train-man."

"Right. She paid me seventy-five dollars for each portrait."

"Really? That seems very fair."

"I guess." I looked off. I wanted to get going.

"You okay?"

"How do you mean?"

"You don't seem your cheery self. In the choir, too, you seemed a little removed."

"Well . . ." I looked down. A flush of heat filled my face, about to transform into tears. What was going on? My throat began to tighten. I couldn't talk. Dr. Bill looked back over to his friends, waved. "Well, okay. You take care of yourself." I nodded, squeaked out, in a gasp, "Right." Dr. Bill patted my shoulder. "Oh, there's Mary. She really was off today but God love her. Let me catch her. Get some rest, Garry, okay?"

He started off, then, "I may talk to you about doing my portrait, okay?"

"Sure." I'd caught it, my breath restored. "Thanks, Dr. Bill."

"Fine . . . Oh, Mary!" He waved. With another pat on my arm, he departed. "You take care, my lyric baritone savior."

I fake laughed as he walked off to catch up with Mary. True. I was a lyric baritone. Not that lyrical this morning. The "savior" reference, when I showed up that Wednesday night, the choir on the brink of dissolution, now felt like eons ago.

I wanted to get out of there. Then, I was glad when Dr. Bill caught me. I wanted to cry and then not. I was glad he saw my inexplicable pain and not. Then I wished he'd said, Let's go have a talk, come on, what's up? He didn't. He couldn't. He didn't know what to do with me or my choked-up state. Better to leave it alone. Which I then tried to do, too.

21

Throughout the next two weeks or so, this choked-up state continued. I was in some sort of bewildered funk. I knew I was very fortunate. I had mornings by the lake, time to read, write in my journal, muse. I finally received a letter from Kathy, also one from Durland. He'd gotten a part-time job near Brooke's home in East Aurora. He'd rented a room, but he would be back in Darlington by the time I'd return.

Some mornings I went for nice, slow runs. Some late afternoons, too. I swam in the lake. I ate apples by the lake, had pancakes at the Snack Shack, or a cheeseburger and strawberry shake at the Burger King.

At the library one day, I argued with Thomas about men going to the moon. Thomas, with his slow, almost mumbled drawl, still believed it was all done in a big film studio or on some backlot in Hollywood. He was sure it was fake. Men didn't really fly off into space, especially not all the way to the moon. Thomas believed in God but not a man on the moon.

Lexie had me over for dinner a few more times during these mysterious weeks. Rosemary continued to be shy and awkward whenever we talked. Sammy remained my biggest fan, and Mike and Perry continued to play catch and argue and make up and be best buddies.

I liked the pen and inks I'd done by the lake, even those I'd done in town of different folks: Trudy at the hair salon; finally, one of Terri at the Snack Shack and, Fred, the cook, too, in back by the grill. Also, a drawing of Mr. Barber at the bank who joked with me about my "millions in savings" and why didn't I open a checking account, too? Most of those ink drawings I liked. The watercolors, too.

But the two weeks I spent trying to find Patricia's likeness and finish her portrait were excruciating. It just wasn't coming. Was I forcing it? Had I lost my creative gift?

I took out a book on John Singer Sargent's paintings that featured his incredible array of portraits, many of high-society folks. Which was how I saw Patricia, as quite noble and dignified, a brilliant intellect and, okay, a high degree of affect, too, even snobbery. She was the kind of young lady who'd never been a tomboy, didn't know boys or sports, and had probably never done yardwork. So, there was something prissy and, also, moody. Every day we met, a different mood. Oh man. I wondered if this was inhibiting me somehow.

Must a portrait painter like the person he's painting? It seemed the people I knew less well, I painted better. That is, their likeness came easily. People I respected a great deal, or I felt were important people, or who I disliked, even in some small way, were not as easy to paint. Terri's husband, a difficult man, his likeness came easily. The reasons around a portrait's success were as mysterious as my own present heartache.

Also, the elements of a face must be factored in: older people, with strong features, were easier to capture than the quick, evanescent red-cheeks of youth. Children's faces, pretty young girls' faces, there weren't a lot of strong, deep lines to latch onto. No big noses or big ears or wrinkled eyes. Very few wrinkles, which for me, were often great footholds for pen and brush. Patricia was a pale porcelain-skinned beauty. And, I was confounded, bewildered. That and, she talked too much. Finally, about fifteen days later, it was finished. More or less. I still wasn't sure. So, we had a look.

It was still pretty bright, but closing in on dusk, when Patricia's mom, Patricia, and I stood on their screened-in porch and looked at the painting, soon to be joined by Patricia's dad. He pulled into their gravel drive and must've seen us, curious about those three huddled on the screened porch, silently staring.

I'd placed the painting, as big as Mike's and Sammy's, 30 x 40 inches, on the white rattan sofa with light green cushions. (With a row of my clean paint rags under it, so none of the wet parts of the picture would mess the cushions.)

Patricia had her right hand to her mouth and chin. Clara's arms were folded, her left hand to her chin. I squinted, wondering about certain areas, the contrast of Patricia's posed figure with the sofa's brightness, the shingled background's grimness. Was it too dark or did it need to be even darker? And, of course, did it look like her?

The crunch of gravel when Henry's car pulled in had broken the silence, as if a cue for Clara to say, "I like it."

"Really, Mom?"

"I really do. Don't you?"

"Well . . ."

I listened. I wanted them to like it, accept it, but I wasn't sure I could. The painting seemed close, but I'd lost my bearings. I was still shaky and funky, and I was sick of meeting with this spoiled, prissy—no question, brilliant—stuck-up young girl.

"Patricia, it's so you."

"Really? I don't look too, like, phony?"

"That's you when you dress up. So pretty. Your shining white face, your favorite black and white party dress, your hazel eyes. The way you sit there, not really posing, but about to say something . . . as if you're just about to respond, or go get your violin."

"OH!" squealed Patricia.

"What?" said Clara.

"My violin! I should be holding my violin! Oh God."

I just stood behind them, listening. Change the painting to include her holding the violin? Two weeks more, at least. Oh God. Change it so that the violin is beside her on the sofa? Another week, maybe less. But, please, God, no.

"No, Pats, this is you. It's about you, lovely you, all alone, not your violin, or, what about the piano, too? Or the clarinet?"

"That's true. Let's see what Daddy says."

The car door slammed. The shuffle of shoes on gravel, then grass. Patricia quickly turned and said, "Hi, Daddy."

"Hi. What's going on? You all about to rise up in song?"

"Hi, honey. We need your input."

Henry, a musician at Dr. Bill's soirees on those special weekends, taught music at Abington State, regular classes as well as summer school. He looked like a teacher: lightweight khaki slacks, a white short-sleeved shirt, undone at the collar, with a lavender tie, and he lugged a beat-up leather satchel. He entered through the screen door, dropped his satchel, got a hug from Patricia, a quick kiss from Clara. He and I, rather formally, with head nods, shook hands. "So, what gives?"

"This gives, Daddy." Patricia stood aside, as did Clara, to reveal the painting leaning there, mute, on the sofa. "Or," added Patricia, "does it?" Another silence. Then, "Wow," said Henry, "I mean," he gave me a quick look, then, "WOW."

"Wow what, Daddy? Whaddya mean?"

"I mean—WOW."

"Henry, please, we need your help."

"I don't think so. Garry's done just fine. Besides, I don't know how to paint."

"Daddy!" Patricia got very intense. "Please, be serious!"

"I am serious. I can doodle, but, no painting. Certainly, not like this."

"Oh, Daddy."

"Does it look like her?" asked Clara.

"Like who?"

"Me! Does it look like me?"

"Oh! That's you?"

"Oh God, Henry."

Henry nudged me as daughter and mother exchanged shook-head grimaces. Then he gave me a wink. "You should pay this young man, thank him enormously—without too much fawning or adulation—and let's get this weekend started."

"Really, Daddy? You like it?"

"I love it! Now I have two daughters. Twins, in fact, and when you run off to some school in the West or the Northeast—"

"I'm also considering Chicago, Daddy."

"Right. Wherever you end up, while you're gone, we'll still have you. Won't we, Clara dear?"

"Yes, Henry, that's a nice thought. It really is her, isn't it?"

"As close to being her without really being her. Yeah."

22

I still was not so sure about her eyes. It might've also been their hesitation, mother and daughter. While Patricia sat there, in the pose, her hands in her lap, her glance a look of readiness, response, because of the black and white dress, perhaps, or her fervor, still, in the eyes, I caught a truth about this young girl's ego and her weakness: that she could be intolerant, a snob. It was not alluring and made her older than her years. That might've been unconsciously why they balked. But, Dad—Henry—had spoken. So, it was decided: this was it. The portrait was painted, finished. Done. And I was done in. I began to gather my brushes, dip and clean them in my turpentine jar. Clara went to write me a check. Henry just plopped into a wicker chair, stared at his daughter, the picture, and out the screen to the dusky lawn and darkening woods adjacent. The light continued to dim.

Patricia ran off. "I've got to call Rosemary!"

I continued cleaning up, putting brushes away, tubes of paint into the box. The damp earthy night air mixed with the smell of linseed oil and turpentine. I still felt inexplicably close to crying. But I was determined to pack up, accept my hard-earned money, and get going.

"Nice work," said Henry, as he sat there, still schlumped, watching the painting.

"Thank you." I continued to clean up, dipping each brush in the turp and eventually my hands, too. Finally, I went to their kitchen sink where I washed each brush with soap and water. The best soap was still simple, old steadfast Ivory. When I came back out onto the porch, Henry asked, "How old are you?"

"I'll be twenty-three in November."

"Amazing. You're twenty-two, my daughter's seventeen, I'm surrounded by artists. By genius."

"Her perhaps but I'm just an apprentice."

"Good. Modesty is good. It lets you learn, grow. This really is a remarkable portrait."

"Thanks." I had three more brushes out of seven to clean.

"You caught her dark beauty and youth but also—I don't think she wants to see it—that little bit of the way she sneers at the world. Her haughtiness, which is perhaps not that attractive, but in a girl trying to make her way in an unappreciative and cynical world, it might just get her through."

I stopped and listened to Henry.

"You think I'm full of shit?"

"No, sir. Not at all."

"Making art—painting, making music, it's not for wimps. You guys have a shot at it."

"Thank you, sir. I hope so."

"No. Don't 'hope so.' Just continue to do it. Every day." He had sat up as he assessed the portrait and his daughter's "sneer." But now he schlumped back in the cushioned wicker chair, sighed, and then said, as if I weren't present and he was thinking out loud, "Yeah . . . every day, without fail . . . wish I had."

Clara returned, did a kind of curtsy bow. "Thank you, Garry. It's a wonderful painting, and we know you're living modestly and that you put a lot of extra time and effort into this painting, so, I hope you're not offended but we gave you a little extra."

"Oh no, that's not necessary."

"Please. The check is written. Please." With both her hands, she squeezed my hand that now held the check. "With our grateful good blessings."

"Oh gosh. Thank you. All of you."

Patricia had returned. She giggled, seemed shy. She hardly looked at any of us, then peeked over her shoulder at the painting. "Oh God, I can't believe it's really finished." Clara turned and watched the painting, too, and said, "I know, honey, but it is. Gosh, what will you do with your remaining summer afternoons?"

"I know," said Patricia, hands to mouth, eyes on the painting.

"Oh, I bet there's a piano or a violin or even a clarinet wishing you'd keep them company."

"Oh, Daddy."

"Well? Am I right?"

I excused myself, went to the kitchen to wash the last of the brushes. What was going on? I saw the kitchen dining table already set for dinner. Saw a vase with yellow flowers on the far end of the kitchen counter. I was holding back this still mystifying sadness. When Clara handed me the check and then held my hand and said, "With our grateful good blessings," I almost broke down sobbing. I needed to get out to the lake. I needed to finish cleaning the brushes, pack up, and get going.

"We'd love to have you join us for dinner, Garry," Clara said as she fussed with napkins and silverware.

"Oh, thank you."

"Oh yes, please join us, Garry," said Patricia, "Rosemary's coming, too!"

It was nice to see Patricia become a normal girl, which made being in her presence almost bearable, but no. I needed to be alone. Or something. I needed quiet. The lake waters. The starry night. Space. Silence. Not this. Not dinner and questions and discussions and showing off and carrying on and all this politeness.

I finished with my brushes, wiped them with a paper towel. Patricia had gone out to the porch.

"Um, Mrs. Willard, I just want to thank you guys again. And, I really appreciate the invitation to dinner but—"

"You've got other plans?"

No. No plans. But I didn't need to explain, so, "Yeah. I kind of do."

"No problem, Garry. Let me get Henry and we'll see you out. Henry?"

All three of them walked me out to the gravel driveway. I placed my paint box, sketchbooks and rags in Titine's back seat. There was another back-and-forth exchange of "Thank you," and "Congratulations" and "Good luck in future endeavors." They watched me as I backed out Titine. Then, as I turned onto the lane and began to accelerate, while Clara and Henry continued to wave good-bye and I waved back, I saw Patricia finish her wave and then bolt back into the house. I think their phone was ringing. Maybe not. But I was gone.

I drove slowly. Their lane was lined with trees, front lawns. It reminded me of the thickly wooded lanes of Connecticut. It was beyond dusk, the night air still humid but mixed with cool breezes, and rich, sweet aromas: cut grass, tangy earth smells, pipe smoke, perfumes, and then a whiff of a grill, a cookout.

The tree-lined roads were darker. Then, leaving this upscale part of town, adjacent to Donelson, the landscape loosened and opened up, with stretches of fields, stone walls, hilly corners, and a more open sky which suddenly seemed brighter, not so black but still a warm blue, a smoky hazy blue with bits of orange and pink, the leftovers of a once-brilliant sun. Still confused and achy, stuck somehow emotionally, I felt I could breathe again, at least. I just needed to get out to the lake. I didn't know why but I was determined. The lake. And quiet. Those waters. And the slow-down night.

23

I had a difficult night's sleep, a lot of restlessness and waking up. The night was not clear, flurries of clouds. The night sounds, owl hoots and birds' slowing coos, were brutally overruled by first one group of campers, and then, an hour later, another. Both groups, loud, drunken. The first sang country songs from the Grand Ole Opry. The second, no singing, just loud, angry, mostly men's voices but for one woman with a high-pitched laugh that would become a pissy angry shriek as they got into it. It went on long enough for me to consider how I was going to go into the woods, over to their campsite and shut them up. As I pondered this and planned my approach, perhaps they finally quieted. It's the last I remembered before waking up in bright sun, sweating.

I was surprised. It was already nine a.m. Several men in Bermuda shorts, hairy legs, traipsed by on their way to the facilities; a woman with several small children slowly wandered by as well. I was glad I'd slept "late," though I hated waking all sticky and wet. I immediately put the bag away, changed clothes, and went for a long run.

I knew my quiet time by the lake that morning would be compromised. So many campers. A hot, humid day in store. Writing, reading by the lake would not be easy or solitary. So, I let myself take time as I ran, going beyond the campsite to the other end of Old Hickory Lake where there was a whole other world: a small deli/liquor store with fishing tackle and bait; a small gas station, and a lovely roadway bridge over to the other far corner of the lake where a fairly upscale marina was situated. Which got me thinking.

The boats, outriggers, cabin cruisers (only a few) but mostly decent-sized sailboats, maybe I'd come back here and do some pen and inks, watercolors. My dad loved boats. Maybe do a painting of these boats for his birthday. I was briefly excited again.

I loved running, working up a good sweat. It felt so good to stretch and breathe and run full out, and, to discover a whole new part of this world. Right here. Just around the corner from my hillside sleeping quarters. A couple miles or so from farms and hayracks and barns.

After, I went for a good, long refreshing swim. The sadness began in me again. I trolled the colder parts of the lake, swam and thought about this change in me, this puzzling sort of heartache. Even though the painting of Patricia had been a real challenge, was I somehow sad or morose over its completion? I did not like things to end. Of course, I was lonely. I thought of Kathy's visit and our time here by the lake, sunbathing, swimming, playing together right here, where I was swimming, in this colder part of the water, not so long ago. But it felt bigger than that, this brooding ache. It wasn't quite manageable or knowable, and it certainly was not nameable. Not yet.

After showering, getting dressed—T-shirt, Bermuda shorts and jog shoes—I was hungry. But I got stuck again: I didn't want to see people. I didn't want to hob-nob or draw pen and inks of people. I wanted to hide out. I wanted to eat a nice breakfast and talk to no one. Which is impossible when all you have for a home is a small, lumpy, grassy hillside. I'd have to choose a diner or coffeeshop, or, if I was willing to sacrifice hotcakes, I could grab an apple and a deli sandwich at that liquor/deli store mart at the far end of the lake, where I'd just jogged to and back.

I sat on the hillside next to Titine and considered my options. A nice thing about a good strong hunger is that it helps you make decisions. But now my hunger seemed pretty confused, too. A rarity. I could blindly stick a finger in the Bible and see what it instructed. Or I could just lie back on the sweet, hot grass, my face in the shade, my legs in the sun, close my eyes and drift and wait and, hopefully, see. I did the latter.

At first, I thought, in vain. But I kept my eyes closed: the smell of earth, grass smells mixed with musky earth. The sun went under, sky full of clouds, nothing ponderous or storm-like. And, it came to me. Get a sandwich or apple, or both, at that deli/mart at the other end of

Old Hickory; have lunch, then drive out to that marina and do a pen and ink, maybe a few, and some watercolors. Or, eat lunch out there, take a nap in the shade somewhere. Then, after the nap, in a slow, steady way, make some art.

And, that's what I did.

The sun was in hiding as I slowly drove over the stone and iron bridge, turned right, and found a big tree next to the marina to park under. It was still mid-day hot plus sticky humid. The air gone slow and still, no breezes. A kind of murky, sunless, stifling heat.

I got out of Titine, carried my brown paper bag of a picnic and looked for a shaded spot to sit in, near the boats. There were none. So, I circled back to Titine, opened the passenger-side door, and sat on the passenger seat, my body leaning out in the welcome shade of this tall, thick-trunked leafy timber. I ate lunch, my back to the boats, the marina, and the lake. My view was of the bridge access toward the road and houses further on, nicely placed among trees, lawns and intersection. I didn't read. I didn't even seem to think. I did note how deserted the marina was, which seemed surprising for the weekend. When I finished lunch, I used the paper bag as a pillow, sprawled under the shade tree, and napped.

24

I slept longer than usual. There was nowhere to dispose of my paper bag/pillow, so I left it in Titine, grabbed my 9 x 12-inch sketchbook and strolled the marina looking for interesting pictures.

It's a strange thing—wonderful, too—this looking at the world, not in a practical way but with an eye to converting three dimensions into two. These shapes, lights, shadows, that I could see on a white piece of paper, excited and pleased me. I was really beginning to learn this. Two years before, the spring of my junior year, I religiously carried a pen and sketchbook with me wherever I went: the five college bus trips; a walk to the PO; my daily walks to classes; the evening chapel talks; even meals, whether in town to grab a slice of pizza, or the college dining hall. Some guys brought books to meals. I brought my sketchbook.

In the marina, what fascinated me were the bold upright masts. Sails furled up at bottom or not evident at all, and how the boats on land, lined up next to each other, created a sort of village, hulls like various-colored blocks, mostly off-white or grey, some baby blue, one forest green. Then, rising from this multi-colored congregation, the tall lonely spires of poles with thin accompanying ropes, and, above and below, the grey metal pullies. I found a spot where one of these groups excited me, visually. Beyond the beached line-up of boats were the boats in water, lengths of dock, horizon of water and, beyond, on the other side of Old Hickory Lake, trees, lawns, and a few small boxy houses.

I did several pen and inks, from varying angles, which only whetted my desire to paint them. Still, no one was about. And the sun was gone. A full sky of neutral, quietly grey clouds. The heat and humidity stayed constant.

After another hour or so, I had three different watercolors of the boats. One in particular pleased me. I was sure it was the one my dad would appreciate. I loved my container of watercolors, although the tin was showing a fair degree of wear and tear, the white pigment piece almost empty. The yellow and cerulean blue, too, were getting thin. I did these boat watercolors on the bigger 11 x 14-inch pad. Not watercolor paper, a heavier rag, these pages remained sturdy even as they dried, with little evidence of the papers stretching, tightening and/or shrinking. Still, the few evident stretch marks worked well with this favorite rendering, joining the horizontal pitch of the side by side-ness of several boats.

I liked the looseness of this one version and the pale, as if worn, colors of the boats, mute, pastel-like: yellow deck, green hull, white hull, and the rugged masts, one straight up. The slight angles of the others. Through them was the broken, distant horizon of lake. Also captured was the dullness of the steamy, quiet afternoon, and the solitary ease of these once vibrant boats, now silent and abandoned beside Old Hickory Lake.

Once the watercolors had dried, I packed up Titine, put everything in the trunk except for my dad's painting, which I leaned against the back seat, on the far-right side, so I could turn from the driver's seat to now and then peek at it and enjoy it, sure my dad would like it. Then I just sat there. It was already after five. There would be no sunset over the lake because there was no sun. That is, there was no blue sky, only a milky, murky grey expanse and increased humidity. I sat in Titine and could feel this grip of sadness, or confusion, begin to take over again. I'd had some relief but now, again, it was as if I had no idea what to do.

Go for a swim? But all those people. I was lonely, maybe even homesick and yet, I wished to see and be with no one. Go for dinner? Again, where? And who might I run into, since now I had become a kind of temporary, and to some, like Rosemary, Lexie and especially Sam, an honorary resident of Donelson? I did not want to partake. Not today. But I had no room to hide in, no little house to get away to and play the recluse.

As I cruised past the campsite beach, I saw that the usual Saturday crowd, with storm clouds festering, had already dispersed. I was in luck. I parked Titine and quickly changed into my swimsuit. It pleased me to have this portion of lake waters all to myself. I did a few flying runs into the water to see if I could shake my melancholy, as if by forcing these whooping, kicking, propeller bellyflops, I might somehow bring back Kathy and our playful day at the beach. Had it only been a few weeks ago? It felt like months. I then just settled into some sturdy strokes out to the lake's center, which helped jar my mood. It scared me to be out so far from the shore. Not only was the sky grey but so was the lake water. Everywhere I looked, nothing, no one. No swimmers, no boats and very few sounds. The clouds darkened and began moving, a kind of up-tempo swirling.

Also, this fear: as I lay on my back, floating, drifting, watching, it was not unlike this dream where I've climbed a ladder but instead of the side of a house that needed painting, I was climbing up, up, up the side of a huge grey building and the ladder continued higher, beyond the edge of the rooftop. Oh no. I quickly began my swim back to shore. As I swam, a big dog appeared along the water's edge not far from my picnic table. He was thick shouldered, dark bristly fur, a blend of brown and black with a lighter underside. He had a wrinkled brow but his eyes seemed quite open. His face, in fact, reminded me of my father's. I switched from a fast crawl to the breaststroke so I could watch him, the way he had loped up to the shore's edge and stopped, his tongue hanging long and pink out of his mouth. As he watched me, I waved to him, mid-stroke, lifted my head, called out, "Hey! Hi!"

I continued to swim toward him but, about twenty yards from shore, I saw him lope off, tongue still dangling. I rose from the water and called again, "Hey, boy! Hey!" He continued on with his slow shouldery stride. He never looked back.

I took a nice hot shower in the facilities, put on some clean clothes, and got in Titine just before the clouds unleashed their gushing torrents. Rain. Slings of it. Unceasing. Ribbons. Grey stripes. An enormous downpour. The loud battering on the car roof, the flanks, the hood. The swishing blur of rivers on the windshield and rear windows, and the slashing splats on the side windows. I sat and watched the grey darken and stir, bursts of streaking, and how my bed-time hillside eagerly soaked up the wet slogs. The green grass become so clean, clear. And very wet.

Where would I sleep tonight? Good-bye, hillside. Good night, stars. I guess I could sleep in Titine. But. What about dinner? What about my dumb art and this stupid life? What was I doing here all alone in this grey maudlin frenzy? Who cared? And why was my life such a failure? I sat there hammering Titine's steering wheel with my clenched fists. Which hurt and, the hurt felt good, felt right. My life was a waste. Who did I think I was? Who cared about me, deep down, really? Kathy was torn between me and Kink. My bud Durland was back up North. Mom and Dad, my sister Carol, brothers Sandy and Chris, they all had full, busy lives. Where was I in the picture, really?

Drawing. Painting pictures. To become an artist, to become a real person, what was going on here? I didn't cry. I sobbed.

When I stopped crying, I used my T-shirt to wipe my face. I was exhausted. And still mopey, sad. It was still raining, the first thunderous crashings had slowed. Just raining now, steady, constant.

Finally, hunger restored me to life. Hunger and memory: there was a motel I'd seen back over toward Hermitage, where my PO box was. I'd buy a sandwich, chips, and soda at a liquor mart on the way. Then, I'd spend my first night in months in a cozy little motel room. Why not? I could afford it. Oh yeah. I was rolling in dough. I decided to splurge: I handed the thin sad-faced woman behind the counter a ham and cheese sandwich. Instead of a small bag of chips, I bought the largest. Not one bag of peanut M&M's but two plus a Peppermint Patty plus a small package of Oreo cookies, and, not one, but two sodas. Party time.

The woman kept eyeing me as we both stood there. I didn't feel like being polite and talkative. Neither did she. The rain continued outside. Somewhere in that dimly lit store, I could hear a steady dripping. The woman wore a pink sweater over a light green jumpsuit. She kept hugging herself. The rain poured, the drip-drip-drip continued.

"We gotta leak."

"I hear it."

"Damn rain. But we need it. Aren't you chilly?"

"A little. Yes." I had on a fresh tee and Bermuda shorts.

She rang me up. "Here you go." She pushed the bag toward me. I handed her a ten-dollar bill. It was half that. "Keep the change," I said.

"For real?"

"Hey, why not, right?"

"Wall, thank yew." She suddenly seemed to speak real Southern.

"Sure." I waved and started out.

"You have a safe night, y'hear? Get dry and warm."

"Thanks. I'll do that."

25

The motel was just on the outskirts of Hermitage, about five miles from Donelson. Not well marked and with very few signs, it was a couple of roads just off the main town road. I don't know how I found the place, except that I remembered that I'd liked how it wasn't a line-up of rooms in one long building, but instead a series of ten separate cottages, in among trees and thin grass, which was mixed with a loamy orange dirt.

Tonight, all that orange dirt was pretty mucky and runny. Thankfully, each cottage had a place to park a car with small round concrete steps that led to a cottage front door.

A dark-haired man with black glasses, black mustache, and very hairy arms checked me in. He wore a light green short-sleeve shirt with a white plastic pen-holder filled with several ballpoints in his left shirt-pocket. As I filled out the small white index card, he returned to the tight corner behind the counter where he continued to watch a small TV, tapping the side of it as he watched. I gave as my address "Old Hickory Lake," Donelson, Tennessee and not my Huckleberry Lane address in Darlington, Connecticut. I continued writing, the man continued tapping.

"Damn reception! It's this shitty rain, but God knows we need it."

"Is it going to rain all night?" I asked.

"Probably. It better. It's been too dry."

"It's been a nice summer," I said as I pushed the white card toward him.

"Has it?" He took the card, eyed it. Then, "Listen," he said, "can you be a little more specific? Gotta street number?" He pulled out one of his ballpoint pens, clicked it, ready to write in my "street number."

"Not really."

"Whaddya live in a tent?" He laughed. I heard his Southern accent then, the way he said "tant" for "tent."

"I stay at the campsite next to Old Hickory Lake. I sleep in my sleeping bag under the stars."

"Really?" His eyes widened. "Difficult to do on a rainy night."

"Yeah."

"Okay. Here ya go. Number 4. Leave here and just pull around to the right, past the three cottages on either side. You'll see it back a-ways on the right."

"Thanks."

"No problem. Enjoy your stay. You gotta TV and a phone, too. Any problems, I'm on till two a.m. Name's William, folks call me Billy."

"Okay. Thanks, Billy."

"Right." He clicked his ballpoint closed, put it back in his plastic pocket, began to place my white info card in a little box behind the counter when the TV's sound and image started acting up again. As I left, I heard him sputter, "Gaw-damn!!" That was soon accompanied by a series of loud whacks and the tinny rattling of his portable black box. I thought maybe my melancholy mood had changed. It hadn't.

I found the #4 cottage (a good sign, I thought, my lucky number was 4). It was back in among some dark, thin-trunked trees. I parked and sat there. It wasn't quite eight p.m. and already it was pretty dark except for now and then the bright flickers of lightning. No sound of thunder. I sat and watched the rain. It continued to stream down the windshield, its pelting of Titine's roof and sides would get intense and heavy, then subside. I sat, watched, listened. I was not a happy camper. Why couldn't I just sleep in Titine? Why'd I pay good money ($28.75) for a motel room? What was I doing? Who did I think I was? Then, from below, to the left of my left foot and the brake, I felt a spattering. Water was puddling under Titine; some of the rain thrusts were slushing water up into Titine, cool air and wet sloshings.

When I bought Titine from Michel, the Frenchman, my junior year at Amherst, I hadn't noticed the small rusted hole there. Winters, salt, corrosion. I was so enamored with the small crowbar-like handle that I could crank to start Titine, any other quirks, like rotting floorboards, were forgiven.

The cold wet, the increasing darkness, and my hunger pushed-pulled me from Titine. I grabbed my watercolor painting of marina boats, closed the pad, quickly exited. I fumbled in the trunk for my books, my journal, my bag of food, and the Bible and light-footed it along the wet and shining concrete circular steps toward my little blue-grey cottage. The key turned easily and I was in.

It was modest but cozy: straight ahead a double bed covered in a bluish coverlet with two pillows, a nightstand at the entry door side with a brassy lamp and a yellowish linen lampshade. I turned it on. Not the brightest but it was fine. A rotary phone beside it.

To the right of the entry door, a window with white curtains and a small round table, two small wood chairs on either side. Along that wall, in the corner, was the big black box TV on a wood stand that had a cabinet door. From that corner, parallel to the foot of the bed, was empty space but for a double window, white curtains. Both sets of windows featured blackness and rain streaks and the constant rat-tat-tat of pouring waters, and now, more winds. The far wall, the other side of the bed, was a single door to a closet. Further up, directly opposite the bed, was the half-opened door to the bathroom. It seemed clean enough, sets of towels, wash cloths, small packages of Ivory soap. The coup de grace was the tub, big, long, white porcelain, and my body was saying, a long hot bath, please!

Body, heart, mind, soul were also saying, all over again, as if I'd just entered a whole other version of this bad mood, that I was cranky, sad, homesick, lonely, depressed. I couldn't quite name it that night but I was stuck in a kind of emotional quicksand.

After surveying my little cottage, I placed the sketchbook, journal, books and Bible on the small table, sat on the bed, still cold, still wet, still drippy. I wanted to cry but couldn't. That's how stuck I was. I just sat. I stared. The lamp's light didn't reach far, a pool of it spread beside the bed and nightstand and a slim edge spilled onto the floor. A slip of it grazed where I sat. This might've been the most alone I'd ever felt in my almost twenty-three years.

I took the sketchpad, opened it to the watercolor of Dad's boats, and carefully placed it in the window next to the round table. Took a minute to get it balanced there until, finally, it stayed in place. I liked looking at it. For a moment, the sullen humid afternoon revived and the quiet beauty of those boats, hulls and masts, came back.

I finally opened the white paper bag, pulled out sodas, sandwich, chips, and began devouring my solitary dinner.

I did take a bath that night but was it before or after I turned on the television? I had not watched TV in several months. But the television. It had been such a habit, even a companion, growing up lonely in the Connecticut suburbs. Less so in junior high and high school, except for sports on TV and the legendary *Million Dollar Movie* or the CBS *Early Show.* College finally broke me of this constancy. This summer? No. I was reading books, sleeping under the stars and actually painting pictures. I did not have that hunger for TV or movies. That would resurrect itself later, in my thirties.

Supper went quickly. I decided to save the M&M's, Peppermint Patty, and Oreos for later. My plan: take a bath, then curl up in bed and see what was on the tube. I was on my way to start running my bath when I realized: I'd better check to see if the TV works, what channels it gets, etc.

The rain sputtered and blew and made its chatty tappings on windows and cottage roof top as if it were calling me to converse. I wasn't interested. I pulled out the far-right nob on the black twenty-two-inch TV. It took a moment, made a low dull moan, letting me know it was firing up, then a bright glow of fuzzy grey static and cross-hatchings, and then, was this some sort of aberrant magic?

There he was . . . Elwood P. Dowd. It was Jimmy Stewart's face. He was just leaving the house. He helped Harvey out the gate. Myrtle Mae and her mother watched from behind window curtains to make sure he was really leaving. Jimmy/Elwood nodded to the mailman, then offered him his card. "Would you like to come for dinner? . . . Oh? . . . When wouldcha?" I sat at the end of the bed. I laughed. I cried. I didn't take my bath.

Harvey.

There he was again, through Jimmy Stewart's eyes, through his believing and our imaginings. Until the head of the asylum, Dr. Chumley, encounters Harvey, too, wants him to stay with him. But, Harvey, like the Muse, is not a constant, not a sure thing. Rather, like a gift, he's mysterious, comes and goes, is nothing as tangible as a good job, security, a picket fence, status, willpower.

Chimera. Muse. Pooka.

What's a Pooka? asks Dr. Chumley's wife. How should I know, answers Mr. Wilson, the white-uniformed asylum attendant. Mrs. Chumley goes to the dictionary, begins paging, realizes she's running late, hands the dictionary to Mr. Wilson, leaves, and there is Wilson looking at the dictionary page, a shaky reader, "Pooka, p-o-o-k-a, a fantastical creature of Celtic origin known to appear to rumpots, crackpots and How are you, Mr. Wilson?" Wilson reacts, looks around, takes the book and shakes it vigorously, mutters, "How are you, Mr. Wilson? Who in the dictionary wants to know?" Then throws the book on the floor as it were on fire.

This film for me was not only profound but very funny.

I want to say "miracle," or is it recognition? That is, the mysterious way in which the Universe seemed to actually see me, touch me and called me further into my seemingly irrational creative life.

I was blessed that night. I felt forgiven, accepted and seen, and, even in this movie's warmth and good heart, loved again. This path I had chosen was such anathema to my dad and a culture that wanted me to make money, to make my bold, imperious, triumphant way.

This movie, this small beacon of light on a miserable rainy night was telling me, Don't give up. Believe. Keep whatever small faith you have and continue to hold dear these brief glimpses of the unseeable, the unknowable, that so many others so cynically, so quickly, so fearfully (root of their pessimism?) pooh-pooh. Which lets them off the hook, since this seems impossible to them, even while it's deeply, as if innately, necessary to me.

I sat on the end of my motel cottage bed, mesmerized. Eventually, I opened my peanut M&M's and munched on those and watched. I had some Oreo cookies, too. I even finished the large Peppermint

Patty. I felt restored, and not so alone anymore.

Mostly, I was a blubbering sweet tooth of sobs and laughs.

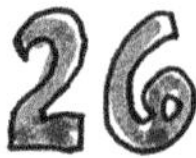

Afterward I sat in the long white tub, in a nice hot bath, and cried some more. What were these tears, really, and why was this movie not just a movie? But then, who and what was it?

Not to exaggerate or overinflate but Jimmy Stewart's Elwood was almost a kind of warm and beatific Christ figure. The fool on the hill. Completely nonviolent, with no agenda, Elwood has this utter and confounding desire to—connect. To see you. To know you. To appreciate you.

He invites the mailman to dinner. At Charlie's bar he invites Mr. Meegles to dinner after he did "a little work for the state," that is, had been in prison. He invites Mrs. Chumley to join Harvey and him as well as Mr. Wilson. Rich, poor, or disenfranchised, no matter, each person is important and worthy of a full encounter.

Not to mention Miss Kelly and Dr. Sanderson, who do find him at Charlie's and when asked "Mr. Dowd, what do you do?" he explains, "Well, Harvey and I go for a stroll and end up here at Charlie's . . . we visit and talk, and you know, no one brings anything small into a bar . . . but when I introduce them to Harvey, well, he's greater and grander than anything they could imagine . . ."

And, at the climax of the film, back at Chumley's Rest, Vita has finally got Judge Gaffney to commit Elwood. But since Elwood wants to go home, he comments, "Ah, an element of conflict is good, everyone gets involved, gets to be heard . . . But, Vita," (his sister's now sobbing), "I'll take the serum" (which will sedate and perhaps ultimately change him), "if you really want me to . . ." (not to over-inflate but in the spirit of metaphor and analogy, it is akin to Christ's sacrifice). And Vita sobs, "Oh, I do want you to take it. I really do."

Elwood goes off with Dr. Sanderson and Nurse Kelly to take the serum while the cab driver comes in, asking for his money. Vita goes to her purse, can't find the money, must interrupt the procedure and ask Elwood for the money, who gives the cabbie the money plus a good tip and has a brief chat with the man, ready to invite him for dinner. The door closes and the cabbie (in a brilliant and touching cameo by Wallace Ford) muses aloud on how the folks he brings there are so sweet on the way: "We stop and smell the roses, watch the sunset, there's no rush, no hurry, it's a sweet easy-going ride . . . but after, oh God—"

Vita interrupts, "What do you mean, 'but after, oh God'?"

The cabbie replies, "I take 'em back, it's watch this, watch that, they're pushing and shouting and carrying on. It's no fun, I tell ya. They're just like every other normal human being—and you know what trouble they can be. I'll wait. Nice to meetcha."

It is Elwood's authentic desire to see you, know you—to push aside labels and titles and judgments—and honor your/my/our humanity. And, Harvey is the leap into the fantastic, the imaginary, dare I say, the spiritual—that piece that is evanescent and greater than the sum of our humble human parts, our squabbles and differences and status-seeking ambitions as well as the even more humbling status quo.

Which is where the human man and this transcendent vision somehow, with such warmth and humor and wisdom (Elwood says to Dr. Chumley, "Oh, Dr. Chumley, I still believe what my mother once told me, 'Elwood,' she said, 'You can be oh so clever or oh so kind.' Well, sir, I choose to be kind . . .") leap off into the glow of what I saw then, and see now, as the creative and art-making, our humanity restored.

I said a prayer of thanks to God, to Harvey, to Jimmy Stewart. And I prayed for Kathy and Durl. I prayed for Mom, Dad, my brothers and their families, my sister and hers.

I prayed for Lexie and Sam and Mikey, for Thomas, the library custodian and for Rosemary, Lexie's assistant.

I thanked God for my life beside Old Hickory Lake. I prayed for Big Jim and his health, for all the salesmen going door to door all over America.

And for Hub and Floyd and Russell, and for Charlie and all the Vietnam soldiers, now coming home and those still over there.

I didn't pray for myself. I felt so thankful, I didn't need to.

The rain stopped sometime during the night while I slept like a rock. When I awoke, the cottage seemed bright, iridescent. The slant of the sun through windows was brilliant, enticing. It was a new day.

I quickly slipped out of bed, flung open my cottage door and stood there inhaling fresh cool summer air. A bit humid but much less than the past week when I'd struggled with Patricia's portrait. No. This was new air. I was reborn. I was excited. I wanted to do everything: write in my journal, read my Bible, look at my art books, read *Wuthering Heights*, which I was two-thirds into. I wanted to go for a long run, swim in Old Hickory Lake. I wanted to eat a big breakfast and say hi to Terri and Stan and Fred, the gang at the Snack Shack.

I looked at my watch: what? It was already past eight-thirty, late for me, and it was Sunday. Omigod! Church and the choir. But what about that run and the lake and some breakfast?

I sat for a moment on the end of my motel bed. The cottage door was still wide open. I'd opened both sets of windows. I was flooded with sun-bright breezes. I sat there, awash, very much alive and present.

I stared again at that magic black box. How had that been possible? I turned the TV on last night. I never even changed channels. I had no notions of a movie being on. I had no notions, period. I was notionless, and dumb and down and then, this transmission, as if from beyond. How does such a thing happen? But I didn't want to muddy this great luxurious delight with too much heady platitude or dogma.

I made a quick plan: church was at ten a.m. I'd forego breakfast, maybe grab a banana at the Quik-Mart on my way back to Old Hickory Lake. I'd go for a short run, take a swim, shower and dress and get to church. I'd have a big Snack Shack breakfast *after* church, when I'd be good and hungry. I had to go sing and praise God and the Universe and these unceasing Mysteries. I'd better get going.

Then I saw it, as if spotlighted against the shadowy cottage walls. It leaned there in the cottage window, still, against a background now of shadows outside, trees, distant cottages in shadow and spots of sunlight: my dad's painting, brightly highlighted and complete—the dolorous afternoon, the buzz of nearby crickets, the quiet counsel of hulls and masts, the lapping waters and lake edge beyond. His birthday gift. I was pretty sure he'd like it.

The day flowed. I didn't think too much. I just lived and relished each and every moment. I was my own youthful version of Elwood P. Dowd. There was time again, and so many lovely flowers to stop and smell.

Reverend Bill's sermon was based on the parable of Mary and Martha and their visit with Jesus, one so busy and intent, the other able to sit and be with Jesus, wash his feet, get slow and quiet, receptive. How perfect was that? All of Sunday, moment by moment, slowed down. Reverend Bill wanted to talk, urged me to come visit next week. Dr. Bill praised my singing and asked about my painting and when was I going to do his pen and ink? And Sarah, the once-aloof Southern belle, smiled at me and then came over to say hi, as folks gathered outside the church. She said I looked quite handsome and, "My, how you sang today. You had such energy, such a strong voice!" I thanked her. Her girlfriends joined her, pulled her away. She waved as they ran off.

That kind of day. Nothing momentous. Just one simple pleasure after another.

The pancakes at the Snack Shack, with a fried egg over easy on top. The OJ tasted as if it were fresh squeezed. Maybe it was. Stan asked about his pen and ink, could he have another look at it? Then he sat down and got all chummy and chatty. Terri came over and scolded Stan. He came right back at her, "Terri, honey, don't start! This is my friend, okay? Garry, did my picture, okay?" She blushed, then laughed. They kissed. Later, they invited me over to their home so I could finally do Terri's pen and ink before I got to be a big famous artist. They both agreed I was headed in that direction.

27

Everything slowed down. I had slow mornings by the lake, slow afternoons at the library, a few more dinners at the Helms', and brilliant nights sleeping again under all those pin-prick stars.

I did drawings out by the lake. Watercolors, too. I did pen and ink portraits of all the people I'd been meaning to—Terri, Thomas, Rosemary, Mikey's buddy Perry. Perry's mom wanted an oil portrait, too. But now I was running out of time. My art exhibition was coming up soon and then, a few days later, I'd be hitting the road.

My big regret: I never got to do an oil or at least a pen and ink of Lexie Helms. She remained elusive. Also, for all her generous, motherly, care-taking bravado, I think she was shy. After all, she was a librarian, with a librarian's sense of service and deference and quiet. Her sons, others, a record of them, held significance.

I had phoned my brother Sandy in Michigan. We decided I'd drive north to join them: spend the night at their home outside Detroit and then we'd caravan east to Connecticut. I'd leave Donelson on Tuesday, get to Dearborn Tuesday night in time for dinner, and then we'd leave early Wednesday. There'd be one layover in a motel in Pennsylvania, Sandy figured, then we'd be in Darlington late Thursday. Dad's birthday was that Friday, August 22.

This meant that, in a few days, I'd begin sorting and choosing from among my drawings and paintings, frame some of them, or, at least, put them into nice cut-out mats. Then, hang the show, so that the weekend before my departure—Friday, Saturday, Sunday and Monday, too—the show of my art could be open to the general public.

This would be it, my final week.

Among my last attempts was an oil rendering of a woman, attractive, sitting and peering out, not at the viewer but beyond, toward the sky or, was it a shelf full of books? With a slow, quizzical stare. A dark grey lush background; her hair a lighter grey. It was painted in shades of grey and flesh-tones, the style of Giacometti, with blurred, smudged strokes, some pencil line showing: it was Lexie. From memory.

I decided to make it the centerpiece. Late on Thursday afternoon, August 14, I finished hanging the show. I'd loved doing it, loved rummaging through my sketchbooks. At that point in the summer, I had something like eleven sketchbooks. Plus, there were eight oils. It was a great way to reminisce, review the summer, and be surprised, too: the vegetable stand girl, the big rocks on the hillside of Old Hickory Lake, and the biggest discovery, the man who resembled James Stewart aka Elwood P. Dowd, off on that cul-de-sac, with his fruit stand, from much earlier in the summer. I had to pause: did I really do that pen and ink? Or, did Harvey do it?

There were no renderings of Harvey but there was something invisible and tender in the air. I felt it most when I asked Lexie—only she was allowed—to come preview the show. It was now around five p.m., an hour before the library was to close.

"Oh, Garry, can't this wait? Can't I see it tomorrow like everyone else?"

"I'll come look," interrupted Rosemary, bright eyed, pushing her black glasses back onto the bridge of her nose.

"No. Only Lexie. Sorry. She is the brain trust behind this event. Lexie? Please?"

"Oh gosh. Okay. Can I come right now?"

"Now. Yes."

"Gimme five minutes and I'll be right down."

I waited at the foot of the stairs. Then I paced, into the large hall where my show loomed, then back to the foot of the stairs. It was a very long five minutes. When I heard the door open above, I ran into the show room and turned off the lights. Only the stairwell remained lit now.

"Garry?"

"I'm here, Mrs. Helms."

Lexie clopped down the stairs and finally arrived.

"Right this way!" We walked a few steps.

"Shouldn't there be a little drum roll or something?" asked Lexie. I watched her bright-eyed anticipation.

"You're right . . . let's see . . ." The lights still off, I began tapping the glass doors with both drumstick-like hands. I then quickly turned on both sets of light switches.

"Oh!" said Lexie. "Oh my."

We both stood there. The beige linoleum floor was also lit up, reflecting back its own version of all forty-one pieces. Lexie slowly entered and said again, "Oh my," this time more meditative, watchful. Then, "You really did all these?"

"I did."

"There's Mikey, his pen and ink, too, but, where's Sam?" She turned quickly, looking, in a slight panic. I started to point.

"Oh, okay. There he is. Nice, on opposite walls from each other. The brothers. Very nice. Close but independent. Sam will like that. Actually, Mike will, too. Oh, there's Perry. That's a great likeness! Oh my, isn't this a wonderful exhibition!"

"You think?"

"Don't you?"

"Well."

"No. It's better to be modest. Let me heap the praise. But . . . who's that woman? Very distinguished. I never saw her before. Do I know her? Wait. Is that your mother?"

This was my Giacometti-like oil portrait of Lexie, the centerpiece, hanging at the far end of the room, painted from memory. But I didn't say who it was. I just looked at it and watched Lexie look at it, walk over to it and eye it a bit more.

"Very interesting woman. I feel as if I know her. A different style, too, looser. All those smudges. I think this is a wonderful exhibition. I really do."

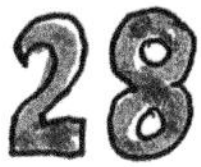

Maybe it was silly of me, the way I stood and/or sat there that first day, Friday, waiting for people to either come down the stairs from the library, or to enter from the back, through the glass doors from the lower parking lot. I'd made a sign that stood on a small easel in the library. It said, "Exhibition of GM Brown's Artwork Below—Down the Stairs—All Are Welcome!" I drew a cartoon, like from *The New Yorker,* of a man in glasses bending close to look at a painting of a pretty girl. Not sure it helped but a lot of people stopped and looked—at the sign. The library opened at ten on Friday morning; it would close at six.

I'd had a good sleep beneath a clear, starry night sky, woke early, sat by the lake, read my Bible, wrote in my journal. No jog. A short swim, then shower, dressed. Didn't have much of a breakfast, a banana and a small Tropicana juice from the Quik-Mart. Then, buzzed into town. Got there at nine-thirty, parked in the lower parking lot and waited until ten. Watched Lexie come from her house, across the damp morning-dewed lawn. She waved hello and then waved me to come on, which I did. I stood with her as she unlocked the upper front library doors.

"You excited?" she asked.

"Gosh, I guess I am."

"Should be. But now, listen. It's Friday. End of the week. People may not come right away so don't get worried or worked up, okay?"

"Yes, ma'am."

"Plus, a lotta folks in these parts just don't appreciate things like drawings and paintings. So, go easy. Right?"

"Right."

She had the doors unlocked, gave a big push and then stopped, looked at me again. "Plus . . ."

"Yeah?"

"It's the weekend. People in this town don't really socialize until Saturday. We're closed Sunday, but then there's Monday. So. What I'm saying is, don't expect too much and don't take it personal, you hear me?"

"I do. Thanks, Lexie."

"Sure. So, let's get downstairs and put those lights on before the art fanatics break down the doors!"

I started downstairs. I put on the lights, then walked around, viewing the show again. It wasn't the best lighting, all those overhead fluorescents, fairly indirect, but it would do. I'd made small white labels, double-sided the Scotch tape, and put them to the left of each picture: the title, the location, the date, and whatever medium used. For example, "'Lakeside,' Old Hickory Lake, Tenn . . . 06.29.71 . . . watercolor." I used my Rapidograph pen and printed as clearly as possible.

That morning, I went around again to check spellings. I liked my drawings and paintings. I liked my art. I liked this, the first showing of my works of art. Ever. I was even kind of proud. Amazed, too. Each time I walked around, looking at all the matted pictures—on the oils I used black masking tape to frame the edges—it was if I had never done them. I had done them and not. I could remember the event of painting or drawing each picture, there was an inner life, or emotion, sometimes a glee or sadness or resistance (when I was so challenged trying to paint Patricia's portrait) and then there was an amnesia. Who did that? Where'd it come from? How did such a picture come into the world? I even felt a loss of confidence, a kind of overwhelm: I did that? Really?

Oh no, I could never do that again. Those brush strokes, the sensitivity of those ink lines—how did the artist do that? Oh. Right. I did that. I did?

Such self-doubts were always diminished once I was immersed in drawing or painting again. Also, I noticed that when others asked me about a particular piece—"How long did it take?" "Do you prefer landscapes or people?" "What's your favorite medium?"—this other part of me, quite confident (and proud) would rise up and speak, knowingly, about whatever piece was being discussed.

Of course, that only occurred if someone came to see my art and ask those questions. By eleven a.m. no one had appeared. As of noon, no one. By then, I had wandered upstairs, to the Fine Arts section of books. I sat in a chair near the stairs, paging through a big art book on twentieth-century painting, while watching to see if anyone was headed downstairs. Nope. I went back downstairs, hoping someone might be coming in the lower entrance. Nope. I decided to go out for lunch, walk over to Burger King. I'd just started back upstairs when I heard voices.

"Hi, Garry, is it okay to come down?" It was Rosemary.

"Hi, Garry. I mean, Mr. Picasso, can I come see my portrait? I miss it terribly!" This was Patricia. They both giggled as they clomped down the stairs. Then they almost toppled me over as I said, "Sure, come on down."

"Hi, how are you? Don't you miss our sittings? Is this it?"

"Over here, Patricia, see? It's the whole room. See?"

They flew past me as I remained by the stairs, a bit stunned. Rosemary looked back. "Garry, will you give us the tour?" The "tour"? "Um. Okay. Sure." I slowly dragged myself to where they stood looking in, waiting. I watched them closely. It was strange: they had come down the stairs like rollicking adolescents but now they stood there, silent, eyes big, taking it all in. They were suddenly quite attractive young women, their faces solemn, radiant. Patricia spoke first, "There are so many."

"I had no idea," said Rosemary. "Mrs. Helms said I'd be surprised. *Impressed,* she said, but—"

"This is like a real, you know, exhibition. Like a concert. Like a symphony or something." Patricia's eyes were very big, very dark.

"Landscapes . . . Faces . . . Real people . . . Portraits . . . Look, that's the woman at the Snack Shack . . . There's Old Hickory Lake. See, Patricia?" Then Rosemary turned to me, her face gone a bit ashen, pale. "Garry, you really did all this, this summer, here in Donelson?"

"Yeah. I did."

She turned back, staring into the room. "I'm sorry," continued Rosemary, "it just doesn't add up, okay?"

"What do you mean?"

"I have to tell you this, Garry, and make an apology." Rosemary spoke to me but faced into the room, as if she were addressing the drawings and paintings. "See, I got to know you, in the library. You took out books, you sat among the art books, you were studious . . . But, I knew, too, that you worked for Mr. Underwood. Russell, his nephew, came in once and said how you were this really hard worker, real strong and athletic. So, I pictured you as a jock, y'know?"

"Russell came in and said that about me?"

"Yes. Let me finish."

"Sorry."

"No, Garry, no, I'm sorry. That's just it. You're so nice, you smile all the time. You're cute. Okay, I think you're more than cute," and here she blushed, "I saw some of your drawings, but *this*? I mean, you are a really gifted artist!"

"You are," Patricia nodded. "I owe you an apology, too, Garry."

"No. Come on, girls."

"I do." Patricia, too, faced into the room as she spoke. "I hated sitting for you, okay? I know I was pissy and petty and I'm really sorry. I didn't realize who I was sitting for, what I was part of. Please forgive me?"

I blushed, didn't know what to say. Finally, "Thanks, you two, you're very sweet."

"Can we go in now and look more closely?" asked Patricia.

"Of course. Please," I made a slight Welcome flourish with my right hand. They both slowly entered.

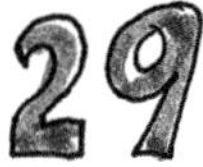

I followed the girls around, fielded their questions, and then, eventually, left them alone to go at their own pace without my hovering.

I made my way to Burger King. When I returned, carrying my dessert—a strawberry milk shake—I stood in the upper parking lot, finishing it, before I entered the library to go check on the exhibition. I'd had this fantasy that on my return, due to the word of mouth of Lexie, Rosemary, and Patricia, the parking lots, upper and lower, would be jammed. That there'd be a line of people, out both the front doors and the lower doors, folks just waiting to enter my show. That Lexie would have to enlist Thomas's help to oversee the crowds and keep tabs on how many could enter at a time, to avoid a stampede and overcrowding. Thomas would have a chrome counter that would click each time another person entered, giving us an actual count day by day over the three days—Friday, Saturday, and Monday—of the show's attendance. I finished my shake, entered the very quiet library and started for the downstairs when I heard Rosemary whisper my name, "Garry! Psst! Garry?" I walked over to the main check-out counter. "Hey, Rosemary."

"Congratulations again. Patricia left but she wanted me to give you this note. Here."

A piece of 8 1/2 x 11 notebook paper, folded in half. I opened it and read:

> *Dearest Garry, again, my sincerest apologies, and, too, my most appreciative thanks. Please forgive me and please know how much I admire you. You were so patient with me during our sittings, and how enormously impressed and moved I was and still am by your great body of work. I'm going to tell every-*

one I know to come see your show and to buy your art.
Thank you again and good luck on your trip back north and to Europe, too. OXOX Patricia
PS—you are SO gifted. I can't wait until one day I can say I knew him and he painted me! OXOX Patricia again

I laughed and folded it shut.

"What?" said Rosemary.

"What?" I looked at her.

"You laughed. Why'd you laugh?"

"Didn't you read it?"

"Yeah but—"

"It was a sweet note."

"Okay but you laughed."

"I dunno. That last part, her being able to say she knew me." I started laughing.

"See? You're laughing again."

"It tickles me."

"No, but this is serious. You have such talent. You mustn't laugh. You must work hard and be humble."

"Is that how you feel about your writing?"

"Well, I'm not that talented but, yeah."

"When am I going to get to read some of it?"

"Oh." Rosemary blushed. "I dunno. Really?"

"That's what we said. One of these days. Remember?"

"Okay." She blushed again, then nudged her black glasses up the bridge of her nose.

"When?"

"You're really serious?"

"You see me laughing?" I smiled.

"You're smiling. And you just were laughing. Twice."

"True. But not now. The smile means I'm friendly, open, receptive and curious to read your poems or—"

"I have a short story?"

"Great. Hand it over."

"You're sure?"

"Now. Before the crowds come and I can never find my way upstairs again."

Rosemary laughed. "Okay. Just a sec." She left the counter and disappeared into farthest of the three office spaces. I waited. Lexie came out of the middle office. She had a napkin and was wiping her mouth.

"Hi, Garry. Need help?"

"Not really."

"How's the show going?"

"Omigod, there's a line outside the lower doors."

"You're joking."

"I am."

"Oh you. Patricia and Rosemary were suitably impressed."

"I know."

"And they're tough cookies. How are my boys doing?"

"In real life or downstairs?"

"Downstairs."

"I'm just headed back down but last I looked, they're just, you know, hanging out."

"Funny. Oh, here's Rosemary." She had a manilla envelope, which she began to put in my outstretched hand. "You're really sure?"

"I'll return it to you Monday."

"Top secret?" asked Lexie as she leaned on the counter between us, folding and unfolding her napkin.

"Remember that story I wrote about my Uncle Nevin?"

"Sure. I like that story."

"Garry wants to read it."

"Oh good. It's a funny story. Her uncle—"

"No, Lexie. Let him read it first."

"Right. Sorry."

Lexie waved her napkin as she strolled off. "Let me go finish my lunch while I can. Bye, y'all."

"How many pages is it, Rosemary?"

"Not long. Thirteen. Typed." Then she blushed. "I'm not real good at hearing criticism but I do want it so don't hold back. Be honest, okay?"

"Sure."

"When will you read it?"

"Over the weekend."

"I mean—at night, before bed, or during the day?"

"Not sure. Why?"

"Think it's better as a bedtime story. I'm thinking of writing a collection of stories all meant to be read before bed and calling it 'Bedtime Tales.'"

"That's a great idea. Alright. I'll read it one of these nights."

"Thanks. I'd better get back to work."

"Yeah. I'd better go see about the crowds lining up downstairs."

"Ha! You watch, once word gets out."

"Right."

"You should write a short bio. I can type it up for you. So that people can know who you are. Hang it near the entry door."

"Okay. But—"

"What?"

"I don't have much of a bio. This is my first show."

"Right, but, you know, your education, where you're from, when you first got interested in art, and that man you studied painting with—people like to know these things."

"Okay. Thanks."

She nudged her black glasses up the bridge of her nose, I waved and we both headed off. I went downstairs, took a brief tour of the show, the room empty and very cold now, the AC going all day. I went back up and asked Rosemary and then Lexie if there was any way to ease up on the AC. There wasn't.

I stayed upstairs, browsing among the art books. Eventually, I wrote some in my journal, a crude version of a bio. Did a few pen and ink sketches, small ones, of the ride in, the duck pond, a house, all quick, playful, from memory. Then I watched people enter and leave the library. Did a bunch of quick sketches of all these different characters, without looking down. I did that until I got tired. Then I decided to read more from this strange and enchanting novel, *Jane Eyre,* until Thomas was tapping my shoulder. "Mr. Garry? We gots to close up now." I lifted my slobbering mouth from my folded arms. "Thomas?"

"Yessuh."

"Was I asleep?"

"Yessuh."

"What was our attendance today?"

"Our attendance? In the library?"

"No. The show. The drawings and paintings?"

"Oh, yessuh. That's a very nice show. You gots me in that show, too. I saw that but—"

"Thomas, sorry. You don't have a chrome clicker, do you?"

"Chrome liquor?"

"Clicker. Sorry. I was dreaming."

"Alright then. We gots to close up, Mr. Garry."

"Right. Can I take just one last look downstairs?"

"Yessuh. Yo' shore can but we turnin' off the lights soon."

"I'll hurry." I made my way downstairs, surveyed the room, all the pictures fine and in place. No one to appreciate them. But hey, it was the first day, a Friday, time to call it a day. I said a simple "Good night, all," flipped the switches for all the fluorescents which, unlike their belabored and sometimes flickering turn-on, all went quickly, instantly out and off. I hustled upstairs and joined Thomas, offered to help him straighten chairs and tables, which he accepted, and then the two of us exited the library together. Six p.m. Still a bright lovely pink sky.

"Okay, Thomas, thanks."

"Thank you, Mr. Garry. 'Preciate your help."

"Lexie and Rosemary left awhile ago?"

"Yessuh. Left me to close up."

"So what are you going to do with your Friday night?"

"Oh, not much. Gots to have some dinner, read my papers, watch a little TV, then get some good sleep. You know. The missus and me don't do too much. Daughter comes to visit from Memphis tomorrow."

"That sounds nice."

"Yessuh. How 'bout you?"

"Oh, you know . . . have some dinner, head out to my lake, sleep under the stars . . . Listen to the Grand Ole Opry . . ."

"Oh yeah! You gots to love that Ole Opry. That's some fine music, you bet."

"Yup."

"Well then."

"See you tomorrow, Thomas?"

"Yessuh."

"Why don't you bring your wife and daughter to the show?"

"The show? What show, Mr. Garry?"

"My art show. Your portrait. Downstairs."

"That's right! That's a pretty good idea. Yessuh. I'll tell her. Yessuh. Well, g'night, Mr. Garry. You be safe now."

"Thanks, Thomas. You, too."

"Yessuh. Gots to always keep your eyes bright and light, as my Pappy used to say, cuz it's a strange dark world out there."

"Very true."

"G'night, Mr. Garry."

I watched Thomas slowly move toward the lower parking lot, carrying his grey lunch pail. He had his red pick-up truck parked down there. I saw him disappear down the tarmac and past the library. It was a beautiful evening. Traffic buzzed along the street beyond, Friday night's hum of eager destinations. Maybe I'd drive, maybe I'd walk over to the Snack Shack for dinner. Read my *Jane Eyre,* watch people, do a sketch, who knows? The show was up and running. I'd had a nice nap, and the evening was still full of dreams. And questions.

30

Saturday morning was slow, sunny, steady. I stayed out by the lake until well after lunch. I decided the show was the show—it was what it was. I didn't need to hover anymore. Plus, things were winding down. I'd be leaving Donelson on Wednesday. Four full days before I'd take Titine back home to Darlington, Connecticut, via Dearborn, Michigan. Also, I was fully immersed in *Jane Eyre,* and wanted to finish it before I packed up and departed.

When I finally pulled into the Donelson Library parking lot, the upper level was completely full. I drove to the lower level and somehow managed to squeeze into a tight spot next to the grey trash bin shed. I was amazed at all the cars. Maybe Rosemary and Patricia did get the word out. I decided to walk around to the front doors and make my heralded entrance. Lexie waved hi as she headed for her rear office. I approached Rosemary as she manned the check-out counter. A mother with two little girls was just finishing, checking out what looked like at least ten books. "Come on, girls," the mom said. She was slim, pretty, her brownish hair done up in pigtails, just like her two girls.

"Hey, Rosemary, thanks!"

"What for?"

"Spreading the word. The parking lot is packed to overflowing."

"Always is Saturdays. But my mom said she'd be coming."

"Oh, so this crowd is just—"

"Saturdays. You know. Families. Kids, parents. Quality time."

"Oh. Right. Of course. Like always."

"Think Patricia's parents were just here. They might still be down there."

"Okay. Thanks."

It was already real chilly downstairs. Thomas was near the stairwell, sweeping.

"Hey, Mr. Garry, how you? Shore gots a nice showing."

"Thanks, Thomas." I looked in. Nobody.

"My wife and daughter, they tryin' to come see it later today."

"Great, Thomas. Thanks."

"Oh sure. My wife, she like the art things quite a lot. My daughter prefer the movies or TV but she say she come, too."

"Okay. Well . . ." No sign of Patricia's parents. Come and gone, I guessed. I started for the stairs, then stopped. "You been down here for a while, Thomas?"

"Yessuh, a little bit."

"Not much activity, I guess."

"No, suh. But they was one couple just here."

"Oh?"

"Yessuh. They liked it fine. Looked at all dem art works. And the man, he seemed to know things. Had a lotta fine things to say. His wife, more quiet. They nice folks."

"Just them?"

"Yessuh. That I could see. But it's still early."

"Early? But it's already afternoon and then there's Monday and that's it."

"Yessuh. Too bad we not open Sundays."

"Yeah." I stood there. Thomas stood leaning on his long-headed sweeper. "Yessuh." "Well," I said, not moving.

"Yessuh." Thomas took a big white handkerchief from his back pocket and wiped his brow.

"Well," I said again.

"Meanin' to ask you, that pictuh of me, I really look that way, Mr. Garry?"

"What way, Thomas?"

"You gots me sittin' there, holdin' this broom pole, and just seems to me I look kinda *dumb*."

"Oh, Thomas." I looked at him. He wiped his brow, looked straight ahead, then turned and side-eyed me.

"No, Thomas. Oh, no. I don't see you as *dumb.* Not at all."

"Naw?"

"No way! Your face. You've got so much character and depth.

You've got what I call a really 'lived-in' face."

"Yeah? Lived in? Lived in what?"

"Lived-in. You know, a lot of living, a rugged maybe even rough life but that's wisdom, I see. Not being dumb. It's more being wise."

"Wise, huh? Ha."

"Those sleepy eyelids of yours, the mouth, those full lips, a little bit open."

"That's what I'm sayin'—my droopy eyes, my mouth catchin' flies, y'see? Looks like a pretty *dumb* man to me."

I just listened, watched Thomas flap his hand as he described his features, as if he were redrawing the picture. I'd never seen him this excited.

"Did someone used to call you 'dumb,' Thomas?"

"Oh, you know . . ." Thomas looked down, the white kerchief in his right hand by his side, the broom pole in his left. For a moment, I glimpsed the trumpet player, Louie Armstrong. Satchmo.

"My daddy, yessuh . . . didn't much appreciate my, I dunno—style? 'Course, I was the last born. Seven kids. He dint have much time for me, I guess."

"Oh?"

"Never knew my name. Always called to me, 'Hey, dummy, come here! Quit catchin' flies and get over here!' Stuff like that . . . On a bad day, wife'll say, 'Thomas, you *so dumb* sometimes' . . . Even my children . . . one time my youngest—our daughter, she comin' by today, she say to me, real angry about somethin', 'Daddy, why you so *dumb*?' . . . Stuff like that, y'see? So I gets to thinkin', hmm, maybe I *am* dumb, y'see?"

"Okay, but, Thomas—"

"Yessuh?"

"A man who stands here thinkin' he might be dumb, is not dumb, you see? He's thinking. He's pondering. That's not a *dumb* man, that's a *thoughtful* man. You see the difference?"

"Hmm . . . I think I do . . . But . . ."

"But what?"

"You just tryin' to make me feels good, ain't ya?" Thomas gave a big white-toothed grin and then lightly tapped my shoulder with his white banner of a kerchief.

The door at the top of the stairs opened. I didn't look right away. Footsteps, down the stairs, in good speed.

"Oh, here you are. Hi, Garry!"

"Mrs. Willard! Hi."

"I wish you'd call me Clara."

"Hi, Garry, glad we found you."

Henry and I shook hands. Mr. and Mrs. Willard, Patricia's parents.

"Rosemary mentioned that you'd come to see my show, but when I got down here, well, I must've just missed you. Oh, and this is Thomas, who keeps an eye on the library and my show, too." They both shook hands, greeted Thomas.

"Well, I'll gets back to it, Mr. Garry. Nice meetin' y'all." Thomas slipped his kerchief into his pocket, assumed his broom-pushing position, nodded good-bye, and departed.

"We're so impressed, Garry. Wow," said Clara.

"Really. A stunning body of work. Congratulations."

"And Patricia's painting looks so nice where it is. Are you pleased with it—the show, I mean?"

"I really am. Thanks for your kind words and for stopping by."

"Are you kidding?" said Henry. "Wouldn't miss it."

"When we pulled in and parked, I told Henry, look at the packed parking lot, what a great turn out for Garry's show, and then—"

"Yeah, I know." I nodded, chuckled.

"We were just so surprised that we were the only ones down here."

"Rosemary set me straight."

"Us, too. After, we book browsed, then talked to her and she told us you'd just arrived. So, it's family day at the Donelson library."

"Let's face it." Henry nodded toward the show. "Most folks in these small Southern towns aren't used to seeing art or going to hear fine music."

"I guess so." I nodded.

"It's not personal," added Henry. "I daresay, it's 'the Way of The World'—the American Southern world. I mean, really, who *needs* Art, right?"

"I do," said Clara, raising her hand.

"I do, too." I raised my hand.

"Hey," said Henry, raising his hand, "I do 'three,' okay? But three, and Patricia makes four—out of how many? Ah, the winds blow cold on the artist's soul, eh?"

The Willards wanted me to give them a tour of all the pictures. They had lots of questions about the landscapes, where were certain locations, and the various portraits, people they didn't know existed in their own town.

"It's like *Under Milk Wood*," said Henry.

I looked at him.

"You know, Dylan Thomas's chorus of town voices, all these different visages, each one a study, but the story of Donelson, y'see?"

"Yes, okay." I nodded.

"I like that, Henry." Clara touched his arm and then pointed. "And this one of Thomas, who we just met. You really captured that sleepy grace of his, that wizened face, so lived in. Remarkable, really." I jumped to attention.

"Say that again, Mrs. Willard. You see a wise, lived-in face, is that right?"

"Why, yes, I do."

I told them about my talk with Thomas, how he saw his own portrait.

"Oh, the poor dear," said Clara. "It's how he was treated. That's what he sees." She pushed off from Henry's folded arms. "It's a striking pen and ink."

"It seems we each bring our own lives to these Rorshachs, don't we?"

"Ooh, Henry dear, that's pretty brilliant!"

Henry nodded, smiled. We visited a little longer. They assured me they'd bring some of their friends on Monday, the last day. Patricia, too, wanted to come again and bring a few classmates before she would head off for almost two weeks of music camp in some sleepy little suburb of Memphis. Henry noted the irony: classical music on the edge of Graceland and Elvis. What a world.

They departed. I browsed at books upstairs, keeping an eye out for any hints of an art show crowd. Few to none. I left the library around five, picked up a Big Whopper and strawberry shake to go.

Once I reached Old Hickory Lake, I parked Titine, changed into my swimsuit, took a nice long swim, swam almost halfway across the lake, in memory of my bud, the Durlando. After I dried off, I sat and munched on my now lukewarm Burger King dinner at my favorite concrete picnic table. A few people still lingered near the beach. But, by the time the sun began its slow sink into dusk, folks had departed or returned to their campers.

I was alone, lakeside. I guess I was a little down, lonely. But I read my *Jane Eyre.* Wrote a few things in my journal. For the longest time I just drifted, keeping a furtive eye on the sun's descent. Once it had dropped behind the trees, houses, lake, horizon, I delighted in its brilliant residual afterglow.

It was a lovely, lonely Saturday night, my last Saturday night beside Old Hickory Lake. I kept counseling myself to appreciate all this—I was writing, I was drawing and painting. I was reading good books. I lived simply but wholeheartedly. I'd made some wonderful new friends, all sorts of acquaintances. And, my art was hanging up on four walls, if not for all to see, at least, for me to review and realize, yes, I was here. One summer, 1971. I went to bed early, stared off, wondering about Kathy, waiting for the stars to take over.

31

Sunday was a blur. I overslept, then got trampled by the campers as they trudged to and from the toilet facilities. A bunch of little kids—a big sister, two brothers, and a toddler little brother—finally woke me. They were playing hide and seek just up from my hillside "bedroom." It was nine-thirty.

The service was at ten o'clock, my final time singing with the Methodist choir. I didn't want to be late and upset or disappoint Dr. Bill. I jogged to the lake, hopped in, swam enough to call myself "wet," relatively "clean," and enough awake to dry off, get dressed, and break a few speed limits to get into town.

Langford's farm. The fields, the rolling hillsides. The duck pond park. The vegetable market dad and his daughter—although on Sunday morning, their wooden cart with its big iron wheels stood empty. It was a beautiful morning, a hint of a cool breeze, just enough to begin me thinking that summer might actually slip away and shiver its way into autumn.

The church was packed. Dr. Bill was glad to see me. Even the pretty brunette gave me a sweet smile. We were missing two of the women but all of us men were present and sang probably the best, most fully and exuberantly, we ever had.

Reverend Bill's sermon was about Jesus in the garden of Gethsemane, his final night on earth. "How do we say good-bye?" asked Reverend Bill. "Some of us just rush off, right? Without even a look back or a wave . . . Some of us can't leave, can't let go, so we sit in our cars, our Gethsemanes, sobbing . . . .and some of us sit and ponder it all, an ending, but a beginning, too . . . It's never easy . . . It feels like such a great loss. And it is . . . We find a comfortable place and stay. As long as we can. Until, that tap on the shoulder. It's time . . . *Think about it: how do you want to leave?* Can you do it as generously and openly and curiously as you arrived? Or, as fearlessly and tenderly as Christ did that next morning?" Reverend Bill cleared his throat, took a sip of water as he continued to look at the congregation, a long pause.

"I think Christ was enormously afraid—and sad—and perhaps stayed up all that night praying in that moon-lit garden, just to savor all the glorious moments He'd had on this earth, His all-too-brief time with us . . . But I tell you, whether old or young or thirty-three, it's all too brief a time we have here on this magnificent earth . . . Think about it. As summer slows to its end, school days soon begin . . . as our loved ones, our sickly, our aged ones, as all of us move on, in some fashion. How do you want to leave? How do you want to say good-bye? And can you trust that God's glory, right here before us, in us, of us, will be in the next moment, too?"

I stared at the choir. I looked below, at all the different families. A slight heartache filled me. I wanted to go home. I wanted to stay. I wanted to see Kathy and Durl and my folks, my sister Carol, my brothers, all their families. And I wanted to stay in Donelson, to keep exploring, drawing, painting, to eat another home-cooked meal with Lexie Helms and Sammy and Mikey, to swim in Old Hickory Lake or just sit there in that lush late summer solitude and read my books, write in my journal, do a pen and ink, and savor all this.

Yet, it *was* time to move on—into my "real life." But wasn't this also *real*? Wasn't all that had gone before also my real life? When was it not real? When, then, did it, or does it, become real? Maybe, living as well as I had growing up, going to good public schools, a good college—maybe that wasn't real because it wasn't quite my own, it belonged to this "American Dream"—this order of prescribed things, of others' expectations, more theirs than my own.

This summer, then, was the marker, or maybe the marker had been two years earlier, when I had quit pre-med, left the secure, prescribed path. Now, two years plus this summer later, I was finally living my own version of a life. A little rough, shaky, even unknown, but something I was appreciating as an adventure instead of a "path"—pre-med, med school, internship, residency, or apprenticeship—work, marriage, kids, that whole dynamic. I still was only sure of a few things. And those few things still needed testing. I pondered all this, inspired by Reverend Bill's sermon. And told him so, after I'd stood in line, waiting to shake his hand.

"Thank you, Reverend Bill, your sermon really hit home."

"Thank you, Garry. Speaking of 'hitting home,' rumor has it that's where you're headed."

"Yes, sir."

"A shame. You've been a fine addition to our community, and a good strong voice from above each Sunday!"

"Thank you, sir."

"We never had our visit, did we?"

"I'm afraid not."

"What's this I hear about you having an art show at the library?"

"Yes, sir. Downstairs. About forty or so drawings and paintings."

"Really? But aren't you leaving soon?"

"Tomorrow's the final day of the show. Then, probably on Wednesday, I'll start driving north."

"It all goes too fast, doesn't it?"

"Yes, sir."

"Maybe I'll stop in tomorrow. I love art. You know what I love? Finger-paints! I do, really. Every now and then, when I'm stuck, especially trying to work up a sermon, I'll pull out my son's old box of finger paints and slosh around for an hour or so."

"Really?"

"Yup. Frees things up, and if doesn't, well, I've just made a mess! But it was fun. How to be a child of God, right?"

"Right."

"Will you be there tomorrow—at the library?"

"Yes, sir. Should be."

"Well, we'll say good-bye now and maybe again tomorrow, okay?"

"Thank you, Reverend Bill."

We started to shake hands again and then Reverend Bill pulled me close, a big firm hug, and said quietly, "You travel safe, you hear, and keep finding ways to love God."

I nodded. I couldn't say anything else because I got teary, so I just waved good-bye. Afterward, I looked everywhere—back in the church, up in the choir, over in the Sunday School rooms, and in the rear and side parking lots—but I couldn't find Dr. Bill to say goodbye. That upset me.

Then, at the Snack Shack for brunch, packed as it was with the post-Sunday services crowd, where was Terri? The thin-as-a-rail waitress was completely new to me. It felt as if I'd already left town, things were already foreign, unfamiliar. Amidst the chaos of chattering families, I quietly ate my pancakes, did an uninspired pen and ink of the plastic yellow flower in the vase, with the salt and pepper nearby. Then, like a small dog with a long tail between his legs, I departed.

The laundromat, too, was unusually quiet, deserted. What with getting the drawings matted, a few framed, along with doing more sketches and watercolors, and then the logistics of figuring out how to hang all of them, I had missed my usual laundry day (Monday afternoons) the last two weeks. So, I had an urgent need for some clean clothes, about two loads' worth. Which was fine. I just about finished *Jane Eyre,* did a pen and ink of Titine out in the parking lot next to the bent grey lamp-post, and remained kind of mystified that I seemed to be the only one doing laundry on a sultry Sunday in Donelson, Tennessee. Just as I finished, a small marching band of three families clamored into the laundromat, kids screaming, chasing each other. Three mothers, heavy set, arms loaded, only one man among them, a red-capped fellow with a beer belly, unloaded a beat-up white station-wagon as I slowly made my way over to Titine.

The sultry weather persisted. I had looked forward to a nice sunset by the lake. But even that expectation was thwarted. It didn't rain but the sky, my beloved Tennessee soon-to-be night sky, gradually filled with row on row of plump dirty pillows, clouds on clouds.

I went for a swim, dried off, ate my sandwich, read and savored a few more pages of Ms. Jane E, and continued to wonder where everybody was. Got ready for bed early. Read some more as I lay on my hillside. Then, without a star to say good night to, I lay head . . . on pillow . . . on sleeping bag . . . on grass, and found sleep much sooner than I'd expected.

32

A good night's sleep changed everything. Maybe all weekend, not knowing it, I'd been saying good-bye to Donelson. Because it felt as if Donelson were leaving me. Now, it was okay. Now, it was time to really say good-bye. I felt a new surge of energy—I was going home!

I had a lot to do to get ready. My bank account to close, my PO box to pay for and let go of, and a bunch of artwork to take down off walls. I'd do the bank and post office that day, Monday, then go catch one last glimpse of my art show before I'd have to take it down on Tuesday. Plus, there would be packing to do, and all the good-byes around town. Then, a good early start on Wednesday morning.

Toward noon, the main thrust of my practical errands completed, I drove over to the library, parked in the rear lot and took one of the paths next to the library in the upper lot, through the trees and pachysandra, into the Shop-A-Lot parking lot, then up Main Street to the Burger King. I sat outside, waited for my strawberry shake to melt and soften so I could finally drink it, ate my Whopper and fries, as I mused on Donelson.

I appreciated the girl behind the counter, with her freckles, ponytail and big white-toothed smile, but I finally decided not to ask her to sit for a pen and ink. I was too energized. I wanted to return to the library. I had art books and poetry books to return, and maybe I'd sit in Lexie Helms's backyard, under tall trees and chirping birds, in that welcome shade (it was already about to hit the high nineties and humid) and finish the last pages of *Jane Eyre.* That book had become a sort of romantic manifesto for this belief I held, expressed in the book, that what we communicate, who we are, how we love, is bigger than us, beyond us, somehow tied into the spiritual realm. It helped me to continue to believe in God, and, of course, in Kathy, too, and all that we shared.

I returned to Titine, gathered my pile of library books (the book on Matisse was a week overdue; the Robert Frost poems, *North of Boston,* was due back in two days) and walked up the side drive to the glass front doors. As I waved to Rosemary and made my way to the return counter, I spotted my elusive friend Elwood P. Dowd or Jimmy Stewart, or, really, this mythic mystery man, James Steward, as he headed through the door, downstairs, to the lower level. Was he on his way to my art show? And was that really him? I hurriedly dropped the books off and moved toward the downstairs door.

"Mr. Brown? *Excuse me*!" It was Lexie Helms's loud whisper. I turned. "Yes?"

"I don't like 'hit and runs,' plus, you owe us some money!"

"But, Lexie—Mrs. Helms—"

"Lexie."

"That man—"

"Mr. Steward. Yes?"

"I want to catch him before—"

"You will. That'll be a buck and a quarter. Hand it over."

"Yes, ma'am." I'd returned to the counter as we spoke. Had to search my wallet for the dollar, my right pocket for the change. "Here you go."

"Thank you. Wanna receipt?"

"Sure." I looked over to the door.

"He'll be there."

"I hope. He's a very elusive fellow."

"Tell me about it. Now then, you really leaving us this week?"

"Yes, ma'am. Day after tomorrow."

"Don't like it. Not one whit bit."

"I'm kind of mixed up about it myself. But I guess it's time."

"Somewhere in the world it's always 'the time,' isn't it?"

"Yes, probably so."

"Listen. You come for dinner tonight, tomorrow night. You pick."

"Oh. Gosh."

"That's not a night, that's an expression of confusion, perhaps. Hesitation? Reluctance?"

"Not at all. I'd be honored. Just—"

"You have other plans?"

"Not really."

"Fine. Tonight, tomorrow night. You can't have both. Don't want to spoil you."

"Tonight. Thank you."

"Tonight it is. Seven p.m.?

"Okay."

"Great. Now go find Mr. Steward. In fact, tell him I'd like to see him, too."

"Sure. Thanks, Mrs. Helms. Lexie."

"You're welcome."

I got halfway across the main room when Lexie, another loud whisper, called my name, "Garry!"

"Yes, Mrs. Helms."

"Lexie."

"Yes, Lexie?"

"What was wrong with tomorrow night?"

"Oh. Nothing really. Just, it's my last night. Think it's important for me to spend it quiet-like, out by the lake. Say good-bye."

"Of course. How nice. Carry on."

I bolted downstairs. Thomas was sweeping near the entrance to the art show hall.

"Hiya, Mr. Garry."

"Hey, Thomas, um . . ." I looked in the hall. Empty. No Elwood, no Mr. Steward. No Harvey, either. "That's strange."

"What's that?" Thomas began to lift his thick broom and swish it in the air as if to wave it or clean the air instead of the floor.

"Well, there was a man—"

"Oh, he come and go. But you should look in there. Someone left a note, Mr. Garry."

"A note? For me?"

"Yessuh. Take a look, way down at the end there."

"Okay. Thanks, Thomas."

"Yessuh. You'd welcome."

I walked in, slowly. The space looked great. The paintings were lit and viewable and I felt somehow proud. Maybe the day away gave me time to miss them a little, appreciate them even more. All these drawings and paintings, they were a kind of family. My own kind of decorous and, also, at times, indecorous, family, throughout days and nights of a challenging, surprising, often lonely, but also gratifying summer.

Even the fluorescent lights had an unexpected warmth to them, or was that just Sentimental Me now saying good-bye to this modest first showing of my art? Funny, even the space felt full, warm, alive, and though I was totally alone, I wasn't, not really. These pictures. I loved seeing them. I wanted to slow down and visit each one all over again.

At the far end, over to the right, taped onto the lower frame edge of my Giacometti-like version of Lexie Helms, was a small pink envelope, fine stationery, high-quality paper. I fingered it as I pulled it off the picture frame. It had a scent, too, as I eyed the graceful cursive on front:

"Garry."

When I opened it, there was even more of a perfumy sweet aroma. The thick pink page was folded in half, embossed in big subtle script were the letters "ALH"—ALH? Who? I opened it. Printed in bold black ink, underlined, and with a question mark surrounded by exclamation points, was one word:

"SURPRISE!?!"

Then, suddenly, behind me, came this voluminous multi-colored CHEER, mixed with squeals and whistles, maybe even some cat-calls—

"SURPRISE!"

33

Everything was in slow motion now. I turned and there, at the other end of the room, the entry way was filled to overflowing—people, faces, arms waving—smiling, beaming faces! Even Thomas's broom waving, with more laughs and screams and cheers and whistles. I stood there, completely dumbfounded. Who were all these people? And where was Mr. Steward? What was happening here? How long did I stand there, stunned?

After the cheers and hoots and hollers, there was applause. I was still nonplussed. As I tried to garble a few words, everyone, as if on cue, broke into laughter. It was Lexie who finally broke the spell: "Well, Garry, we couldn't let you leave without a proper send-off. So . . ."

The crowd parted and Lexie came forward bearing a big glass bowl, filled with a pink liquid and a ladle. Thomas followed her with a folding table, which he placed in the center of the room.

"Come on, everyone, we've got some punch, some cookies, some snacks. Let's let this poor stupefied boy come back to earth, and I know, eventually he'll talk to us . . ."

Rosemary came running over with Patricia. Rosemary spoke first, eager, excited, "Were you surprised?"

"Omigod," I stammered.

"Isn't this amazing?" said Patricia, "*I'm* amazed. Look how many people know you!"

"Yeah?" I could barely move.

"Look who also came," said Patricia. As she waved her arm, I could see her folks. With them was Dr. Bill.

"Oh, Dr. Bill! I looked for you yesterday."

"I had to run off. Knew I'd see you today. How about this? Surprised?"

"Oh God, I still can't speak."

"I know. Overwhelming. Lovely crowd." He looked back among the throng, now beginning to mingle and line up for punch, cookies. Dr. Bill continued, "Wonder if any of them sing. And are Methodists!" He turned to me. "Though I don't think we'll find anyone to replace you." Patricia's mom hugged me. Her dad shook my hand.

"Hey, Garry." It was Sam the dentist.

We shook hands, he slapped my back. "See? It's not about the money, is it? If you do good work, people get it, right?"

"Hey, Picasso," a dark gravelly voice called to me.

"Hi, Garry, you sure did a lot of drawing and painting this summer." It was Stan and a lovely, freckled, and very dressed-up Terri.

"Terri, Stan, hey, you two! I was at the Snack Shack yesterday but no sign of you?"

"Yeah, Stanley wanted to go fishing. I took the day off. We went to the far side of your lake, took a picnic. It was a nice day. Wasn't it, Stan?"

"No sun. No fish. But, otherwise, sure."

"Oh, Stannie! You had a good time, admit it."

"I suppose."

"We really like Stan's picture, by the way."

"Yeah, but how come you never did Fred's or Terri's?" asked Stan.

"I know." I blushed. "What am I going to do about that? And I leave early Wednesday."

"Well," said Terri, "there's still tomorrow. I'm working all day, till six p.m. most likely."

"Okay. Maybe I'll drop in."

"Real early or real late. When things are slow is the best time."

"Okay. I'll try to get all my packing and errands done in the morning and, what's four p.m. or so like?"

"Yeah, between four and six is real good."

"Great."

"I want one like that 'Vegetable Stand Girl.' She's so sweet. So pretty."

"You got it."

Terri flashed her big smile.

34

Eventually, I returned to earth. Most of the people I knew—some from the Methodist choir, the Snack Shack, a few regulars from the library. Emmy from the PO dropped in, and Mr. Wallace, from my bank, came. He carried a glass of punch with him as he nosed up to one after another of my pictures.

Reverend Bill did show up, with his wife and two daughters. She was very formal and the girls were almost too polite—they did little curtsies when I met them. Reverend Bill gave me a card with his mailing address. "Use that little typewriter of yours, please? You know, how you used to show up and sit typing in the children's classroom? Well, you type me one of your letters one of these days, you hear? And we'll have an epistolary talk about God and Art and the Spirit that runs through all this mess."

"Thank you, Reverend Bill. I'll do that."

We both nodded and smiled, shook hands. His wife—was it Eleanor?—held out her hand. I wasn't sure if I was to shake it or kiss it or bow to it. I shook it. She pursed her lips, fluttered her eyelashes and then nodded good-bye, without a word about my artwork. Both girls curtsied.

As I watched them walk off, I spotted Mr. Steward, bent over my small pen-and-ink of the five trees beside Old Hickory Lake. Before I reached him, Mr. Steward turned toward me, singing the refrain of a song, "Three coins in the fountain . . . da-da-da . . . da-da-da . . . that song keeps running in my head . . . goes with this picture, I think: 'Five trees by the la-ake' . . . you see?"

I nodded, a bit curious.

"Nice pen and ink. You have the gift . . . Harvey's clearly been keeping you company . . ."

"You think?"

"I do think, perhaps too much. Easy to do in a small town. Well, it's necessary in small towns. You can also overthink, which tends to happen in big cities. Of course, that's what big cities are for, not really overthinking, but BIG thinking. What do you think?"

I was a bit flustered, not sure what I thought since I was just so pleased to really be talking with Mr. Steward again. Before I could answer—

"Someone said you're leaving our little town. Is that right?" asked Mr. Steward.

"Yes, sir. Heading back to Connecticut. My dad's sixtieth birthday is this Friday."

"Really? Good for him, and that you want to be there. For him. With him."

"I think so."

"You *think* so? See, you're doing it."

"Doing it?"

"Thinking, thinking. A nasty business. Gets us into all sorts of difficulties and deviations."

"Okay."

"No paintings of Harvey? I see his influence, certainly."

"Well, he's pretty hard to—I mean, he's so—you can only catch glimpses of him."

"You're saying he's—elusive?"

"No, sir. You're *elusive.* Harvey's more *ephemeral.*"

"Ah, *ephemeral*! Isn't that a wonderful word? I'll say it again, '*ephemeral.*' Yes. That *is* Harvey. That is, in fact, life itself, don't you think?"

"I do."

"But 'elusive'—me?"

"Which reminds me, sir—Mrs. Helms, the librarian, wanted a word with you."

"You don't say. A lovely woman. Husband's always gone. Train man, rides the rails. Now there's a soul who's elusive."

"Mrs. Helms?"

"Her husband. Have you ever met him?"

"Actually, I haven't."

"Nice man. Quiet. Lexie certainly adores him. And those two handsome boys of hers, which, I might add, you've portrayed wonderfully."

"Thank you, Mr. Steward."

We were, in fact, now standing next to those two portraits. Why I didn't put them next to their mom's, I'm not sure. Well. Hers was more experimental, from memory and the erasings. Not as formal as the guys', which were painterly but more conventional.

"I love the light on the lawn in this one, behind Sam, as he sits there rather proud, the would-be dentist."

"That's my favorite part, those paths of light."

"Which only works so well because of this rangy patch of shaded greens. Wonderful! A real summer evening backyard, way down in Tennessee of all places!"

I watched James Steward. I listened. He didn't seem quite real and I wondered again if I was a little bit mad or just off in some fantasy, some elaborate imagining.

"It's your longing," said Mr. Steward as if in response.

"My 'longing'?"

"It's evident. These paintings, this great heartache for connection, for intimacy. I know it because I feel it, too, which is why I'm so lucky to have Harvey. He's a lonely man's refuge. Perhaps these creations are yours."

"Really?" I stopped breathing for moment. Was this true? If I were no longer lonely, would I stop painting, have no need to create?

"It's a deep ache that is never finally resolved. Just either reinvigorated or reinvented. It gets assuaged at times, on an occasion like this. Or a return home, or even marriage, is my guess. A brief stay against confusion. But then, in time, it resurfaces and then it must be renegotiated. A new motif, a reinvention of the self, or selves. Or—divorce, an affair, you know. It's our incessant curiosity and avidity, right?"

"Right." Oh man, some of this was registering, a lot was not.

"Thank God for Harvey."

"Where is Harvey?" I asked.

"Harvey? Oh. Well. Let's see . . ." Mr. Steward left off staring at

Mikey's portrait. He seemed to be quite intrigued by my rendering of the American flag and stood very tall as he surveyed the room. "Oh, that's him. See him? Over there, coming in the glass doors."

I looked. There were two men with big smiles waving, pushing a man in a wheelchair, a woman with a sullen expression walking beside. Big Jim! Eddie was pushing him in the wheelchair, Chuck continued to wave and smile. Eddie smiled, nodded, and Big Jim's wife—was her name Kelly?—looked very unhappy.

They wheeled over and we stood there, staring at each other. Big Jim wore a short-sleeve shirt, dark slacks, and a steady smile.

"Big Jim! Wow!"

"Garry. Hey, man." He offered his hand. I shook it.

"Chuck, Eddie and hi—um—"

"Kelly. Big Jim's wife. We met the evening you and John came for supper?"

"Of course. Hi." I nodded, she nodded. Then, we all just stood there. I'm sure I was beaming. Both Chuck and Eddie began to survey the room. Kelly seemed quite shy, lowered her eyes. Big Jim looked over at the snack table, then watched my face again.

"'What I Did Last Summer' by Garry Brown . . . heh, heh." This was Eddie, who then looked at me and winked.

"And we thought you were just lying around among hayfields and lakes, staring at the clouds," nodded Chuck, as he continued to look about.

"You did all these?" asked Big Jim.

"Yes, sir. By the way, Big Jim, I'm sorry you've been through such a rough patch."

"Naw, naw. No big deal. I coulda died. I shoulda died, but Kelly here, she's the one. She's the gutsy one."

"Jimmy, stop. It wasn't your time, honey. That little rabbit made sure of that."

"You mean . . ." I was going to say "Harvey," but then I realized I hadn't seen Harvey. I briefly looked about. Where was Harvey? In fact, where was Mr. Steward?

"That rabbit, you know," said Big Jim. "Remember?" He cradled an imaginary bunny in his two big thick hands. "In my cousin's barn back in July, remember? When you and your hay crew came barreling in on my, you know. Remember?"

"Oh, okay. Sure," I said. "That bunny."

"Saved this big lug's life." Kelly patted Big Jim's shoulder.

Big Jim looked off, puzzled, said, "You know, that little bugger, I think he really did."

"When'd you come home from the hospital?"

"It's a couple weeks now. But look, who cares? I wanna look at your art." Big Jim started looking a little more carefully. "I see now why selling books might not be your cup of tea. These are really *good.* Any of me and the guys or Durland?"

"You know . . . I don't think so. Well," I pointed, "there is one from that week in Nashville. A view of the city skyline, from our hotel rooms."

"Oh, where is that? I wanna see."

They followed me over to the far wall. I pointed to it, a big horizontal picture that included the window frame and big thick rivulets of curtains, pulled to either side, with a big reveal of roof tops, church spires, water tanks and, in the distance, more roof tops, a cupola, even a few trees at the edge of a park.

"That's Nashville?" said Big Jim. "Looks a lot nicer than I remember it. Even looks like a real city, huh, Kell?"

"It is a real city, honey."

"Sure, but this view. Makes it look like a city where people really live, y'know?"

"I remember that view," said Eddie. "That's from the window at the end of our floor, right?"

"Right."

"That fateful fifth floor," mused Chuck.

"That's only five floors up? Looks higher," said Big Jim. "Pretty nice view, I'd say."

"That was done on . . ." Eddie leaned in and eyed the date on the lower right corner, ". . . June seventeenth. That was only two months ago. Doesn't it seem like light years?" Big Jim, Kelly, Chuck, and me, too, all four of us stood there eyeing the drawing, this vista of cityscape, nodded our heads, and then, as if on cue, gave out in unison an extended, "Yeahhhhhh . . ."

We visited a little longer, and then I backed off, slipped away. I don't know why, exactly. I was so overwhelmed, so touched. I wanted to just quietly take in this basement exhibition room, and all these people, who were real friends to me now, who had appeared, and who seemed authentically interested, curious, even appreciative. This room that had felt so empty for the past five days, since I began putting up the show, was now so full of life. Small groups gathered at the snack table but also throughout the room. Next to the pen and inks I did of the rocks and trees near Old Hickory Lake. Or the series of drawings of Langford's farm. The various views I'd drawn from the library, looking into town. Also, of course, the array of ink portraits as well as, with some of them, their companion versions in oils. Next to each of these, small groups talked and browsed. Some looked like serious discussions, and then there were folks, usually the men, cracking jokes, slapping shoulders, having some good laughs.

35

As things began to wind down, folks came over, shook hands, continued their praise and congratulations, said their good-byes. It seemed as if just about everyone I knew in Donelson, Tennessee, had shown up for my art show. I went out to my car to put away my pad and notebook before walking over to the Helms'. Both parking lots were now almost empty. But there, leaning against the rear end of his big white Caddy, was none other than Floyd Underwood.

"Christ, it's hot!" Floyd wiped his face with his white kerchief.

"Mr. Underwood, hey!"

"Hey, yourself! We got more hay. You ready to work again?"

"Really?"

"Russell, get out-chere and say hello." Russell quickly slinked out of the Caddy. This time he had a real basketball under his arm. "Christ, leave the ball."

Russell, in one undulant, almost snake-like move, dropped the ball back into the front passenger seat, then stood and waved. "Hey, you still got your art going on?"

"Hi, Russell. Yeah. You really came to see my art show?"

"You think we come to see *you*?" said Floyd, who gave a snarl toward Russell but then looked back at me with a deft wink.

"Where's Charlie? He couldn't make it?" I asked. We all just stood there. Well, I stood, Floyd leaned and wiped his face, and Russell was now leaning next to him.

"Don't lean on my car, son."

"Well, you are, Uncle Floyd."

"Thass right. It's *my* car. Behave yourself. Straighten up. We're going to an Art Show."

"Oh man." Russell stood up. "Charlie's here. Hey, *Charlie*!"

"What?" came quick and muffled, until Charlie appeared in the car window of a beat-up red Chevy, two cars over. *"What?!"*

"Hey, Charlie, how ya doin'?" I called to him.

"Purty good. I'd be better with a beer and a girl." He snapped open his car door. It creaked. He got out.

"I can't believe this. You all came! This is amazing!"

"What's amazin'?" said Floyd, holding his kerchief to his forehead.

"That you guys are here."

"It was Russell's idea," offered Charlie, who was licking his hands and wiping his dark hair, as he walked over.

"No, it wasn't! I ain't no faggot. I just was leavin' church and this woman was talkin' about some guy at this *other* church—the Methodist church—who was down from the North and had this show of his art at the library . . . and when she said the guy's name, I thought it might be you . . . and so, yeah, I see it is you. So. That's all."

"Well, thanks, Russell. I really appreciate that. Why don't I take you guys down to the show before the library closes?"

"What time is it? Christ." Floyd tried to find his watch.

He had on his big white cowboy hat, a blue dress short-sleeved shirt, and tan slacks, with his big black cowboy boots. He looked quite solid, put together, even as his handkerchief kept flopping over his wrist.

"It's after five-thirty, I know that," said Russell.

"How ya know that, boy?" said Charlie, spitting his words at Russell.

"God, Charlie, say it, don't spray it! Shit!" Russell wiped his face and arms. "Jesus."

"Well?" Charlie looked at me, nodded, grinned. I could see the gaps where he was missing teeth. They were still at it. God, it was good to see them.

"I just know, okay?"

"It's five forty-five," said Floyd, straightening the huge gold watch on his wrist. "Are we in time? It didn't close at five or nothin', did it?"

"No, no. We're good. It officially closes at six, but I've got connections, so we can stay later."

"'Cause you're the artist, right?" asked Charlie.

"That's right, Charlie. I'm the artist and what I say goes!"

We were already inside the library, headed for the stairs. Lexie spotted us and waved. I waved back. I thought about making introductions but decided it'd be better to do that later. Just as we started down the stairs, it hit me. "What about Hub? Was he thinking of coming?"

"I dunno," said Charlie, who was just behind me.

"I dunno either," added Russell.

"Think so," said Floyd. "Was going to bring Hazel, his wife. God, this AC feels damn *good*."

When we got downstairs, the room was pretty empty. The lights were still on. As we opened the glass doors, there at the far end was Thomas, leaning on his broom, talking to a last lingering couple, a sturdy-looking man and a woman with a small white bonnet with tiny pink blossoms on it.

"Shit, lookee there," said Floyd.

"What?" I said, assuming Floyd was impressed with all the artwork. Floyd looked down, fingering his shirt pocket, "Okay to smoke in here?"

"Gee, I'm not sure."

"Guess it's like church, better not."

"Oh man, Uncle Floyd, y'see this one over here?" Russell was already crossing the room, pointing to the view of Langford's farm.

"That punch, them cookies." Charlie pointed to the table in the center of the room. "Okay if I have some?"

"Please, Charlie, help yourself."

"Thank ye." Charlie marched over to the table, slicked back his hair, wiped his hands on his jeans, and then took the punch ladle and a cup and began to help himself.

Lifting the filled cup and showing it, Charlie called out, "Punch anyone?" Which is when Thomas looked our way. Then the couple turned, too. It took me a moment but there, in white shirt and tie, dark suit, tanned and smiling, was—

"Hub!" I called out.

"Hey thar!" Hub waved, nodded to his wife. "That's the feller."

"Hub, you came. You really came to my show, too!"

"Yes, sir. Talkin' here to Mr. Thomas about you and your art and how you made this here picture of him, which my wife here really likes."

"I sure do."

"This here's my wife, Hazel."

Floyd and I had walked over. Now, Hazel, wearing bright red lipstick, was all smiles. She held out a white-gloved hand to me and did a small curtsy, as we shook hands. Funny, I never pictured Hub being married. He always felt like such a solitary man, quiet, watchful, hard working. But here was Hazel, tall, very dressed up, very ladylike and seemingly proper. The more verbal and maybe even the more educated of the two.

"So nice to meet the artist in person—and living!" she exclaimed, nodding and smiling, looking to me and then at Hub.

"No, please, this means so much to me, having you here."

"Really?" Hazel, sweetly sincere, blushed.

"And meeting you, Hub's wife, and seeing Hub again. Hey, Hub." We shook hands. I wanted to give him a hug but stopped myself. I felt like I was going to cry all over again. "And seeing Floyd and Russell and Charlie. This is real special."

"I bet it is," said Hazel, "I heard tell of your helping these men with their hay work but Herbert never mentioned you were an artist."

"Hazel, how'm I gonna tell you somethin' if I don't know it myself?"

"Well, that's true, Herbert dear."

"And we had no time for drawing, right, Hub? Not the way Mr. Floyd cracked the whip and kept us moving from field to field and barn to barn!"

Hub gave a sly smile, nodded.

"I show you my whip?" asked Floyd, quite seriously.

"Your whip?" I looked at him. "I just meant—"

"Gotcha!" And Floyd slapped my back. "How you doin', Hazel? You gonna buy one of these here pictures?"

Hazel eyed Floyd quite coolly. Then, "I dunno. Are we, Herbert?"

"Well now, that's a big question. How much are they and which one you want?"

Then Thomas spoke up, "They's all marked, y'see? In the corner, near the title and all." Thomas leaned on his broom handle and pointed.

"Oh, why sure they are!" said Hazel as she leaned close. "Mr. Thomas, this one of you costs fifty dollars. Oh my!"

"Fiddy dollars?" said Floyd. "Christ, that ain't hay, is it, huh, Hubber?"

"Guess not, Mr. Floyd, since we do know hay, don't we?"

Everyone laughed.

"But it's got a little red dot." Hazel spotted it.

"Which means it's sold," I offered.

"To me," said Thomas. "But Mr. Garry gimme it, if I want it. Not sure I do."

"Oh?" Hazel looked at Thomas. "Oh, Mr. Thomas, you mustn't look a gift horse in the mouth!"

"Alright, maybe I will take it."

Everyone laughed again.

“I’d like one of these pictures, Uncle Floyd,” called Russell, from the far side of the room. “This girl here is very pretty. Can we get it, Uncle Floyd?”

“What girl, Russell? These ain’t pin-ups, y’know!”

“I know. She’s just real pretty. Sweet-like.”

He was standing beside the big oil and smaller pen and ink of Patricia. If Russell only knew. We all headed over and joined Russell. “See, Uncle Floyd? Ain’t she a beauty?”

“Yeah.” Floyd stood there, intently looking. “Mighty fine.”

“What, you gotta crush on her, Russell?” Charlie again sprayed his words at Russell.

“Charlie! Jesus!” Russell wiped his face.

“Which you like better,” Floyd looked at Russell and pointed, “this big one in color or that drawing?”

“I like them both.”

“Actually, Russell, the painting is already sold. Her parents wanted me to paint her and they paid me. So that big one belongs to her folks.”

“Oh,” said Russell.

“But the pen and ink’s for sale. I put both in the show to kind of demonstrate how a painting starts as a sketch and then becomes this other, more elaborate thing.”

“Right,” said Floyd, nodding. Floyd took off his big white hat, wiped his brow and said, “So you want that drawing, Russell, or what?”

“I dunno. I kind of liked the painting more.”

“I like that drawing of her a lot,” said Hazel. “Don’t you, Hub?”

“You want me to buy that one for you?” asked Hub.

“Oh no, Russell’s got his eye on it. There are plenty of others to choose from. They're all so wonderful!" Hazel turned and took in the whole room.

"Oh boy," said Hub.

"Thanks," I threw in.

"Well, Russell, we ain't got all day," said Floyd as he put his hat back on.

"I know, Uncle Floyd, I know."

"I like these beside Old Hickory Lake. See, Herbert? Oh, and I love those fiery sunsets. Is that what they are?" asked Hazel.

"Yes, ma'am. Watercolors. Old Hickory Lake, one beautiful night not so long ago."

"That is a beautiful lake out there, isn't it, Herbert?" Hub nodded. "We don't get out there enough, do we, honey?" continued Hazel.

"I'm out there all the time, hayfields all over the place."

"I know. I mean the lake, to go swimming and such like."

"'I s'pose," said Hub.

"Is that Langford's farm?" called Charlie. "Where we worked?"

"Yeah, Charlie." It was the big 18 x 24-inch pen and ink with the line-up of hayrack, flatbed, mower, tractor, and Titine parked nearby, with the partial fence and frayed grass stands dotting the foreground.

"That's your car, right?" asked Russell.

"Titine, my grey Peugeot."

"Funny lookin'," commented Charlie.

"The car's name is Titty?" asked Hazel.

The men laughed.

"Tit-*tine*," I corrected. "Bought it from a French student in college. He named it Titine."

"Funny name, huh, Uncle Floyd?" Russell chuckled.

"It's French, Russell. I like it," said Floyd.

"I like this drawing, Herbert. I want this one," said Hazel, in a serious tone.

"This one with the machines and such," nodded Hub.

"Really, Hazel?" said Floyd. "I kinda like this one myself. Those fields and them machines, see? Those are *my* machines!"

"Aw, Uncle Floyd, I don't want that one."

"I know, Russell, but I do. You pick the one you want."

"Maybe it's this one then, too."

"For you?" asked Floyd.

"I want this one, Herbert. Didn't I say so first?" Hazel looked over at Floyd with a frown.

"Well, Hazel dear, okay, but—"

"I don't think this is up for discussion. This is the one I want, Herbert. How much is it?" Curiously, Hub's wife, Hazel, her polite and proper veneer had vanished, become quite stern, even cold. Hub leaned down and then, "Looks like thirty dollars."

"Really?" said Hazel, surprised.

"Tell you what there, Hazel. I'll buy it for thirty bucks and then you can buy it from me for fifty!" said Floyd.

Hazel did not blink, all eyes still on Floyd.

"Just jokin'. Ha!" Floyd wiped his brow, Hazel stared at him.

"Come on, honey, let's find you another fine picture."

"No, Herbert. I want this one. Don't I, Floyd?"

"Tell you what, I'm going to buy this here picture and give it to this fine lady, right here, Hubber. Whaddya say to that?"

"Well now."

"I'd like to give her a gift. Can I do that, Hubber? You think she'd like that?"

"I don't rightly know, Mr. Floyd Underwood. Why don't you ask her yourself."

Floyd cleared his throat, took off his big white hat. "Excuse me, fine lady . . ." Here, he slowly bowed. "May I present you with this very fine picture, as a token of my respect and appreciation?" Floyd stayed bowed. Hazel kept watching all this, arms folded. She looked at Hub, then down at the still-bowed Floyd.

"I don't appreciate your making fun, Floyd," came Hazel's darkened voice. Almost in a whisper, she continued, *"You are an under-paying, over-working sum bitch! I don't want no gifts from you! In fact, you can shove this very fine pitcha right up your, y'know, where the sun don't shine!"*

"Hazel honey—*Jesus*!"

"I'm sorry, Herbert. And I'm sorry to you, young man. You got a mighty fine show here. I'm sorry I have to leave under such ill-mannered and unforgivable circumstances. Good-bye . . . I'll be in the car, Herbert."

I hadn't noticed Hazel's bright red high-heels. They briskly clicked and clacked their way across the harsh linoleum floor, out the glass doors, up the stairs. We could still hear her echoing up and out, all of us, stunned, silent. She was gone.

37

Floyd slowly straightened from his bow. "Jesus H. Christ . . . what'd I do?"

"Dunno but I'd better excuse myself, too." Hub tugged on his tie, nodded, started out, then stopped. He looked at me, looked toward the glass doors, and then quickly shuffled over to me. "Um . . . so, congratulations on your art, Garry . . . Guess it's a lot like them hayfields. Some days it's just damn hard work, other days there are fields, great beautiful fields, to mow and hay and bale. It all takes time . . . You're a damn hard worker, I know that, and I wish you more good days than bad . . . Good luck and I hope we see you in these parts again." Hub gave my hand a solid sturdy shake, nodded, and then traipsed out the glass doors, up the stairs.

Floyd started wiping his neck and chin. "That woman has never liked me. She acts all polite and ladylike but I knew her daddy, her brothers, too. Every time I try to do something kind for her, I just don't get it."

"So which one we gonna buy, Uncle Floyd?"

"None. I'm just disgusted. Got me a sour mood now, dammit all to Hell." Floyd said this with a certain sadness as he wiped the inner headband and quickly doffed his hat.

"But, Uncle Floyd."

"Nope, Russell. Not today. Sorry, Brown, but, well, we got to get goin', too . . ." Then to Charlie, over by the snack table, "Whyn't you eat *all* them cookies, Charlie?"

"Might just do that. Damn good." Charlie took two more in his right hand.

"Come on, boys."

"But, Uncle Floyd—"

"You heard him, Russell." Charlie came over, his saliva flying.

"Charlie, will you quit? *Shit—*" Russell quickly charged out the glass doors and up the stairs. Floyd stood there, did another, final wipe of his inner hat rim, put on his hat, stared at Charlie.

"What?"

"Let's go."

"Right." Charlie pocketed the cookies, wiped his face, then turned to me. "Nice pictures, Brown. Keep this up, you might could be an artist one day." Charlie nodded and walked off.

"We'll miss you at that pig farm, Brown. If you change your mind, you know my whereabouts, don'tcha?"

"Yes, sir."

"Like Charlie said, real nice pictures."

"Here, Mr. Underwood, why don't you take this one?" I went over to the drawing of the fields and the machines and began to lift it from its hook.

"No, sir. Appreciate the thought but that picture—no, sir—it's wreaked enough havoc. Don't need no more."

"But, Mr. Underwood—"

"Thanks, but no thanks."

"How about that small one, of the girl, for Russell?"

"No, sir. We done with pictures for today. Best get going. You take care and have a safe trip." Floyd nodded, tapped his hat, even did a herky-jerky little bow, turned and walked as fast I'd ever seen him walk, not that I-own-the-earth kind of saunter but a real beeline for the doors. Until he abruptly stopped.

"You're a good young man. Don't know about all this art stuff but I know a hard worker, like Hubber said. You keep doin' that, you'll do fine. Good luck and don't forget us, y'hear?"

I nodded. "Thanks, Mr. Underwood."

"Alright then. Bye." He was through the glass doors, up the stairs—gone.

I stood there holding the 18 x 24-inch pen and ink. I looked through the glass doors, toward the now empty stairs. I looked down at the picture, the hint of those expansive hay fields, with Floyd Underwood's machines lined up at the edge of all that earth and green and yellow and big inviting sky. There was Titine, too, sitting quietly, next to all those farm machines. Just a pen and ink, black and white, but I could see it all in color, and I could remember the sweat and the smell of cut grass. And the constant steady movement—bodies, machines—the humidity laced with now and then a sweet breeze.

I stood there looking at this picture. I began to quietly cry. I felt quite alone, and, I also felt excited. I was headed home in two days. On the road again. Back to Michigan, where I was born. Then, back to Connecticut, where I grew up. Then, eventually, in the autumn, with Kathy, I'd be off to backpack through Europe. To visit cities and museums, see art, see Van Gogh and Rembrandt and Matisse and meet all kinds of people. But, which life was mine? These men, those fields of hay and harvest. This library—and where was Thomas? I'd have one last dinner with Lexie and Sam and Mikey. They were not my family and yet, I'd miss them. I'd known them. I knew them. And now I'd carry them with me, but—what would become of all of us?

If this were a movie, the camera would pan down from my teary face to close in on that pen and ink, the whole panoramic view of fields, machines, and then get even closer until all we see is the black ink outline of my dear old car, Titine . . . very gradually the ink outline would turn light grey, then darker grey until it *is* Titine, my grey Peugeot. And it's bumping along country roads until there she is—full tilt boogie, and I'm driving, windows open, hot Tennessee air blasting, now on the highways going east and north, to Michigan, and then further east, to Connecticut.

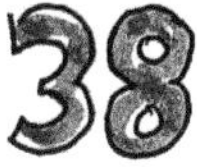

I did say good-bye to Thomas, the next day as I packed up my art show. I did have that final Monday night dinner with Lexie and Sam and Mikey, Southern fried chicken and all the fixings. A delicious meal. And when I returned Rosemary's short story about her Uncle Nevin, I could see her beam as I told her how much I appreciated it and all the surprises revealed about her beloved and quirky "Unc' Nev."

I slept under the stars that night and Tuesday night. I woke early Wednesday morning, a little nervous, and very antsy. It was time to go. I was packed and ready. I took a quick dip in the lake, washed and dressed, had an apple to snack on but didn't eat it. Just got on the road with the idea that I'd stop for lunch somewhere along the way. I didn't. I just kept driving. And driving.

I don't even remember arriving in Michigan that night. Did we have a cookout? Did I sing songs with nephew and niece, Chip and Jenny, as Jenny played the piano? Did we all get to bed early? All I remember is driving, on the road again the next day, my little old Titine, following Sandy and Judy's car, heading east to Connecticut. Did we stop at a motel, somewhere in eastern Pennsylvania, an imaginary halfway point? I think so. It was less humid, even balmy. And, while Sandy and Judy lounged poolside with drinks from the bottles of liquor Sandy had packed for them, did I swim and play in the pool with Chip and Jenny? No memory.

Except that we arrived on Friday afternoon, in coolish, fragrant weather on Huckleberry Lane, and Mom came running out from the garage as we pulled in, squealing and smiling, waving her arms and then eagerly hugging each one of us as the cars were parked, car doors flying open, each of us emerging, motors turned off. My dad, too, appeared and trudged steadily over to the cheery family.

But where was brother Chris? He'd arrived the day before, after driving up from Kentucky, his summer at grad school completed. His wife, Judy, and two sons, Chris Jr. and Matt, were back home in Pennsylvania. He came alone.

It was late August, moist and hot in Connecticut, too. But this was tame compared to the heat and humidity of Tennessee. My attic bedroom seemed small, dark and cramped. I'd been sleeping under the stars. What was I doing here? Was this really still my home?

Durland was home, too. He'd phoned the house asking about me, Mom said. After we unpacked the cars and settled in our assigned bedrooms, the kids (myself included) swam in the pool while the adults fixed drinks. Mom scurried about, making appetizers and starting to ready dinner. It had been decided: hamburgers and hot dogs tonight, Friday night, and a nice big, juicy steak for Dad's birthday dinner tomorrow, Saturday night. After my swim, while everyone sat on the big screened-in porch, nursing drinks and catching up, I called Durland. I sat in Mom's pink kitchen and tried for some privacy.

"Garry, you can use the phone in our bedroom if you want privacy."

"Thanks, Mom." I hustled upstairs, closed the bedroom door and sat on the edge of their huge king bed. Everything seemed too close, intrusive. Already I felt myself longing for the wide-open night world of my small, grassy hill near Old Hickory Lake.

"Brown."

"D-man."

"You're back."

"*You're* back."

"Almost a week. So, Gar, how ya doin'?"

"Oh man, Durl, what happened to our summer?"

"I know . . . Hey, you wanna go for a run tomorrow?"

"Sure. Listen, I'll run with you if you'll come to my dad's birthday dinner tomorrow night."

"Tomorrow night? I don't have a gift for him or anything."

"No problem. I gotta gift that can be from both of us."

"Okay. What time?"

"Let's say seven. What time for the run?"

"You gotta choice, early morning or late afternoon."

"Hmm. How about late afternoon? Then we go for a pool swim and shower here and join the party?"

"Great. Meet you at five p.m. at Wee Burn."

"Got it. I've missed you, D-man."

"Me, too, Gar."

Curious: during Friday night's dinner and on into Saturday's breakfast and lunch, as the family would gather, mingle, come and go, no one seemed at all interested in where I'd been and what I'd done all summer. It didn't really bother me. I realized how each person holds their own life very close so there's not a lot of room for another's, especially those of us just beginning to enter "real life." Or, was it because I wasn't following the conventional "real life" path? It did seem as if I were being intentionally overlooked. Like one who is sick or, even, infectious? Leprous? Okay. I *was* bothered.

Only Mom kept quizzing me. And, when he was drunk enough, my brother Chris would launch into these inquiries which he called "Existential. Y'know, Monk, the profound questions of a life that every man must answer for himself, sooner or later, right?" Right.

And, while I loved Chris's questions, and I loved him, I felt saddened by his flirtations with profundity. We'd start in talking—I've always listened carefully to both of my older brothers—but then the talk would go only so far. Chris would lapse into a kind of murky drunken silence. Or he'd just get up and go fix himself another drink and end up talking to our brother Sandy, then joking and flirting with Sandy's wife, Judy, who I called "Judites." When I'd finally get up to leave, Chris stood there and called to me, "Hey, Monk, where ya goin'? I thought we were talkin'?"

"Yeah," I called back, "I thought so, too, but—"

"No, no, it's okay." He'd wave me off. "We'll get back to it, right?"

Right. We never did. I have to admit, all three men—my dad, Sandy, Chris—left me hanging. We would kind of touch on things and then poof! Either the subject changed, another drink got refilled or any one of them, or all three of them, would go silent and give that sullen two-thousand-mile stare.

Only Mom and Judy remained curious. Both were bubbly, effervescent, had lots of questions. Although, it sometimes felt as if they weren't really asking *me* questions so much as they were eager to just ask questions. Keep the ball in the air, moving, bouncing, jostling along. No silences, no pauses.

Judy was helping Mom in the kitchen, Mom making the hamburgers, counting hot dogs; Judy fussing over the salad. "So, I thought you and John were going to spend the summer together."

"We did, too."

"You never sold any dictionaries? At all?" continued Judy.

"Not a one."

"So, okay. No bookselling. But, then what?" asked Judy.

"Wait, Garry." Mom flapped a hot dog at me. "I thought you spent a week learning to sell."

"That's right, Mom. But then, we quit the books, camped out by this lake for a weekend. Then John came back North and I stayed in Donelson."

"Donelson?" said Judy, munching some carrot herself. "I thought you'd gone to Nashville."

"We did. That first week. Then, oh God, it's a long, crazy story."

"Okay, okay, but what did you *do*?" Judy stopped cutting carrots and looked right at me. "I mean, how did you survive? Did you *work* or something?"

"I did, yes . . ." I nodded, finished my carrot piece, as I considered how I'd explain it all. Then Judy said, "Oh God, Petie, is this salad going to be big enough?" And that was that. End of inquiry. Although Mom tried to keep the ball in the air a little bit longer. "No, Judy, he did work. On this farm. With hay and pigs and tractors and farm machines. And he was painting. He did portraits and people actually paid him."

"Really? Is this true, Gar?"

"Kind of. Yeah."

"Wow, Gar . . . how much money did you make?" Dad walked in as Judy asked this. Not missing a beat, as he went over to pour himself another Scotch, he said, "Not enough to pay me back for the work they did on that junky old foreign car. Am I right?"

"Well, but, Dad—"

"I know, I know. I'm throwin' that in with your Europe trip money. But Christ, two hundred bucks! You should have a new car for that much money. Jesus!"

"Oh, Brownie."

"Hey, think about it."

I said nothing, just blushed. Still chopping carrots, Judy bent close and confidentially asked, "So you had car problems, Gar?"

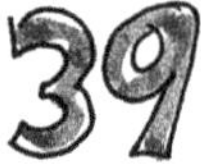

Mom's pink kitchen. The blue living room, blue dining room, up the stairs into the bedrooms, all the bedrooms—except for my attic hideaway, which was wood-paneled—blue. The big greyish/purplish screened-in porch, nestled out among the summer twilight of trees, shrubs, so many hints of forests and bedtime fables. But, all of it, the drinking, the small talk, everything that led up to the meal and away from it, felt purposeless, false, a distraction. Where was real life?

These rooms, not unlike Lexie Helms's home, were comfortable, cozy, but I continued to want space, air, a vivid night sky. I had a hard time sleeping in my bunk bed. My bedroom was no longer a getaway but felt more like a small tower prison. I was restless, uneasy, confused: how often had I had bouts of homesickness, a desire to return home? Okay, a few. Even in college a few, and when I returned for the holidays, I was pleased, content, satisfied. But something had changed.

The next day, late morning, I began a nice-sized oil (24 x 30 inches) of Judy. She was in the backyard, lying out in the red-painted wood lounger, sunning herself. Suntan cream was smeared on her face. With her black sunglasses on, she sat up, a drink resting on the wood arm near her right hand, a big hardcover novel in her lap, both legs raised a bit. Over the book was her full figure, her pink two-piece, her tan cleavage. I did a pen and ink first. Then I saw how I could make it a painting. The novel was John Updike's *Rabbit Redux.*

Mom fixed tuna salad sandwiches for lunch, iced tea. I ate a half sandwich and then asked Judy if she'd want to come sun herself some more.

"Oh, Gar, I'll become a lobster."

"I'm so close, though."

"Well, okay."

My lovely sister-in-law sat for another hour. We talked about books. She asked more questions. She wanted to know about the librarian and the haying and my art show. But finally, she'd had enough sun. I painted some more without her, the background areas. I liked this painting. I was hopeful.

Then I went for a dip in the pool. Tossed Jenny in the water. Then Chip wanted me to toss him, too. He was afraid at first, so I held him up and then plopped him down, never letting go. He liked that. Soon he wanted to be tossed like his big sister. Chris took his car and went to revisit Pear Tree Point, and, he was curious to see the new high school. I left the pool area and the kids and Sandy, who was watching the kids as he paged through *The New York Times.* I took one of Mom's big flowered towels and lay out in the back yard. Nodded off, half in the sun (my lower half), half in the shade. Had a great nap.

Close to four-thirty p.m., it was time to pull things together, go meet Durland. I put the towel back, then wandered over to look again at Judy's painting. Still liked it, still hopeful. I had already washed the brushes. I put everything in my box, the brushes, paints, rags, turpentine and linseed oil, and carried them to the garage. Then I hustled upstairs and got dressed. In jog shorts and tee, Titine and I headed for Wee Burn.

I liked the drive over there. Hot, a little humid—nothing like Tennessee. Windows open, radio on, hoping for some Oldies-But-Goodies. Up Pembroke to Mansfield. It felt good to be alone again, quiet, watching the different houses, the "landmarks," remembering a few things. Like my paper route, certain customers. Also, old "girlfriends." The Kavoojians over near the Hunt Club, Anahid, that dark beauty, a sophomore when I was a senior, so sweet, so down to earth. It always surprised me to see such a big, fancy well-to-do house. Or Dotty Pierpont, who I had a crush on and never got to kiss when we played spin-the-bottle at her twelfth birthday party. She had lazy dirty-blonde curls and dimples, this impishness that I couldn't resist. I cruised along relishing all this, the Kingdom of My Youth and Foolishness, my longings, my foibles.

Five p.m. on a Saturday, late August. Wee Burn Country Club seemed quiet. I pulled in and parked beside Durland's Green Monster. John stood up from bending over, nodded, then bent down again into a deep leg stretch. He was all business.

"Gar, you're late."

"Durl." I looked at my watch: five past five.

"Well?"

"Five past five."

"Like I said, you're late."

"Wow, Durlie, what bee got in your bonnet? I thought you missed me. Thought you'd be glad to see me."

"I am, Gar, I am. Hey . . ." We briefly hugged. High-fived. "You're still late."

"Oh man." I spread my legs, swiveled my hips. Bent over, touched toes. I leaned into my spread legs, first the right side, then the left. It felt good to stretch. I pulled each leg up into a curl, into my chest, first the right, then the left.

"You ready?"

"Well."

"Come on. We'll do a real light jog, that'll warm us up. Then, like at the fifth hole, we'll get a good pace going, okay?"

"How long we going for?"

"Whaddya think? Five, six miles?"

"That's like—"

"Half-hour, forty-five minutes? We'll just run, see how it feels. Okay?"

"Yeah, but y'know, things will start around seven. It's five fifteen now. We might want to take a swim before we shower."

"Come on, Gar, don't worry. We won't be late. 'You think too much, Butch. Leave the thinking to me, okay?'"

"Okay, Sundance. Okay."

"Come on, nice and easy."

A light jog. Through the parking lot, a few cars. Where were all the golfers?

Strange. Along a section of gravel that blended into grass, over some old log beams, which indicated the end of the parking lot and down a gentle grassy slope onto the Wee Burn Country Club golf course.

Durl loved to run. He took it very seriously. He had a very distinctive style, which I might call "princely." He ran, not quite rigid, but as if he must keep that plate on top of his head at all costs. He was so straight-backed, so poised. Yet his shoulders remained lowered, relaxed, as his arms and hands kept a low steady ballast, right along his waist, a rhythmic pumping. All of this had the effect of keeping his chest full and out, as if he were leading with it. It was a relaxed gait within this sturdy, almost rigid posture. Of course, if you watched his legs, you'd be easily impressed, even intimidated. Not so much as we jogged along, but once in full stride, watch out. They were sinewy pistons, stretched to their max, black hair accenting their muscular grooves, their striations.

I was a year older than Durlie. In high school, I'd been a leader, visible, vocal, a bit of a joker but president of our class, QB on the football team, co-captain of the basketball team. John Durland had seemed almost passive, faintly visible, although for me, and many others, he was one of those silent but deep guys, as in "still water runs deep." He was following the high standards of Doc Robbins, as the vigilant, almost morally superior captain of the track teams—cross-country, indoor and outdoor track.

I wanted what seemed like John's profound ability to remain observant, restrained. I tended to be all impulse and reactivity. Durl, of late, having gone door to door for the last three summers, had begun to find that part of him that was more outgoing, expressive. In the context of running, well, Durl was the leader and I was clearly the jokey, mock-whiney sidekick. We truly did complement one another.

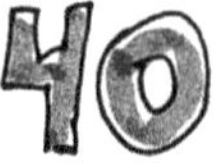

It was a lovely early evening, humid but cool. The sun would set in another two hours. The Wee Burn fairways and greens were laced with tall evergreen trees. Sunlight filtered through so that the yellow grasses were lined with long dark green shadows.

We were now in full stride, the fifth hole had come and gone, and I was surprised: I was keeping up, matching John stride for stride, feeling good, my body hungry for a good workout. We silently clipped along, up long hills, down beside short clumps of thicker grass, beside sand pits, and finally, in among the back fairways. There, we saw four men marching up to a flat-top of hole with "flag-pole" fluttering, each of them in short sleeves and navy slacks, eyeing the hole, looking for their respective white balls. Of course, the irony was that, as we strode past on the far side, their balls were not on the green flat but back on the thicker grass where we'd just come from. I watched the men and when one of them looked our way, I waved to him and then pointed backward. He waved back, nodded, and started talking to the other three men.

As we approached the final fairway, I sensed what was in store. I saw John's steely eyes gleam. I felt his competitive entitlement. This was his realm, how dare I threaten it? How dare I keep up and not whine but even shine? The smooth grass swooped up to the final hole and clubhouse beyond. By now it had a frosting of light along its edges, though mostly it was a dark, cool, trim green.

John was ready. Strangely, I was, too. Casually, as if commenting on the fine sunset, in a deep husky whisper, he said, "Shall we kick it in, Gar?" I acted a bit abashed, caught off guard (though I really wasn't) and replied, "Oh, really? Well" (pant-pant), "okay." John nodded, bowed his head as his body dipped into the charge. Instead of backing off or giving up or just plain flapping my arms and collapsing,

I again matched him. I was feeling strong and playful, even feisty. I did not blow past him. Nor did John's big burners leave me behind. Again, stride for stride, we ascended the green slope, until I decided to make a move. There was something extra stirring in me. Suddenly I roared up the hill, calling out in a cheery voice, "Come on, Durlie!" I was twenty feet ahead of him at the top, where I slowed and allowed Durl to catch me. We finished stride for stride in a dead heat.

It didn't feel right to not have John in the lead, or, at least, close, and I'd made my point. It was in me. To do it consistently? No. But to know it was there, in me, a force to be reckoned with, felt very satisfying. Also, to remember again, that in ways athletic as well as social, I was still the elder, the leader of sorts. And that such power wasn't always necessary. Or was it? We bent over and caught our breaths, then paced and stretched and through all this, coughed words.

"Jesus, Brown."

"Yeah, huh?"

"Christ, Gar."

"I know, huh?"

"You been—? Jesus."

"Yeah. A little."

"Workin' out? In Tennessee?"

"Some jogs. Swimming. That haying work."

"Oh, right. But still."

"I know. Surprised me, too."

"That was a first."

"What?"

"You took over."

"Well . . ."

"Think you nosed me out."

"Naw. No way."

"Yes 'way.' BIG way. Man!"

"Durl, we tied."

"You slowed down. Waited."

"But, D-man—"

"It's okay, Gar. It was fine."

"Yeah. It felt good."

"You looked great, Gar. So strong."

"Really?"

"Best I've seen you."

"Yeah?"

"Nice, Gar. Really nice."

"Thanks, Durlie. I learned from the best."

"I mean it."

"I do, too."

We made a light jog back over to our cars. Then John's Green Monster followed my grey Titine. We made like a small caravan over to Huckleberry Lane. We parked in the driveway. With no conversation, we made our way through the garage, through the TV room, and out into the pool area. We both took quick rinse-off showers before we plunged into the pool.

Where was everybody? The clock on the pool wall—big, battery run, with black arrow hands like a library clock—said it was past six-thirty. No matter. John and I took turns doing cannonballs off the stiff sandpapery diving board. We laughed, we cried out. John asked if I had my Frisbee handy, or even a tennis ball would do. I went looking in the closet next to the shower/changing room. Finally, I found a small plastic orange football with a black stripe on either end.

"Perfect, Gar—throw it!"

I mock-called signals. "Se-et! Hut one—three—forty-eight! Set . . . Hut- hut-HUT!"

John raced off the board. I pretended to backpedal, looked downfield as I threw a sidelong glance as Durl launched high off the board, spotted him, and, with a solid whip-motion—his arms reaching, calling for it—I planted it—THWAT!—into his hands as his body, hands, ball, face were swallowed by bluish pool water. I cheered. John was submerged. My mother appeared, in her pink bathrobe. John rose from the water, both hands raised, the orange pigskin in his right hand. "Hey, Mom," I said and called out, "Touchdown!"

"OH YES!" called Durl followed by, "Hi, Mrs. Brown."

"Hi, John." She waved, tried to smile. "Oh Garry, when did you get home?"

"Maybe twenty minutes ago."

"Okay. Great."

"Where is everybody?"

"Oh, you know . . . lunch was late, we had drinks, too. People swam, and then when the kids went for their naps, the adults did, too. So, everyone's slowly getting up, showering, you know."

"Right. Were we too loud—did we wake everyone?"

"No, it's time for everyone to get ready. Did you and John have a nice run?"

"Real nice."

"Gosh, it's been so long since I've seen the two of you."

"I know, all summer. I missed you, Ma."

"Oh, you don't have to say that."

"I did. It's nice being home."

"Well, we're so glad you're home safe . . . It's so good having everyone. Carol and Dick and the kids'll be over soon. So, I'm going to go get dressed and then start in the kitchen."

"Okay."

"Would you want to look at the grill? Maybe put the charcoal in, get the fire ready for your father, the Chef?"

"Sure, but usually Dad likes to do it."

"I know. But, just have a look."

"Sure."

While John showered and dressed, I went and checked on the grill. Years ago, Dad had a brick and iron grill built into the back patio side of the house joining the indoor fireplace in the TV room. The patio seemed small and lonesome compared to the now looming purple screened-in porch on one side and the more recent big yellow (plastic, steel and concrete) pool area to the other side. The dogwood tree still arched nearby, a constant companion. The backyard extended beyond, warmed by streaks of early evening's last sunlight. And the grill? Dad had been there already: the charcoal was placed in its neat and modest pyramid of black cubes. The ashes already cleaned out, a metal tray laid beside lined with knives, big metal forks, prongs, skewers, one metal spatula, one pink plastic. Surgeon-like, Dad's instruments were at the ready.

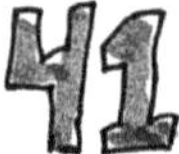

Dad didn't even eat any of his own birthday cake. He blew out the candles. Mom cut the cake for him while he went to refill his drink, another Scotch on the rocks, with very few "rocks."

Dinner plates cleared, we were all assembled among tables and chairs on the big screened-in porch, eating Mom's angel food cake with chocolate frosting. Dad raised his glass to us all as he sat, beside him a small pile of birthday gifts. He would open a gift, then Mom or Judy—Carol just watched—would push the next gift toward him.

The kids—Jenny, Chip, Dave, Laura and Jess—eagerly watched at first and then, as things slowed and got boring, they gradually, one by one, made their way downstairs to the TV room to see what was on.

Judy and Sandy's gift was opened first, a small silver jigger cup with the inscription, a parody of the Maxwell House slogan, "Good to the Last Drop!", which Dad held up and slowly marveled at, then chuckled, "That's right, huh, Pete?" (Pete or Petie was Mom's nickname, given to her by Grandpa Clyde). Mom nodded. "Get it? 'Good to the last drop,' right?"

"I suppose," said Mom. She held her drink up to his bright jigger cup, her fake smile become a dour expression.

Johnny D didn't touch his cake. He drank orange juice, watched my folks' reactions, and saw how the family slowly devolved into a sodden alcoholic blur. The kids had made crayoned birthday cards which were bright and cheery. Carol and Dick had given Dad a new spy thriller from John Le Carre. Then mine, wrapped in brown paper, a piece of baby blue ribbon tying it together. I'd found a piece of pre-cut mat board while in Donelson, had it reconfigured to fit the watercolor (11 x 14 inches) so that it overlapped the edges by a quarter-inch on all four sides. Dad slowly unwrapped it, sipping at his drink. The brown paper falling away, he held the matted watercolor in both hands. “Lookee there, huh, Pete? Boats.” Dad looked at it slowly, dully, then said, “Huh. Boats.” He then gave it to Mom, who got very excited and showed it to the rest of us. “Oh, Garry, what a lovely painting! Your dad loves boats!”

“I do?” said Dad as he fingered the one ice cube in his drink.

“Of course you do, Brownie,” nudged Mom, valiantly.

“Oh, right. Love boats.” He drained his drink.

“Oh, Gar, this is a great painting!” Judy lit up.

“Thanks, Judy.”

She was the first to hold it as the picture was passed around. “Were these boats on the lake where you camped?” asked Judy, still holding the picture, watching it.

“Well yeah, the other side of the lake from where I camped out.”

“Nice, Gar,” Durl nodded, raised his eyebrows.

“I thought you said this was from you and John,” said Dad, standing up, jiggling his empty glass. “Who wants a refill?”

“Oh, Brownie, haven't you had enough?”

“Never enough, my dawlin', never enough.”

“I'll join ya, Dad.” Chris stood, a bit unevenly.

“Sit. I'll get it. What's your poison?”

“Whatever you're having.”

“Scotch-rocks it is.” Dad began to turn, then stopped. “Huh, John? Those boats are from you, too?”

“Um,” Durl gave a sly grin toward me, and then continued, “well, Mr. Brown, who was responsible for getting Garry all the way down to Tennessee so he could hate selling books, leave Nashville, and instead of staying in some stuffy furnished room because of my nudging and enormous love for the Great Outdoors—we ended up beside Old Hickory Lake, camped under the stars?”

John paused, gave me a wink, and then again, eyed my dad and spoke right to him, “And there, lo and behold, after a number of good long jogs, on the other side of that same Old Hickory Lake, Gar found those boats and painted them. Just for you . . . So, yeah, I'd say those boats are from the both of us.”

Everyone laughed, clapped.

“Well done, Durlie.” I nodded.

"Here, here!" said brother Sandy.

Mom, Judy, and Carol all laughed. Dick, too, who said, "Bravo, John, well spoken. A wicked web you weave, or something like that."

"I'll drink to that," said Chris, still somewhat wobbly next to Dad. After the applause and huzzahs died down, Dad took a moment, sized John up, and then looking him hard in the eye, said, "Guilt by association, is that what you're saying?"

John nodded, laughed, "Ha! Right, Mr. Brown. Exactly."

"Riiigght," said Dad as he and Chris turned, both headed for the kitchen and more booze.

42

John and I sat in the TV room downstairs. The TV wasn't on. We just sat there. I had my legs up on the coffee table. There was noise coming from the kitchen, just out the door and up the eight stairs. Dad and Chris were talking loudly. I could hear Judy's laugh, then Sandy's voice. Carol and Dick had already departed; little Dave walked blurry eyed beside Carol as she carried Jess. Dick had Laura draped over his shoulder.

John and I just sat there. We didn't talk for a long time.

"You wanna go for a swim, Gar?"

"Naw. You?"

"Not really."

We sat there some more, staring at the big grey TV screen. It was a big color TV, on the extended slate ledge, with the fireplace to the left. Mom's black rocker was to the right of the TV. Ruth White's framed quilt hung on the wall, also to the right. A great piece of patchwork quilting, mostly reds, browns, rust colors, yellows, even some silk pieces. Dated 1888. Pretty impressive. But we weren't looking at that now. Maybe Durl was looking into the empty fireplace mouth. I dunno. I looked at the television.

"You okay, Gar?"

"Not really."

"You wanna talk about it?"

"Not really."

"You want me to go home?"

"No. Not at all."

"Gar, you're supposed to say 'Not really.'"

"Oh. Right. Ask me again."

"You want me to go home?"

"Not really. Funny, Durl."

"I thought so."

"Oh man, Durlie."

"Oh woman, Brownie."

"Yeah. That—her—too."

"Come on, Gar, it's your old bud, the D-man, right?"

"Ah, Durl, I dunno. I just don't get it."

"Get what?"

"This. Him. My dad. This family. It's weird."

"Yeah?"

"I got all homesick. Then I did all these paintings, right?"

"Right."

"And when I did this one, of the boats, and I do think it's one of my best watercolors—"

"Yeah."

"I mean, I really thought he'd like it. He used to love boats. I thought, coming home, you know, well, I just missed everybody so much but, is it me, or have things radically changed?"

"Yeah." Durl nodded and just stared off. Both of us stared at the blank TV screen.

"Well," said John, "I think . . ."

"Yeah?"

"It could be us."

"What do you mean?"

"We broke the spell."

"The 'spell'?"

"We went away. I feel it, too. And then came back, and now we see things that we couldn't see before."

"But, Durlie, we've been doing that for the past four years, all through college."

"Not the same. I went to East Aurora this summer to be with Brookie. You—we both went South to Tennessee—I mean, we're out of college, we're starting our own lives now. It's not the same. It's like we're finally swimming in the ocean. We come home and everyone's—it's like slow motion. They're all kind of stuck in this muck, you know?"

"Precisely. Wow. Very good, Durl. Wow."

"Thanks, Gar."

"I don't think I belong here anymore."

"Yeah."

"Thank God I'm not staying too long anyway."

"Where you going?"

"Europe. With Kathleen. Remember?"

"Right. How soon?"

"Soon. She flies East next week, Labor Day weekend."

"Wow."

"Yeah."

"You ready for that?"

"I don't know. I do miss her. I'm ready to not be here anymore. My bedroom, I mean, after those Tennessee night skies? Feels like I'm in some cramped little wood box."

"I know. Doesn't it?"

"You, too?"

"Yeah."

The voices in the kitchen got louder. Glasses clinking, music playing from the living room.

"Jesus, sounds like a party up there."

"Well, Gar, I guess it is."

"Right. You wanna watch some TV?"

"Not really. I should get going."

"Me neither," I said as I went over and turned it on. I started to switch the channel.

"Wait, Gar, isn't that your guy?"

"What 'guy'? Who?"

"Go back." I was at the TV. I'd already starting changing channels.

"No. Too far back. Just go one channel."

I did. A TV commercial. Some new whiz-bang cutting device. All kinds of blades. The announcer, "Now let me show you how it peels an onion, okay?"

"This guy, Durlie?"

"No, no. You know. Whatever that movie is. Just wait."

We waited. Onions, bread, carrots—really fine, thin slices of carrot. Then, prices, a phone number. "Okay. Here it comes," said John. Another commercial—for hair shampoo. "Oh Jesus," said Durl. "Try the next channel. I swear." The next channel had a Tarzan movie with a chimpanzee making a big smiley face while he made high-pitched grunt noises, jumped up and down, and pounded his chest.

"Funny, Durl. That's 'my guy'?"

"No, no, not this. Go back."

I did. Omigod. That voice. The young nurse watching him, the young fresh-faced doctor somewhat mesmerized, too: ". . . It's a funny thing. Everyone has problems. No one brings anything small into a bar. But then I introduce them to Harvey . . ."

"Durl—"

"Right, Gar, see?"

"Oh man." Warmth around my eyes, they began to water. Durl was saying things but I couldn't speak. I tried but it felt as if small pebbles were stuck in my throat—

"Gar—hey, buddy, you okay?" Durl leaned in close. He saw that I was crying. "Ah, Gar, it's okay, buddy." He patted my shoulder. He squeezed it. "Good ol' Harvey, right, Gar? And Jimmy Stewart."

I nodded. I wiped my eyes. I watched Elwood P. Dowd. And the young adoring nurse and also how the young dutiful doctor tried to make sense of Elwood and then how that once-blind doctor saw that young nurse as a lovely woman for the first time, as he fell in love.

I wanted to explain to Durl that this wasn't just a movie anymore—not for me. That these were somehow, well, a few of them had become characters in my life this past summer. That Dowd and Jimmy Stewart and Harvey had offered me some sort of code, and another way of being in the world, as a young man trying to figure things out and find my way, but also as an artist trying to be true to my vision. They gave me courage, fortified my ability to go forth in the world, to believe in art and my life, to be devoted to loving art and people and this earth, and even my somewhat distraught—lost?—family.

But I couldn't talk. I sat there with my wet face, leaning forward, watching this movie, touched again by Jimmy Stewart's comforting warble. John sat beside me, watching, too. Both of us leaned over our bent knees, at the edge of the sofa. Now and then, Durl would either bump my knee or nudge my shoulder with his and say, "Huh, Gar, that's your guy, right? Right, Gar?" Through tears, I nodded, grinned. We went on watching.

43

A week later, just after Labor Day, Kathy flew in to LaGuardia. I drove down alone and picked her up. Not in Titine. Titine was not doing so well.

"She's a piece o' junk," Dad said.

"I don't think that car's safe, Garry. Please don't drive it anymore," said Mom. "Please?"

"Piece o' junk. Scrap it. Now." Dad was adamant. Mom offered her Ford Fairlane.

Then Dad said, "Hell, if it's on the weekend, take my Mercedes but not that piece of scrap metal. No way."

It was the Tuesday after Labor Day. I took Mom's Ford. Dad's fancy green 220s scared me. God forbid anything should happen to it. I'd be in debt for life. It did catch me off-guard, though, that Dad offered it to me. It meant a lot of things, that he trusted me as a driver and, in his crusty way, he loved me, wanted me to be safe. I appreciated that.

I don't remember Kathy arriving in Darlington. I only remember our driving over to a junkyard in Norwalk and selling Titine for something like five dollars as they turned her into scrap metal. I keep picturing Kathy standing there beside me—but is that what really happened? Or, did I just wish she'd been with me when I said good-bye to Titine?

It was a big, rangy, more than an acre lot, old cars, old trucks, old appliances strewn all about. One section where a huge derrick and plunger, from at least thirty feet above the ground, came down and pounded on whatever lone, forsaken heap of metal was caught in its—literally—iron grip. Down and up. Down and up. Over and over—pounding, pounding—and then it stopped.

And sweet Titine, once a modest grey bowler hat shape, emerged as a six-foot cube, still grey but with streaks of chrome running throughout. She—it—was then lifted and conveyed slowly, steadily on to a pile of other cubes and rectangles, a mountain of reshaped boxy metals, these amalgams, anonymous, returned to their sources of indistinguishable metals.

The day was sunny and bright, a few clouds, even a few breezes, but it didn't feel like summer to me. It felt grey and wintry and humorless. Kathy must've driven my mom's Ford, following me as I drove Titine for the last time. Then, after, on the drive back to Huckleberry Lane, "Good-bye, Titine," called Kathy, out the window and to the junkyard lot and its grey malaise.

"Yeah. Damn. I loved that car."

"She was a very special car, Gar."

"What is that with cars? They hold our lives, our histories."

"Like houses. Homes."

"But different. Because we're on the move with them. They join us. They take us. I went places with Titine."

"Like a friend. Like me?" asked Kathy.

"Like you."

"Like Titine."

"Yes. Like Titine."

"A French friend."

"A French friend from college."

"From Massachusetts. And Connecticut."

"From Tennessee."

"Right, Gar, or, as you like to say, 'from Tin Sea.'"

"Yeah. From 'Tin Sea.' Oh shit." It hit me.

"What?"

"I'm missing her. Almost as much as I missed you all summer."

"Really?"

"Did you miss me, too?"

"But I was so busy."

"You didn't miss me?"

"I missed you, sure."

"But Kink, Greg Kinkel."

"Oh Gar."

"Tell me."

"I was looking forward to this. Ellie's wedding in London, our trip to Europe, you know."

"Were you?"

"I still am."

I still was, too. But I knew, deep down, that it wasn't clear to me who Kathy was and why I loved her so. Who I was and why I was so determined to become an artist, a painter, a visionary of sorts. I had gained enormous confidence from my summer days and nights in Tennessee. Also, this longing that was a mix of love, homesickness, craving, and ambition. It contained a desire to see and experience great art, memorable paintings, the great cities and art museums of Europe, but also this unfathomable and, most of the time, unmentionable, longing and love for Kathy.

Were we truly meant for each other or not? I couldn't quite ask her if she felt this, too, or even define it, but I sensed that we had something special. I sensed, too, that she didn't quite believe it. Didn't quite believe in us. Perhaps, back then, as she navigated between her love for camp and kids and science and biology, she didn't quite believe in herself yet, either.

And, I wasn't the sort of young man to force the issue, not really. I certainly had pursued her, from spring of our freshman year on. Until I read one day—was it during college or years after?—that it's finally the woman who chooses, who says Yes or No.

What was Kathy telling me? I was busy and I missed you. I love you and there's Greg Kinkel. Come to Ellie's wedding but don't get any ideas. We'll backpack in Europe so you can be inspired, see great art. Not: We'll backpack in Europe so we can deepen our love and grow and one day make a life together. But. Did I really want that myself? And yes, that's another story.

The story never ends, really. Every story is either prelude or semicolon or aftermath or segue. It all continues on and on until it comes to a place where it doesn't. Or, where it looks as if it doesn't. That wave peaks and crashes—whoosh! And? Comes another wave.

Enough. For now.

Or, as Elwood P. Dowd might say, "When? When can you come for dinner?"

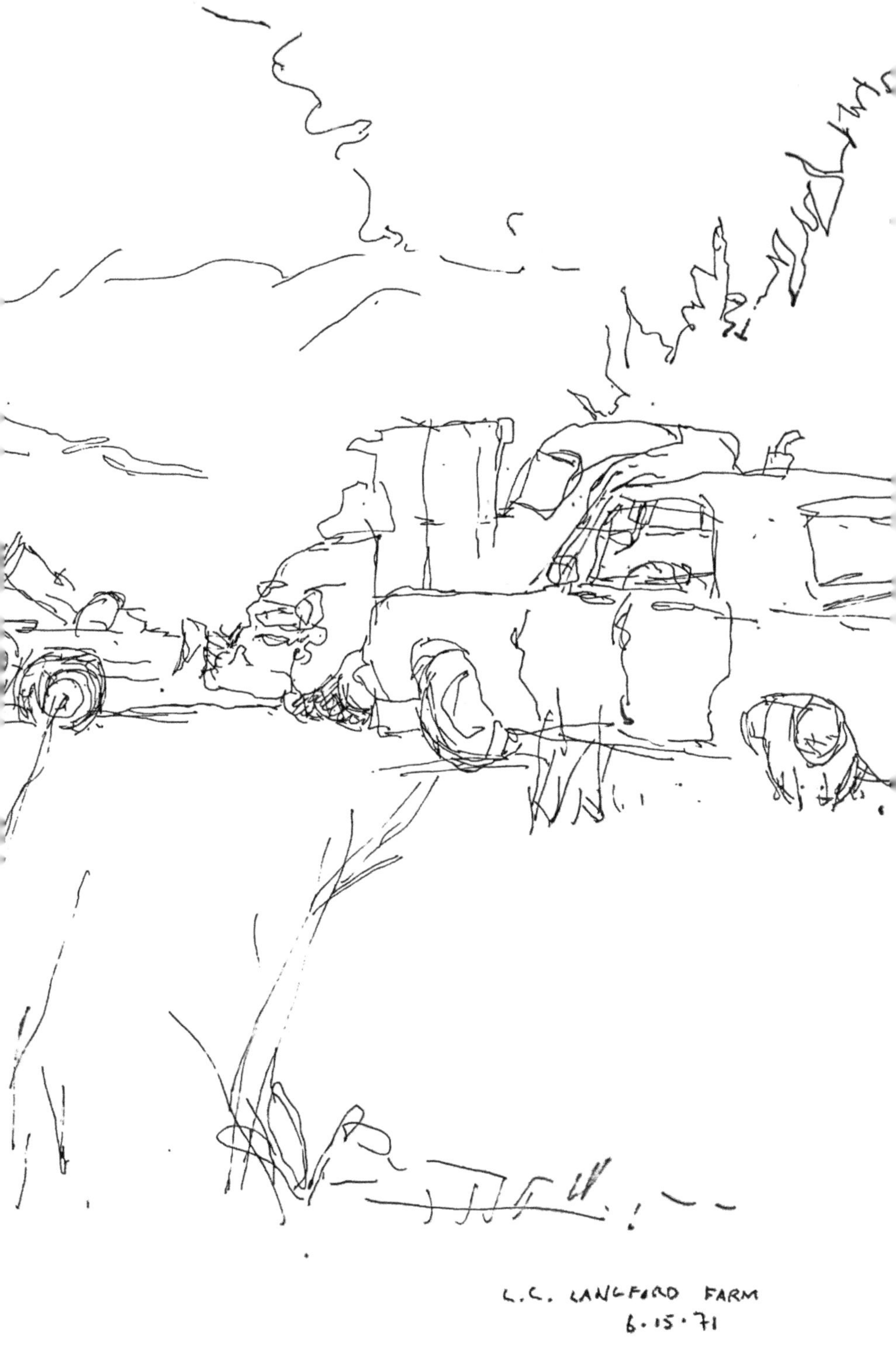
L.C. LANGFORD FARM
6.15.71

Acknowledgments

Early in 1983, my daughter not yet two years old, in a small nook study across from her bedroom, I first began to write about that summer of 1971 in Tennessee—as a play. I grappled with it there in Park Slope, Brooklyn, and then put it aside. Five years later, now divorced, I'd found a summer rental in Amagansett, on Long Island. Just a bike ride from the ocean, I'd resumed making notes about that Tennessee summer, filling two three-hole, wide-ruled notebooks (dated August 11, 1988 until November 20, 1989)—not sure if it was going to be a play, a novel, or a memoir. Again, I put it aside. Finally, living in Los Feliz, the eastern part of Los Angeles, having rewatched the movie *Harvey* the night before, on Sunday, August 6, 2006, what began in long-hand in my journal eventually moved into five more three-hole, wide-ruled notebooks, the final handwritten pages ending in May 2009. I didn't begin typing those notebook pages into the computer until nine years later. All this to say—and marvel at—all the life and lives that have been tangential to this Tennessee fable. For which I continue to be grateful.

Portions of this book were read at Ensemble Studio Theatre LA in Winterfest, 2019; I'm grateful to my dear friend, Terry Andrews, who gave the then bulky and unedited manuscript a generous and thoughtful read; also, up-and-coming comedian, Greg Miller, thanks to him for offering to read it.

Richard Heller, through the years, my thanks for his steadfast appreciation and belief in my writing efforts—he and our fellow writers as well as beloved writing mentor Holly Prado, in our ongoing Tuesday night workshops, not one of them ever read *Tin Sea* in any of its manifestations. My wife Marie remembers my working on it on our trip to Germany in 2009 when I called it my "secret writing." Though none of them knew what I was concocting, all of them were instrumental, by example and exhortation, in inspiring this strange and tender alchemy for writing.

It's one thing to write voluminous notebooks, type them up, and call it a manuscript, but a whole other task, also a kind of magic, to have a very insightful editor, grasp it, love it, and very gingerly cut and paste and shape it into the book you hoped to create. For this I owe enormous thanks to Cecilia Woloch, poet, novelist, teacher, and friend.

Thanks, too, to April Eberhardt who introduced me to Susannah Noel who straightened me out about "The Seven Editorial Roles." I was referred to one of those real angels of the publishing world, an insightful and perspicacious proofreader, Christa Evans—a keen-eyed and talented "language mechanic."

The design of this book, so inviting, so creative, is all due to the grace and artistic efforts of book designer, Michael Ellison, of Ellison/Goodreau. This is Mike's fourth book with Lagoon House Press and I remain ever grateful.

My ongoing thanks to Barbara Crane, novelist and short story writer, and Bill Davis, peripatetic photographer, who week in, week out, continue to be beloved friends, colleagues, and along with my wife, Marie Pal-Brown, steadfast movers and shakers of our Lagoon House Press.

My wife, the writer, Marie Pal-Brown, has been such a vivacious and luminous power of example—not just her own evocative writing but her daily gracious blessing as she sees me, wounds and pockmarks and wisecracks and all. Thank you, my beloved Marguerite (yes, her name is Marie and the "Marguerite," that's another wonderful story).

Finally, it was my first wife's late father, Ted Martens, who, a retired Navy man, in his later years, was always working on this book, called "The Book." We thought it was a memoir but no one was sure. It was a bit of a joke, since no one ever saw it, he never

---

read excerpts from it, and at any mention of it, he'd just cryptically, with a tiny grin, nod his head. I'm not sure it ever was completed, and of course, looking at my own timeline, you do begin to wonder. As my father says in this book, "You're a sentimental fool," which is true, and perhaps it's the sentimental fools that help create, maybe not a legislated world, but a magical one. This is also the sentimental piece, dear Dad, because there are a lot of us—may our tribe increase—that do dream and do scribble or jot or sketch or vocalize, even in closets and before mirrors, but we keep at it. This book is also for them, with my thanks.

Garry's Art Show

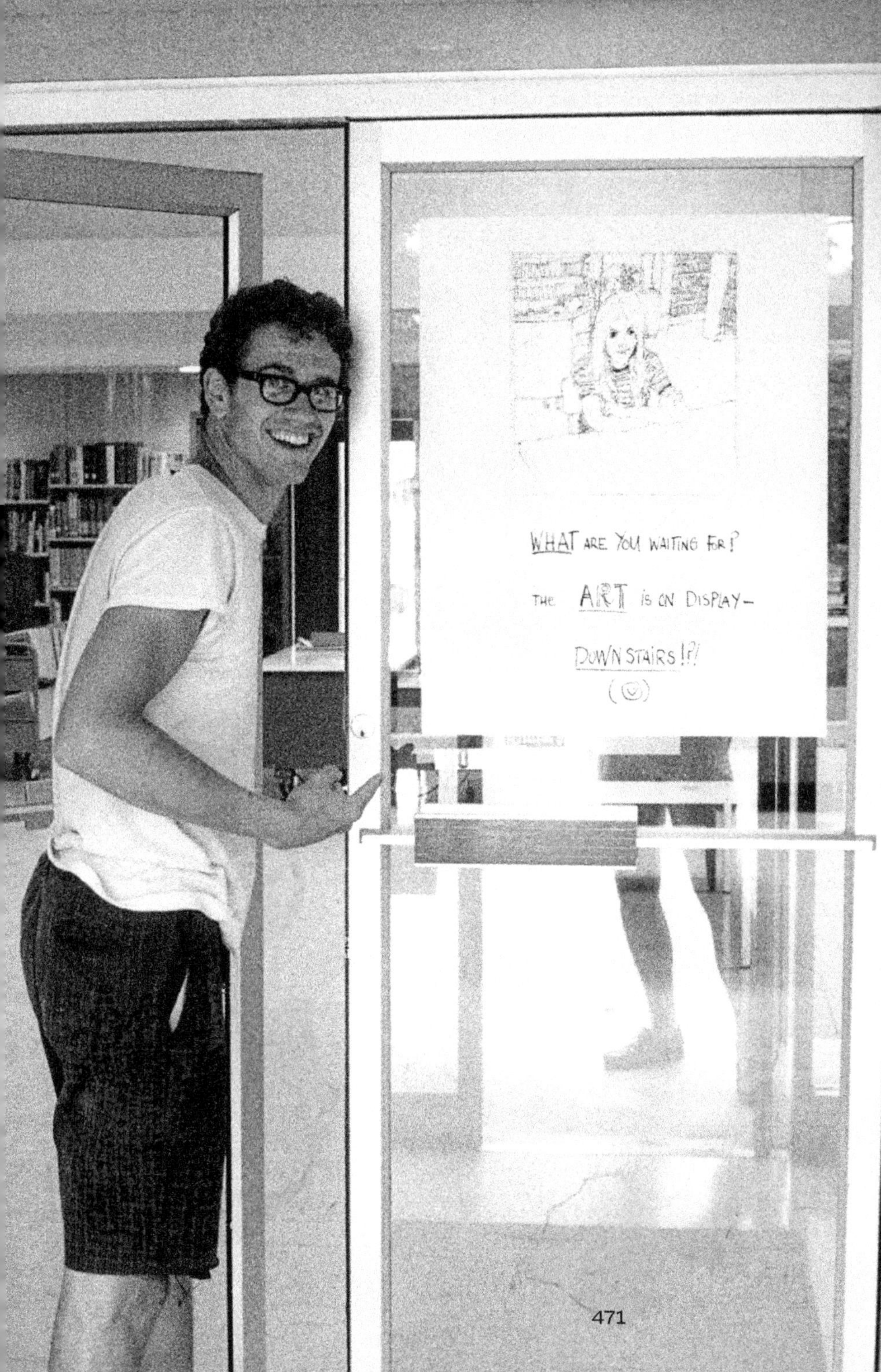
WHAT ARE YOU WAITING FOR?
THE ART IS ON DISPLAY–
DOWNSTAIRS!?!

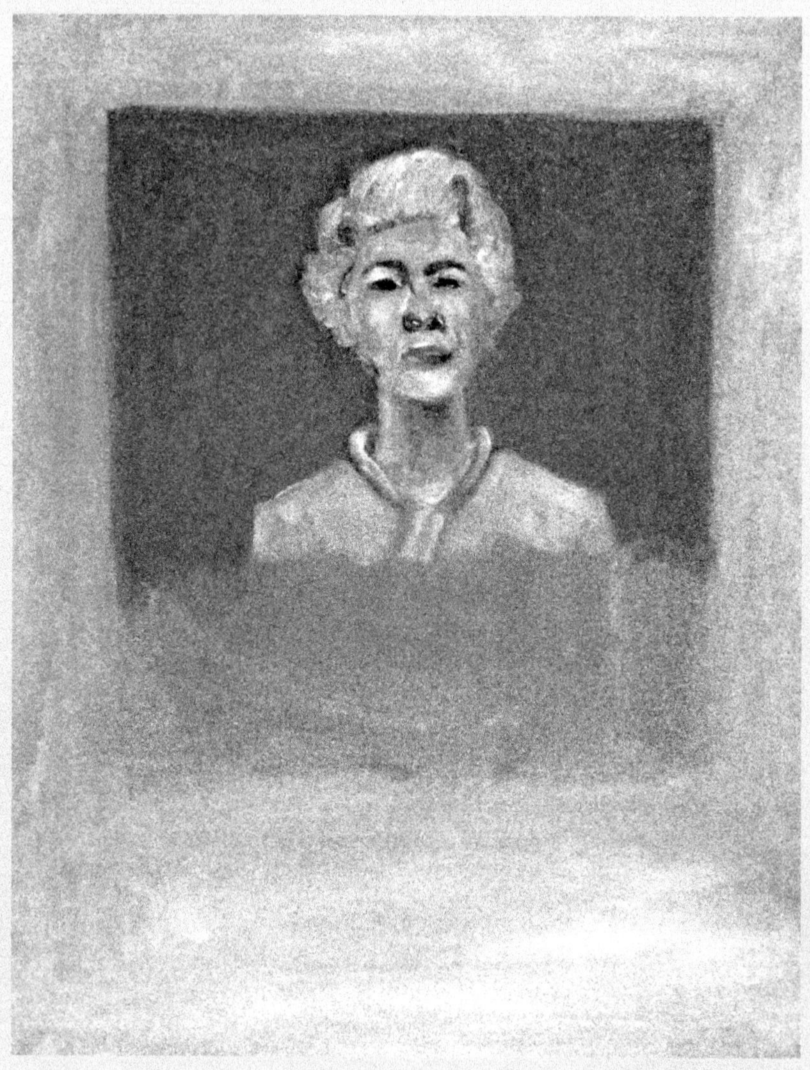

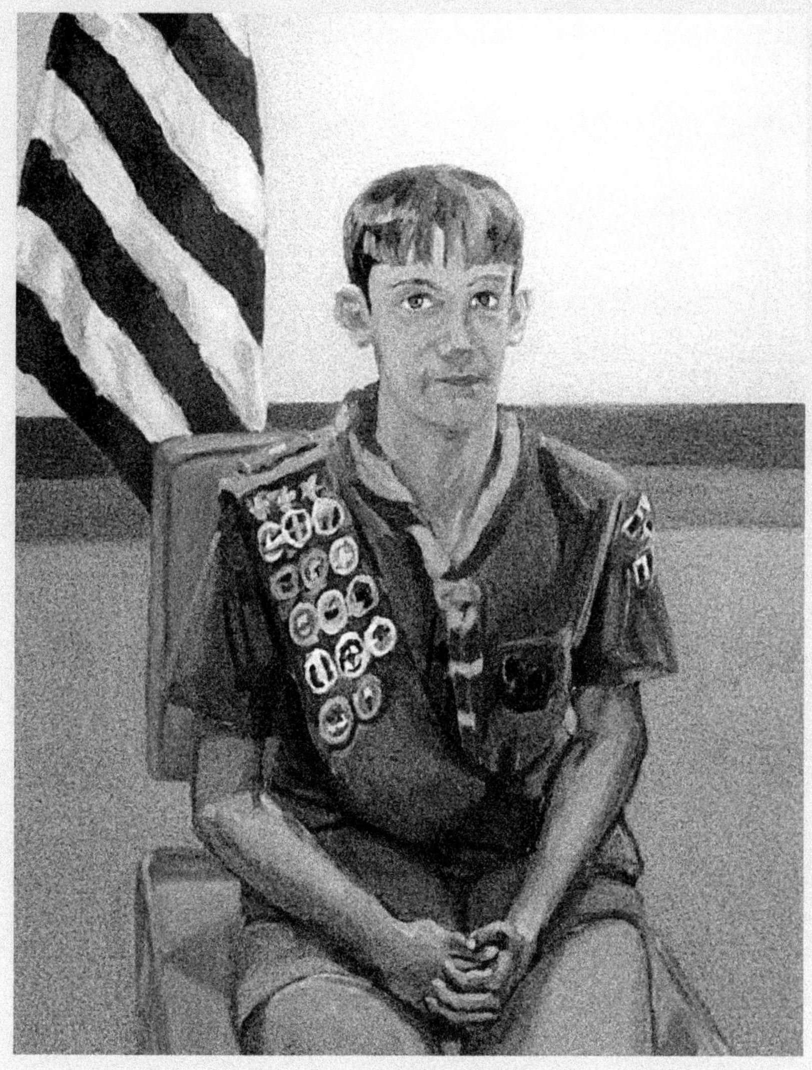

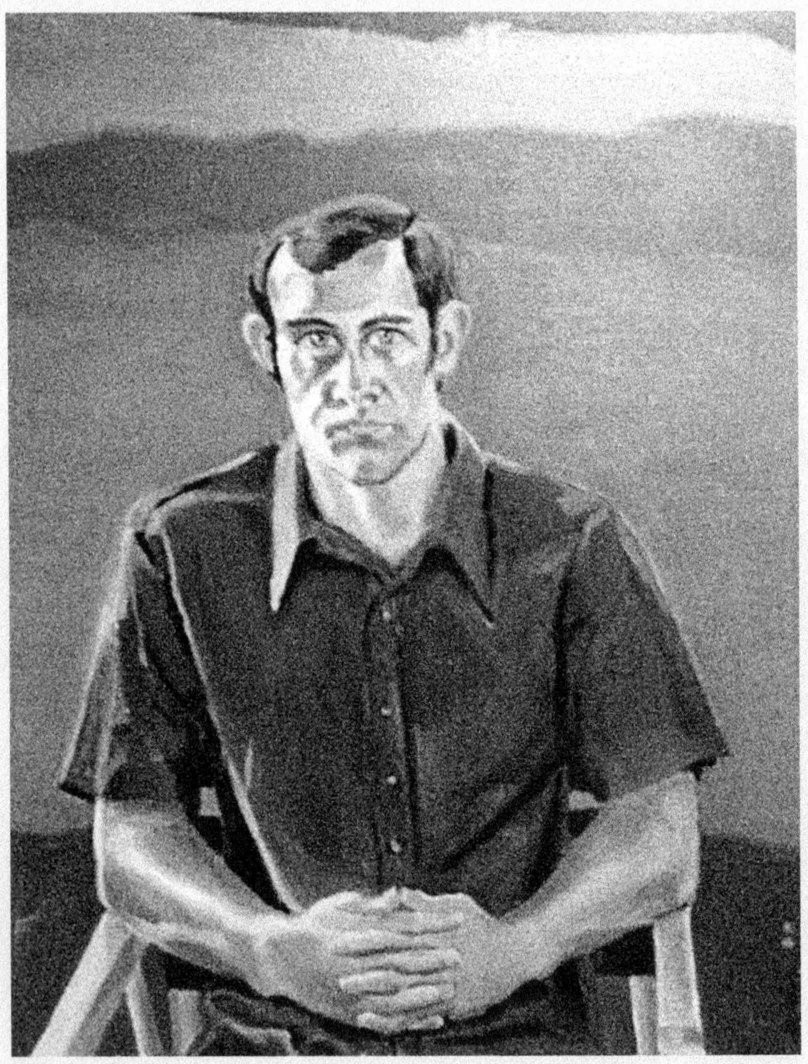

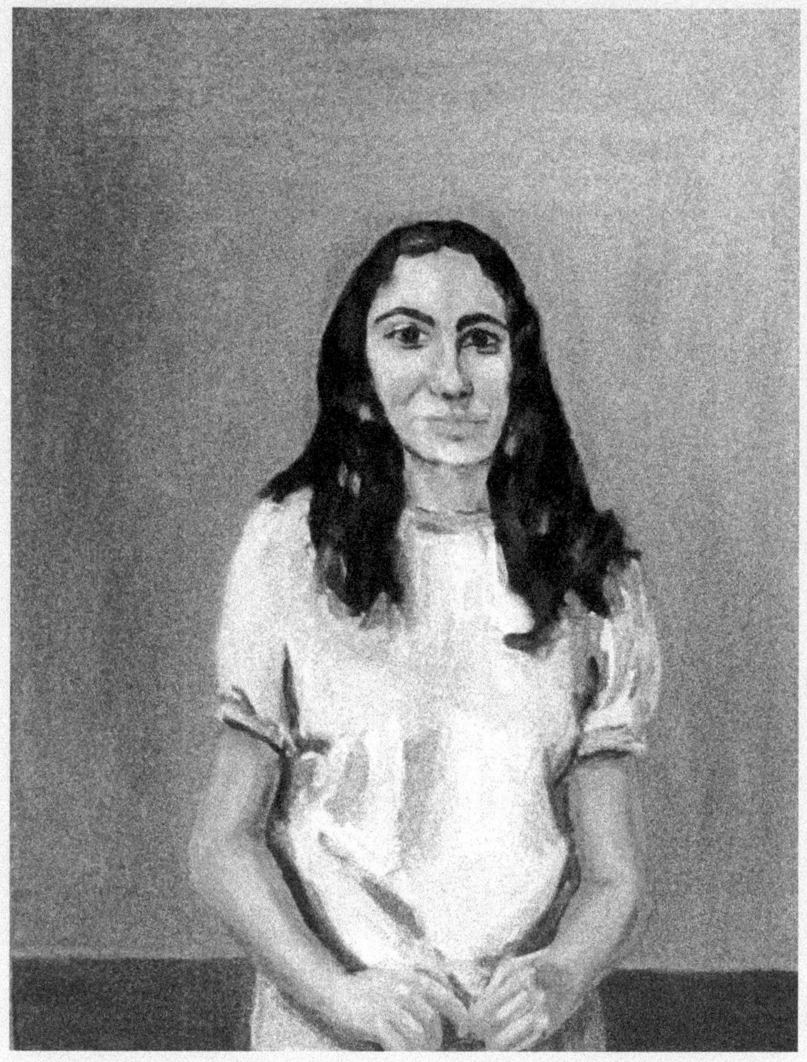

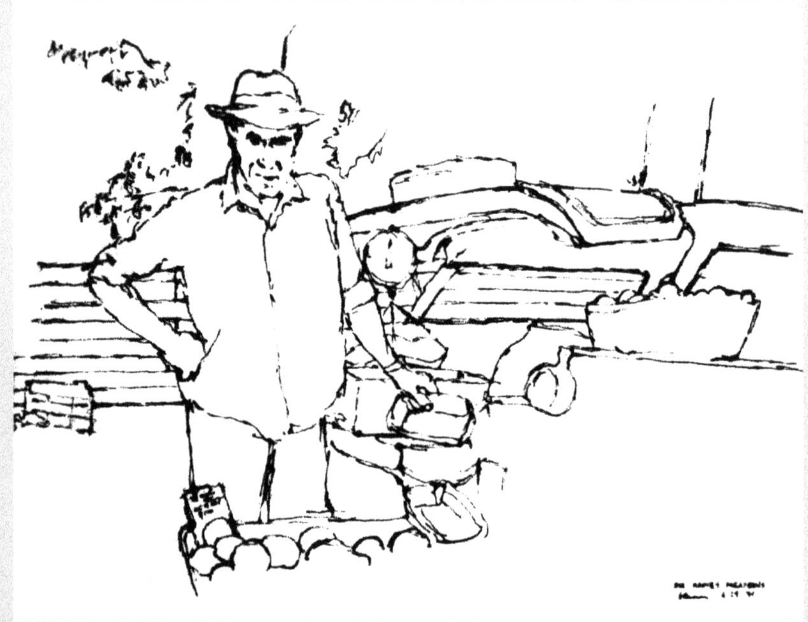

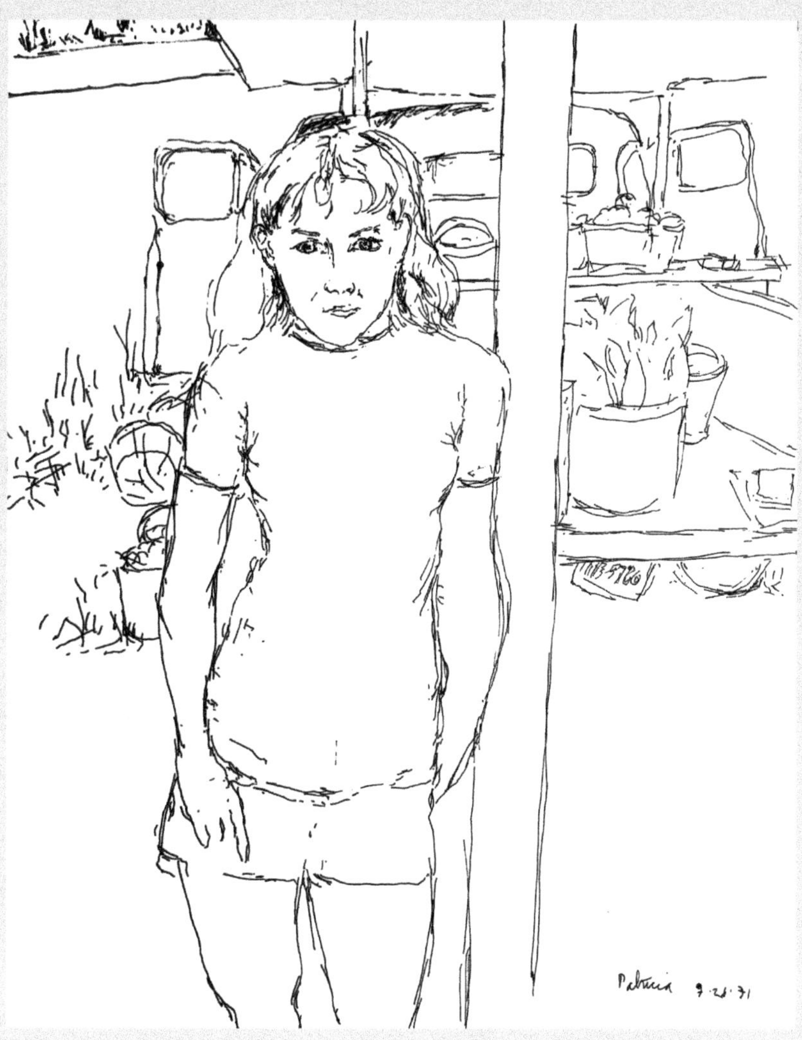

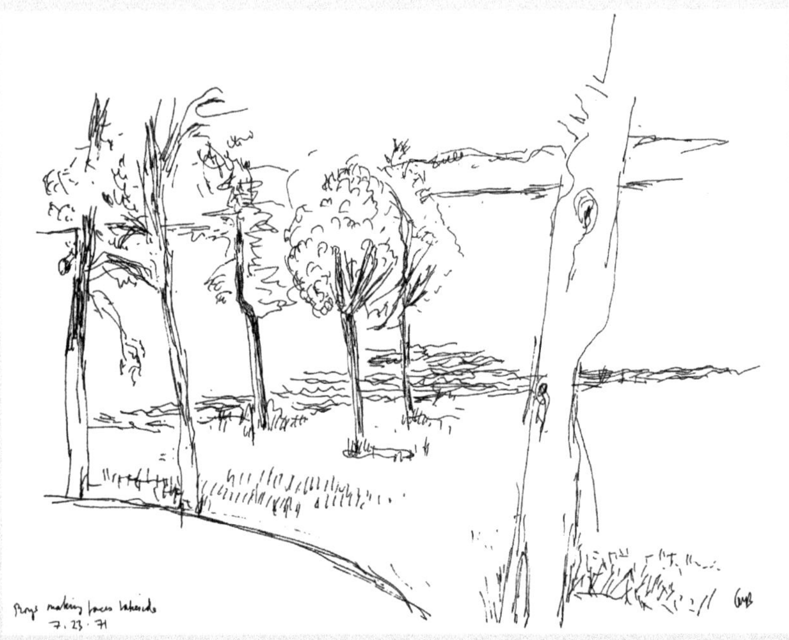
Boys making faces lakeside
7.23.71

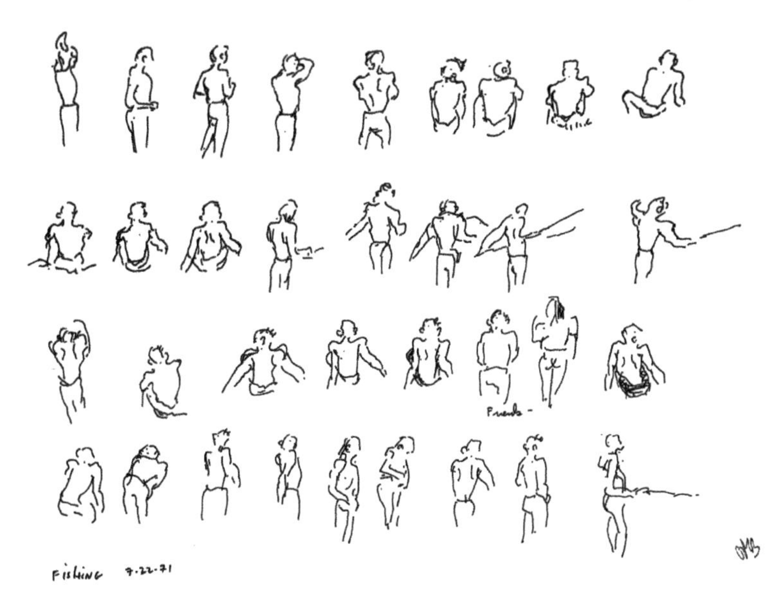
FISHING 7.22.71

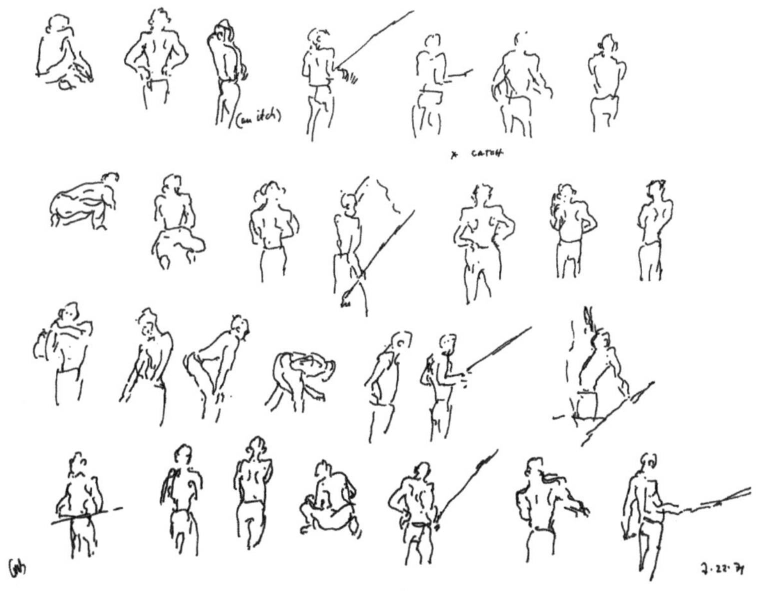
(an itch)
x CATCH

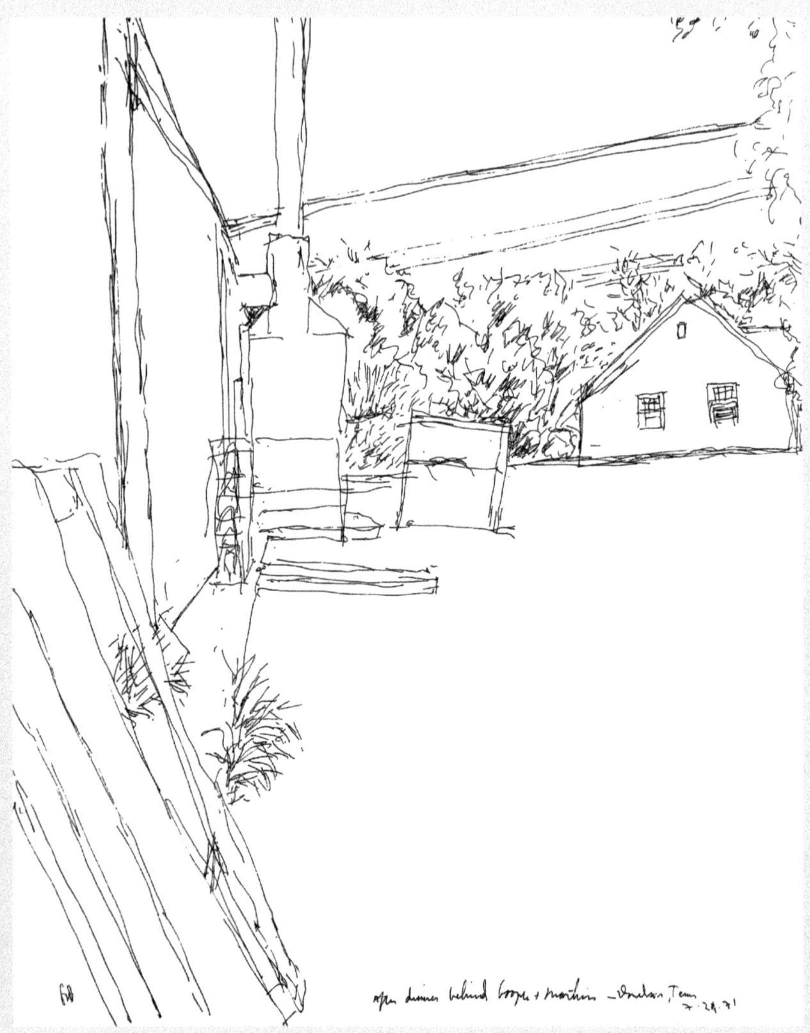
after dinner behind Cooper + Martin's — , Tenn
7·29·81

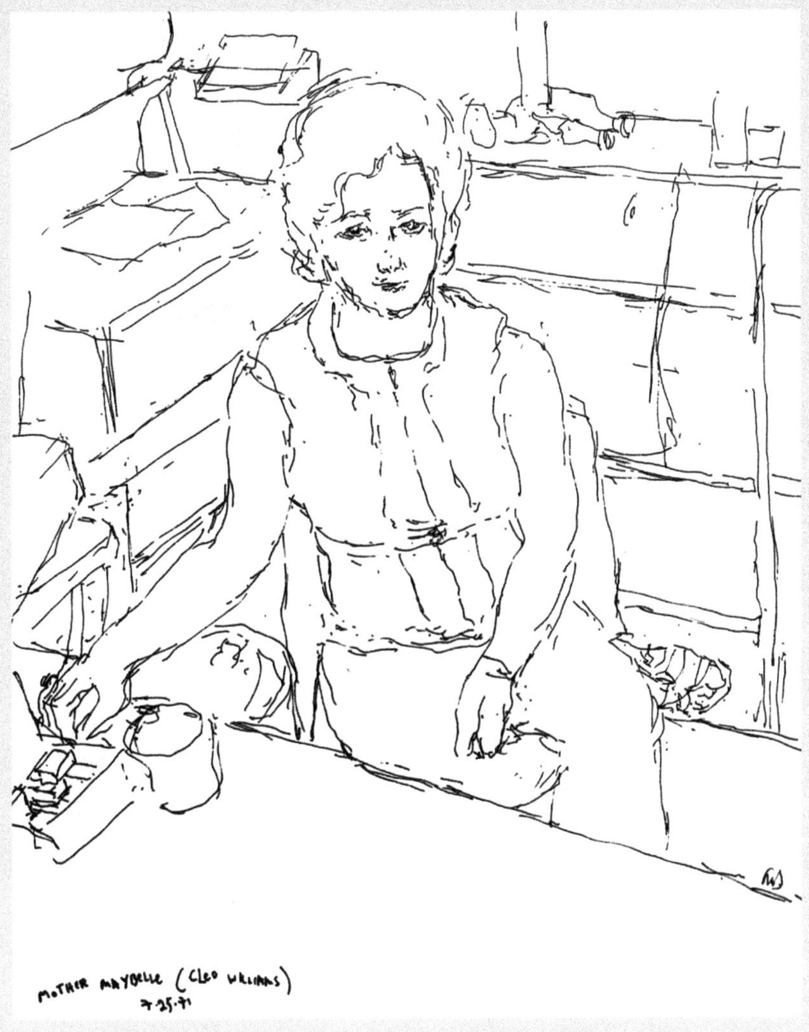
MOTHER MAYBELLE (CLEO WILLIAMS)
7.25.71

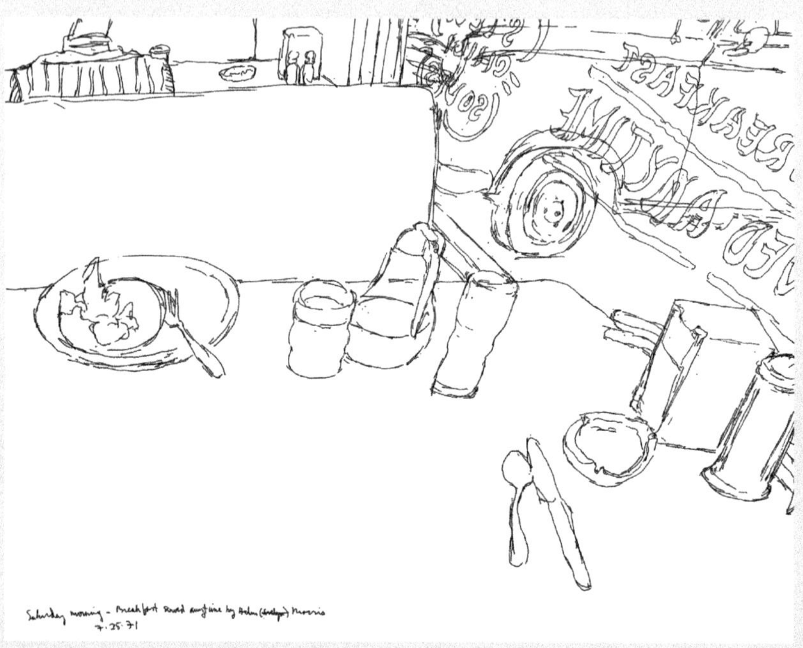
7.25.71

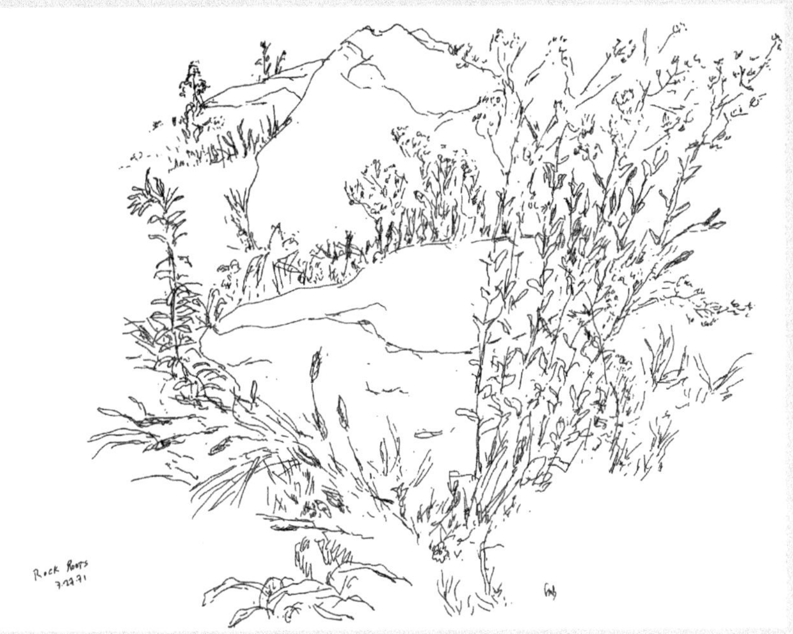
Rock Roots
7.22.71

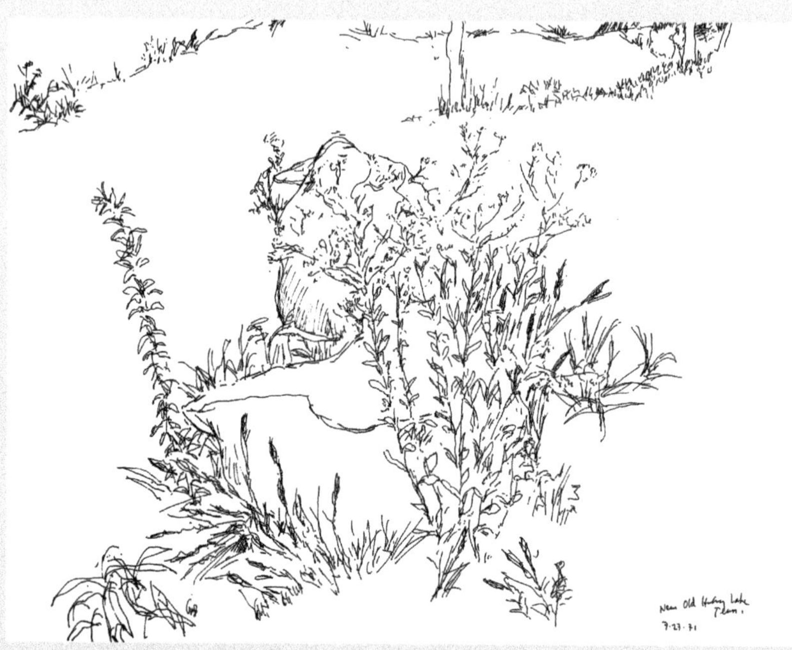
Near Old Hickory Lake Tenn.
7·27·71

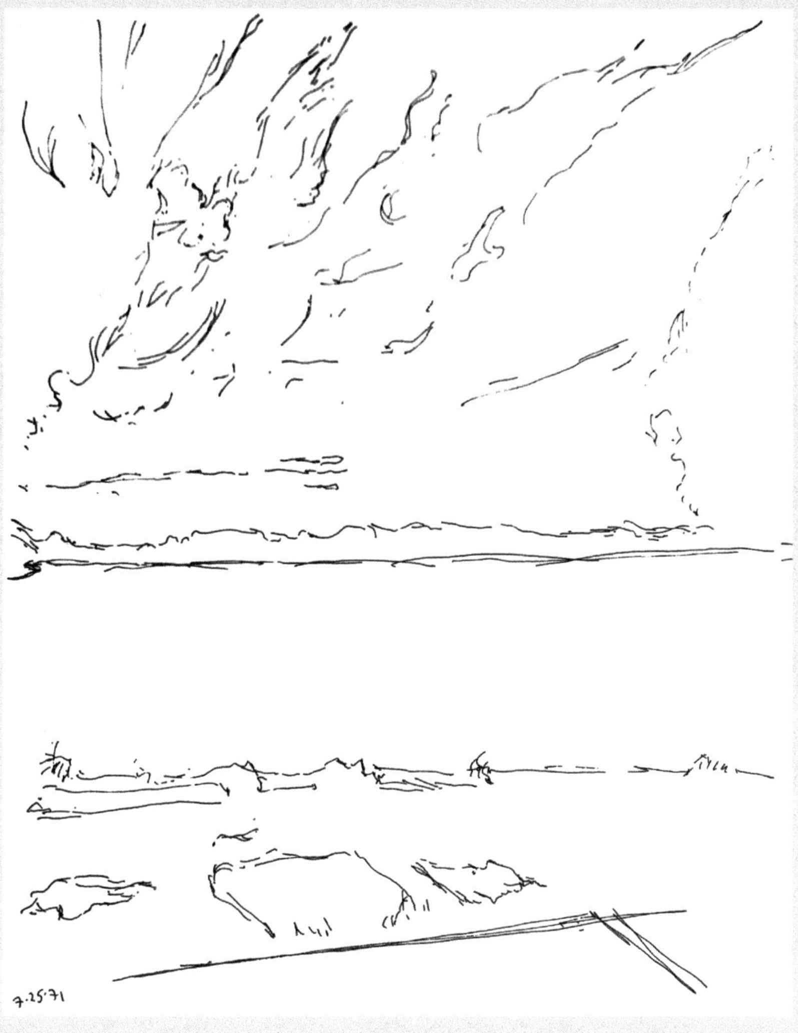
7.25.71

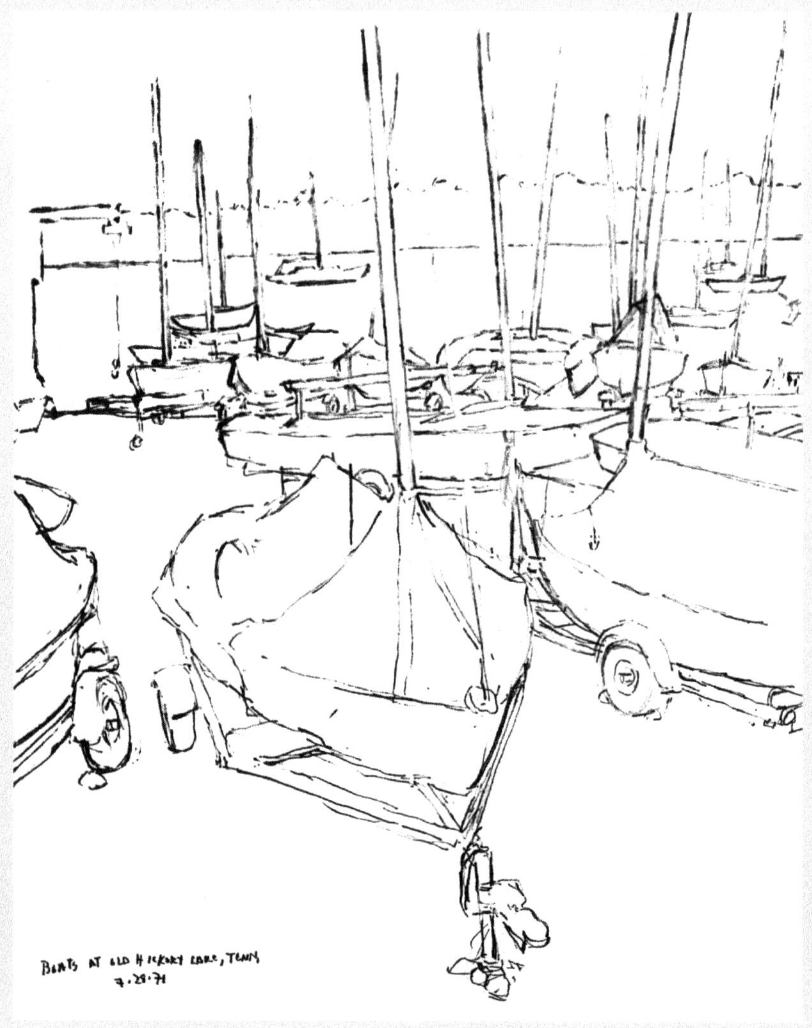
BOATS AT OLD HICKORY LAKE, TENN
7.28.71

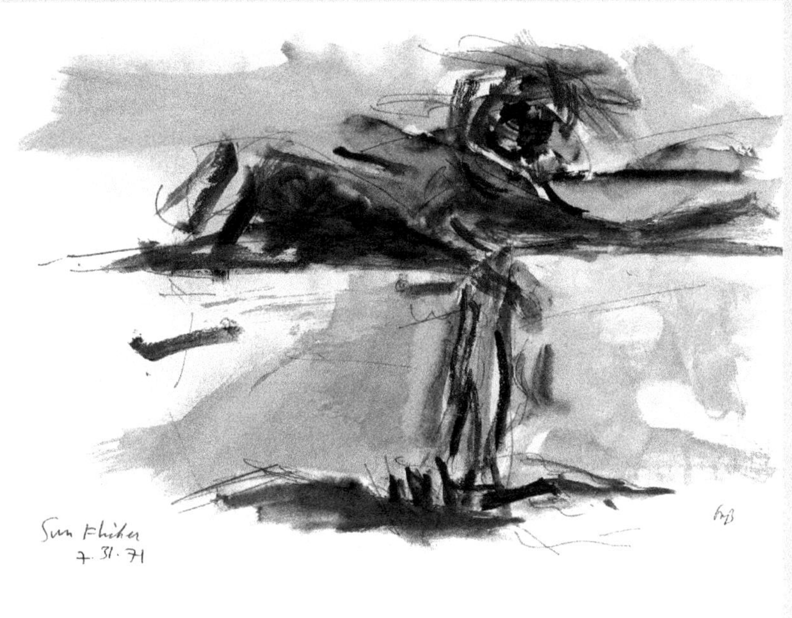
Sun Flicker
7.31.71

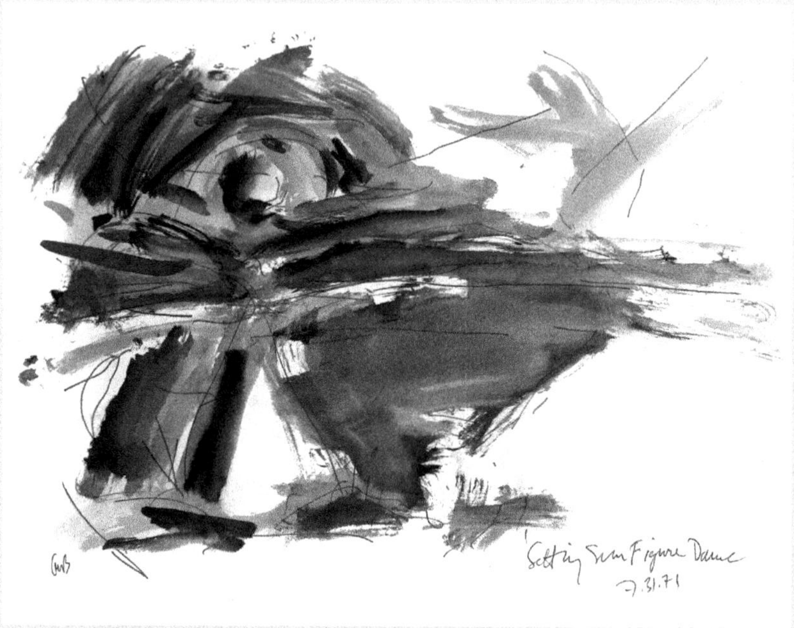
Setting Sun Figure Dance
7.31.71

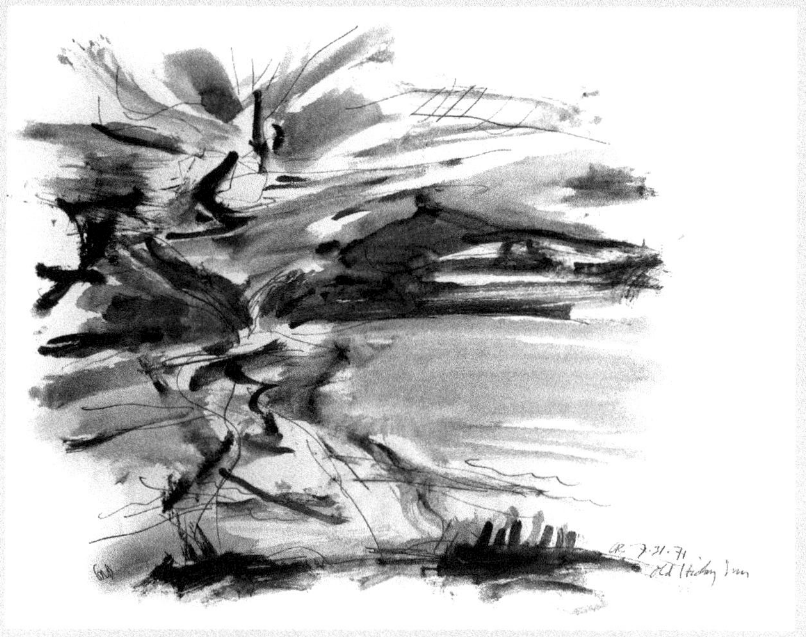
7.31.71

Garry's Art Show, pages 470 to 489:

p. 471 — Garry and poster invitation, "What Are You Waiting For? The Art Is On Display—Downstairs!"
p. 472 — *Lexie Helms*, oil, summer, 1971.
p. 473 — *Mikey Helms*, oil, summer, 1971.
p. 474 — *Sam Helms*, oil, summer, 1971.
p. 475 — *Patricia Willard*, oil, summer, 1971.
p. 476 — *Vegetable Man, Harvey Meadows (or is that James Steward?)*, pen and ink, summer, 1971.
p. 477 — *Patricia, cucumber girl*, pen and ink, summer, 1971.
p. 478 — *Trees / Boys Making Faces Lakeside*, pen and ink, summer, 1971.
p. 479 — *Boy Fishing*, diptych, pen and ink, summer, 1971.
p. 480 — *The "Shop-A-Lot,"* pen and ink, summer, 1971.
p. 481 — *Mother Maybelle (or is that Marlene?)*, pen and ink, summer, 1971.
p. 482 — *Snack Shack*, pen and ink, summer, 1971.
p. 483 — *Old Hickory Lake Rocks 1*, pen and ink, summer, 1971.
p. 484 — *Old Hickory Lake Rocks 2*, pen and ink, summer, 1971.
p. 485 — *Old Hickory Lake Sky*, pen and ink, summer, 1971.
p. 486 — *Boats, Old Hickory Lake*, pen and ink, summer, 1971.
p. 487 — *Sunset 1, Old Hickory Lake*, watercolor, summer, 1971.
p. 488 — *Sunset 2, Old Hickory Lake*, watercolor, summer, 1971.
p. 489 — *Sunset 3, Old Hickory Lake*, watercolor, summer, 1971.

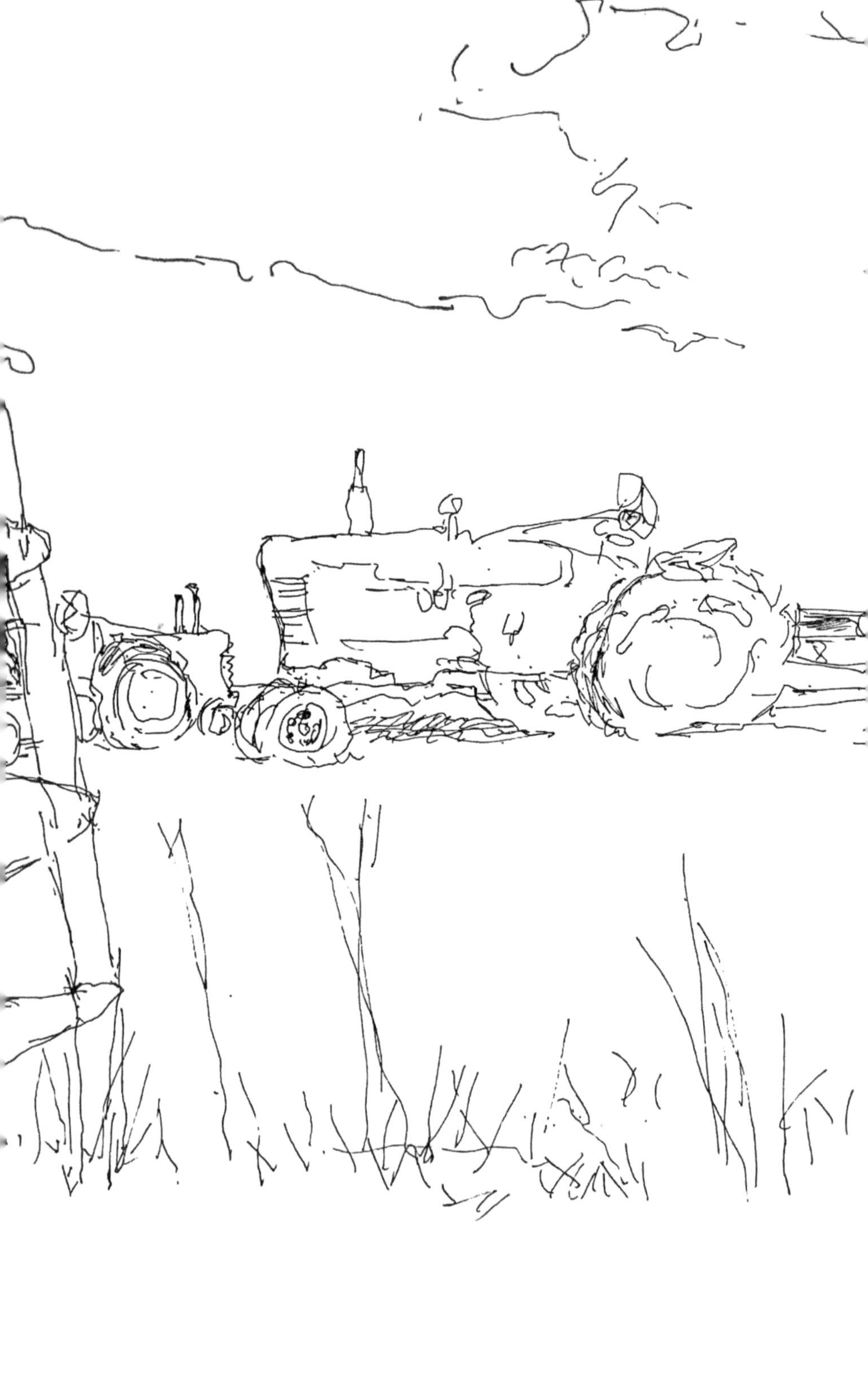

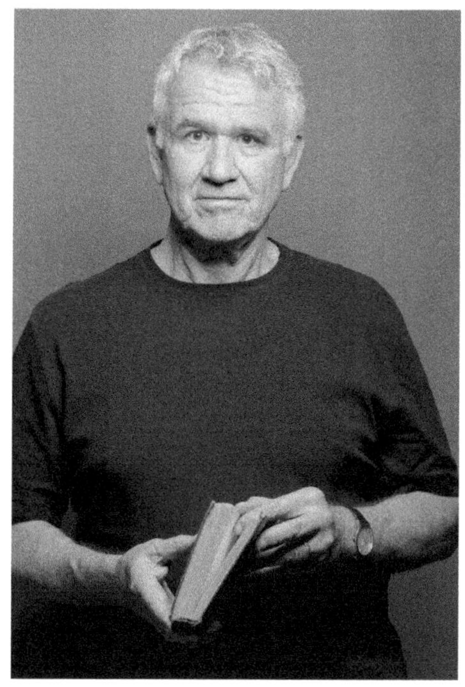

Garrett M. Brown is an actor, writer, playwright, and visual artist. His poems have been read at Ensemble Studio Theatre LA and published in the *Valyermo Chronicle*, his plays have been produced in Los Angeles and New York City, his drawings and paintings have been exhibited around the United States, and three of his stories are part of Lagoon House Press's fourth book, *Three Writers/One Photographer,* published in 2023. He's married to the writer and poet, Marie Pal-Brown; they live in Long Beach, and like his creative comrades of Lagoon House Press, he, too, was mentored by the writer and poet, Holly Prado Northup.

www.ingramcontent.com/pod-product-compliance
Ingram Content Group UK Ltd.
Pitfield, Milton Keynes, MK11 3LW, UK
UKHW062306290726
14090UKWH00018B/906